GOVERNANCE AS RESPONSIBILITY

This book undertakes a specialised analysis of a topic that is highly significant both theoretically and practically.

At the theoretical level, it discusses questions that have remained insufficiently answered in the fields of international human rights and institutional law. Notably, it clarifies how international human rights law conditions member States' governance role within international financial institutions and how this role is to be accommodated in the regime of international responsibility.

Furthermore, the book's thorough discussion of member States' human rights due diligence duties offers a practical contribution to the understanding of what tools may be used by States to secure their human rights obligations when participating in international financial institutions. Its practical significance also relates to the examination of the various elements that must be demonstrated by an individual wishing to invoke member State responsibility for alleged human rights violations in the context of international financial institution operations.

Ana Sofia Barros is a lawyer and researcher in public international law. She is currently working for the United Nations High Commissioner for Refugees. She obtained her Law degree at the University of Lisbon, a Master's degree in Human Rights and Democratisation from the European Inter-University Centre for Human Rights and Democratisation and her PhD from the Catholic University of Leuven. Ana Sofia worked in a Portuguese Law Firm (CSCA), having qualified as a lawyer in 2012. She also worked as a jurist at an international NGO (IRCT) and at the European Commission (OLAF).

Governance As Responsibility

MEMBER STATES AS HUMAN RIGHTS PROTECTORS IN INTERNATIONAL FINANCIAL INSTITUTIONS

ANA SOFIA BARROS

CAMBRIDGE
UNIVERSITY PRESS

CAMBRIDGE
UNIVERSITY PRESS

University Printing House, Cambridge CB2 8BS, United Kingdom

One Liberty Plaza, 20th Floor, New York, NY 10006, USA

477 Williamstown Road, Port Melbourne, VIC 3207, Australia

314–321, 3rd Floor, Plot 3, Splendor Forum, Jasola District Centre, New Delhi – 110025, India

79 Anson Road, #06–04/06, Singapore 079906

Cambridge University Press is part of the University of Cambridge.

It furthers the University's mission by disseminating knowledge in the pursuit of education, learning, and research at the highest international levels of excellence.

www.cambridge.org
Information on this title: www.cambridge.org/9781108492867
DOI: 10.1017/9781108675109

First published 2019

Printed and bound in Great Britain by Clays Ltd, Elcograf S.p.A.

A catalogue record for this publication is available from the British Library.

Library of Congress Cataloging-in-Publication Data
NAMES: Barros, Ana Sofia, author.
TITLE: Governance as responsibility : member states as human rights protectors in international financial institutions / Ana Sofia Barros.
DESCRIPTION: Cambridge [UK] ; New York, NY : Cambridge University Press, 2019. | Includes bibliographical references and index.
IDENTIFIERS: LCCN 2019008014 | ISBN 9781108492867 (hardback)
SUBJECTS: LCSH: Social responsibility of business – Law and legislation. | International law and human rights. | Financial institutions, International – Law and legislation. | Financial institutions, International – Social aspects. | Human rights – Economic aspects.
CLASSIFICATION: LCC KZ1266 .B37 2019 | DDC 341.4/8–dc23
LC record available at https://lccn.loc.gov/2019008014

ISBN 978-1-108-49286-7 Hardback

I dedicate this book to my mom, my light,
and to my dad, my ground.

Contents

Foreword

A NEW DIMENSION OF INTERNATIONAL RESPONSIBILITY

It is with satisfaction that I write this brief foreword to this book by Dr Ana Sofia Barros, *Governance As Responsibility: Member States As Human Rights Protectors in International Financial Institutions*, for two particular reasons. First, the topicality of the subject requires closer attention in our days, such as that devoted to it by the author in her present work. And second, I have been accompanying the author of the book – at distance, from the World Court here at The Hague – in her earlier years of academic formation and professional work, and I value her vocation and dedication to facing challenges with a humanitarian outlook, so as to safeguard the rights of those more vulnerable.

Since I started reflecting on international responsibility at the University of Cambridge in the seventies, I have deemed it to constitute a most important chapter of international law, ultimately the backbone of the discipline (*The Application of the Rule of Exhaustion of Local Remedies in International Law*, Cambridge University Press, 1983). Along the last decades, I have seen the topic gather steam and expand, and have contributed to it. In effect, contemporary international law, as I have been stressing in my own writings, bears witness of the expansion, altogether, of international jurisdiction, of international responsibility, and of international legal personality and capacity.

The expansion of international jurisdiction is evidenced by the co-existing multiple contemporary international tribunals nowadays. The expansion of international responsibility can be seen in their work (as for State responsibility, e.g., in the decisions of the International Court of Justice and of international human rights tribunals, and as to individuals' responsibility, in those of international criminal tribunals), as well as in the work of the UN International Law Commission (e.g., its articles on responsibility of States, 2001, and of international organisations, 2011).

And the expansion of international legal personality and capacity can be examined in the work mainly of international human rights tribunals, and also of international criminal tribunals.

The work of contemporary international tribunals in distinct domains of the law of nations (e.g., also the law of the sea), as well as the work of the International Law Commission in its endeavours of codification, has been contributing to that complex expansion (inter alia, of international responsibility). Despite all advances achieved, there have subsisted points which call nowadays for further examination, such as that of the allocation of the responsibility between international organisations and their member States.

In her present book, Sofia focuses her attention not exactly on the responsibility of international organisations, but rather, and more precisely, and irrespectively of that, on the obligations and responsibility of their member States under international law. In order to clarify this point, already in the first chapter she addresses the distinction between international organisations and member States in their relationship, as subjects endowed with international legal personality.

In dwelling further on the complex topic in the following chapters, Sofia analyses in depth, in logical sequence, the governance role of member States of international financial institutions, concentrated on their own responsibility for conduct performed in the course of the latter's operations. She singles out such international financial institutions as background for her investigation given the fact that they are rarely scrutinised in current discussions on international responsibility. Her book thus comes to fill a gap in expert writing.

Attentive to the human rights impacts of the activity of international financial institutions, Sofia addresses the topic from the perspective of individuals and their needs of protection. In turning attention to the terms in which the responsibility of member States can be invoked, she considers the legal argumentation to render viable the access of individuals to justice. As she comprehensively shows, human needs ought to be taken into account in all steps of the project cycle, calling for effective mechanisms of redress in case of ensuing harm.

In effect, providing effective access to a remedy to the identified victims, or potential victims, of the operations at issue constitutes a basic pillar of the rule of law in a democratic society. In my own trajectory in two international jurisdictions, I have appealed countless times to the pressing need to strengthen the individual's access to international justice, as also expressed in my books (e.g., *The Access of Individuals to International Justice*, 2011; *Le Droit international pour la personne humaine*, 2012).

I am thus very pleased to see that a scholar of the new generation, Sofia, devotes her endeavours to an aspect of a matter calling for development, namely, that of the consideration of the obligations of member States of international financial institutions, so as to render them amenable in practice, in light of the International Law of Human Rights. The author is duly attentive to the issue of the attribution of conduct to member States of international financial institutions, seeking to contribute to the safeguard of the human rights at stake.

Along her work, the author remains attentive to the attribution of conduct to member States of international financial institutions, which is essential to the understanding of how to distinguish the two subjects of international law. Relying on the role of Executive Directors as State representatives, and their exercise of voting rights as State action, she thus signals an independent locus of international responsibility (of member States), concomitant to the responsibility of the aforementioned international institutions.

Sofia's book constitutes a noteworthy contribution to this effect, in the framework of multilateral development cooperation: in clarifying the terms whereby the responsibility of member States of international financial institutions may be invoked, it puts forward the possibility of a legal claim by individuals before domestic and international courts, against such an allegedly wrongdoing member State.

The already mentioned adoption by the International Law Commission of its Articles on the Responsibility of States (in 2001) and of International Organizations (in 2011) contributed to the systematisation of the matter, but such Articles cannot pretend to be exhaustive, nor the final work on it. While the responsibility of member States was widely discussed, some matters remained somewhat unclear, attribution of conduct having been an illustration to this effect.

Sofia attempts to fill a gap in the debate on attribution of conduct in the context of member State participation in the representative organs of international organisations, with a focus on international financial institutions. It should not pass unnoticed that this focus on member State responsibility may enhance legal accountability, as the author sustains, in that, in her outlook, there are currently more dispute-settlement mechanisms available for complaints against (member) States than for complaints against international organisations themselves.

With her book, Sofia offers an original insight to the ongoing thorny debates around the responsibility of member States of international organisations. In a constructive reasoning, she furthermore sheds light on the application of the International Law of Human Rights to member States of international financial institutions, so as to safeguard the rights of individuals in situations of vulnerability. Her book constitutes a valuable contribution to the matter, and deserves wide readership, also and mainly on the part of the new generation of scholars.

Antônio Augusto Cançado Trindade
The Hague
10 October 2018
Antônio Augusto Cançado Trindade is Judge of the International Court of Justice; Former President of the Inter-American Court of Human Rights; Emeritus Professor of International Law of the University of Brasília, Brazil.

Preface

Over the last two or three decades, international lawyers (and others) have started to realise that while international organisations may still manifest the turning of 'swords into ploughshares' and may still be harbingers of the 'salvation of mankind', nonetheless, as political actors, they merit the same sort of scrutiny that accompanies other political actors. If decisions taken by States can provoke debates in terms of accountability or responsibility, so too can decisions taken by international organisations. Examples may include the activities of the North Atlantic Treaty Organization (NATO) outside its member States, in Serbia, in Afghanistan, off the Somali coast; the involvement of peacekeepers deployed by international organisations such as the United Nations (UN) in sexual abuse, or in torture, or in smuggling; or the way refugee settlements are managed by staff operating on behalf of the UN High Commissioner for Refugees (UNHCR).

Several professional organisations of international lawyers – formal as well as informal – have studied the topic in great depth and have developed methods to try to institutionalise the legal control of acts (and, not unimportantly, omissions) on the part of international organisations. The most authoritative of these, though of limited scope, are the Articles on the Responsibility of International Organizations, adopted by the International Law Commission in 2011: these are authoritative in that they were formulated by the closest body the world has to a legislative preparatory committee, the International Law Commission; but they are limited in scope in that they merely apply in relations between organisations and States or other international organisations. This may cover some of NATO's actions in Afghanistan or Serbia but not all, and does not seriously cover any of the other examples mentioned above.

Less authoritative perhaps, but of broader scope, are the Recommended Rules and Practices adopted by the International Law Association (ILA) in 2004. These aim to address also the situation where the organisation's acts (or omission) affect mostly individuals, such as when UNHCR operates refugee settlements, or UN peacekeepers engage in sexually abusive practices. And a similarly broad scope underpins several large-scale academic projects, such as the Global Administrative

Law approach pioneered at universities in Rome and New York, or the International Public Authority approach emanating from the Heidelberg Max Planck Institute.

Whatever the merits of these projects (and their merits are considerable), they all struggle with one of the central questions in the law of international organisations – the question of legal obligation. Why, and on what basis, can international organisations be said to be bound by international law, to such an extent that their activities can be evaluated against international law? To be sure, there are other unresolved issues, ranging from problems of attribution (if a UN-deployed peacekeeper engages in sexual abuse, is this something that can be attributed to the UN? His home State? The peacekeeper himself? All of these?) to questions of immunity from jurisdiction – domestic courts are notoriously reluctant to pierce the immunity veil covering international organisations. But the question of the basis of legal obligation is a foundational one: if an organisation is not bound by international law to begin with, it cannot be held responsible under international law either, and if international law cannot be the applicable yardstick, then all that rests are subjective conceptions (so the argument goes, however implicitly usually) relating to moral obligations, or proper behaviour, or desirable behaviour.

The International Court of Justice has shed some light on the issue, but not much. In its 1980 advisory opinion on the World Health Organization's regional office in Alexandria, it opined that international organisations are bound by obligations incumbent on them under treaties to which they are parties, under their constitutions, and under 'general rules of international law'. Far from suggesting a proper basis of obligation, this merely states the reasonably obvious (the references to treaties and internal constitutional orders), or begs the question: what is the import of the reference to 'general rules of international law'? Some suggest this is a reference to the entire corpus of customary international law; others feel that such a conclusion is unwarranted – if the Court had wanted to say that international organisations are bound by customary international law, it could simply have said so, without having to resort to obfuscating terminology.

It is this debate about controlling international organisations that Dr Sofia Barros has jumped into, and she has done so with vim, vigour and intelligence, as the book in front of you testifies. Originally defended as a doctoral thesis at the Catholic University of Leuven, the book zooms in on the responsibility of international organisations – in particular the financial institutions – via their member States, and makes a contribution to discussions on State responsibility as well as the responsibility of international organisations. It starts from the *topos* that the law abhors a vacuum: if the financial institutions do something wrong, it seems only fair that somehow someone should incur responsibility. Given the above, it is not all that obvious that organisations can be held responsible in their own right. Hence, perhaps responsibility may rest elsewhere, for instance with the member States.

Earlier work on the responsibility of member States for the acts of international organisations tends either to focus on a responsibility to repair (once a wrongful act has taken place), or to enable the organisation to repair the organisation's wrongful act, and, while useful, this is but one possible aspect of the *problematique*, if only because it still presupposes that obligations rest on international organisations separately – it is the violation by the organisation of an obligation resting on it that triggers responsibility. But it is precisely this aspect, as discussed above, that is so difficult to demonstrate.

What Dr Barros adds to the literature is an exhaustively researched different approach, concentrating on the behaviour of member States when they decide on acts of questionable legality. The member States, after all, do not leave their sovereignty and their own obligations behind when they enter the headquarters of the World Bank or the International Monetary Fund: they play an important role in the governance of those institutions, and for that role (and within the limits of that role), Dr Barros investigates whether those member States may incur responsibility under international law. She does so with elegance and understanding, in a study brimming with useful insights and, importantly, without conflating the obligations of member States and those of their organisations. Instead, the member States are held responsible for acts committed in breach of their own obligations, as members of the organisations concerned.

Like all legal arguments, this one too raises questions and possible rebuttals, and in raising such issues Dr Barros provides new impetus to long-standing debates. As noted, the responsibility of international organisations has been on the agenda for quite some time, and quite a few studies have been devoted to the human rights obligations (*vel non*) of the international financial institutions. Some of those suggest, not entirely persuasively perhaps as a matter of legal analysis, that the financial institutions are bound to respect human rights because human rights are inherently worthy of respect, and it would be unacceptable that public actors could disrespect human rights with impunity. Others suggest, also not entirely persuasively perhaps legally speaking, that the obligation resting on the World Bank and the IMF to respect human rights derives from customary international law. Yet others focus (and again, in law not entirely compellingly perhaps) on the internalisation of those norms by the organisations themselves. In the established chorus of opinions it was difficult to imagine that a new and original voice could make itself heard, but Dr Barros's work proves otherwise: this is an excellent, highly accomplished and innovative legal analysis of an issue that has been puzzling various generations of international lawyers, approaching it from an unexpected but fruitful angle, and doing so with intelligence and diligence.

Jan Klabbers
Helsinki
5 October 2018

Jan Klabbers is Professor of International Law at the University of Helsinki

Acknowledgements

Acknowledgements allow us to look back in time and revive moments. The process of writing this book, which is based on my PhD thesis, was built by uncountable, little moments: the legal discussions at a coffee bar; the shoulder to lean on when the mind got lost; the dinner that was prepared for me so that I could keep on working; the sharing of an ideal and, with it, of plans to make the world a better place. What seemed little turned out to be precious on its own.

Prof. Cedric Ryngaert, who supervised my thesis, deserves my first and foremost ovation, for my gratitude to him is boundless. His support was unwavering from the beginning; his remarks prompt and wise; his engagement genuine. Above all, I thank Cedric for his enduring trust in my work and for encouraging its publication. Prof. Geert de Baere became my supervisor along the way, and I must thank him wholeheartedly for having accepted this task. If my thesis bettered, it was certainly also due to his thorough reviews.

My infinite gratitude extends to Professors Jan Klabbers, Pierre Klein and Niels Blokker, for their guidance and support, very insightful comments, trust and friendship. This book would possibly not exist today if it were not for them. I am likewise infinitely grateful to Judge Antônio Cançado Trindade, above all, for inspiring belief. To Judge Trindade and Prof. Klabbers I owe special thanks, for giving me the honour of writing this book's foreword and preface, respectively.

My book is in the end an accomplishment of many hands. I thank unreservedly Prof. Jan Wouters and all the dear administrative staff and colleagues from the Leuven Centre for Global Governance Studies for allowing my research to flourish in such an enriching and vivid environment. Discussions with my cherished colleagues proved very fruitful along the way – be it in seminars, in the corridors or in the park. Inspiring academic insights came from other places as well. I thank wholeheartedly the GLOTHRO group for the opportunities granted to me within this project, in particular Prof. Wouter Vandenhole and Arne Vandenbogaerde. I owe a fantastic research stay at the Lauterpacht Centre for International Law (Cambridge) to the bright and nice colleagues I found there and, of course, the administrative staff who made it all so easy-going. A big thanks must also be extended to all those who accompanied me at the Erik Castrén Institute of International Law and Human Rights (Helsinki), including Prof. Marti Koskenniemi, for reading and commenting a text included in this book. I moreover owe a debt of gratitude to Dr Mota Pinto for providing me an outstanding research experience at the World Bank, and to all members of Executive Director Office 21 for their very warm welcoming. Access to the life of international financial institutions proved invaluable for this research and I must thank wholeheartedly all the member State representatives, their legal advisors, general counsels and jurists from such organisations for their time and explanations provided during interviews or more informal talks.

This book would of course not exist without the support of Cambridge University Press. I am particularly grateful to Prof. Jean D'Aspremont, to Tom Randall and Gemma Smith for making it all a reality and also for their kindness and patience.

Engaging in such an academic roller coaster would not have been possible without the love of my family and friends. They filled the whole process of writing this book, and the thesis on which it is based, with their warm support and encouragement, their smiles, their stories, their care. From being roots to being sky, they meant, and mean, everything to me, in all their big and little ways of manifesting and shaping moments.

Abbreviations

ACHR	American Convention on Human Rights
AfDB	African Development Bank
AIIB	Asian Infrastructure Investment Bank
AOBs	Absence of Objection Basis
AOI	Arab Organization for Industrialization
ARIO	Articles on the Responsibility of International Organizations
AsDB	Asian Development Bank
ASR	Articles on the Responsibility of States for Internationally Wrongful Acts
BMZ	Federal Ministry for Economic Cooperation and Development
BSTDB	Black Sea Trade and Development Bank
CAO	Compliance Advisor and Ombudsman
CEDAW	Convention on the Elimination of All Forms of Discrimination against Women
CESCR	UN Committee on Economic, Social and Cultural Rights
CFI	EU Court of First Instance
CFSP	Common Foreign and Security Policy
CIEL	Center for International Environmental Law
CJEU	Court of Justice of the European Union
CESCR	Committee on Economic, Social and Cultural Rights
COREPER	Committee of Permanent Representatives
CSO	Civil Society Organisation
DFID	Department for International Development (UK)
EBRD	European Bank for Reconstruction and Development
ECB	European Central Bank
ECHR	European Convention on Human Rights
ECJ	European Court of Justice
ECOFIN	Economic and Financial Affairs Council
ECtHR	European Court of Human Rights

EDS	Executive Director's Office
EEC	European Economic Community
EGC	EU General Court
EIA	Environmental Impact Assessment
EIB	European Investment Bank
ESC	Economic, Social and Cultural (rights)
ESM	European Stability Mechanism
ESF	Environmental and Social Framework (World Bank)
EU	European Union
FRY	Federal Republic of Yugoslavia
FYROM	Former Yugoslav Republic of Macedonia
G7	Group of Seven
G11	Group of Eleven
G20	Group of Twenty
GAL	Global Administrative Law
HRIA	Human Rights Impact Assessment
HRW	Human Rights Watch
IACHR	Inter-American Commission on Human Rights
IACtHR	Inter-American Court of Human Rights
IBRD	International Bank for Reconstruction and Development
ICAO	International Civil Aviation Organization
ICESCR	International Covenant on Economic, Social and Cultural Rights
ICJ	International Court of Justice
ICTY	International Criminal Tribunal for the former Yugoslavia
IDA	International Development Association
IDB	Inter-American Development Bank
IDI	Institut de Droit International
IEG	Independent Evaluation Group (World Bank)
IEO	Independent Evaluation Office (IMF)
IFAD	International Fund for Agricultural Development
IFC	International Finance Corporation
ILA	International Law Association
ILC	International Law Commission
ILO	International Labour Organization
IMF	International Monetary Fund
IMFC	International Monetary and Financial Committee
IRM	Immediate Response Mechanism
ITC	International Tin Council
JICA	Japan International Cooperation Agency
KFOR	Kosovo Force (Kosovo)
MIGA	Multilateral Investment Guarantee Agency
NATO	North Atlantic Treaty Organization

NGO	Non-Governmental Organisation
NIB	Nordic Investment Bank
OAS	Organization of American States
OECD	Organisation for Economic Co-operation and Development
OHCHR	Office of the United Nations High Commissioner for Human Rights
OSCE	Organization for Security and Co-operation in Europe
PCIJ	Permanent Court of International Justice
PRGT	Poverty Reduction and Growth Trust
SCM	Subsidies and Countervailing Measures
TEU	Treaty on European Union
UDHR	Universal Declaration of Human Rights
UN	United Nations
UNGA	United Nations General Assembly
UNMIK	United Nations Mission in Kosovo
UNSC	United Nations Security Council
UK	United Kingdom
US	United States
WB	World Bank
WHL	Westland Helicopters Ltd
WTO	World Trade Organization

Introduction

1 INTERNATIONAL FINANCIAL INSTITUTIONS, THEIR MEMBER STATES AND THE CLAIM FOR HUMAN RIGHTS RESPONSIBILITY

1.1 *The World Problem*

All year long, representatives of the member States of international financial institutions[1] sit at the latter's decision-making bodies[2] to approve projects and programmes aimed at furthering global development. Through the loans thereby made available, dams and oil pipelines are built, public administrations are reformed, general balance of payments support is provided, and programmes for the promotion of basic service delivery, such as health, education or water supply, are implemented.[3] Ultimately, all such cooperative

[1] The expression 'international financial institutions' is used in this book to generally refer to organisations with a developmental or monetary mandate, aimed at offering qualifying member States a range of financial instruments, technical expertise and advisory services. Although they differ in membership, in their specific functions or operational focus, all international financial institutions serve a public purpose, related either to general development goals or to macroeconomic policy. Except for the International Monetary Fund (IMF), most examples referred to in this book relate to the operations of institutions with a developmental mandate (and not, for example, to funds dedicated to a special sector such as the International Fund for Agricultural Development (IFAD)). These are at times termed 'multilateral development banks' and include institutions such as the World Bank (WB) and regional banks such as the Asian Development Bank (AsDB) or the smaller Black Sea Trade and Development Bank (BSTDB). See: M. Ragazzi, 'International Financial Institutions', in *Max Planck Encyclopedia of Public International Law*, last updated May 2014; and D. Bradlow, 'International Law and the Operations of the International Financial Institutions', in D. Bradlow and D. Hunter (eds.), *International Financial Institutions and International Law* (2010) 2, 3.

[2] The expression Executive Board or Board of Executive Directors will be used in generic terms to refer to the decision-making body of an international financial institution. In some cases, this organ can be termed differently: in the Council of Europe Development Bank, for example, it is termed Administrative Council.

[3] This financing assistance is granted in terms that allow international financial institutions to exert significant influence upon the borrower States' governance and policy-making structures (D. Bradlow, 'Developing Countries Debt Crises, International Financial Institutions, and International Law:

undertakings are presumed to nurture the needs of individuals in developing countries.[4]

Reality, however, is sometimes at odds with such a view of a better world, in that institutionalised forms of multilateral development cooperation do not automatically contribute to the promotion of, and respect for, human rights. As has been noted, '[m]any activities undertaken in the name of "development" have subsequently been recognized as ill-conceived and even counter-productive in human rights terms'.[5] This counter-productivity can come about where the best policies and practices are set in place.[6] Given the prominent role of States as

Some Preliminary Thoughts', 51 GYIL (2008) 111, 140) and thereby, to keep a strong hold over the latter's independence to use the loans received (A. Reinisch, 'Aid or Assistance and Direction and Control between States and International Organizations in the Commission of Internationally Wrongful Acts', 7 IOLR (2010) 63, 69).

4 Taking the WB as an example, its main purposes, as currently defined, are to 'end extreme poverty by decreasing the percentage of people living on less than $1.90 a day to no more than 3%' and 'promote shared prosperity by fostering the income growth of the bottom 40% for every country' (see the WB's website: www.worldbank.org/en/about/what-we-do, last consulted 15 October 2018). See also the description of the Bank's purposes contained in Article I of the International Bank for Reconstruction and Development Articles of Agreement, 2 UNTS 134, 27 December 1945 (IBRD Articles of Agreement). The achievement of poverty alleviation through the promotion of economic growth and social equity undoubtedly entails important human rights dimensions and is inextricably linked to the notion that global development is necessarily a sustainable process. See, inter alia: outcome document of the United Nations Conference on Sustainable Development, 'The Future We Want', annexed to the Resolution adopted by the General Assembly on 27 July 2012, UN Doc. A/RES/66/288.

With regard to the IMF, although it is generally mandated under Article I of its Articles of Agreement (2 UNTS 39, 27 December 1945) to promote macroeconomic stabilisation and surveillance, which point to the exclusive consideration of economic or financial factors in its work, para. (ii) does refer to the 'promotion and maintenance of high levels of employment and real income'. The scope of the Fund's mandate has in reality been widened so as to embrace human rights-related aspects: firstly, its financial assistance policies include variables such as 'good governance', equity, the role of women and environmental protection – all of which are deemed to serve the purposes of long-term economic growth (see: M. Darrow, *Between Light and Shadow: The World Bank, the International Monetary Fund and International Human Rights Law* (2003) 170–86); secondly, the IMF provides support to low-income countries via, inter alia, concessional financial support through the Poverty Reduction and Growth Trust (PRGT) (see: IMF Factsheet, 'IMF Support for Low-Income Countries' (2018), available at: www.imf.org/en/About/Factsheets/IMF-Support-for-Low-Income-Countries, last consulted 15 October 2018); and thirdly, increased attention has been paid within the IMF to its role in social protection (see: Independent Evaluation Office of the IMF (IEO), 'The IMF and Social Protection' Issues Paper for an Evaluation by the Independent Evaluation Office (2016)). Next to this, it has been noted that the IMF's debt financing activities can contribute to the establishment of conditions for the realisation of human rights, provided certain requisites are met. See: UN Human Rights Council, Report of the Independent Expert on the effects of foreign debt and other related international financial obligations of States on the full enjoyment of all human rights, particularly economic, social and cultural rights, Cephas Lumina, *Guiding Principles on Foreign Debt and Human Rights,* UN Doc. A/HRC/20/23 (2011) 3 (*UN Guiding Principles on Foreign Debt and Human Rights*).

5 Committee on Economic, Social and Cultural Rights (CESCR), General Comment No. 2 on International Technical Assistance Measures, UN Doc. E/1990/23 (1990) para. 7.

6 UN Office of the United Nations High Commissioner for Human Rights, *UN Guiding Principles on Business and Human Rights* (2011) commentary to Principle 12, 24.

creators and participants in the boards of international financial institutions, the question arises of how their international responsibility may be engaged when things go wrong. For instance, is the Board of Executive Directors internationally responsible for approving a loan to a member State that is used for a project during the implementation of which human rights violations occur? This book will attempt to answer this sort of query, premised on the notion that, after adhering to international financial institutions, member States do not leave their international human rights obligations 'at home'.

Scenarios liable to trigger human rights concerns abound. As an example, the financial and economic crisis witnessed in Europe in the past years has had a sweeping impact on human rights (disproportionately affecting the most vulnerable), and the terms in which it has been managed by international institutions and their member States have contributed to a worse status quo in some countries.[7] With the imposition of austerity policies and conditionality upon indebted States as a response to recession, socioeconomic rights have suffered the most, in that debt service obligations are often fulfilled at the expense of social investment.[8] For instance, a study commissioned by the European Parliament[9] surveying the impacts in Portugal of austerity measures negotiated with the so-called Troika[10] traced severe interferences upon a wide range of human rights, among others, children's rights and notably the right to education,[11] the right to health and healthcare,[12] the right to work[13] and the right to pensions.[14] With particular regard to labour rights, a 2016 Report of Independent Expert Bohoslavsky shows how austerity-related labour law reforms, such as the flexibilisation of the labour market through deregulation, the downsizing of the public sector and the reduction of wages and work-related social benefits, have often resulted in the contravention of States' international human rights obligations, the erosion of labour rights and increased discrimination in the labour market towards

7 See, inter alia: UN Human Rights Council, Report of the Independent Expert on the effects of foreign debt and other related international financial obligations of States on the full enjoyment of human rights, particularly economic, social and cultural rights, Juan Pablo Bohoslavsky, UN Doc. A/HRC/31/60 (2016) 13–17 (UN Human Rights Council 2016 Report on Foreign Debt).

8 *UN Guiding Principles on Foreign Debt and Human Rights*, *supra* note 4, 3.

9 M. Canotilho, Study for the European Parliament LIBE Committee, 'The Impact of the Crisis on Fundamental Rights across Member States of the EU: Country Report on Portugal' (2015) (European Parliament Country Report on Portugal).

10 The Troika comprises the European Commission, the European Central Bank (ECB) and the IMF.

11 As noted, Portugal's expenditure on education has been significantly reduced – with children who have special needs or learning disabilities being particularly affected (see 20–5 of the European Parliament Country Report on Portugal, *supra* note 9).

12 Owing to the closure of hospitals and other health units, the rise in healthcare fees and the reduction of free transportation of non-urgent patients (ibid., 26–33).

13 The Report notes that this right has been the most affected one, on the basis of pay-cuts, reduction of severance payments and an expansion in working hours without additional pay (ibid., 34–40).

14 As reported, this right suffered pay-cuts and the rules for calculating the amount of pension became more severe (ibid., 41–3).

young and older persons and individuals belonging to marginalised social groups.[15] With such types of macroeconomic and structural policies being pursued, failures of the past seem to linger[16] – and this to the detriment of 'citizen solidarity', as observed by former IMF Managing Director Strauss-Kahn.[17]

The human rights implications of multilateral development bank operations are likewise extensive. Older accounts of WB-financed projects[18] have extensively condemned the environmental and social damages arising therefrom. These include broader claims of accelerated deforestation of the tropics and neglect for rural farmers in agriculture projects,[19] the forced resettlement of large numbers of people and inundation of areas of great environmental and scientific importance stemming from hydroelectric projects,[20] and more specific allegations such as that of arsenic poisoning deriving from a project intended to provide groundwater from tube wells.[21] Here, as elsewhere, the past seems to haunt the present, and, despite the

15 UN Human Rights Council, Report of the Independent Expert on the effects of foreign debt and other related international financial obligations of States on the full enjoyment of all human rights, particularly economic, social and cultural rights, Juan Pablo Bohoslavsky, UN Doc. A/HRC/34/57 (2016) especially 8–14.

16 Consider, e.g., the East Asian crisis, where unemployment rates were seen to rise exponentially, reaching levels which were three to five times higher than they had been before the crisis, despite the IMF's interventions. See: J. Stiglitz, 'Democratizing the International Monetary Fund and the World Bank: Governance and Accountability', 16 *Columbia Academic Commons* (2003) 111, 112, 113, and the IMF's own assessment of its 2010 intervention in Greece, entitled 'Greece: Ex Post Evaluation of Exceptional Access under the 2010 Stand-By Arrangement', IMF Country Report No. 13/156 (2013), asserting that 'the burden of adjustment was not shared evenly across society' (24), that its programme left 'taxpayers and the official sector on the hook' (28), and – on account of the deep recession and 'exceptionally high unemployment' – conceding that '[t]he program did not restore growth and regain market access as it had set out to do' (32).

17 In an open letter addressed to Germany in 2015, drawing on the Greek bailout deal, Dominique Strauss-Kahn affirms that 'the demon that makes us repeat our errors of the past is never far away . . . In counting our billions instead of using them to build . . . in preferring to humiliate a people because they are unable to reform, and putting resentments – however justified – before projects for the future, we are turning our backs on what Europe should be, we are turning our backs on Habermas' citizen solidarity.' The letter may be found at: http://en.protothema.gr/former-imf-chief-d-strauss-kahns-inspirational-address-to-germans/, last consulted 15 October 2018. The IMF's failure to apply lessons from past crises, notably the Asian one, was corroborated in a recent study of the IEO. See: Report of the Independent Evaluation Office of the IMF, 'The IMF and the Crises in Greece, Ireland, and Portugal' (2016) 38. It is of note that the imposition of strict conditionality by the IMF is not required by its Articles of Agreement, as observed by J. M. Boughton, 'Many Borrowers; How Many Sizes? IMF Lending and Program Design', in *Tearing Down Walls: The International Monetary Fund 1990–1999* (2012) 193.

18 The WB refers generally to the International Bank for Reconstruction and Development (IBRD), the International Development Association (IDA), the International Finance Corporation (IFC), the Multilateral Investment Guarantee Agency (MIGA), to the exclusion of the International Centre for the Settlement of Investment Disputes.

19 B. M. Rich, 'The Multilateral Development Banks, Environmental Policy, and the United States', 12 Ecology LQ (1984–5) 681, 689 et seq.

20 Ibid., 701, 702.

21 L. A. Kornhauser, 'Incentives, Compensation and Irreparable Harm', in A. Nollkaemper and D. Jacobs (eds.), *Distribution of Responsibilities in International Law* (2015) 144–8.

improvement of the Bank's operational policies,[22] still today 'far too many violations' of the rights to water and sanitation stemming from large-scale development projects are brought to the attention of the Special Rapporteur on the right to food,[23] to name but one example. While projects involving infrastructure, extractive industries and energy stand out as the types of project that lead to most complaints against international financial institutions, even those that are explicitly tailored to produce direct social benefits have raised serious human rights concerns.[24] This is exemplified by the 'villagization' initiative in Ethiopia, where the WB's Promoting Basic Services Program, aimed at supporting education, health, water, sanitation, rural roads and agriculture extension services, has allegedly been linked to 'arbitrary arrests and detention, forced evictions, beatings, torture, killings . . . and inadequate access to food, health care and water'.[25]

In sum, international financial institutions deal with a multitude of matters, ranging from taxation to environmental protection, which almost unavoidably interfere with the enjoyment of human rights – often economic, social and cultural rights. As will be argued in this book, it is essential to ensure that the human rights impacts of all such operations satisfy proportionality tests and that development processes are equipped with procedural safeguards for an effective protection of the rights of their beneficiaries.

1.2 *The Book's Focus*

The abovementioned examples evince the pertinence of judging the impact of international financial institution operations against human rights standards.[26] At the same time, they bring to the fore complex questions when it comes to

22 For a good synthesis of how the WB's operational policies have evolved, see: N. Bugalski, 'The Demise of Accountability at the World Bank?', 31(1) Am U L Rev (2016) 1, 5–9.

23 UN Human Rights Council, Report of the Special Rapporteur on the right to food, Hilal Elver, *Access to Justice and the Right to Food: The Way Forward*, UN Doc. A/HRC/28/65 (2014) para. 31.

24 C. Daniel, K. Genovese, M. van Huijstee and S. Singh (eds.), 'Glass Half Full? The State of Accountability in Development Finance' (2016) 36 ('Glass Half Full Report'), available at: www.ciel.org/wp-content/uploads/2016/01/IAM_DEF_WEB.pdf, last consulted 15 October 2018.

25 Human Rights Watch, 'Abuse-Free Development: How the World Bank Should Safeguard Against Human Rights Violations' (2013) 1–3, 36, 38 (hereinafter 'HRW Abuse-Free Development Report'). This case led to the submission of a Request to the WB Inspection Panel by the state of Gambella's Anuak Indigenous Peoples. In its Investigation Report, *Ethiopia: Promoting Basic Services Phase III Project (P128891)*, Report No. 91854-ET, 21 November 2014, the panel conceded, inter alia, that the programme's design had not sufficiently assessed and mitigated the risks deriving from Ethiopia's resettlement operations, particularly in the delivery of agricultural services to the Anuaks, thereby producing grave impacts upon the villagers' livelihood and their food security (see: paras. 214–22).

26 That the operations and decisions taken within the remit of international financial institutions must be compatible with international human rights law has been extensively emphasized by legal scholars and practitioners. See inter alia: UN Human Rights Council, Report of the Special Rapporteur on Extreme Poverty and Human Rights, Philip Alston, UN Doc. A/70/274 (2015); Letter of 28 Special Rapporteurs to the WB President Jim Yong Kim in the context of the process of review of the Bank's

determining which entity is to be held internationally responsible for human rights harm. The problem is general in nature, and essentially relates to the question of how to reorganise sites of power (and thereby ponder international responsibility) in a global governance structure whereby new actors have played increasingly influential roles.[27] It is thus conceivable to impute human rights responsibility to the various international legal subjects involved, i.e., to the borrowing State, to the international financial institution and to its member States. Recently, an argument of the sort was made by De Schutter and Salomon when analysing the Troika's imposition of macroeconomic adjustment conditions for the provision of financial assistance to Greece.[28]

The human rights responsibility of the borrower State is an obvious focus of attention: as a party to a range of human rights treaties, it has undertaken to protect the human rights of individuals under its jurisdiction and, thus, is not to ignore its obligations in the negotiation and conclusion of agreements with its creditors.[29] As a matter of fact, cases have recently been brought against Greece, with success, before the Council of Europe's European Committee of Social Rights, for having violated the right to social security through the adoption of austerity measures.[30] Part of Greece's defence was based on the argument that the restrictions upon social protection complained of had been effected due to its obligations vis-à-vis the Troika.[31] While the Committee rejected this argument,[32] it is true that, indeed, the responsibility of the European Commission, the ECB and the IMF may have also been at stake.

safeguard policies (2014), available at: www.ohchr.org/Documents/Issues/EPoverty/WorldBank.pdf, last consulted 15 October 2018; UN Human Rights Council, Report of the Special Rapporteur on adequate housing as a component of the right to an adequate standard of living, and on the right to non-discrimination in this context, Mission to the World Bank, Raquel Rolnik, UN Doc. A/HRC/22/46/Add.3 (2013); M. Salomon, 'Of Austerity, Human Rights and International Institutions', 21(4) Eur LJ (2015) 521; HRW Abuse-Free Development Report, *supra* note 25.

27 D. Held and A. Mcgrew, *Globalization / Anti-Globalization: Beyond the Great Divide* (2007) 2–4.

28 O. De Schutter and M. Salomon, Legal Brief Prepared for the Special Committee of the Hellenic Parliament on the Audit of the Greek Debt (Debt Truth Committee), 'Economic Policy Conditionality: Socio-Economic Rights and International Legal Responsibility: The Case of Greece 2010–2015' (2015) (hereinafter 'Legal Brief on the Case of Greece'). See also: M. Salomon, *supra* note 26, 537–40.

29 See, e.g.: Committee on the Elimination of Discrimination against Women, Concluding Observations on the seventh periodic report of Greece, UN Doc. CEDAW/C/GRC/CO/7 (2013) para. 6, referring to the detrimental effects of the measures taken by Greece, in cooperation with the EU and the IMF, to address the financial crisis and the country's persisting human rights obligations.

30 *Federation of pensioners IKA-ETAM* v. *Greece*, European Committee of Social Rights, Decision on the Merits, Complaint No. 76/2012, 7 December 2012. As noted in para. 7 of the decision, the complaint was one in a series of collective complaints regarding the same facts, namely those registered as Nos. 76/2012 to 80/2012.

31 Ibid., para. 10.

32 Ibid., paras. 50, 51, arguing that said international obligations do not remove domestic measures from the ambit of the European Social Charter.

This brings to the fore a parallel locus of responsibility: that of the international (financial) institution. The question has, yet again, recently been raised within the context of the European crisis, this time before the Court of Justice of the European Union (CJEU). It concerned the financial assistance facility provided to the Republic of Cyprus and the attendant responsibility of the European Commission and the ECB.[33] Focusing on the institutions' conduct, performed on behalf of the European Stability Mechanism (ESM),[34] the CJEU remarkably asserted that 'the Charter [of Fundamental Rights of the European Union] is addressed to the EU institutions, including ... when they act outside the EU legal framework'.[35] These are certainly interesting developments. They are, however, quite specific to the EU context, notably, the obligations of EU institutions. Although it is widely accepted that international organisations are bound by international law, including international human rights law, it remains unclear which obligations under the latter field specifically apply to them. Thus far, lawsuits filed against international financial institutions for alleged human rights violations have proved unsuccessful.[36] More research is needed in this respect, in that much (in the size of another monograph) is still to be discussed: while international (financial) institutions are certainly responsible for their own conduct, the contours of invocation of said responsibility remain uncertain.

Despite the plurality of centres upon which responsibility for the protection of human rights may be imputed, this book will not address them all. It will rather focus on the member States of international financial institutions as global development actors in their own right. It will notably explore how the human rights framework shapes the creation and participation of member States in institutional operations and how secondary rules of international law may be engaged in cases of failure to comply with human rights requirements. A key trigger for the present monograph lies in the basic assumption that if member States, acting as international legal subjects, and the organisations they create *affect* individuals, then the former must make sure that this impact does not occur to the detriment of the international

33 Joined Cases C-8/15 P to C-10/15 P, *Ledra Advertising Ltd and Others* v. *European Commission and European Central Bank*, 20 September 2016.

34 The ESM is an international financial institution created in 2012 to mobilise funding and provide stability support under strict conditionality to ESM members. See: Treaty Establishing the ESM, signed on 2 February 2012, Articles 1 and 3.

35 *Ledra* v. *European Commission and European Central Bank*, *supra* note 33, para. 67. It is of note that the question had been left unresolved in Case C-370/12, *Thomas Pringle* v. *Ireland*, 27 November 2012.

36 Lawsuits have been filed against international financial institutions for alleged human rights violations stemming from policy mistakes. Mention could be made of a claim filed by a group of South Korean labour unions against the IMF, blaming the organisation for giving wrong advice when austerity measures were imposed on the country, thereby causing businesses to fail and unemployment to rise (see: Brettonwoods Project, 'Korean Workers Lawsuit Against IMF Thrown Out', 15 April 2000, available at: www.brettonwoodsproject.org/2000/04/art-15638/, last consulted 15 October 2018). The lack of success of these lawsuits is mostly owed to immunity questions, of course (see Section 3.4.2.2, C).

human rights obligations they are bound to observe. As will be seen, such a guaranteeing role is substantiated by procedural requirements of due diligence.

It is sometimes observed that the main reason why member State responsibility is pondered relates to the difficulties around the establishment of international organisation responsibility.[37] Not only are the latter's internal accountability mechanisms underdeveloped, but also, the fact remains that their conduct is hardly liable to judicial adjudication: at the international level, since no standing international court or tribunal enjoys jurisdiction to do so; and at the domestic level, as courts will inevitably grapple with issues of immunity. While all such hurdles might indeed steer third parties towards claiming reparation from member States in cases where international organisation responsibility is quite likely at issue, it is submitted here that the parallel sphere of responsibility of the member States cannot be overlooked. Indeed, as this book will demonstrate, notably in Chapter II, there may very well be valid reasons to claim member State responsibility for/in connection with international organisation conduct and, principally, for their own acts performed in institutional settings. To be sure, to discuss member States' responsibility does not in any way negate the separate legal personality of international organisations and their own responsibility under international law; rather, discussing member States' responsibility for their own behaviour *solely* brings to view a parallel sphere of conduct (to that of the organisation), which is liable to judgement against international legal prescriptions.

In the grand scheme of things, then, this book – focusing as it does on member State responsibility – responds only partially to the question of how to establish international responsibility when it comes to international financial institution operations and attendant injurious human rights impacts. In other words, it solely explores one piece of the responsibility puzzle. Indeed, responsibility in the contexts addressed in this book mainly lies in the hands of the organisation, as decision-maker and executor of programmes and projects. International financial institutions comprise thousands of staff members that make decisions on a daily basis, determine benchmarks and priorities in project implementation, mobilise resources on the ground, evaluate risks and create data. For all this, said organisations will be held responsible if things go wrong. This fact, notwithstanding, does not invalidate the possibility of inquiring into whether the member States were in some way involved in said wrongs.

A few instances of international responsibility therefore arise: as already mentioned, it is highly likely that in most cases only the responsibility of the international

37 See, e.g.: N. Blokker, 'Member State Responsibility for Wrongdoings of International Organizations: Beacon of Hope or Delusion?', in A. S. Barros, C. Ryngaert and J. Wouters (eds.), *International Organizations and Member State Responsibility: Critical Perspectives* (2016) 34; C. Ryngaert and H. Buchanan, 'Member State Responsibility for the Acts of International Organizations', 7 ULR (2011) 131, 146; R. Wilde, 'Enhancing Accountability at the International Level: The Tension between International Organization and Member State Responsibility and the Underlying Issues at Stake', 12 ILSA J Int'l & Comp L (2006) 395, 408, 409.

financial institution for its own wrongful conduct will be at stake; exceptionally, the responsibility of member States may be invoked for/in connection with the wrongs committed by the organisation; exceptionally, again, the responsibility of member States may be invoked for their own wrongful conduct performed in an institutional setting. It is not this book's purpose to address the first hypothesis, that is, the responsibility of international organisations. It will take it as given that international organisations are responsible for their own conduct and that this responsibility can be invoked separately. When it comes to the member States, the book will test, to the extent possible, their responsibility for/in connection with the conduct of international organisations; still, the major part of the analysis will concentrate on member States' responsibility for their own wrongful behaviour.

The book will examine member States' responsibility from the viewpoint of their governance role. It will draw on a novel sphere in which State power has been institutionalised and reconstruct the political reality of the State as a global actor within multilateral cooperative undertakings.[38] Said 'novel sphere' can, for instance, be discerned in the WB's official description of its governance bodies: 'The organizations that make up the World Bank Group are owned by the governments of member nations, which have the ultimate decision-making power within the organizations on all matters, including policy, financial or membership issues. Member countries govern the World Bank Group through the Boards of Governors and the Boards of Executive Directors.'[39] Member States' role as governors thus relates to the notion that they *own* the organisation and have decision-making power on all institutional matters.

The concept of governance has been said to stem from the Greek *kybernan*, which means to pilot, steer or direct.[40] It relates to how actors are capable of providing direction and control for society,[41] thereby yielding collective goods for a particular community.[42] In this book, the notion will be picked up to depict the

[38] Political scientists have explored at length the shifting role of States in the global order by noting the transition from a world of 'government' to one of 'governance'. Various 'theories of the State' have been advanced to describe this phenomenon, notably those of 'governance as the hollowing out of the State', 'degovernancing', 'state-centred governance' and 'big governance', which is marked by the notion of regulatory States. According to the last two perspectives, States still play a leading role in global governance without, however, monopolising authority. This is the understanding that is embraced in this book. See: D. Levi-Faur, 'From "Big Government" to "Big Governance"', in D. Levi-Faur (ed.), *Oxford Handbook on Governance* (2012) 3, 10–14.

Yet, an important distinction must be made between the role that States assume at the global level in a unilateral fashion (think of the exercise of universal jurisdiction under Articles 5 and 7 of the UN Convention Against Torture) and their role in multilateral settings – which includes their participation in international organisations. The latter form of international cooperation can be said to bring about a 'new' role for States, as their subjectivity is defined (for international law purposes) in light of their relationship with the international organisation wherein they operate.

[39] The website is available at:www.worldbank.org/en/about/leadership/members, last consulted 15 October 2018.

[40] D. Levi-Faur, *supra* note 38, 5.

[41] B. Guy Peters, 'Governance As Political Theory', in D. Levi-Faur (ed.), op. cit. *supra* note 38, 19.

[42] T. Risse, 'Governance in Areas of Limited Statehood', in D. Levi-Faur (ed.), op. cit. *supra* note 38, 700.

steering role assumed by States in international financial institutions and the terms in which their actions serve common developmental needs.[43]

But is this not, after all, a matter of politics? As has been observed, there is an 'inherent conflict between law and politics at the heart of the practice of States conferring governmental powers on international organizations'.[44] Drawing on member State governance could thus be seen as 'unduly cloaking the exercise of power within concepts of legality'.[45] Yet, it is submitted here that leaving the matter unexplored in legal terms, which is currently (almost) the case in the literature, is tantamount to unduly cloaking member State exercise of power within concepts of politics. As will be demonstrated in this book, State adherence to international financial institutions does have human rights implications which merit careful attention. Said implications may in some cases lead to the invocation of member State responsibility. If politics are also a question of legitimacy and credibility, the truth is that, in creating and participating in international financial institutions to strengthen cooperation in global development, member States can only be fully credible in what they do if they are prepared to assume responsibility for it.

1.3 *Member State (Human Rights) Responsibility As an Ongoing Discussion*

The main concern underlying this book relates to the fact that the operations of international financial institutions and their member States may produce negative impacts upon human rights, without there being clear criteria, in international law, to establish member State responsibility in said contexts. The absence of a consistent analytical framework to notably assess the creation, by member States, of international financial institutions, and their participation in the latter, runs counter to

43 Some level of generalisation when referring to the 'member States of international financial institutions' is unavoidable, as it would be impractical to cover even half of the existing international financial institutions. Governance dynamics within these organisations (e.g. powers, functioning and bureaucratic institutionalisation) will necessarily differ if a more in-depth account is undertaken. For example, the BSTDB does not have a resident Executive Board, in contrast with the Bretton Woods institutions. However, for the purposes of this book, which works upon *legal categories* and is meant to provide a general conceptual framework to determine the responsibility of the member States of international financial institutions, such differences do not seem to matter much. Indeed, the governance structure of all these organisations can to some extent be analogised to the corporate model, with shareholders and a weighted voting system that is based on the number of shares or quotas that each member State has subscribed, which, in turn, is linked to the relative size of each member's economy (see M. Ragazzi, *supra* note 1, para. 13). Importantly, the regional financial institutions that were created in the post–World War II era generally followed the institutional set-up of the Bretton Woods organisations, with the Boards of Governors (plenary organ) and Executive Directors (executive organ) assuming the governance and representative functions of these organisations (see Chapter II).

44 D. Sarooshi, *International Organizations and Their Exercise of Sovereign Powers* (2005) 31.

45 I. Venzke, 'International Bureaucracies from a Political Science Perspective – Agency, Authority and International Institutional Law', 09(11) GLJ (2008) 1401, 1423.

an effective protection of human rights, and inescapably hampers individual attempts to obtain reparation for damage, or the risk of damage, caused by wrongdoing member States.

Such a state of affairs is owed to various factors, all of which bring about intricate legal questions that have not been sufficiently addressed in the literature. This holds true for scholarly work on either primary rules or secondary rules of international law[46] – even if it is generally claimed that the member States of international (financial) institutions indeed bear human rights obligations and, thereby, responsibility under international law.[47] What remains underdeveloped in academic writings is how to legally (i.e., technically) construct said claim.

A more profound problem lies perhaps in the intersection between international human rights law and international institutional law: while interpretations of the former may at times sound rather vague in their – somewhat idealistic – attempt to blame member States for *everything*,[48] scholars from the latter field may sometimes pay too much deference to the functionalist needs of the international organisation (i.e., the preservation of its legal personality and autonomy) when discussing responsibility matters.[49] In order to find an appropriate response to this book's topic, a balance must thus be sought between both international legal fields.

When it comes to primary law, the question arises of how to extend the scope of application of international obligations to the new forms in which States operate at the global level. Through their membership in international organisations, States exercise public power, and, thus, it is first of all sound to inquire whether such exercises endure (international) constitutional limitations. Doctrinal attempts to introduce elements of the rule of law tradition in international institutional contexts mainly draw, however, on the exercise of power by international organisations, and

46 As explained by Crawford, primary rules are to be distinguished from secondary rules in that the former place obligations upon States, while the latter generally determine the conditions under which those obligations have been violated and what the consequences of such violations are. See: J. Crawford, *State Responsibility: The General Part* (2013) 64–6.

47 See, inter alia: notes 899 and 900 *infra*, for references to CESCR general comments and concluding observations and note 950 for bibliography references.

48 See, e.g.: Appeal submitted by The Global Initiative for Economic, Social and Cultural Rights, Rights Action and the International Human Rights Clinic at Western New England University School of Law, on behalf of the Survivors of the Río Negro community and similar Chixoy Dam harmed communities in the Chixoy river basin, Guatemala (Petitioners), Case P-894-04, 7 December 2011 (hereinafter *Chixoy Dam* petition), alleging several human rights violations owed to the construction of a hydroelectric dam, available at: http://209.240.139.114/wp-content/uploads/2012/01/120119ChixoyPetition.pdf, last consulted 15 October 2018. This case is further discussed in Section 2.1.3.1. For an academic example, see: S. Yee, 'The Responsibility of States Members of an International Organization for Its Conduct as a Result of Membership or Their Normal Conduct Associated with Membership', in M. Ragazzi (ed.), *International Responsibility Today: Essays in Memory of Oscar Schachter* (2005) 435.

49 See, e.g.: Articles on the Responsibility of International Organizations, with commentaries, in Report of the International Law Commission, Sixty-Third Session, UN Doc. A/66/10 (2011) (ARIO), and the discussions preceding its adoption, as well as the positions defended by A. Pellet in, inter alia, ILC, Summary record of the 2892nd meeting, UN Doc. A/CN.4/2892, YILC, 2006, Vol. I., 156.

not the member States.[50] Rule of law-based procedural standards certainly apply to the latter, in terms that can be best understood by resorting to international human rights law, as will be further examined in this book.[51] What begs further discussion then is, firstly, to whom such member State obligations are owed and, secondly, what contours they specifically assume in institutional settings. The former query poses conceptual and practical challenges to international human rights law, in that it ventures into extraterritoriality issues[52] and begs for a solid understanding of how these issues are affected by the position of power held by member States vis-à-vis international organisations.[53] As regards the second query, although the case-law of human rights bodies hints at the imposition of due diligence duties upon member States (i.e., duties to monitor and secure the human rights conformity of the organisation's operations),[54] it does not offer comprehensive normative guidance on how they concretely apply in an institutional setting. In the literature, references to this particular topic are made only in passing,[55] and general international legal studies on due diligence fall short of operationalising such a standard in institutional contexts.[56]

At the level of secondary rules of international law, knowledge gaps likewise exist. They revolve around the implications, for international responsibility purposes, of the

[50] See, inter alia: A. Von Bogdandy, R. Wolfrum, J. V. Bernstorff, P. Dann and M. Goldmann (eds.), *The Exercise of Public Authority by International Institutions: Advancing International Institutional Law* (2009); N. Walker, 'Post-Constituent Constitutionalism? The Case of the European Union', and B. Fassbender, 'We the Peoples of the United Nations' Constituent Power and Constitutional Form in International Law', both in M. Loughlin and N. Walker (eds.), *The Paradox of Constitutionalism: Constituent Power and Constitutional Form* (2008); and International Law Association, Accountability of International Organisations Committee, Final Report, Report of the Seventy-First Conference held in Berlin, 2004 (ILA Report on Accountability of International Organisations).

[51] Section 3.2 will briefly discuss the relationship between the rule of law and human rights.

[52] W. Vandenhole and W. V. Genugten, 'Introduction: An Emerging Multi-Duty-Bearer Human Rights Regime?', in W. Vandenhole (ed.), *Challenging Territoriality in Human Rights Law: Building Blocks for a Plural and Diverse Duty-Bearer Regime* (2015) 1.
As will be discussed in Section 3.3.1.2, the circumstances under which human rights are seen to apply extraterritorially in the case-law of the European and Inter-American human rights regimes are hardly applicable to the context of member State participation in international financial institutions.

[53] The few contributions in this respect include: S. Narula, 'International Financial Institutions, Transnational Corporations and Duties of States', in M. Langford, W. Vandenhole, M. Scheinin and W. V. Genugten (eds.), *Global Justice, State Duties: The Extraterritorial Scope of Economic, Social, and Cultural Rights in International Law* (2013) 120–8, 131–5; Maastricht Principles on Extraterritorial Obligations of States in the area of Economic, Social and Cultural Rights, adopted by international experts on 28 September 2011, especially Principles 9(c) and 15 (hereinafter Maastricht Principles).

[54] See *infra* Section 3.3.

[55] Rare references can be found in: A. Khalfan, 'Division of Responsibility amongst States', in M. Langford, W. Vandenhole, M. Scheinin and W. V. Genugten (eds.), op. cit. *supra* note 53, 311, 312; P. De Sena, 'International Monetary Fund, World Bank and Respect for Human Rights: A Critical Point of View', 20(1) Italian YB Int'l L (2010) 247, 257, 258, 264, 265.

[56] See, inter alia: ILA Study Group on Due Diligence in International Law, First Report (2014) (ILA Due Diligence Report); and R. Pisillo-Mazzeschi, *'Due Diligence' e Responsabilità Internazionale Degli Stati* (1989).

institutional veil – which symbolises the transparent legal set-up of international organisations, with member States to some degree being visible behind the veil that clothes them.[57] For member States to be found responsible under international law, they must have acted as sovereign States (i.e., as international legal subjects) and not as integral parts of the organisation, which entails a thorough understanding of how the legal distinctness of both subjects comes about. Herein lies the crux of the application of attribution rules. Yet, the role played by both actors, and their interaction, has not been sufficiently captured in legal scholarship dealing with international responsibility questions. Said gap notably extends to the participation of member States in the governance bodies of international organisations in general.[58] To be sure, most discussions around the establishment of member State responsibility draw on the role of States either as troop contributors or as implementers of institutional decisions (see *infra* Section 2.1.2.2), in institutional settings such as the UN,[59] NATO[60] and the EU.[61]

The composite character of international organisations[62] – made up as they are of member States – somehow gives the impression that there will always be a multi-layered contribution to the wrong. This creates the risk of embarking into a spiral of responsibility buck-passing,[63] which this book precisely aims at avoiding. The solution cannot

57 C. Brölmann, *The Institutional Veil in Public International Law: International Organisations and the Law of Treaties* (2007) 1. The author further addresses the implications of the institutional veil for international responsibility purposes in: 'Member States and International Legal Responsibility: Developments of the Institutional Veil', in A. S. Barros, C. Ryngaert and J. Wouters (eds.), op. cit. *supra* note 37, 72–94, without, however, delving much into the governance role of member States.

58 See, exceptionally: A. S. Barros and C. Ryngaert, 'The Position of Member States in (Autonomous) Institutional Decision-Making: Implications for the Establishment of Responsibility', 11(1) IOLR (2014) and A. S. Barros, 'Member States and the International Legal (Dis)order: Accounting for the Notion of Responsible Governance', in A. S. Barros, C. Ryngaert and J. Wouters (eds.), op. cit. *supra* note 37. Member State power within the governance bodies of international organisations has otherwise found a place for analysis in political science writings, which are of some use for this book. See, inter alia: R. Stone, *Controlling Institutions: International Organizations and the Global Economy* (2011); Report of the Independent Evaluation Office of the IMF, 'Governance of the IMF: An Evaluation', 2008, 6, available at: www.ieo-imf.org/ieo/pages/CompletedEvaluation110.aspx, last consulted 15 October 2018 (IEO Report on IMF Governance).

59 See, inter alia: A. Tzanakopoulos, 'Sharing Responsibility for UN Targeted Sanctions', in A. S. Barros, C. Ryngaert and J. Wouters (eds.), op. cit. *supra* note 37; C. Ryngaert, 'Apportioning Responsibility between the UN and Member States in UN Peace-Support Operations: An Inquiry Into the Application of the "Effective Control" Standard after Behrami', 45(1) Israel L R (2012).

60 See, inter alia: T. Stein, 'Kosovo and the International Community: The Attribution of Possible Internationally Wrongful Acts: Responsibility of NATO or of Its Member States', in C. Tomuschat (ed.), *Kosovo and the International Community: A Legal Assessment* (2002).

61 A. Sari and R. Wessel, 'International Responsibility for EU Military Operations: Finding the EU's Place in the Global Accountability Regime', in B. Van Vooren, S. Blockmans and J. Wouters (eds.), *The EU's Role in Global Governance: The Legal Dimension* (2013); P. J. Kuijper and E. Paasivirta, 'EU International Responsibility and Its Attribution: From the Inside Looking Out', in M. Evans and P. Koutrakos (eds.), *The International Responsibility of the European Union: European and International Perspectives* (2013).

62 P. Reuteur, *Institutions Internationales* (1969) 71.

63 R. Pierik, 'Shared Responsibility in International Law: A Normative-Philosophical Analysis', in A. Nollkaemper and D. Jacobs (eds.), op. cit. *supra* note 21, 53.

but be found in the delineation of clear criteria to establish member State responsibility. Still, the regime, as currently devised, does not offer the desired results. Early debates on the matter, followed by the authoritative work of the *Institut de Droit International* (IDI),[64] mainly focused on the international legal personality and autonomy of international organisations – member State responsibility coming in only as a derivative factor. What the majority agreed upon was that member States should not be held responsible for institutional wrongs by virtue of their membership alone.[65]

Such a legacy was kept in the framework construed by the International Law Commission (ILC) in Part V of the ARIO.[66] While the ILC undertook the important task of further developing criteria to establish member State responsibility for/in connection with the acts of international organisations,[67] these only apply to a limited set of circumstances. Besides, they do not offer comprehensive guidance as to how to establish member States' responsibility for their own wrongful behaviour. The ARIO undoubtedly constitute a useful starting point to investigate member State responsibility, but do not specifically respond to the question of how to engage States' responsibility for their governance role performed in international (financial) institutions. In any event, the ARIO acknowledge that '[n]ot all the questions that may affect the responsibility of a State in connection with the act of an international organization are examined in the present draft articles',[68] thereby leaving open for consideration the application of the ILC's Articles on the Responsibility of States for Internationally Wrongful Acts (ASR).[69]

Against this backdrop, the present study explores possible future avenues for the questions left unregulated by the normative framework so far devised by the ILC. Drawing on the member States of international financial institutions, it seeks to frame the former's governance power vis-à-vis the organisation under international (human rights) law and to subsume it in a coherent set of secondary rules of international law.

2 APPROACH TO THE TOPIC: POWER, THE INDIVIDUAL AND THE LAW

A commentator once raised the question: 'What is the relationship between one's motive for imagining power and the image one ends up with?'[70] Far from being an

64 Institut de Droit International, 'The legal consequences for member states of the non-fulfilment by international organizations of their obligations toward third parties', in Ann IDI, Session de Lisbonne, Vol. 66-I (1995) 465 et seq. (IDI Resolution on Member State Responsibility).

65 Ibid., Article 6(a).

66 *Supra* note 49, 50–170.

67 Through aid or assistance (Article 58), direction and control (Article 59), coercion (Article 60) and circumvention (Article 61).

68 See: para. 2 of the introductory commentaries to Part V ARIO.

69 Articles on Responsibility of States for Internationally Wrongful Acts, with commentaries, Yearbook of the International Law Commission, Vol. II (Part Two), *Fifty-Third Session*, UN Doc. A/CN.4/SER.A/2001/Add.1 (2001).

70 W. Said, 'Foucault and the Imagination of Power', in D. C. Hoy (ed.), *Foucault: A Critical Reader* (1986) 151.

abstraction, this question is important for the present analysis on member State responsibility. A correlation can indeed be found between this book's reasons for imagining member State power and the image it ends up with. Inasmuch as responsibility constitutes a formal mode of legal reasoning that is employed to determine and allocate injurious exercises of power,[71] its 'dynamics, potential, and limitations cannot be understood without considering the particular normative interests it serves'.[72]

Admittedly, there is an ideal of justice that is captured in this book, one that is centred on the protection of the human rights of those who are affected by institutional operations. This is reflected throughout its various chapters: in the constitutionalist lens through which member State governance functions are addressed; in the interpretative extension of international human rights law extraterritorially; or in the conceptualisation of the regime of member State responsibility. Yet, in allowing such an ideal to guide the analysis, one should not fall into the traps of 'human rightism', as put by Pellet, notably, of taking certain desires for realities as legal truths and presenting political projects as scientific certainties.[73] While such *tendencies* may at times be found in legal writings, they certainly go beyond the use of international law in a purposive fashion. To be sure, this book seeks for scientific rigour in the interpretation of international law.

It is important to note, along Higgins, that when it comes to uncertain areas of international law such as that of the international responsibility of international organisations and their member States, looking into policy considerations comes forth as an 'entirely appropriate' exercise.[74] As the evolution of legal debates on the matter shows (see Chapter II), this means that one may take the position of either favouring the international organisation or the member States, or, in opposition to both, favouring third parties.[75] The question thus turns into *who* should bear the loss caused by institutional activity: the international organisation, the member States or the injured individuals. As noted by Hirsch, there is no vacuum, as someone has to bear this loss.[76]

71 J. D'Aspremont, 'International Responsibility and the Constitution of Power: International Organisations Bolstered', 12(2) IOLR (2015) 382, 385.

72 A. Nolkaemper and D. Jacobs, 'Shared Responsibility in International Law: A Conceptual Framework', 34 Mich J Int'l L (2013) 359, 364.

73 A. Pellet, '"Human Rightism" and International Law', 10 Italian YB Int'l L (2000) 3, 5, 16.

74 R. Higgins, 'The Legal Consequences for Member States of the Non-Fulfilment by International Organizations of Their Obligations toward Third Parties – Preliminary Exposé and Draft Questionnaire', in *Annuaire de l'Institut de Droit International*, Session de Lisbonne, Vol. 66-I (1995) 288 (Preliminary Exposé).

75 Without endorsing a specific normative presupposition, it is harder to say which view is the better one. In a way, then, the interpretation and application of international institutional law to some extent also entails pursuing an argumentative strategy based on policy preferences. See: J. Klabbers, 'The Changing Image of International Organizations', in J. Coicaud and V. Heiskanen (eds.), *The Legitimacy of International Organizations* (2001) 233, 234.

76 M. Hirsch, *The Responsibility of International Organizations toward Third Parties: Some Basic Principles* (1995) 174.

But does this mean, as inquired by Higgins: 'If international law is not the mere application of neutral rules in an impartial fashion, but requires choices to be made between alternative norms that could, in context, each be applicable, then do we really have something other than a justification of the end by the means?'[77] Higgins's response is negative, partly out of the belief that not all means arise as possible choices, given, for example, the importance of judicial precedent.[78] All in all, members of the legal community are required to test and prove the validity of their legal contentions. Regardless of the interests that law may seek to advance, the practice of professional judgment in applying them is of undeniable importance.[79]

The current regime on member State responsibility, as devised by the ILC, certainly implies definitional choices as to how to attribute legal meaning to a social phenomenon, in particular, choices about how to interpret institutional dynamics and translate sociopolitical factors into a normative framework. Quite straightforwardly, the ILC's decades-long discussions on international responsibility (which find their origin in the reports of Special Rapporteur F. V. García-Amador, written in the 1950s)[80] have been described as a 'protracted architectural work involving a variety of actors dialoguing with one another and struggling to make international responsibility serve their respective agendas'.[81] This is not to say that the ILC's ASR and ARIO are not significant contributions to the codification and progressive development of international law. To the contrary: while the former's wide acceptance is unquestionable, the ARIO, even if sometimes criticised, have the audacity to finally introduce a proper legal framework to deal with claims against international organisations. To be sure, the latter have already found their way in a few judicial decisions, such as the well-known 2013 *Nuhanović* and *Mustafić* cases, where the Dutch Supreme Court found the Netherlands responsible for acts committed by Dutch soldiers under the command of the UN peacekeeping force in Srebrenica.[82] Still, looking at the ARIO as an end product of ten years of swaying debates, where the perceptions and preferences of some were endorsed to the detriment of other legally sound ones, it is arguable that 'legalisation' endeavours are, to some extent, also a product of who wields final enunciative authority.[83]

The enterprise of categorising instances of member State responsibility – which is what the ILC did in Part V ARIO – is, in any case, no easy affair. As noted by

77 R. Higgins, *Problems and Process: International Law and How We Use It* (1994) 5, 6.
78 Ibid., 6.
79 M. Koskenniemi, 'Constitutionalism As Mindset: Reflections on Kantian Themes about International Law and Globalization', 8 *Theoretical Inquiries in Law* (2007) 9, 18.
80 See: Analytical Guide to the Work of the International Law Commission on State Responsibility, available at: http://legal.un.org/ilc/guide/9_6.shtml, last consulted 15 October 2018.
81 J. D'Aspremont, *supra* note 71, 386, 387.
82 *Nuhanović* v. *Netherlands*, Judgment, BZ9225, and *Mustafić* v. *Netherlands*, Judgment, BZ9228, Supreme Court of the Netherlands, 6 September 2013.
83 M. Toufayan, 'Between Solipsism and Empire (through Law): International Organizations and the Politics of Formalized Mimetism', in *Responsibility of Individuals, States and Organizations: Proceedings of the 35th Annual Conference of the Canadian Council on International Law* (2006).

D'Aspremont, 'however ubiquitous [power] may be, [it] is extremely fluid and can hardly be subjected to formal descriptive categories which can then be mechanically deployed in the formal modes of legal reasoning associated with responsibility'.[84] The provisions envisaged in the ARIO have, at least, the merit of ensuring that a certain level of legal security and predictability is attained. Their stringency, however, implies that not all exercises of power by member States vis-à-vis international organisations engage the former's international responsibility.

It will be contended in this book that the ILC's approach to member State power is not an entirely satisfactory one, first and foremost because it does not take sufficient account of the position of the individuals affected by institutional operations.[85] While the ILC's codification endeavours do not have to serve a pro-victim normative agenda, the reality is that the ARIO lean towards the opposite direction, as they are overly protective of international organisations and their member States (see Chapter II). How, then, should a better balance be sought between all the interests at stake when it comes to the assessment of member State power for responsibility purposes?

Any assessment of an agent's power entails two judgements about what is significant to the assessment, i.e., judgement about the scope of the concept of power that is being used and judgement about the relevance of the outcomes the agents are capable of effecting.[86] Hence, the wider the scope of what counts as power in a given conceptual framework, the more power in the world one will be able to identify.[87] In this book, the crux of the question lies in the power, or influence, that member States wield as creators and participants in institutional operations, which allows them to condition institutional performance and, as a result, its impact on the lives of individuals. The notion that 'power breeds responsibility',[88] or, more generically, that governance breeds accountability,[89] is well known. And if different types of power trigger different types of responsibility in different situations,[90] an appraisal is surely warranted of the concrete terms in which member States' conduct is to be legally constrained in view of their human rights obligations.

As the following sections will show, the relational power between member States and the individuals affected by institutional operations is key to understanding various aspects of member State responsibility and the terms in which the regime

84 J. D'Aspremont, *supra* note 71, 393.

85 Rather tellingly, the title of an academic paper authored by A. Von Bogdandy and M. S. Platise reads: 'ARIO and Human Rights Protection: Leaving the Individual in the Cold', 9 IOLR (2012).

86 S. Lukes, *Power: A Radical View* (2005) 72.

87 Ibid.

88 The expression is owed to Clyde Eagleton and is further explored by Nollkaemper in the intricate context of shared responsibility, in: A. Nollkaemper, 'Power and Responsibility', in A. Di Stefano (ed.), *Un Diritto Senza Terra? Funzioni e limite del principio di territorialità nel diritto Internazionale e dell'Unione europea* (2015).

89 For example: J. A. Scholte, 'Global Governance, Accountability and Civil Society', in J. A. Scholte (ed.), *Building Global Democracy? Civil Society and Accountable Global Governance* (2011) 15–32.

90 A. Nollkaemper, *supra* note 88, 22–4, 39.

can broadly serve the normative interest of ensuring an effective human rights protection. This is true for both primary rules and secondary rules of international law. With regard to the former, it conditions not only the scope of application of international obligations but also their content; as to the latter, it has a bearing on the attribution of conduct, the finding of wrongfulness and the allocation of responsibility.

3 OUTLINE OF THE CHAPTERS

In broad terms, this book is about governance and international responsibility. The structure of its various sections, distributed along three chapters, attempts to respond logically to the need to understand, first, what the former means and, second, how the latter operates. In order to hold member States responsible under international (human rights) law, it is essential to grasp the conditions under which they act as international legal subjects in institutional settings. This implies clarifying the dynamics inherent in the relationship between international organisations and their member States, and, thereby, the terms in which both entities may be distinguished from one another. This task is taken up in Chapter I. Using, to the extent possible, international financial institutions as examples, this chapter starts by analysing the legal implications – first from a domestic and then from an international law perspective – of State adherence to international organisations. As will be shown, a defining element of the latter phenomenon is that States remain continuously engaged in the exercise of powers that they transferred to international organisations. Member State pursuit of sovereign preferences is, of course, limited, and the second part of the chapter attempts to clarify this by calling attention to the personhood of international organisations and the autonomy with which they lead a life of their own. The demarcation of both spheres of subjectivity is crucial to understanding the terms in which member States remain legally visible underneath the institutional veil. When it comes to the relationship between international financial institutions and their member States, it will be contended that the latter's visibility reveals itself at the 'macro' level of governance of these organisations. Their oversight and 'authority management' role is thus unveiled – a role that is concrete enough to allow assessment of their responsibility under international law.

Chapter II embarks on a discussion of how the governance power of member States is to be subsumed in secondary rules of international law. It begins by taking stock of early doctrinal debates and case-law on the matter, with a view to clarifying the conceptual underpinnings of the current regime devised by the ILC. As will be seen, although said power has been acknowledged all along, different responsibility criteria have been upheld, on the basis of different policy considerations. These have shifted between the prioritisation of institutional independence and the protection of third parties. Against this backdrop, the chapter undertakes a critical analysis of

Part V ARIO, and the instances it exceptionally foresees for the establishment of derived member State responsibility. It will be observed that they do not solve the specific problem of how to engage member States' responsibility for their participation in institutional decision-making, and, thus, the book asks whether the latter phenomenon may rather lead to a finding of member States' responsibility for their own wrongful conduct. It thus turns its gaze to the operation of attribution rules and analyses the treatment these have merited in the case-law and doctrine. While attribution has not been comprehensively addressed with relation to member State participation in the representative bodies of international financial institutions (and international organisations in general), it is deemed useful to assess its functioning in contexts where member States emerge as troop contributors or implementers of institutional decisions. Based on these findings, the chapter proceeds to a thorough investigation of the international legal status of Executive Directors, notably inquiring whether they can be qualified as State organs, as opposed to officials of the international financial institution, and tests the qualification of their exercise of voting rights as conduct attributable to the State.

Grounded on the conclusion that, through their representatives in international financial institutions, member States remain powerful international legal actors and may be held responsible for their own behaviour, Chapter III examines how this power should be framed and tamed by international human rights law. It does so premised on the notion that whilst adhering to international organisations, States do not leave their international human rights obligations behind. Concerned with the need to ensure that the interests of the beneficiaries of multilateral development cooperation are effectively accounted for, the chapter first explores member States' duty to preserve legality from a constitutionalist lens. It notably discusses the values of representation and responsiveness. As these values are seen to translate into human rights protection duties, the chapter proceeds to an analysis of the human rights regime and interpretations thereof advanced by human rights bodies. An important point in the assessment consists in determining how member States' human rights obligations extend to their relationships with international financial institutions. It will be argued that member States' relational power vis-à-vis the latter brings with it the proceduralisation of said obligations, as imposed by the due diligence standard, and so too their extraterritorial applicability. The second part of Chapter III is concerned with the specific contours of member States' human rights due diligence obligations. Based on the application of the due diligence standard in different areas of international law, it undertakes to operationalise it in the international financial institutional context. As will be contended, human rights due diligence conditions member States in two main instances: in their participation in institutional decision-making processes, as well as in the use of the institutional and operational apparatus they set up to provide individuals with access to justice. Finally, the third part of Chapter III concentrates on the possible failure of member States to comply with the required conduct and explores a range of elements that should inform human rights claims against them. It notably assesses the terms in which a breach of due diligence may be established and articulates the legal consequences of such an internationally wrongful act. To terminate, the chapter briefly discusses a number of matters that complicate the invocation of responsibility. These pertain not only to the fact that the conduct of various member States might be at stake, but also to the need of identifying the individuals that are to be considered victims of human rights violations and are thereby to be granted standing before a dispute settlement mechanism.

The book concludes by summarising the main findings and wrapping them all together in an attempt to provide a 'bigger picture' of the debate on the responsibility of the member States of international financial institutions. On a more conceptual note, the concluding section recollects the notion of power and how it affects different aspects of member State responsibility. And in a more pragmatic tone, it suggests a constructive perspective from which to address member State responsibility: by locating member States' governance role in the global public space, the final section gives note of a more predictable relationship between them, international organisations and third parties; moreover, by clarifying the legal implications of said role, it approximates States to the attainment of the very aims that led to the creation of international financial institutions in the first place, that is, of better serving the development needs of individuals all around the world.

I

The Relationship between International (Financial) Institutions and Their Member States

States' engagement in institutionalised forms of international cooperation brings about intricate legal questions when it comes to defining their position vis-à-vis international organisations for the purposes of establishing international responsibility. These mainly concern the tension between, on the one hand, the preservation of sovereignty and, on the other hand, the unavoidable limitation of States' freedom of action, to give way to the life of the organisation thus created.[91] Rather than an instrumentality in the hands of member States, international organisations emerge as sources of authority[92] in the international scene, with competences and purposes that must necessarily be respected by their members. Their international legal personality thus becomes the main vantage point from which to discuss international responsibility in institutional contexts. The fact of international legal personality, notwithstanding, is far from fully explaining the relationship between international organisations and their member States underneath the institutional veil.

Keeping the aforementioned tension in mind, Chapter I analyses how international organisations and their member States operate as subjects of international law and what it *means*, legally speaking, to transfer the exercise of sovereign powers to international organisations. The various sections are meant to convey one of the main messages of this book: the understanding that sovereign powers, rather than being inexorably transferred to international organisations, are instead 'shared' between the latter and their member States. This means that after adhering to international organisations, (member) States remain powerful actors in their own right, rather than disappearing behind the veil of the international organisation's legal personality. As will be seen, this has obvious implications for the application of international responsibility rules.

Section 1.1.1 begins with an account of the impact, in domestic legal systems, of State adhesion to international organisations. Drawing on a few examples (selected

[91] M. Virally, 'La Notion de Fonction dans la Théorie de l'Organisation Internationale', in *Mélanges Offerts à Charles Rousseau – La Communauté Internationale* (1974) 296.

[92] The concepts of authority and power are used in this book interchangeably.

on the basis of pertinence, geographic considerations and availability of information), it demonstrates how the State apparatus is engaged when it comes to the pursuit of national interests in international multilateral forums. Section 1.1.2, in turn, elaborates on the transfer of the exercise of sovereign powers to international organisations from an international law perspective. Its purpose is to highlight the notion that member States (still) partake in the exercise of the powers that were transferred, including in more advanced forms of intergovernmental integration.

The understanding that such a conferral of powers is a continued process undergirds Section 1.2. In this dynamic, however, it is fundamental to distinguish the conduct of international organisations from that of its member States as subjects of international law. Section 1.2.1 thus discusses the contours of international organisations' personhood. In this respect, the question of how their legal distinctness comes about (i.e., of what is the potential for the development of a separate will) emerges as a more profound one which is explored in Section 1.2.2, dedicated to the concept of institutional autonomy. Grounded on the understanding that autonomy is not a watertight concept (as it is systemically permeated by member State influence), the last section, Section 1.2.3, deepens the notion of member State visibility underneath the 'institutional veil' by pointing out instances of manifestation of such visibility.

While Section 1.2.1 resonates with constructivist approaches to international organisations theory, the second and third sections invoke realist-like notions to highlight the legal visibility of (member) States underneath the institutional veil.[93] The choice is intended, as both theories resort to elements or features of what is, at the end of the day, a complex phenomenon. A theoretical legal framework of international responsibility (based as it is on assumptions) that is intended to be meaningful (in the sense of reflective of the empirical conditions of international organisations, and, therefrom, susceptible of application in real-life situations)[94] cannot but be devised with such complexity in mind, only to ultimately find the appropriate balance between both views.

93 It is of note that, despite being grounded in an established academic legal tradition, this book also resorts to other fields of knowledge. Even jurists like Virally would claim that '*pour le juriste plus que pour tout autre spécialiste, l'étude des Organisations Internationales présente nécessairement un caractère inter-disciplinaire*'. See: M. Virally, *supra* note 91, 278. As further noted by Lagrange, '*[l]e jurist qui aborde la representation institutionnelle est aussitôt débordé par un afflux d'images, précipité vers les confins de sa discipline et du discours politique ou philosophique*'. See: E. Lagrange, *La Représentation Institutionnelle dans l'Ordre International: Une Contribution à la Théorie de la Personnalité Morale des Organisations Internationals* (2002) 3.

94 A legal (responsibility) regime that does not meaningfully capture the behaviour of the subjects it is meant to regulate may otherwise become utopian and lose its relevance. See: M. Koskenniemi, *From Apology to Utopia: The Structure of International Legal Argument* (2005) 2–5. Along these lines, McCorquodale notes that 'it is necessary to ensure that the conceptual bases for the international legal system reflect the reality of changed international social relations'. See: R. McCorquodale, *International Law beyond the State: Essays on Sovereignty, Non-State Actors and Human Rights* (2011) 403. Cf., however, Hirsch, noting that '[r]ules of law, generally, do not aim to reflect accurately the existing situation prevailing in a given community'. See: M. Hirsch, *supra* note 76, 177.

As this chapter will attempt to demonstrate, although international organisations and the phenomenon of membership have transformed the way State sovereignty is perceived,[95] notably for the substantive limitations imposed upon it, the State remains a powerful actor in the international scene when participating in international organisations. Capturing such a reality is essential for attribution purposes, and to the understanding of the scope of application of primary international legal rules to member States. The fact that the exercise of powers is shared between international organisations and their member States essentially entails that each international legal actor will be responsible for its own 'share' in such an exercise.

1.1 BEHIND THE SCENE OF MEMBER STATE RESPONSIBILITY: THE TRANSFER OF THE EXERCISE OF SOVEREIGN POWERS TO INTERNATIONAL ORGANISATIONS AS A PROCESS 'IN CONTINUUM'

The present section looks into the implications of the transfer of the exercise of sovereign powers to international organisations from both a domestic and an international law perspective. In so doing, it aims at clarifying the position of member States vis-à-vis international organisations, and, notably, the fact that State adherence to international organisations does not imply the former's disappearance behind the institutional veil. This is of utmost importance for the understanding of international responsibility, for its rules will apply to member States only where they act as subjects of international law.

Section 1.1.1 will explore how the role played by States as both creators and participants in international organisations is conditioned by domestic checks and balances. To that end, it starts by providing an overview of the sort of constitutional requirements that limit State adhesion to international organisations (Section 1.1.1.1). Based on the understanding that State participation in international organisations corresponds to the exercise of governmental action on foreign affairs, Section 1.1.1.2 moves on to a discussion of how it may be subjected to domestic legal constraints and parliamentary oversight. The analysis is meant to demonstrate that the pursuit of national interests constitutes a defining element of States' engagement in international cooperative undertakings.

Viewed from the perspective of international law, the significance of such a finding is especially revealed. As will be discussed in Section 1.1.2, it means that despite the conferral of powers to international organisations, the latter inevitably remain forums for the contestation of sovereignty by their member States. This translates into different manifestations of control (in the sense of influence) being

95 J. E. Alvarez, 'International Organizations As Law-Makers', in W. P. Heere (ed.), *From Government to Governance: The Growing Impact of Non-State Actors on the International and European Legal System* (2003) 14.

exerted over the exercise of powers by international organisations, which cannot be neglected when determining how a member State responsibility regime should look.

1.1.1 *The Impact of State Adhesion to International Organisations in Domestic Legal Systems*

1.1.1.1 Constitutional Limitations over the Transfer of Powers to International Organisations

Constitutions worldwide envisage the transfer of the exercise of sovereign powers to international organisations for the benefit of international cooperation.[96] In contrast with the lenience of international law,[97] however, constitutional texts may provide for this competence in significantly more limited terms.[98] In some instances, the extent to which limitations on State sovereignty are constitutionally allowed is not immediately discernible: it suffices to recall the *Solange* case-law of the German Federal Constitutional Court, BVerfG, and its questioning of the autonomy and supremacy of EU law over the protection of core constitutional values.[99] More recently, in a case unrelated to constitutional rights, but in any event linked to Germany's constitutional identity, the same court considered the *ultra vires* character of an act of the ECB, describing it as a usurpation of the budgetary sovereignty of the German Bundestag.[100] This and various other constitutional court pronouncements from different

96 See, inter alia: Article 11 of the Italian Constitution; Article 79 of the Russian Constitution; Article 7 of the Singaporean Constitution; Article 14 of the Vietnamese Constitution; Article 110 of the Zairean Constitution; Article XXVIII(ii) of the Ugandan Constitution; Article 12(j) of the Cuban Constitution; Article 3 of the Ecuadorian Constitution. Such a transfer is mainly done through the adoption of treaties which normally correspond to the constituent instruments of the organisations, but it can also occur on an ad hoc basis (see: D. Sarooshi, *supra* note 44, 19–27). See also: commentary to Article 2, para. 4 ARIO, where it is noted that international organisations may also be established by States on the basis of resolutions adopted by an international organisation or by a conference of States; and also F. Seyersted, 'Objective International Personality of Intergovernmental Organizations: Do Their Capacities Really Depend upon the Conventions Establishing Them?', 37 NJIL (1964) 3, 49, 50 for more examples.

97 In principle, States may grant the exercise of virtually any power to international organisations.

98 In analysing several constitutional provisions envisaging the transfer of powers to international organisations, Martin Martinez identifies three types of conditions for such a transfer to occur: procedural conditions to validate the act of transfer, such as parliamentary approval by a qualified majority; conditions to be fulfilled by the organisation to which powers are being transferred, such as the pursuit of specific goals; and conditions to be fulfilled by all the other future members, for instance, equal treatment within the organisation. See M. Martin Martinez, *National Sovereignty and International Organizations* (1996) 15–61, 67, 68.

99 *Solange I*, BVerfGE 37, 271, 2 BvL 52/71, 29 May 1974; *Solange II*, BVerfGE 73, 339, 2 BvR 197/83, 22 October 1986; *Solange III*, BVerfG 89, 155, 2 BvR 2134/92, 12 October 1993 (also known as the *Maastricht* decision); and *Solange IV*, BVerfG 102, 147, 2 BvL 1/97, 7 June 2000.

100 The decision refers to the ECB's 'Outright Monetary Transactions' programme, designed to assist troubled euro-zone member States. The proceedings were suspended as the BVerfG referred to the CJEU for a preliminary ruling. See: BVerfG, 2 BvR 2728/13, 4 January 2014, particularly, paras. 44–54. In Case C-62/14 *Peter Gauweiler and Others* v. *Deutscher Bundestag* [2015], the EU court asserted that

countries[101] reflect the emergence of an interesting dialectic between national and international institutions as to how sovereign powers are to be exercised at the international level.[102] In particular, they manifest upfront the unclear contours and legal implications of membership in international organisations.

Admittedly, the general and anticipatory terms in which constitutions authorise the transfer of the exercise of sovereign powers to international organisations do not say much about the precise impact of State adhesion to international organisations on domestic legal systems. Constitutional endorsement, notwithstanding, does have something to say about how the position of member States vis-à-vis international organisations is perceived in domestic legal orders: inasmuch as it allows the legislative and the judicial powers to exert some kind of control over the executive's activity on foreign affairs (for one, to examine whether the constitutional conditions for the transfer of competences have been met),[103] it shows that, at least from a domestic law perspective, State participation in international organisations constitutes legally relevant conduct in its own right and can thereby be subjected to the scrutiny of competent authorities. As will be discussed shortly, such type of scrutiny not only is present at the initial stage of the transfer of competences to the organisation but also can endure, and has been seen to endure, throughout the participation of States in institutional operations.

the ECB bond-buying programme fell within the monetary policy framework laid down by primary EU law, and, thus, upheld its legality. The interpretations of the CJEU were ultimately endorsed by the Second Senate of the Federal Constitutional Court in 2 BvR 2728/13, 2 BvR 2729/13, 2 BvR 2730/13, 2 BvR 2731/13, 2 BvE 13/13, 21 June 2016.

101 As observed by Hilpold, the Solange jurisprudence seems to have influenced significantly the large majority of European Constitutional Courts when it comes to questions involving the protection of core constitutional values, such as fundamental rights or the rule of law. See P. Hilpold, 'Solange I, BverfGE 37, 291, 29 May 1974; Solange II, BverfGE 73, 339, 22 October 1986; Solange III, BverfGE 89, 155, 12 October 1993; and Solange IV, BverfGE 102, 147, 7 June 2000', in C. Ryngaert, I. Dekker, R. Wessel and J. Wouters (eds.), *Judicial Decisions on the Law of International Organizations* (2016) 181.

102 See, e.g., para. 48 of BVerfG 2 BvR 2728/13, referred *supra* note 100, where the court highlighted that 'Parliament may not cede the power to decide whether and to what degree sovereign powers are to be transferred, and it may not transfer this power to the institutions of the European Union. It is, in fact, obliged to decide on its own and in formal proceedings about the transfer of powers in the scope of European integration, in order to avoid that the constitutionally required principle of conferral is undermined.' See also: D. Sarooshi, 'The Essentially Contested Nature of the Concept of Sovereignty: Implications for the Exercise by International Organizations of Delegated Powers of Government', 25 Mich J Int'l L (2004) 1107–18.

103 Including with regard to the approval of amendments to the foundational treaties of international organisations, an issue which was addressed by BVerfG in 2 BvE 6/99, 22 November 2001 (and, similarly, in 2 BvE 2/07, 3 July 2007). Here, the court was called upon to determine, inter alia, whether NATO's New 1999 Strategic Concept constituted an amendment of the NATO Treaty of 1949, in which case parliamentary consent for ratification would have been required on the basis of Article 59(2) of the German Basic Law. See: B. Schlütter, in ILDC 134 (DE 2001).

1.1.1.2 Domestic Checks and Balances upon the Exercise of Governmental Powers in International (Financial) Institutions

State adhesion to international organisations brings with it the development of a government apparatus responsible for formulating – in more or less detail – the national positions that are to be pursued by State representatives in institutional undertakings. The main actors in this context are the ministries of foreign affairs of member States.[104] Yet, when it comes to international organisations dealing with specific matters, such as the international financial institutions, other ministries play the leading role, notably, ministries of finance or ministries for economic and development cooperation (see Section 2.2.2.2).

The engagement of governments with State representatives participating in institutional operations indicates that the transfer of the exercise of sovereign powers to international organisations unfolds in a 'continuum', i.e., as a dynamic (rather than static) process. As noted by Martin Martinez, this continued process 'starts once the authorizations to transfer State's power on behalf of international institutions are put into practice' and 'is accomplished by means of the day-to-day effective application of the powers and functions attributed to I.O.'s in their constitutive treaties'.[105]

A fundamental element underlying the notion of 'continued transfer' – one which will often be recalled throughout this book – is that national interests are continuously engaged when it comes to the conduct of government representatives in institutional settings. The impact this has on policy formation in international financial institutions is important to the understanding of the relationship between the organisation and its member States and how the latter become legally visible behind the institutional veil.

It is in fact interesting to note how the notion of 'continued transfer' has been translated into different forms of domestic control over governmental action – parliamentary oversight constituting a case in point. Indeed, conceptions of 'vertical' democracy entail the involvement of citizens, through their parliamentary assemblies, in intergovernmental law-making and decision-making processes.[106] Without turning a blind eye to the fact

104 This is the case in 'capital-based coordination systems', i.e., systems where national policies and instructions are formulated by the country's authorities based in its capital. Next to this, there are mission-based coordination systems, where the major parts of national decisions are formulated by diplomats on the ground, dealing with the negotiations in question. See: D. Panke, 'Getting Ready to Negotiate in International Organizations? On the Importance of the Domestic Construction of National Positions', 4(2) *Journal of International Organizations Studies* (2013).

105 M. Martin Martinez, *supra* note 98, 2.

106 J. Wouters, B. De Meester and C. Ryngaert, 'Democracy and International Law', XXXIV NYIL (2003) 137, 177–9.

Interestingly, there are at least sixty-seven inter-State organisations of parliamentarians of States, created at the global, regional and interregional levels, as a means to counteract the dominance of governments in conducting the foreign relations of their States. See: C. F. Alger and K. J. Kille, 'How Are, and Should, Parliamentarians of States Be Involved in Global Governance?', 5(2) *Journal of*

that a democratic deficit may be inevitable in institutional settings,[107] it is still noteworthy that the scope of domestic participation in institutional affairs has been widened.

Arguably, parliamentary control – or, at least, its formative influence – features more prominently when it comes to deeper levels of intergovernmental integration, such as the participation of States in the EU.[108] Accordingly, all EU member States' parliaments include bodies specialising in Union affairs,[109] although, in practice, the degree of engagement of these bodies will unavoidably diverge.[110] With regard to parliamentary oversight of State participation in international financial institutions, various examples could be given. In Denmark, for instance, there is extended parliamentary supervision: under the Danish Constitution (Article 19(3)), the Government is required to consult the Parliament's Foreign Affairs Committee 'prior to the making of any decision of major importance to foreign policy'. As explained in the website of the Foreign Affairs Committee, development aid 'plays a prominent role in the committee's work' and is closely monitored via the tabling of questions, orally or in writing, to the minister, or through consultation questions.[111]

In Germany, politically sensitive projects under discussion at the Executive Boards of multilateral development banks will often engage the Bundestag. In what concerns decision-making at the WB, in particular, the Executive Director is regularly subjected to inquiries held by the Parliament.[112] Institutional policy reforms are likewise of concern to the Bundestag, which is illustrated by the input it provided to the BMZ (Federal Ministry for Economic Cooperation and Development) in its 2014 consultations organised in the framework of the WB's environmental and social safeguard review process (launched in 2012).[113]

International Organizations Studies (2014). Among these platforms for parliamentarians, the Parliamentary Network on the World Bank & International Monetary Fund should be mentioned. It was founded in 2000 and gathers parliamentarians from over 140 countries. See: www.parlnet.org/, last consulted 15 October 2018.

107 E. Stein, 'International Integration and Democracy: No Love at First Sight', 95 Am J Int'l L (2001), 489, 490–3. See also 524, 525 and 531 on the possibility of exercising control over international organisations via national parliaments, with a particular focus on EU institutions. Regarding the WB and the IMF, see: N. Woods, 'Making the IMF and the World Bank More Accountable', 77(1) *International Affairs* (2001) 83, 84, 85, explaining how the 'chain of representative accountability' is a 'long and imperfect one' in these institutions. See, however, the points made in R. Kehoane, S. Macedo and A. Moravcsik, 'Democracy-Enhancing Multilateralism', 63 *International Organization* (2009) 1, about how international organisations (and other multilateral frameworks) can also be democracy-enhancing.

108 From the European example it can be stated that higher degrees of transfers of powers to international organisations lead to an increase in the political pressure exerted by domestic branches of government over institutional decision-making processes. See, inter alia: D. Sarooshi, *supra* note 44, 121.

109 A list of these bodies may be found at: www.cosac.eu/national-parliament-european-c/, last consulted 15 October 2018.

110 See, e.g.: C. Stratulat, J. A. Emmanouilidis, T. Fischer and S. Piedrafita, Discussion Paper on 'Legitimising EU Policymaking: What Role for National Parliaments?' (2014) 4, 5.

111 See: www.thedanishparliament.dk/en/committees/committees/uru, last consulted 15 October 2018.

112 This information was provided by a BMZ official, Interview #VIII, 23 April 2015.

113 Ibid. The process of review will be mentioned sporadically in this book.

The Belgian Parliamentary Foreign Affairs Committee is fairly proactive in monitoring the participation of Belgium in international financial institutions, in particular, the WB. Inquiries, which are of a considerable number,[114] can be made orally or in writing to the Minister of Finance, as well as to the Minister of Development Cooperation. In an inquiry from June 2016, members of the Parliament did not shy away from criticising Belgium's participation in the WB, for its lack of transparency and the nonconformity of the policies pursued therein with the country's international legal commitments, including respect for human rights.[115] In addition, when it comes to the adoption of new operational policies, like Germany, the process of review of the Bank's Safeguard Policies has also attracted considerable attention in the Parliament.[116]

A last example is that of Japan, where issues concerning the affairs of international financial institutions fall under the control of the Ministry of Finance. The ministry is subjected to the oversight of the Finance Committee of the Lower House (Zaimu Iinkai) and the Finance Committee of the Upper House (Zaisei Iinkai) of the Diet (Japanese Parliament), and is thereby required to answer any queries raised by the latter. Moreover, whenever there are capital increases in the abovementioned institutions, the ministry is responsible for laying a bill before the Diet containing the legal grounds for expenditure, which must be duly approved by the competent committee.[117] On the latter point, Japan is obviously followed by the other member States: inasmuch as capital increases in international financial institutions necessarily impact upon the national budget, parliamentary approval is called for.

At the end of the day, the role played by national parliaments as watchdogs of their governments' participation in institutional settings may vary considerably: it will depend on a number of factors such as the degree to which parliaments are actually constitutionally afforded the leeway to exert such a scrutiny and the extent to which

114 Interview #XXI, 17 June 2015.

115 It is instructive to quote an excerpt of a question posed by the Socialist Party to the Belgian Minister of Development Cooperation: 'Malgré la loi de 2013 sur la cohérence des politiques en faveur du développement, les orientations prises par la Banque mondiale sont de plus en plus critiquées, de même que certains des projets ainsi financés. Ceux-ci posent en effet parfois question au regard des enjeux du développement durable et des engagements nationaux et internationaux pris par la Belgique (respect des droits de l'homme, cohérence des politiques, sécurité alimentaire, etc.). De plus, il apparaîtrait que l'institution ne respecte pas certains traités internationaux ratifiés par la Belgique.' See: De Kamer/La Chambre, Commissie Voor de Buitenlandse Betrekkingen van Dinsdag 7 Juni 2016/Commission des Relations Extérieures du Mardi 7 Juin 2016, para 04.02 et seq. (available at: www.dekamer.be/doc/CCRI/html/54/ic437x.html, last consulted 15 October 2018).

116 Interview #XXI, 17 June 2015.

117 Communication with an official of the Japanese Ministry of Foreign Affairs, on file with author.
In the case of the US, when it comes to replenishments of international financial institutions, the Secretary of the Treasury is required to consult the Committee on Banking, Finance and Urban Affairs of the House of Representatives, the Committee on Appropriations of the House of Representatives, the Committee on Foreign Relations of the Senate, the Committee on Appropriations of the Senate, and the appropriate subcommittee of each such committee. See: 22 US Code § 262g–3.

the legislature is controlled by the executive.[118] In the US, Congress has the ultimate authority over the criteria that govern US participation in these institutions, the level of US financial commitments and the general framework for US policy,[119] which means that it is almost 'obsessively' concerned with how taxpayers' money is being spent.[120] In the UK, the same concern often subjects both State representatives and the Government's Department for International Development (DFID) to monitoring by internal and external scrutiny bodies.[121] In contrast, in countries such as Angola or Brazil, national Parliaments have engaged in only a limited amount of affairs, usually through informal inquiries.[122] Among borrower countries, a remarkable exception is that of Costa-Rica, where congressional approval is required for every loan it negotiates with multilateral development banks.[123]

Next to parliamentary control, the formulation of government positions on action within international organisations can be assessed by national courts for its conformity with domestic legislation. The British case provides an illustration of this. The UK's positions taken at the WB are formally decided by the UK Delegation to the WB, with thorough guidance by the DFID, sitting in London, and analytical support from country offices and policy division teams. Given that all UK government departments are required by the 1998 Human Rights Act[124] to pursue respect for human rights in their work, the DFID, as a public authority, is bound by the Human Rights Act. Hence, in case an act or a failure to act is incompatible with the European Convention on Human Rights (ECHR),[125] a human rights claim can be brought against the Secretary of State.

In nearby Belgium, a concrete example is provided by its 2013 Act on Development Cooperation, which determines that the country's participation in multilateral organisations is contingent upon the pursuit, by the latter, of developmental objectives that generally meet the Belgian ones.[126] These include: 'consolidation de la démocratie et de l'état de droit, en ce compris la bonne gouvernance, ainsi qu'à l'objectif du respect de la dignité humaine, des droits humains dans toutes

118 D. Sarooshi, *supra* note 44, 76.

119 R. M. Nelson and M. A. Weiss, 'Multilateral Development Banks: How the United States Makes and Implements Policy', Congressional Research Service Report (2014) 1 (available at: www.fas.org/sgp/crs/misc/R41537.pdf, last consulted 15 October 2018).

120 Interview #XV, 11 June 2015.

121 Interview #VII, 10 April 2015; Interview #X, 27 May 2015; Interview #XIII, 5 June 2015.
See a publication of the Independent Commission for Aid Impact (ICAI) – which reports directly to Parliament through the House of Commons International Development Committee – evaluating how the DFID works with multilateral organisations such as the WB, entitled: 'How DFID works with multilateral agencies to achieve impact', Report 44, June 2015.

122 Interview #XIV, 8 June 2015; Interview #XVII, 12 June 2015.

123 Interview #XVI, 11 June 2015; Interview #XXXIII, 31 June 2015.

124 Human Rights Act, 9 November 1998. The act incorporates the European Convention on Human Rights into UK domestic legislation.

125 Convention for the Protection of Human Rights and Fundamental Freedoms, 213 UNTS 222, 4 November 1950.

126 Article 25 de la Loi Relative à la Coopération [belge] au Développement, 19 March 2013.

leurs dimensions et des libertés fondamentales'.[127] Belgian positions advocated in the WB could thus very well be judged for their conformity with domestic legislation on development cooperation.

A final example is that of the US, where there is an impressive, and possibly unparalleled, set of legislation conditioning the behaviour of State representatives in institutional settings.[128] For instance, the delineation of its assistance policies with international financial institutions – in which the Secretary of the Treasury assumes a fundamental role – is shaped by numerous provisions contained in the US Code.[129] Considering US practice as a member of international organisations, it is striking how far domestic legal documents (reflecting national preferences) have the potential to affect its behaviour in institutional contexts[130] – an illustration of this being the US's 'institutionalised' practice within the WB of not supporting loans to Iran, on the basis of domestic legislation imposing sanctions on the latter.[131] This is a clear example of 'internationally important internal law' indicating the course of conduct to be adopted by the State vis-à-vis its counterparts[132] in the framework of international organisations.

The brief overview lends itself to the conclusion that following States' adhesion to international organisations, what States *do* within such contexts constitutes a matter of concern in domestic legal systems. Regarded as governmental activity on foreign affairs, the role played by States as both creators and participants in international organisations is, as such, conditioned by legal constraints, and is thereby susceptible – to a higher or lower degree – to domestic checks and balances. For present purposes, just how such control is exercised is not so relevant. Rather, the fact that it is, in some instances, exercised is merely invoked to reinforce the notion that the pursuit of national interests constitutes a defining element of States' engagement in international cooperative undertakings, and, thus, that membership of international organisations cannot be dissociated from the State apparatus.[133] The subsequent sections address these matters from an international law perspective.

127 Ibid., Article 4.
128 See the various sections and subsections of 22 US Code § 262, which encompass the International Financial Institutions Act, as amended through Public Law 113–188, 26 November 2014.
129 See: 22 US Code § 262h and § 262p-4.
130 Domestic legislation cannot, of course, govern international organisations or any of their organs, as institutional operations could otherwise be hindered by entanglements in domestic laws and judgments. See, inter alia, the decision of the World Bank Administrative Tribunal *Aida Shekib*, Decision No. 358 (2007), para. 27.
131 See Sec. 10 of S. 970, the Iran Counter Proliferation Act of 2007, and Sec. 12 of S. 3227 Iran Sanctions Act of 2008. As clarified in various interviews with WB Executive Directors, such practice is not questioned by the Board. For more information on the US's lending practice to Iran, see: M. A. Weiss and J. E. Sanford, Congressional Research Service Report, 'The World Bank and Iran' (2008).
132 J. Rousseau, *Droit international public*, 331, quoted in ILC, Special Rapporteur Cedeño, *First Report on Unilateral Acts of States*, UN Doc. A/CN.4/486 (1998) 332.
133 See Section 2.2.

1.1.2 *Interplay between Conferrals of Powers to International Organisations and Member State Sovereign Power*

When thinking about the transfer of the exercise of powers to international organisations and how it impacts the position of (member) States in the international scene, a question that arises is how it particularly affects the notion of sovereignty. A glance into the past shows that, despite the enthusiasm surrounding the creation of international organisations, which was particularly evident around the second half of the twentieth century,[134] there have always been expressions of concern with this phenomenon – of which the Frankenstein metaphor is a telling representative.[135]

The suspicion of legal thinkers is owed to the alleged 'erosion' of State sovereignty that comes with the transfer of powers to international organisations.[136] Seidl-Hohenveldern, however, rejects the idea of a real transfer of sovereign rights. In the author's view, the allegedly transferred power is instead retained by States, but remains 'dormant', which implies the 'temporary suspension of the exercise of an otherwise indisputably existing sovereign right'.[137] Others, as noted by Cassese, perceive conferrals of powers as 'limitations on State freedom', noting that sovereignty can only truly be transferred whenever, in addition to legislative and judicial powers, international organisations are vested with executive powers.[138] More recently, Sarooshi suggested three different modalities of conferrals of powers to international organisations, which would vary in degree: the agency relationship, the delegation of powers and, to a deeper extent, the transfer of powers to international organisations proper.[139] Within this framework, the last form of conferral would grant international organisations an exclusive right to exercise the powers bestowed upon them.

[134] J. Klabbers, 'The Life and Times of the Law of International Organizations', 70 *Nordic Journal of International Law* (2001) 287, 298–302.

[135] The expression was used by J. E. Alvarez, *supra* note 95, 11. The expression also made its way to the title of a later article authored by A. T. Guzman, namely, 'International Organizations and the Frankenstein Problem', 24(4) EJIL (2013) 999.

[136] See A. T. Guzman and J. Landsidle, 'The Myth of International Delegation', 96(6) Cal L Rev (2008) 1693, 1694, 1695.

Interestingly, some constitutional texts use such type of wording to express the phenomenon of State adherence to international organisations. See, inter alia: Article 11 of the Italian Constitution, whereby 'L'Italia ... consente, in condizioni di parità con gli altri Stati, alle *limitazioni di sovranità* necessarie ad un ordinamento che assicuri la pace e la giustizia fra le Nazioni' (emphasis added) and Article 110 of the Zairean Constitution, entitling the Republic to 'conclude treaties and agreements of association which involve *partial abandonment of its sovereignty*' (emphasis added). Next to these examples, case-law also reflects the notion that State adherence to international organisations implies a 'permanent limitation of [States'] sovereign rights', as exemplified by the CJEU Case 6/64, *Flaminio Costa* v. *E.N.E.L.*, 15 July 1964.

[137] I. Seidl-Hohenveldern, *Corporations in and under International Law* (1987) 70–2.

[138] A. Cassese, 'Modern Constitutions and International Law', 192 RCADI 1985/III, 341, 416.

[139] D. Sarooshi, *supra* note 44, 28–32. For an overview of other doctrinal proposals attempting to explain the question of conferrals of powers to international organisations, see the literature referred by Guzman and Landsidle, *supra* note 136, 1697, 1698.

Having a look at practice, it is clear that States are generally reluctant to transfer powers to international organisations in the sense used by Sarooshi.[140] Intimidated by the limitation of autonomous decision-making in their own legal orders, they *solely* entrust international organisations with the necessary competences to ensure the latter's effective functioning as a matter of constitutional existence.[141] While the EU and the UN Security Council (UNSC) might constitute exceptions to this, they still depend on complementary State conduct to function, which in the end entails that sovereignty has not been fully transferred to these institutions after all.

It is significant to retain the notion that the transfer of the exercise of powers to international organisations cannot be dissociated from different manifestations of control (in the sense of influence) over such an exercise by member States.[142] Ultimately, conferrals of powers are invariably permeated by 'the important role of States *as actors* in contesting sovereignty within international organisations'.[143] Anxious to preserve their sovereignty and maintain their freedom of political choice, member States will hardly lose an opportunity to assert their power over the organisation.[144] In fact, as explained by Sarooshi, the contestations of sovereignty that occur within States are often 'the very same contestations that are now taking place within international organizations. They are about the central problem of sovereignty: what are powers reserved to government; who exercises which of them, and how should they be exercised?'[145]

In the view of some commentators, such forms of affirmation of member State sovereignty are not necessarily legally relevant. As has been vocally argued with regard to the EU, the notion of conferral of competences is key to the understanding of responsibility (and attribution) issues thereof. Accordingly, as long as the EU has competence to act in a certain field, and to be the bearer of international obligations, State control over the exercise of competences by the EU or the implementation of EU decisions does not give rise to controversy, as responsibility for the breach of any such obligation will in principle lie with the EU.[146] This understanding is

[140] See: A. T. Guzman and J. Landsidle, *supra* note 136.

[141] C. Ahlborn, 'The Rules of International Organizations and the Law of International Responsibility', 8 IOLR (2011) 397, 422.

[142] Just how these manifestations of control may translate into international responsibility will be addressed in Chapter II.

[143] D. Sarooshi, *supra* note 44, 6 (emphasis in original).

[144] As described by Plantey: 'Even when not deployed in the service of the States which, alone or together, dominate an international organization, the cohesion of its bureaucracy cannot fail to provoke a reaction on the part of governments anxious to maintain their freedom of political choice. *States lose no opportunity to assert their authority over a system with a tendency to free itself from their control and set itself up as an independent technical or diplomatic power*' (A. Plantey, *International Negotiation in the Twenty-First Century* (2007) 220 (emphasis in original)).

[145] D. Sarooshi, *supra* note 44, 7, 8.

[146] See, inter alia, the contributions of P. J. Kuijper and E. Paasivirta, *supra* note 61, 54–63 and of F. Hoffmeister, 'Litigating against the European Union and Its Member States – Who Responds under the ILC's Draft Articles?', 21(3) EJIL (2010) 723, 743–5.

questionable,[147] however, in that it seems to regard 'transfers of powers' as inexorable phenomena, wherein there is no margin left to consider the extent to which member States were involved in the operationalisation of those powers.[148] As this book will attempt to demonstrate (albeit with a focus on other institutional contexts), such State involvement – in the form of complementary exercise of competences by domestic institutions – cannot simply be bypassed on competence grounds and is of utmost importance when discussing international responsibility questions.[149]

In general, member States' role as creators and participants in international organisations is echoed in various critical aspects: they delineate their purposes, institutional design and rules of procedure; they finance and provide material support for the operations of international organisations; they second their nationals to the latter's organs; they affect the composition of management bodies;[150] they control the accession procedure of new members;[151] they participate in institutional decision-making processes; and they implement institutional decisions. Member States thus assume diverse roles which are indispensable for the effectiveness of institutional operations. In addition, provided certain conditions are met, States can ultimately withdraw,[152] or threaten to withdraw, from the organisation in case they disagree with the way in which it is exercising its

147 That the understanding of the EU as a special case in the law of international responsibility is controversial finds expression in the fact that the ILC barely took into account the views expressed by the EU throughout the discussions preceding the adoption of the ARIO (see, specifically on attribution: ILC, *Responsibility of International Organisations: Comments and Observations Received from International Organisations*, UN Doc. A/CN 4/545 (2004) 28–32). Admittedly, the *lex specialis* rule laid down in Article 64 ARIO does not dispel the controversy either. On the latter question, see: C. Ahlborn, *supra* note 141.

148 See D. Sarooshi, *supra* note 44, 65.

149 In a rather colloquial – but elucidating – tone, Klabbers alerts to the difficulties inherent in the allocation of responsibility between the EU and its member States by presenting a scenario where a Dutch customs officer, acting under the supervision of Dutch authorities, illicitly seizes a shipment of goods whilst implementing a regulation in an area of exclusive EU competence. See J. Klabbers, *An Introduction to International Institutional Law* (2015) 319, 320.

150 See the exposition contained in E. Lagrange, *supra* note 93, 218–30, showing how institutional organs ('organes intégrés'), such as management bodies, are permeable to the political influence of member States, notably owing to the rules of composition of these organs and the procedures for the nomination of higher positions thereof.

151 See K. D. Magliveras, 'Membership in International Organizations', in J. Klabbers and Å. Wallendahl (eds.), *Research Handbook on the Law of International Organizations* (2011) 85–90.

152 To assess whether unilateral withdrawals from membership are lawful, resort must be made to the constituent instruments of international organisations. A significant number of instruments, including the WB and the IMF Articles of Agreement (but not the UN Charter), expressly envisage that possibility, with some nuances in what concerns the requirement of prior notice. Regarding the EU, which is the organisation with most supranational features, it is interesting to note that, contrary to the previous founding instruments, the Lisbon Treaty (Consolidated version of the Treaty on European Union, *OJ C* 83/13, 30 March 2010 (TEU)) finally included a withdrawal clause in Article 50. At the time of writing, interesting developments are taking place with discussions around the UK withdrawal from the EU. For a legal analysis of the operationalisation of Article 50 in the Brexit context, see, inter alia: E. Szyszczak and E. Lydgate, UK Trade Policy Observatory, Briefing Paper 4, 'Triggering Article 50 TEU: A Legal Analysis' (2016). For more examples, see: H. Schermers and

powers.[153] To some, these are reasons enough to regard conferrals of powers as a natural extension of member States' rights, and, thus, as means to enhance the ability of States to exercise their sovereignty.[154]

From an international law perspective, it therefore remains valid to uphold the notion that the transfer of the exercise of sovereign powers, rather than freezing at the moment of adoption of the organisation's constituent instrument, brings about a process of interaction between international organisations and their members that unfolds in a 'continuum'. This enables the capturing of diverse sorts of action throughout the exercise of sovereign powers – whether performed by the international organisation or its member States, or both, as subjects of international law – each of which may be legally relevant for responsibility purposes. D'Aspremont pictured this notion as a manifestation of a flux of powers between international organisations and their member States.[155]

To a considerable extent, as creators, States remain the 'owners' of the powers whose exercise was transferred,[156] and in that condition they should *have a say* on how these powers are being, or are to be, exercised by the international organisation.[157] This is so, for the simple reason that States carry with them international law obligations once they adhere to international organisations – obligations which do not obviously fade away upon such adhesion (see Chapter III).

And yet, a word of caution is required at this point: the above observations should not be interpreted as supporting the idea that international organisations are ultimately mere tools or vehicles in the hands of their member States (particularly the most powerful ones), as realists would generally argue.[158] To the contrary, State adherence to international organisations necessarily implies a limitation of freedom of action, to give way to the life of the new international legal person thus created. Otherwise, it would not be of much use to set up such forms of institutionalised cooperation in the first place.[159] It is essential to provide the means for an

N. Blokker, *International Institutional Law: Unity within Diversity* (2011) 99. In any case, as also noted by Schermers and Blokker, the absence of a withdrawal clause has not prevented withdrawals in the past (see, ibid., 103, 104). These constitute violations of international law unless they fit in one of the exceptions contained in Articles 56(1) of the 1969 Vienna Conventions on the Law of Treaties, 1155 UNTS 331, and of the 1986 Vienna Convention on the Law of Treaties between States and International Organizations or between International Organizations, 25 ILM 543.

153 Some cases of withdrawal from membership are presented in H. Schermers and N. Blokker, ibid., 99–110.

154 See: D. Epstein and S. O'Halloran, 'Sovereignty and Delegation in International Organizations', 71 Law & Contemp Probs (2008) 77, 91.

155 J. D'Aspremont, *supra* note 71, 395.

156 See Section 1.2.1 on the question of 'mission-creep'.

157 The identification of an obligation to this end will be discussed in Chapter III.

158 See, inter alia: J. Mearsheimer, *The Tragedy of Great Power Politics* (2001), 363–6.

159 That international organisations do constrain member State behaviour through the exercise of conferred powers should not, in any case, be mistaken for the fact that constraints exist that result merely from international politics. These might as well occur in the framework of institutional operations, but not be *owed to* the latter, as explained by Guzman and Landsidle, referring to the

international organisation to manifest its autonomous will: given the latter's representational role of a given community of interest, this is, as a matter of fact, a necessary condition to ensure the prevalence of the principle of sovereign equality among the organisation's members.[160] A deeper insight into the terms in which the personhood of international organisations comes about will thus be given in the following section, to the extent that it is relevant to the understanding of the position of member States in relation to the organisations they create.

1.2 THE INSTITUTIONAL VEIL AND ITS IDIOSYNCRASIES

Having clarified that adherence to international organisations does not bring about the demise of the member State as a subject of international law, Section 1.2 digs further into the question of how the legal distinctness of both international legal subjects is to be understood. The matter is not without its difficulties, in that, as will be seen, the legal personality of international organisations has commonly been used as a powerful legal trope in responsibility discussions. Such tendency is only logical, and the merits of it are not herein questioned. It has, however, impeded an analytical account of member State action underneath the veil of institutional operations.

Sections 1.2.1 and 1.2.2 will thus attempt to delineate the boundaries of international organisations' personhood. Firstly, the contours of the powers of international organisations will be analysed, with a view to clarifying how their subjectivity comes about. Secondly, attention will turn to the concept of autonomy, and the terms in which international organisations can be said to express a *volonté distincte*. This exercise is deemed of utmost importance to the demarcation of an international organisation's responsibility for wrongful behaviour. At the same time, it is essential to the understanding of the position of member States vis-à-vis the international organisation, which will be discussed in Section 1.2.3. Using international financial institutions as background for analysis, it will be contended that the legal visibility of member States lies in the margin that is left for them to pursue sovereign preferences in institutional settings. As will be further explored in this book, it is in said margin that member State conduct – for attribution, and thereby responsibility, purposes – may be found.

1.2.1 *The Emergence of International Organisations' Personhood*

The post-war period witnessed an exponential growth in the creation of international organisations. Precedents of this phenomenon date back to the nineteenth century, however, when international public unions and international commissions (both

debates held by States at the UN General Assembly. See: A. T. Guzman and J. Landsidle, *supra* note 136, 1701.

160 Cf: E. Lagrange, *supra* note 93, 56.

functional and riparian commissions) were established.[161] Various reasons may explain States' undertakings of joint cooperation in the international scene.[162] Whatever these may be, an underlying factor will surely relate to the existence of an interest that is shared by the creators of the organisation and is perceived as being best attained collectively. Accordingly, to carry out tasks that States individually cannot, or which they believe international organisations can more effectively pursue at the global level,[163] the latter are equipped with mechanisms that (purportedly) allow them to pursue their goals with autonomy, and express a 'distinct will' from their members. Apart from their character as 'communities of interest',[164] international organisations have become sources of authority, and may appositely be regarded as actors[165] in the international scene. In international law, this image is captured through the notion of international legal personality.[166]

International legal personality has been hallmarked as an essential feature of international organisations, and was given a particularly prominent place in the ICJ 1949 *Reparations* case, when it came to determining whether the UN possessed the capacity to bring international claims for damages.[167] As the Court famously held: 'the Organization was intended to exercise and enjoy, and is in fact exercising and enjoying, functions and rights which can only be explained on the basis of the possession of a large measure of international personality and the capacity to operate upon an international plane'.[168] Yet, the added value of defining the status of international organisations as international legal persons has been questioned,[169] and so too the usefulness of identifying the inherent institutional traits of said

161 D. B. Michaels, *International Privileges and Immunities: A Case for a Universal Statute* (1971) 12. An example is the International Commission for the Cape Spartel Light, established in 1865. The life (and demise) of the organisation is discussed by D. Bederman, 'The Souls of International Organizations: Legal Personality and the Lighthouse at Cape Spartel', 36 Va J Int'l L (1996) 275.

162 See: M. Virally, *supra* note 91, 283–8. It is also useful to look into the work that has been done in this respect from a social sciences perspective. See, notably: K. Abbott and D. Snidal, 'Why States Act through Formal International Organizations', 42(1) JCR (1998) 3.

163 As synthesised by P. Bekker, *The Legal Position of Intergovernmental Organizations: A Functional Necessity Analysis of Their Legal Status and Immunities* (1994) 47.

164 The term was used by the Permanent Court of International Justice (PCIJ) in the *Case Relating to the Territorial Jurisdiction of the International Commission of the River Oder*, Series A-No.23, No. 16 (1929) 27, to refer to the common interest of riparian States which generated a common legal right in the use of the whole course of the river Oder. D. Bederman, *supra* note 161, retrieved the notion to highlight the transactional or relational character of international organisations.

165 In the sense of international bureaucracies which exercise public authority in contemporary world politics through both their rational-legal form of administration and their technical expertise and information. See the study of M. Barnett and M. Finnemore, based on Weber's work on bureaucratisation, in 'The Politics, Power, and Pathologies of International Organizations', 53(4) IO (1999) 699, 707–10. See also: I. Venzke, *supra* note 45, particularly 1410–16.

166 N. White, 'Discerning Separate Will', in W. P. Heere (ed.), op. cit. *supra* note 95, 31.

167 *Reparation for Injuries Suffered in the Service of the United Nations*, Advisory Opinion, ICJ Reports 174 (1949).

168 Ibid., 179.

169 According to Jenks, it is questionable whether the invocation of legal personality for the purpose of defining the legal capacity and powers of international organisations is necessary. However, when compared to the alternative of developing new terminology, it can still be deemed convenient for

concept.[170] At any rate, it can safely be asserted that the international legal personality of an international organisation entails that it may incur responsibility for any wrongful acts attributable to it.[171]

International legal personality thus signals (unquestionably) the existence of a new subject in international law,[172] which can be assessed as an objective, social phenomenon.[173] By the same token, the constituent instruments of international organisations cannot simply be thought of as embodying a contractual relationship between States: these instruments rather constitute a 'treaty +', giving rise to a new international legal entity through an act of legal personification,[174] which is thereby

practical reasons, as conceded by the author (see: C. W. Jenks, 'The Legal Personality of International Organizations', 22 BYIL (1945) 267, especially 271). Following this line of thought, but more bluntly perhaps, Klabbers contends that international legal personality does not constitute a threshold condition for the performance of legal acts, thus suggesting that it may be merely declaratory (see: J. Klabbers, 'The Concept of Legal Personality', in F. Johns (ed.), *International Legal Personality* (2010) 6). Some authors have even avoided the notion of international legal personality, preferring the conception of 'actor' or 'participant' in the international scene, whereby all entities exercising effective – as in factual – power in international decision-making processes are to be considered international persons. See: R. Portman, *Legal Personality in International Law* (2010) 208–13.

170 As explained by Lauterpacht, attributing 'personality' to an entity does not have any meaning as such, its significance depending on how the concept is perceived within a specific system of law (see: E. Lauterpacht, 'The Development of the Law of International Organization by the Decisions of International Tribunals', 152 RCADI 1976/IV, 377, 403). In the international legal context, Klabbers has classified personality as a purely descriptive and normatively empty concept, inasmuch as neither rights nor obligations derive automatically from it (see: J. Klabbers, *An Introduction to International Institutional Law* (2009) 51 (in the latter, 2015, version of his monograph, 69, Klabbers observes that this discussion has now shifted the focus of attention to the powers of the organisation, as these more satisfactorily explain personality in functionalist terms). Regarding the jurisprudence of the ICJ, the powers and competences of certain international organisations were assessed in seminal cases such as the abovementioned *Reparations* case, *supra* note 167; *Effects of Awards of Compensation Made by the United Nations Administrative Tribunal*, Advisory Opinion, ICJ Reports 47 (1954) (hereinafter *Effects of Awards* case); *Certain Expenses of the United Nations (Article 17, paragraph 2 of the Charter)*, Advisory Opinion, ICJ Reports 151 (1962); and *Legality of the Use by a State of Nuclear Weapons in Armed Conflict*, Advisory Opinion, ICJ Reports 66 (1966). Here, resort was consistently made, albeit with some nuances, to the notion of functional necessity as a yardstick to determine which rights and obligations flow from international legal personality.

171 By the time the ICJ *Cumuraswamy* opinion was given, it already seemed settled that international responsibility was a direct consequence of the international personality of an international organisation (see: *Difference Relating to Immunity from Legal Process of a Special Rapporteur of the Commission on Human Rights*, Advisory Opinion, ICJ Reports 62 (1999) 88, 89, para. 66), as noted by R. Portman, *supra* note 169, 109. See also Articles 2(a) and 3 ARIO, where it is made clear that in order to be held internationally responsible, international organisations must enjoy international legal personality.

172 If anything, the recognition of a group qua group in any given legal system is of immense symbolic value, and shields such an existence from possible interference by outside authorities, as conceded by Klabbers. See: J. Klabbers, *supra* note 169, 30, 31.

173 C. Brölmann, *supra* note 57, 96.

174 The term 'treaty +' is borrowed from R. Wessel, 'Dissolution and Succession: The Transmigration of the Soul of International Organizations', in J. Klabbers and Å. Wallendahl (eds.), op. cit. *supra* note 151, 346. The dual nature of the constituent instruments of international organisations as contracts

able to act vis-à-vis its member States, as well as, in principle, other international legal persons.[175]

International legal personality is often conflated with the notion of 'separate will'. And yet, legal scholars seem to disagree on how the will of international organisations comes about. Some pay deference to the limits of international organisations' power and claim that such organisations have 'no existence except through the will of [their] member States' (as expressed or implied in their founding treaties).[176] Less stringently, others see in constituent instruments the 'ground rules for a living body, the practical operation of which may increasingly go beyond the intention of its creators'.[177]

The latter is, in fact, visible when considering how the mandates of international organisations have evolved beyond their (original) purposes and (attributed) competences through administrative adaptation.[178] Regarding the Bretton Woods institutions, it is indeed interesting to note how – through the leadership of both organisations' heads – the IMF, which is mandated to promote macroeconomic stabilisation and surveillance, has recently been putting forward an environment agenda based on the understanding that 'environmental damage has macroeconomic implications, and implications for the design and impact of fiscal policy';[179] and how the WB's purportedly apolitical development mandate[180] came to integrate the fight against corruption as one of its benchmarks.[181]

As explained by Alvarez, inasmuch as the interpretations generated by institutional organs of their constituent instruments remain unchallenged – and thereby gain *general acceptance* – a gradual body of institutional precedents is produced,

between States and as constitutions governing the life of a new legal entity has merited considerable attention in legal writings. For an overview of the literature, see: C. Ahlborn, *supra* note 141, 408–10.

175 The issue of whether international organisations have objective personality is, according to the ILC, a settled one, as was made clear in para. 9 of its commentaries to Article 2 ARIO.

176 C. Chinkin, *Third Parties in International Law* (1993) 95, 96.

177 H. Schermers and N. Blokker, *supra* note 152, 728.

178 R. Wessel, *supra* note 174, 351, explaining how NATO shifted from a collective defence organisation into a collective security one, and how it has claimed the power to perform new activities in the absence of legal basis.

179 Christine Lagarde, 'Promoting Responsible Energy Pricing', Center for Global Development, 31 July 2014, available at: www.imf.org/external/np/speeches/2014/073114.htm, last consulted 15 October 2018. See also the information provided on the IMF's website: www.imf.org/external/np/fad/environ/, last consulted 15 October 2018.

180 Note that the Articles of Agreement prohibit the provision of loans based on considerations other than 'economic' ones (IBRD Articles of Agreement, *supra* note 4, Article III, Section 5(b); International Development Association Articles of Agreement, 249 UNTS 439, 24 September 1960 (IDA Articles of Agreement), Article V, Section 1(g)), as well as interference in the 'political affairs' of States (IBRD Articles of Agreement, Article IV, Section 10 and IDA Articles of Agreement, Article V, Section 6).

181 The mainstreaming of anti-corruption at the WB was ignited by former President James Wolfensohn by the end of the 1990s, as explained in the World Bank Group Annual Report prepared by the Department of Institutional Integrity on 'Investigations and Sanctions of Staff Misconduct and Fraud and Corruption in Bank-Financed Projects' (2005) 1.

typically in favour of expanded institutional competences.[182] And yet, this expansion may even occur without it being possible to relate to a specific constitutional provision susceptible of extensive interpretation: at the WB, while decision-making authority for loan approval is clearly vested in the Board of Directors,[183] the reality is that some projects (which are not necessarily less significant in terms of the size of the loan involved) are not included by management in the Board meetings' agendas, so that they are instead processed on an absence-of-objection basis.[184] The so-called AOBs are thus considered approved if none of the Executive Directors raises an objection. It is, of course, true that any Executive Director unsatisfied with this classification may request that the AOB project be integrated in the following Board meeting agenda for discussion.[185] However, AOBs can go unnoticed,[186] which means that, in practice, management has arrogated to itself some sort of decision-making power, even if to a very limited extent.

That international organisations become living bodies which may operate beyond the intention of their creators is also observable in the role they sometimes play as standard-setting entities – even if not *constitutionally authorised* to make law. Such a role may manifest itself in subtle ways but still tangibly contribute to developments in international law. For instance, in the execution of their mandates, international financial institutions are guided by a set of operational policies, which, albeit closely linked to international legal regimes, often do not explicitly refer to them.[187] In this vein, their staff are provided with the leeway to interpret and apply these policies on the basis of their own institutional culture and understanding. Unavoidably, the organisations' discretionary interpretations of certain international legal norms,

182 J. E. Alvarez, 'Constitutional Interpretation in International Organizations', in J. Coicaud and V. Heiskanen (eds.), *The Legitimacy of International Organizations* (2001) 113. The author notes, however, that it is dubious whether the lack of member State contestation of institutional practices should be equated with members' consent of these practices, as the passiveness of a given member State can be owed to extraneous reasons such as, for instance, the fear of confronting powerful members or organs (see 120).

183 See, for example, Article V of the IBRD Articles of Agreement, *supra* note 4.

184 It should be noted that AOBs are quite rare in the IMF, as confirmed in Interview #XXVII, 25 June 2015.

185 Field notes, 8 June 2015.

186 Tracing the AOBs really depends on the capacity and proactivity of the officials that staff Executive Directors' offices.

187 Consider the WB's new Environmental and Social Framework (ESF), adopted in August 2016 and in effect since 1 October 2018, which merely refers to the UDHR in its non-binding preamble, entitled 'A Vision for Sustainable Development'. The ESF is available at: http://pubdocs.worldbank.org/en/837721522762050108/Environmental-and-Social-Framework.pdf, last consulted 15 October 2018. To name but one example, the Environmental and Social Standard 7 on Indigenous Peoples/Sub-Saharan African Historically Underserved Traditional Local Communities does not contain any reference to the UN Declaration on the Rights of Indigenous Peoples, adopted by UNGA Resolution A/61/L.67 and Add.1 (2007). Cf., however, the European Bank for Reconstruction and Development Performance Requirement 7 on Indigenous Peoples, last updated in May 2014, which does refer to the UN Declaration in para. 4. The latter bank's Environmental and Social Policy is available at: www.ebrd.com/news/publications/policies/environmental-and-social-policy-esp.html, last consulted 15 October 2018. It is of note that this policy is under review in 2018.

principles and standards ultimately influence the evolution and interpretation of those very norms, principles and standards.[188]

Perceived by some as undesired by the principals (i.e., the member States), the phenomenon of 'mission-creep' has been described in IR literature as 'agency slack',[189] as well as dysfunctional or pathological institutional behaviour.[190] It proves, indeed, that member States are incapable of clearly defining at the outset the scope of the international organisation's powers, and that there is a limit as to what member States can *control* in institutional affairs.[191] Yet, at least formally, the claim can be made that, in joining the international (financial) institution, the member States consented in advance to the institutional aspect of autonomy,[192] and, thus, to not being able to exercise control over *everything*.

It remains no less true that the organisation's powers must always find their justification in functional necessity,[193] or, more broadly, in the purposes set out in the organisation's constituent instrument, however vague these may be.[194] Less ambiguous is the fact that the international organisation's 'separate will' cannot go as far as to dictate institutional or fundamental changes to its constitution, modify institutional structures such as the relationship between the various organs, or alter the rights and obligations of member States.[195] As straightforwardly put by Queneudec, the juridical personification of international organisations has as its limit the fact that it must remain at the service of member States' interests, 'parce qu'une organisation internationale n'existe que dans l'intérêt de ses membres et parce que son intérêt propre, lorsqu'il est reconnu, est encore au service du leur'.[196]

In sum, the exercise of powers by international organisations – within, and sometimes beyond, the framework of their founding treaties – constitutes a product of (and, at the same time, informs) their personhood. Their organic and

188 D. Bradlow, 'The Reform of the Governance of the IFIs: A Critical Assessment', in *The World Bank Legal Review: International Financial Institutions and Global Legal Governance* (2012) 37, 53, 54. As explained by the author, such a state of affairs is facilitated by the remaining uncertainty surrounding the content of international legal norms and standards and the terms in which they apply to the complex development issues implicated in institutional operations.

189 D. G. Hawkins, D. A. Lake, D. L. Nielson and M. J. Tierney, 'Delegation under Anarchy: States, International Organizations, and Principal-Agent Theory', in D. G. Hawkins, D. A. Lake, D. L. Nielson and M. J. Tierney (eds.), *Delegation and Agency in International Organizations* (2006) 8, 9.

190 M. Barnett and R. Finnemore, *supra* note 165, especially 715–19.

191 The question of the EU's accession to the ECHR shows that, sometimes, there may be a clash of autonomous actors within a given internal legal order. Indeed, in its Opinion 2/13, ECLI:EU:C:2014:2454, 18 December 2014, the CJEU rejected the draft Accession Agreement that would allow the EU to accede to the ECHR, invoking its incompatibility with EU law. This can be seen as an expression of institutional autonomy against the will of member States who supported the EU's accession.

192 I. Brownlie, *Principles of Public International Law* (2008) 272.

193 A. T. Guzman, *supra* note 135, 1006.

194 J. Alvarez, *supra* note 182, 119.

195 Ibid.

196 J. Queneudec, Préface, in E. Lagrange, *supra* note 93, VI.

permanent character[197] brings about manifestations of a *volonté distincte* (i.e., a 'distinct will'), and thus allows for the identification of an independent sphere of conduct, which must be demarcated from member States' conduct, qua sovereigns, for the purposes of establishing international responsibility.

In this connection, it is interesting to note how (full) autonomy has been perceived in legal practice as a prerequisite for the identification of the organisation's separate will[198] – the presupposition being that an entity can be considered as a separate subject of international law only if it is autonomous from other entities. Autonomy, however, is far from being an opaque concept: it rather shields within the intricacies related to the internal dynamics of international organisations and the way in which these actors come to operate as corporate-like structures in the international scene.[199] As will be discussed in the following section, the idea of autonomy does not translate into a 'zero-sum' member State and institution contest, but is instead more contingent and complex.[200]

1.2.2 *Institutional Autonomy As an Intricate Concept*

Albeit intimately related with the concept of international legal personality, autonomy can still be interpreted differently: while legal personality refers to the capacity of the

197 The term is borrowed from A. McNair, 'The Functions and Differing Legal Character of Treaties', 11 BYIL (1930) 100, 117.

198 See, e.g.: the older Judgment of the Italian Corte di Cassazione of 26 February 1931, 5 Ann. Dig., 414, as quoted in D. Bederman, *supra* note 161, 353, where the Court, in order to classify international administrative unions as international legal persons, found it essential to establish whether they remained autonomous and removed from State interference.

199 Autonomy, as herein perceived, is therefore linked to the political independence of the organisation from its member States. A distinct concept of autonomy refers to the legal order of an international organisation and its independence from the general international legal order. See, inter alia: J. D'Aspremont, 'The Multifaceted Concept of the Autonomy of International Organizations and International Legal Discourse', in R. Collins and N. White (eds.), *International Organizations and the Idea of Autonomy: Institutional Independence in the International Legal Order* (2011), particularly 70–86. With regard to the EU's institutional autonomy, for instance, mention should be made of the well-known *Kadi* cases, where the EU Court of First Instance (CFI), now the General Court of the EU (EGC), and then the CJEU, had to decide upon the independence of the EU legal order from external institutional interference, particularly from a Chapter VII UNSC Resolution (see: Case T-315/01, *Yassin Abdullah Kadi* v. *Council of the European Union and Commission of the European Communities* [2005] ECR II-3649, 21 September 2005 (hereinafter CFI, *Kadi I* 2005); Joined Cases C-402/05 P and C-415/05 P, *Yassin Abdullah Kadi and Al Barakaat International Foundation* v. *Council of the European Union and the Commission of the European Communities* [2008] ECR I-6351 (hereinafter ECJ, *Kadi I*); Case T-85/09, *Yassin Abdullah Kadi* v. *European Commission* [2010] ECR II-5177 (hereinafter EGC, *Kadi II*); Joined Cases C-584/10 P, C-593/10 P and C-595/10 P, *Commission and United Kingdom* v. *Yassin Abdullah Kadi*, Judgment of the Court (Grand Chamber) of 18 July 2013 (hereinafter ECJ, *Kadi III*)). See, also with regard to the EU, N. Tsagourias, 'Conceptualizing the Autonomy of the European Union', in R. Collins and N. White (eds.), ibid., 339–52.

200 R. Collins and N. White, 'International Organizations and the Idea of Autonomy: Introduction and Overview', in R. Collins and N. White (eds.), op. cit. *supra* note 199, 3.

international organisation to act as an independent subject of international law and thereby manifest a separate will from its members, autonomy reflects the extent to which member States can influence the functioning of the organisation.[201] Autonomy thus refers to self-government, and the degree of authority asserted by international organisations to regulate themselves.[202] This implies that an international organisation may well have separate legal personality, but that some of its organs may not act in a fully autonomous fashion vis-à-vis the member States.

The legal and factual autonomy of international organisations is thus measured with reference to two opposing (and at the same time coexistent) forces: on the one hand, the influencing power of the staff (Section 1.2.2.1); and, on the other hand, the presence and influence exerted by the member States upon institutional affairs (Section 1.2.2.2).[203]

1.2.2.1 The Staff's Role in the Ascertainment of Institutional Autonomy

The concept of institutional autonomy is inextricably linked to the process of formation of institutional will and its magnitude is contingent upon the organisation's capacity to act in insulation from the control of its member States. As Judge M. Alvarez put it in his individual opinion on the 1948 ICJ *Admissions* case, the extent of institutional autonomy depends on whether the institution, once established, has 'acquired a life of its own', and has developed 'not in accordance with the views of those who created it, but in accordance with the requirements of international life'.[204]

The identity of international organisations as independent subjects that have 'acquired a life of their own' is necessarily reliant upon the influencing power exerted by their staff over institutional operations. This power is undoubtedly significant, and can vary depending on a few factors, such as the staff's capacity to mobilise technical expertise, forge strategic alliances and raise public awareness, their leadership role in negotiations, and their agenda-setting capacity.[205] For example, the more than fifteen thousand officers composing the WB's bureaucracy play a non-negligible role in

201 T. Gazzini, 'The Relationship between International Legal Personality and the Autonomy of International Organisations', in R. Collins and N. White (eds.), op. cit. *supra* note 199, 196–200. Although the UN was characterised by the ICJ as possessing 'a large measure of international personality' in the abovementioned *Reparations* case, *supra* note 167, it bears emphasis that, unlike the notion of autonomy, international legal personality is not a measurable concept: an actor either has international legal personality or does not have it.

202 A. Sari, 'Autonomy, Attribution and Accountability', in R. Collins and N. White (eds.), op. cit. *supra* note 199, 258.

203 The following sections draw on a previous publication by: A. S. Barros and C. Ryngaert, *supra* note 58.

204 Individual Opinion by Judge M. Alvarez, *Conditions of admission of a State to membership in the United Nations (Article 4 of Charter)*, Advisory Opinion, ICJ Reports 57 (1948) 68.

205 See: B. Reinalda and B. Verbeek, 'Policy Autonomy of Intergovernmental Organizations: A Challenge to International Relations Theory?', in R. Collins and N. White (eds.), op. cit. *supra* note 199, 95, 96.

shaping its development practice: they are responsible for preparing the project-related reports on the basis of which the Executive Board makes its loan decisions, and they are the ones who establish priorities in project implementation and mobilise resources on the ground. Grounded on an entrenched institutional culture[206] – that shapes their own allegiances and behaviour – the Bank's staff are significantly involved in problem-definition and problem-solving. In structuring knowledge, classifying and organising information,[207] and developing policy preferences of their own, bureaucracies thus bring about institutional ontological independence.

The importance of a dedicated and autonomous international staff is undeniable. Notably, if an international organisation is to genuinely act in the common interest of all its members, it can only do so if it operates as a neutral actor and is not subjected to their control.[208] The need to shield international organisations and their staff from member State interference and thereby ensure efficiency in their functioning is precisely the reason why a robust framework of institutional privileges and immunities has been set in place, especially in treaties such as the headquarters agreements of these organisations[209] and both the Convention on the Privileges and Immunities of the United Nations and the Convention on the Privileges and Immunities of the Specialized Agencies.[210]

In this light, while the international organisation is under a legal obligation to fulfil its attributed functions, its member States are legally bound to respect the autonomous performance of such functions and, generically, to act in accordance with the purposes set out in the organisation's constituent instrument.[211] States, qua members of the international organisation (i.e., in their *internal* capacity), are in this sense required to act in good faith so that the 'primacy of common aims over manifestations of excessive individualism by States which are incompatible with them' is ensured.[212]

206 Safarty provides a thorough account of the WB's institutional ethos, explaining how the predominance of economic rationality has hampered a more human rights-friendly culture, in: G. A. Sarfaty, *Values in Translation: Human Rights and the Culture of the World Bank* (2012).

207 See: M. Barnett and R. Duvall, 'International Organizations and the Diffusion of Power', in T. Weiss and R. Wilkinson (eds.), *International Organization and Global Governance* (2014) 56, explaining how international organisations' institutional power allows them to guide behaviour through classificatory practices.

208 P. Bekker, *supra* note 163, 100. See also: Y. Haftel and A. Thompson, 'The Independence of International Organizations: Concept and Applications', 50(2) JCR (2006) 253, 255–7.

209 See, inter alia: Headquarters Agreement between the Food and Agriculture Organization and the Italian Government, 1409 UNTS 521, 31 October 1950.

210 Convention on the Privileges and Immunities of the United Nations, 1 UNTS 15 and 90 UNTS 327 (corrigendum to Vol. 1), 13 February 1946 and Convention on the Privileges and Immunities of the Specialized Agencies, 33 UNTS 261, 21 November 1947. For a comprehensive overview and detailed discussion of both documents, see the various contributions contained in: A. Reinisch and P. Bachmayer (eds.), *The Conventions on the Privileges and Immunities of the United Nations and Its Specialized Agencies: A Commentary* (2016).

211 H. Schermers and N. Blokker, *supra* note 152, 121–3.

212 R. Kolb, 'Article 2(2)', in B. Simma, D. Khan, G. Nolte and A. Paulus (eds.), *The Charter of the United Nations: A Commentary* (2012) 174, with regard to the obligation of good faith in the framework of the UN Charter. Within the EU context, good faith is expressed through the duty of sincere cooperation

1.2.2.2 The Permeability of International Organisations to Member State Influence

Next to the role played by the staff, the presence and influence exerted by member States upon institutional affairs cannot be overlooked in the ascertainment of the autonomy of international organisations. Autonomy is thus idiosyncratically limited, when compared to the autonomy of States.[213] Indeed, in current sociological theory, autonomy has even been criticised as an inappropriate term to describe institutional behaviour, for an international organisation can never be truly autonomous.[214] In this variation, the international organisation–member State balance is lost where States (informally) exert influence in a manner amounting to interference with, and even hindrance of, institutional operations, thus overstepping the minimum threshold of autonomy required for the organisation to act as an independent actor on the international scene.[215]

The institutional set-up of the international organisation is an important factor to capture the degree of its (im)permeability to member State interference. Apart from the existence of a powerful secretariat (already discussed), the design of decision-making procedures can also be of relevance to determine the extent of institutional autonomy.[216] Accordingly, permeability to member States is most conspicuous where unanimity voting applies or where decisions are taken by consensus. The possibility to dissent and the use of the veto power inexorably impede institutional action, and thus leave States a rather large margin of discretion to protect their sovereign preferences while acting within the framework of the organisation. By contrast, in international organisations where the majority rule is employed, it is possible for the organisation to adopt institutional decisions notwithstanding the objection of a few member States, which certainly limits the possibility of member State interference and increases the degree of autonomy of the organisation.[217]

and the principle of Union loyalty. See: Article 4 TEU (*supra* note 152) and, for an overview of the principle's implications, P. J. Kuijper and E. Paasivirta, *supra* note 61, 39–42.

As recalled by Judge Rezek in his separate opinion in the ICJ *Cumuraswamy* opinion, *supra* note 171: 'the fact of membership … requires that every State, in its relations with the organization and its agents, display an attitude at least as constructive as that which characterizes diplomatic relations between States'.

213 On institutional autonomy as a relative concept, see A. Sari, *supra* note 202, 258–60.

214 S. Brechin and G. Ness, 'Looking Back at the Gap: International Organizations as Organizations Twenty-Five Years Later', 4 *Journal of International Organizations Studies* (2013) 14, 22.

215 As noted by Stone: 'there is an accepted range of legitimate deviations from formal rules, and an outer range of illegitimate deviations, and the difference turns on the circumstances of domestic politics or international strategic concerns that create the temptations' (R. Stone, *supra* note 58, 44).

216 ILA Report on Accountability of International Organisations, *supra* note 50, 9. See also: Y. Haftel and A. Thompson, *supra* note 208, 257–62.

217 It is, at any rate, interesting to note that in some international organisations, such as the ICAO, a member State that does not agree with a decision taken by a committee of member States can always appeal this decision. See: Article 52 of the Convention on International Civil Aviation, 15 UNTS 295, 7 December 1944.

In the former case, where the unanimity rule applies, institutional autonomy is perceived as rather limited. This has led some authors to assert that in such cases the organisation has 'no life independent from the will of its members'.[218] Some have even gone as far as to question the (external) legal personality of such an organisation, maintaining that it hardly enjoys any degree of (internal) autonomy from its member States.[219] Likewise, in IR literature, the question has been raised as to whether it can properly be said that States with veto power actually delegate powers to international organisations.[220] One need not go so far, however. On the one hand, unanimity necessarily constitutes a limitation on States' autonomous decision-making power; on the other hand, it does not impede the emergence of the organisation's *volonté distincte* or an institutional will expressed, and seen to be expressed, by a competent organ of the organisation.[221] The use of the veto power, unless systematic, simply delimits the possibilities for a collective will to be expressed.[222]

The example of unanimity voting illustrates that the political autonomy of an international organisation can sometimes be undermined, which, in any event, does not mean that its legal personality is lost.[223] What it could mean, however, is that conduct performed under the institutional cloth may in reality find its origin in – legally meaningful – *interference* by the member State, and, in that sense may: be attributed to the latter rather than to the international organisation; be concurrently attributed to the international organisation and to the member State; engage the responsibility of the latter even if performed by the organisation, as will be discussed in Section 2.1.

To assess institutional autonomy, it is essential to examine the de facto extent of member States' interference. Standard operating procedures such as the *de jure* majority rule are not, as such, decisive to argue for a pronounced degree of autonomy, inasmuch as informal rules, allowing for member State *manipulation* of negotiations (usually by the most powerful), may also play a significant role in decision-making.[224] It has been widely reported how formal voting rules are

218 D. Bederman, *supra* note 161, 358. See also: J. Klabbers, *supra* note 149, 48.
Guzman has similarly stated that, in consensus decision-making, institutions cannot be said to use delegated authority in any meaningful sense, and, thus, described the rules adopted thereof as 'having been created by the states'. See: A. T. Guzman, *supra* note 135, 1013.
For a critical account of earlier doctrinal and jurisprudential views in this sense, see: E. Lagrange, *supra* note 93, 276–80.

219 See, e.g., as regards NATO: T. Gazzini, *supra* note 201, 201–5. The author is mainly concerned with the strict control over NATO decision-making processes exerted by its members. See also: T. Gazzini, 'NATO Role in the Collective Security System', 8 JCSL (2003) 231, particularly 240–2.

220 See: D. Epstein and S. O'Halloran, *supra* note 154, 82, 83.

221 See, inter alia: R. Wessel, 'Revisiting the International Legal Status of the EU', 5(4) EFAR (2000) 507, 518 and N. White, 'Decision-Making', in J. Klabbers and Å. Wallendahl (eds.), op. cit. *supra* note 151, 227.

222 E. Lagrange, *supra* note 93, 281.

223 J. D'Aspremont, *supra* note 199, 69.

224 Cf.: M. Virally, *supra* note 91, 278.

sometimes bypassed and actual decision-making takes place on the 'backstage', where the margin left for member State political interference can be quite significant.[225] A case in point is the recourse to consensus decision-making, which often occurs in organisations where a weighted voting system is applied,[226] e.g., in the Bretton Woods institutions.[227] As a pattern for decision-making, consensus has been characterised as 'essentially institutionalized diplomacy',[228] and while it could seem that it smoothens power imbalances between member States – and accordingly limits the potential for State interference – the reality is that 'a weak State will reluctantly acquiesce in the decision being discussed [by powerful States]'.[229] As noted by Escarameia, when it comes to politically controversial matters, the consensus method corresponds, in practice, to the exercise of veto power by the most influential States.[230] In this vein, considering that the US together with the EU member States hold more than 40 per cent of the voting power in the IMF,[231] or that the G7 hold about 40 per cent of votes in the organisation, it is indubitable that the economically powerful States *dominate* the IMF – a domination that has visibly been transposed to the less formalised decision-making formats adopted in this institution[232] (see Chapter II). The informal governance mechanism set up by the IMF to respond to systemic crises is a notable example of this, inasmuch as it shifts decision-making out of the Executive Board into a small network of senior government officials (often the G7), who practically negotiate in secrecy.[233]

From the above, it follows that the functional independence and political autonomy of a given international organisation lie in its impermeability to the imposition of policy preferences and ideological biases by member States, as may or may not be reflected in the decision-making set-up of the organisation. As a matter of fact, to admit that member States may significantly condition the formation of institutional will is to acknowledge, in other terms, that member States remain *visible* underneath

225 See, inter alia: R. Stone, *supra* note 58, discussing informal governance mechanisms at the IMF, the WTO and the EU.

226 Such a system constitutes a pertinent example of an institutional arrangement whereby the influence of the most powerful States can be maintained.

227 See Article XII(5) of the IMF Articles of Agreement and Article V(3) of the IBRD Articles of Agreement, *supra* note 4.

228 E. Stein, 'Democracy beyond Nation-State: On World Trade Organization and European Union', in *The Dean Rusk Lectures* (2002) 11.

229 N. White, *supra* note 221, 229.

230 P. Escarameia, *Reflexões sobre Temas de Direito Internacional: Timor, a ONU e o Tribunal Penal Internacional* (2001) 199.

231 According to the latest data available, the US holds 16.52 per cent of the voting power whereas EU member States hold around 25 per cent. See the IMF website: www.imf.org/external/np/sec/memdir/eds.aspx#2, last consulted 15 October 2018.

232 D. Bradlow, *supra* note 188, 39.

233 As further explained in the IEO Report on IMF Governance, *supra* note 58, 6, once a tentative solution is reached, IMF staff work closely with relevant stakeholders to delineate the details, and management subsequently brings the proposed package to the Executive Board for review and approval.

the cloth of institutional operations. In this vein, the outright attribution of conduct (and responsibility) to international organisations under the assumption of autonomous behaviour might not capture in sufficiently comprehensive terms the whole spectrum of conduct that is legally relevant for an assessment of responsibility. As already hinted at and will be further discussed in Chapter II, the pervasiveness of member States may well bring to the fore a new, supplementary locus of responsibility.

1.2.3 *The Legal Visibility of Member States behind the Institutional Veil*

1.2.3.1 State Action in Institutional Settings As *Dédoublement Fonctionnel*

From the previous sections it transpires that the relationship between international organisations and their member States is marked by tension. Given the prominence of member States as drivers and participants in institutional affairs, alongside the organisations' autonomous conduct, it sometimes becomes unclear where the international organisation begins and its member States end.[234]

That there is indeed a 'thin veil through which the member states are clearly visible'[235] is reflected in various accounts in the jurisprudence, legal and soft-law instruments where reference is made to 'States acting through international organisations' or to 'State actions as members of international organisations'.[236] Importantly, then, one should examine under what circumstances the conduct of (member) States becomes legally visible, i.e., 'addressed from, and involved in, the general international plane'.[237] In such an exercise, it is fundamental to keep in mind that States act in the framework of international organisations in a dual capacity, also termed, to borrow from Scelle, *dédoublement fonctionnel*:[238] they

[234] J. Klabbers, *supra* note 149, 310.

[235] N. Blokker, 'International Organizations and Their Members', 1 IOLR (2004) 139, 144.

[236] See, inter alia: *Prosecutor* v. *Dusko Tadić*, IT-94-1-AR72, Appeals Chamber of the International Criminal Tribunal for the former Yugoslavia, 2 October 1995, para. 47; *Prewitt Enterprises Inc and ors* v *Organization of Petroleum Exporting Countries*, Appeal Judgment, 353 F3d 916 (11th Cir 2003), p. 11, ftn 9; Article 139(3) of the United Nations Convention on the Law of the Sea, 10 December 1982, 1833 UNTS 397; and General Comment No. 19 on the Right to Social Security, UN Doc. E/C.12/GC/19 (2008) para. 58.

[237] C. Brölmann, *supra* note 57, 255.

[238] The expression is owed to G. Scelle, whose doctrine can be found in various publications including *Précis de Droit des Gens. Principes et Systématique*, Vol. I (1932) 42–57 and Vol. II (1934) 10. An important remark should, however, be made: Scelle's doctrine was developed in a context where, in the absence of 'institutions constitutionelles organiques spéciales aux milieu interétatiques' (Vol. II, 10), and thus, where 'les institutions étatiques fonctionnent comme institutions internationales' (Vol. I, 47), the need was felt to explain the role played by government officials in the international arena. According to Scelle, such a role would be 'split' depending on whether government officials acted within the national legal system or, rather, the international one. As noted by Cassese, Scelle's theory

act, on the one hand, as members or organic parts of the organisation, and, on the other hand, as sovereign States upholding their own domestic preferences.

This duality is perhaps most visible in the model of institutional design used by most international organisations: the plenary organ, ordinarily the principal decision-making body (and often the highest political one), in which all members are represented and are entitled to vote. In these organs, as noted by Klabbers, 'there is always an element of artificiality in making a distinction between organizations and their members'.[239]

To be sure, in non-plenary bodies deciding on behalf of the whole membership, the issue is likewise present: in the Executive Boards of international financial institutions, for instance, the dichotomy inherent in the role of the Executive Directors is clearly noticeable. Accordingly, a study conducted in 2008 by the IEO confirmed that '[m]ore than half of Board members reported that they occasionally face a conflict between their role as representatives of their authorities and their role in upholding the Fund's institutional interests ... [W]hile in practice all Directors clearly understand their representational role, their status as officers of the Fund is less clear.'[240] A more recent appraisal conducted by the author of this monograph indicates that the role of IMF and other international financial institutions' Executive Directors as State representatives is indeed strongly felt – an opinion that was expressed by representatives of both powerful and less powerful member States.[241]

The dual capacity of States is mirrored by the multifaceted identity of international organisations which not only emerge as independent actors on the international scene (as seen in Sections 1.2.1 and 1.2.2), but can also be regarded as forums for States to engage in international relations. Klabbers picked up this image as one positing the character of international organisations as classical *agoras*,[242] and so did Plantey, highlighting their role as instruments for diplomacy.[243] Along the same

failed to account for instances where State agents behave as international organs and nevertheless 'take action for the exclusive purpose of safeguarding *national* (or short-term, self-centred) interests' (emphasis in original). See: A. Cassese, 'Remarks on Scelle's Theory of "Role Splitting" (*dédoublement fonctionnel*) in International Law', 210 EJIL (1990) 210, 219. As applied to the role played by State representatives in the framework of international organisations, the concept of *dédoublement fonctionnel* comes closer to the instances mentioned by Cassese, with the important adjustment that it does not refer to the behaviour of State agents *as* international organs, but, rather, *in* international organs.

239 J. Klabbers, 'Autonomy, Constitutionalism and Virtue in International Institutional Law', in R. Collins and N. White (eds.), op. cit. *supra* note 199, 121.

240 IEO Report on IMF Governance, *supra* note 58, 16.

241 Interview #IV, 3 June 2014; Interview #VI, 23 March 2015; Interview #XII, 5 June 2015; Interview #XIII, 5 June 2015; Interview #XIV, 8 June 2015; Interview #XV, 11 June 2015; Interview #XVI, 11 June 2015; Interview #XVII, 12 June 2015; Interview #XVIII, 12 June 2015; Interview #XXI, 17 June 2015; Interview #XXIV, 19 June 2015; Interview #XXV, 22 June 2015; Interview #XXVI, 22 June 2015; Interview #XXVII, 25 June 2015; Interview #XXIX, 26 June 2015; Interview #XXX, 26 June 2015; Interview #XXXI, 29 June 2015; and Interview #XXXIII, 31 June 2015 (see *infra* Chapter II).

242 J. Klabbers, 'Two Concepts of International Organization', 2 IOLR (2005).

243 A. Plantey, *supra* note 144, especially 198–222. As noted by the author, 'the temptation is strong for some great powers to see international organisations as instruments of their own global policies' (221).

lines, Brölmann referred to the transparent legal set-up of international organisations, wherein the geopolitics of the 'institutional veil' become patent.[244]

The notion of international organisations as a domain of political interaction is crucial to retain, inasmuch as this is precisely the domain in which the legal significance of State participation in institutional affairs is brought to the fore.[245] It is here where, in parallel with institutional conduct, there is a margin left for (member) States to act with a certain degree of autonomy and discretion; where, in other words, the State apparatus is engaged and the pursuit of national preferences is made possible; where, in sum, member States exercise public power and can thus be said to act as subjects of international law.[246]

Such remnants of sovereignty come as no surprise. To be sure, the mere fact of membership represents for the member State the materialisation of a national interest: the acknowledgement that collaborating with other States (or entities) towards the attainment of a common purpose is in the State's best interest. Ultimately, as 'instruments' of States,[247] international organisations can survive in the long term only if they are somehow perceived to be pursuing joint (national) interests.[248] This explains why a purely constitutional model of international organisation – as opposed to a contractual model – has not yet been set in place. Instead, to prevent Frankenstein-like situations, States have ensured forms of institutional design whereby State-to-State bargaining is made possible, as is their capacity to *informally* influence decision-making processes.[249] As the next section will show, this remains no less true in the context of international financial institutions.

1.2.3.2 The Legal Visibility of the Member States of International Financial Institutions

Within international financial institutions, the dynamics of membership cannot be dissociated from the pursuit of sovereign preferences (recall Section 1.1.1). The very choice of institutional design made by the member States attests to that. Looking back at the Bretton Woods debates, it is clear how the US pushed for a model of institutional design that would allow it to heavily influence the operations of these institutions – not only through its quota share, but also by ensuring sufficient leeway for informal influence – and thereby promote national objectives within such

244 C. Brölmann, *supra* note 57. The author focuses on treaty-making within international organisations, as this subject-matter illustrates the problems related to the geopolitics of the 'institutional veil' particularly clearly.

245 See *infra* Section 1.3, on the role of Executive Boards of international financial institutions as a political counterweight to the staff's technical operations.

246 Recall what was said in Section 1.1 regarding the contestation of sovereignty by member States.

247 M. Virally, *supra* note 91, 278, 291.

248 R. Stone, *supra* note 58, 18.

249 Ibid., especially 2–32.

contexts.[250] Similarly, it is interesting to note how the model of quota distribution in the Asian Infrastructure Investment Bank (AIIB), spearheaded by China, was designed so as to grant the latter the position of largest shareholder, with a 'veto' power akin to that currently held by the US in the Bretton Woods institutions.[251] To put it simple, models of institutional design whereby Executive Boards and their most powerful members are granted a wide margin of control and oversight constitute an obvious choice when it comes to international financial institutions, in that 'those who contribute the bulk of the financial resources will only do so if they can be assured a certain degree of control over their use'.[252]

Membership of international organisations can thus be said to constitute a means for States to pursue foreign policy objectives.[253] Indeed, at an elementary level, membership in multilateral development banks emerges as a foreign policy choice to engage in multilateral cooperation in the field of development.[254] Inevitably, then, the participation of States in these institutions cannot but be permeated by their own vision of development, its meaning and implications – up to a point where the institutions sometimes become 'battlefields for debates about development policies'.[255] The process of review and update of the latest WB environmental and social safeguard policies constitutes a clear example of this: the process was highly politically charged, and while some (Western) countries consistently upheld the mainstreaming of human rights in the policy framework to be adopted, other (Eastern) countries vehemently blocked such an approach.[256] Also, when it comes to member States' views on the environment, some

[250] R. Mikesel, *The Bretton Woods Debates: A Memoir*, Essays in International Finance, No. 192 (1994) 52. As noted by Woods, there is a general perception that the IMF is mostly a US-led organisation, based on various factors including the veto power it holds on major institutional changes. See N. Woods, 'Global Governance after the Financial Crisis: A New Multilateralism or the Last Gasp of the Great Powers?', 1(1) GP (2010) 51, 56.

[251] China's voting share within the AIIB is of 26.5872 per cent, as enunciated in the Bank's website, available at: www.aiib.org/en/about-aiib/governance/members-of-bank/index.html, last consulted 15 October 2018.

[252] L. Martinez-Diaz, 'Executive Boards in International Organizations', in R. Lamdany and L. Martinez-Diaz (eds.), *Studies of IMF Governance: A Compendium* (2009) 117.

[253] R. Stone, *supra* note 58, 3. This was also acknowledged by member State representatives of the IMF, the WB, the Inter-American Development Bank (IDB) and a senior official of the NIB (Interview #II, 3 October 2013; Interview #XIV, 8 June 2015; Interview #XXI, 17 June 2015; Interview #XXXI, 29 June 2015; Interview #XXXIII, 31 June 2015).

[254] The webpage of the US Treasury dedicated to the participation of the US in multilateral development banks reads: 'America's leadership in these institutions ensures that the United States can help shape the global development agenda, leveraging its investments to ensure effectiveness and on-the-ground impact.' See: https://home.treasury.gov/policy-issues/international/multilateral-development-banks, last consulted 15 October 2018.

[255] J. Strand, 'The Regional Development Banks and Global Governance', in T. Weiss and R. Wilkinson (eds.), op. cit. *supra* note 207, 601, providing the example of Japan and other East Asian governments, which attempted to replicate their post–World War II development experiences – based on State-centric economic growth strategies – in other developing countries, as an alternative to the neoliberal economic orthodoxy that is typically pursued in these institutions.

[256] See a confidential statement submitted during the process of review of the Bank's safeguard policies by six Executive Directors to the WB's Committee on Development Effectiveness, where they criticised the absence of references to human rights standards in the Bank's proposed draft, available

members strongly supported clean energies and the decarbonisation of development, whereas coal-dependent countries were less receptive to the idea. As admitted by former WB President Kim Jong Ying, the bank's safeguard review process brought about 'extremely strong opinions that come from different parts of the world with different frames together'.[257] It thus comes as no surprise to hear within Bretton Woods circles that the idea of these institutions as apolitical creatures is even 'naïve'.[258]

The argument that international organisations constitute means for States to pursue foreign policy objectives can be stretched further, to encompass the notion that the pursuit of economic (and other) objectives also plays a role when it comes to State participation in international financial institutions. This is, for instance, reflected in US law: in a section of the US Code regarding multilateral development bank procurement, it is prescribed that '[t]he Secretary of the Treasury shall instruct the United States Executive Director of each multilateral development bank to attach a high priority to promoting opportunities for exports for goods and services from the United States'.[259] This explains why several US Executive Director offices in international financial institutions include staff from the Department of Commerce, responsible for the identification of procurement opportunities for US firms and for monitoring procurement issues.[260]

The promotion of national goods, services and corporate interests seems, at any rate, to be common – and well accepted – practice among member States, and not just the US, or the most powerful members.[261] There is, moreover, an explicit reference to this aspect in the WB Code of Conduct for Board Officials, according to which: 'Board Officials . . . may take appropriate action at the Organizations *in the interests of governments, organizations, entities and individuals in their respective constituencies*, provided that such measures are consistent with the rules and procedures of the Organizations. Whether taking such actions or otherwise, they shall not attempt to exert undue influence on management and staff of the Organizations with respect to: (i) the awarding of contracts for the procurement of goods or

at: https://sjc-cjs.org/wp-content/uploads/2015/11/ED-statement-on-safeguards-draft.pdf, last consulted 15 October 2018.

257 See: Devex news article, 'No Easy Path for the World Bank's Safeguards', 9 December 2014, available at: www.devex.com/news/no-easy-path-for-the-world-bank-s-safeguards-84887, last consulted 15 October 2018. These stories certainly repeat themselves in other international financial institutions. See, e.g.: J. Strand, *supra* note 256, citing examples regarding the AsDB and the European Bank for Reconstruction and Development (EBRD).

258 The expression was used by a Senior Advisor to an Executive Director, in Interview #XXVIII, 25 June 2015.

259 See: 22 US Code § 262s.

260 R. M. Nelson and M. A. Weiss, *supra* note 119, 4.

261 This information was confirmed in interviews with Executive Directors, Alternates and Advisors of offices representing both powerful and less powerful WB member States, as well as with an EBRD Alternate Executive Director. Interview #III, 2 June 2014; Interview #VI, 23 March 2015; Interview #XII, 5 June 2015; field notes from 16 June 2015.

services.'[262] Similar stipulations can be found in the codes of conduct for Executive Directors of other international financial institutions.[263]

Although the quoted provision attempts to constrain the margin left for Board Officials to pursue national interests, the boundary between due and undue influence is not easy to delineate. This means, in practice, that commercial or other geostrategic objectives may sometimes take priority over the common objectives and criteria that are officially declared by these institutions.[264] African countries, for example, are known to occupy a 'special place' in the foreign policy strategies pursued in the IMF and the WB by former colonial powers such as France, the UK and Portugal.[265] With regard to France, for instance, the IMF has even (informally) accommodated the country's strong economic, political and military interests in francophone Africa, allowing it to interfere on behalf of its former colonies to help them secure IMF support, and to significantly influence the development of IMF conditionality decisions in these countries.[266]

To add complexity to the picture, one should mention the phenomenon of 'institution shopping'. Accordingly, critical shareholders own 'equity' shares across international financial institutions, which entails that they coordinate their strategies with a view to combining their international institutional and financial assets with

[262] Article 5(a) of the WB Code of Conduct for Board Officials, adopted 1 November 2007 (emphasis added).

[263] The African Development Bank (AfDB) Code of Conduct for Executive Directors, adopted as amended in September 2007, foresees, in para. 8, cases of conflict between the interests of Executive Directors' constituencies and those of the AfDB and determines that 'Executive Directors may take appropriate action at the Bank in the interests of governments and private persons in their respective constituencies, provided such measures are consistent with the rules and procedures established by the Bank.' In the General Counsel's Explanatory Note accompanying the Code, it is stated that this provision was included to respond to the 'need to prescribe standards with respect to the conflict between the official interest of governments in their constituencies in securing positions, contracts, procurement and other benefits from the Bank for their nationals and the Bank's objective criteria and procedures in this regard'. See also: IDB Code of Ethics for the Board of Executive Directors, adopted as amended in 15 April 2009, 7. In contrast, Article 31(2) of the Agreement Establishing the Black Sea Trade and Development Bank, 30 June 1994 (Agreement Establishing the BSTDB) exceptionally establishes that Executive Directors 'shall, in their decisions, take into account only considerations relevant to the Bank's purpose, functions, and operation'.

[264] See, inter alia: A. Clapham, *Human Rights Obligations of Non-State Actors* (2010) 140–2; C. Tan, 'Mandating Rights and Limiting Mission Creep: Holding the World Bank and the International Monetary Fund Accountable for Human Rights Violations', 2(1) HR&ILD (2008) 79, 93.

The prevalence of geopolitics over macroeconomic objectives (or development objectives, in the case of the WB) is testified in numerous accounts in the literature. See, inter alia: R. Faini and E. Grilli, 'Who Runs the IFIs?', Development Studies Working Papers, N. 191 (2004). Also, in R. Stone, *supra* note 58, 188, it is for instance noted how US interests regarding Pakistan have significantly influenced IMF and WB financing to the latter: a long suspension from IMF and WB financing occurred during the Clinton administration, which was punishing Pakistan for the development of nuclear weapons, but was brought to an end when the Bush administration called for Pakistan's support in the 2001 war against Afghanistan.

[265] Interview #IV, 3 June 2014; Interview #XIII, 5 June 2015; Interview #XXXIV, 9 July 2015. See also: R. Stone, *supra* note 58, 173–8.

[266] R. Stone, ibid. This information was confirmed in Interview #XX, 15 June 2015.

their national ones.[267] This has implications when it comes to the governance of these institutions: as the 'finance ministers of the critical shareholders set agendas for the IFIs more like a portfolio of investments than as a holding company', the votes cast by a member State representative in a given international financial institution will not be independent of the vote of his or her counterpart in a different institution.[268]

National interests, be they economic, geopolitical, security or other, thus find their echo in State participation in institutional decision-making. To be sure, policies and votes on particular issues may affect member States' relations with individual countries.[269] Hence, as a corollary of bilateral relations, former colonial powers will not, by default, vote against, or abstain from supporting, the financing of a project in a former colony.[270] Moreover, in order to avoid a clear conflict of interests, Executive Directors remain silent in meetings whenever a company from the country(ies) they represent is involved in a project under discussion for IFC loan approval.[271]

Member State visibility is particularly prominent in decision-making processes regarding crucial issues such as membership,[272] institutional structures and the policy framework guiding institutional operations. In these cases, change mostly depends on what is determined by member States,[273] who have the authority to provide independent direction and impetus on the basis of direct political responsibility.[274] The creation of the WB Inspection Panel in 1993 so illustrates: intensive external pressure by CSOs as well as the findings of two Bank-commissioned reviews regarding the Bank's lack of compliance with its social and environmental policies ignited the initiative of a group of Executive Directors from both donor and borrowing countries to circulate a proposal for a new accountability mechanism and, ultimately, the US's forceful engagement (marked by the threat to withhold its contribution to the 10th replenishment of IDA's resources) led to the issuing of a resolution in that regard by the Bank's Executive Directors on 22 September 1993.[275]

267 M. Fratianni, P. Savona and J. Pattison, 'Governance and Conflicts of Interest in International Financial Institutions', in M. Fratianni, P. Savona and J. Kirton (eds.), *Corporate, Public and Global Governance: The G8 Contribution* (2007) 132.

268 Ibid. The phenomenon of choosing between international organisations as negotiating forums is in any case broader, as noted by J. A. Alvarez, 'International Organizations: Then and Now', 100 Am J Int'l L (2006) 324, 330, 331.

269 In the US, this matter is dealt with by the regional bureaus of the Economic and Business Bureau. See: R. M. Nelson and M. A. Weiss, *supra* note 119, 4.

270 Interview #IV, 3 June 2014.

271 Ibid.

272 K. D. Magliveras, *supra* note 151, 101.

273 For a thorough account of how policy-making unfolds in international financial institutions, and the role of member States as driving forces of change (and thereby responsible actors in such context), see *infra* Sections 2.2.2 and 3.4.2.

274 A. Plantey, *supra* note 144, 216.

275 D. Clark, 'Understanding the World Bank Inspection Panel', in D. Clark, J. Fox and K. Treakle (eds.), *Demanding Accountability: Civil-Society Claims and the World Bank Inspection Panel* (2003)

That policy change is deeply interconnected with member States' preferences is clearly noticeable in replenishment negotiations. As has been reported, these constitute useful tools in the hands of (donor) member States for the latter to significantly influence the direction and content of the institutions' operational, financial and internal administrative policies.[276] Notably, member States condition their support 'on being satisfied that their own *donor conditionalities and priorities* – often subtly and sometimes not so subtly expressed during replenishment negotiations – as to what the MDBs … will do, how they will do it and how they are to be run, will be met by MDB managements'.[277]

It is, at any rate, important to note that it is not necessary to trace the promotion of a specific, strategic national interest (economic, security, political or other) by member State representatives to claim member State visibility: the national interest may simply lie in aligning one's position with a particular member State or group of members.[278] As regards the EU (euro area) member States, certain positions may even be collectively delineated and politically filtered, out of a sense of common identity and obligation. The European Commission has actually taken steps to strengthen the coordination of common positions in order to ensure that the euro area systematically speaks with one voice on all IMF policy, country and surveillance issues of relevance to the euro area.[279] Currently, EU member States meet at the WB on a weekly basis and at the IMF at least once a month, in the so-called EU coordination meetings.[280] These meetings serve as an informal forum for member State representatives to share views on issues listed in the Board's agenda and to discuss written positions on programmes, projects or reports to be adopted. In these meetings, Executive Directors test the possibility of expressing unified positions on varied matters and, when that is the case, they issue a joint 'grey' (written statement, often used as an alternative to oral statements), co-signed by all.[281] Less systematic but still

2–9. See also: Resolution No. IBRD 93-10 and Resolution No. IDA 93-6, 'The World Bank Inspection Panel', adopted on 22 September 1993.

276 P. Mistry, *Multilateral Development Banks: An Assessment of Their Financial Structures, Policies and Practices* (1995) 118–20. See also: N. White, *The Law of International Organisations* (2005) 151.

277 P. Mistry, ibid., 118 (emphasis in original).

278 See: D. Panke, *supra* note 104, especially 28, 29.

279 Article 138(1) of the Consolidated version of the Treaty on the Functioning of the European Union, *OJ* C 326/47, 26 October 2012, states: 'In order to secure the euro's place in the international monetary system, the Council, on a proposal from the Commission, shall adopt a decision establishing *common positions* on matters of particular interest for economic and monetary union within the competent international financial institutions and conferences …' (emphasis added). Also relevant is the article's para. 2, whereby: 'The Council, on a proposal from the Commission, may adopt appropriate measures to *ensure unified representation* within the international financial institutions and conferences …' (emphasis added). The Commission has taken up this task in 'Proposal for a Council Decision laying down measures in view of progressively establishing unified representation of the euro area in the International Monetary Fund', COM (2015) 603 final, 21 October 2015.

280 As the relevance of these meetings has grown over time, the EU now counts with a permanent representative at the WB.

281 In the IMF, joint 'greys' are issued, for instance, with regard to Eurozone programme countries. When it comes to other countries, (EU) Executive Directors either issue their own 'grey' or co-sign one with another counterpart with whom they share the same views. For example, the French and the

significant are the G11 meetings, where developing countries gather for the same kind of purpose, usually once a month.[282]

In addition, it should be emphasized that the legal visibility of member States does not depend on the political character of the question or interests at stake. Actually, the delineation of State positions often regards specific technical questions pertaining to environmental risk assessments, fiscal policy choices, or the like. Accordingly, the link between the conduct of Board Directors and the States they represent rather derives from the fact that policy formation is – in a more or less detailed manner, and for whatever purpose – domestically driven, thereby emerging within a sphere of State interaction. Acknowledging that the concrete preference or objective pursued by the member State might deviate from the general purposes of the organisation only reinforces the notion that a link with concrete sovereign preferences can be established.

In pursuing sovereign interests, member States thus become legally visible. It is in the margin left for member States to exercise public power that member State conduct – for attribution, and thereby responsibility, purposes – may be found. It is thus, here as elsewhere, reiterated that the transfer of the exercise of sovereign powers to international organisations unfolds in a 'continuum', i.e., as a dynamic process, wherein member States remain systemically engaged.

1.3 TRANSLATING MEMBER STATE POWER INTO RESPONSIBLE GOVERNANCE

In the framework of the binary member States–international organisation relationship, one is left to wonder: what are the contours of each actor's governance functions so that they operate effectively and become distinct from one another? To reproduce Kuper's broader inquiry, '[a]t which levels and loci of power should governing institutions be situated so that they are stable, enabling office-holders and citizens to operate in these justifiable ways on an ongoing basis?'[283] For this book's purposes, the question thus turns into an investigation of how the international legal order responds to the need for a 'complex and contextualised state, with the capacity to know when to do nothing, when to regulate and when to provide'[284] when it acts within the framework of international organisations. Sovereignty, then, is used less for the sake of definition than for the identification of a 'conceptual locus for intervention'.[285]

UK Executive Directors often co-sign 'greys' for questions regarding African countries (Interview #XXVII, 25 June 2015).

282 Interview #XXIX, 26 June 2015.

283 A. Kuper, *Democracy beyond Borders: Justice and Representation in Global Institutions* (2004) 192.

284 P. Gready and W. Vandenhole, 'What Are We Trying to Change? Theories of Change in Development and Human Rights', in P. Gready and W. Vandenhole (eds.), *Human Rights and Development in the New Millennium: Towards a Theory of Change* (2014) 5.

285 D. Kennedy, 'The International Style in Postwar Law and Policy', 7 Utah L Rev (1994) 7, 15.

As has already been hinted at, and will be further explored in the subsequent chapters, member States are deemed to have enough *leverage* to condition institutional outcomes. In political science terms, borrowed from Barnett and Duvall, this would mean that the member State 'working through the rules and procedures that define those institutions, guides, steers, and constrains the actions (or non-actions) and conditions of existence of others'.[286] And because the member State stands in a particular relation to the relevant international organisation, it exercises power over the latter.[287] In this vein, one is forced to agree that if member States, acting as international legal subjects, and the organisations they create *affect* (or *determine*)[288] individuals, then the former must make sure that this impact does not occur to the detriment of the international human rights obligations they are bound to observe.[289]

In this setting, the most important manifestation of member States' (remaining) power is their role as 'authority managers'.[290] Some authors have noted how member States have a vital interest in policing the public power that is exercised within international organisations[291] and that, as a matter of fact, their oversight role is built into the heart of the founding treaties of multiple international organisations.[292] Still, the argument can be stretched further, to make way for the claim that managing authority constitutes an obligation inherent in member States' role as creators of, and participants in, international organisations.

The parallelism between governance and authority management can easily be identified in the role played by the Executive Boards of international organisations.

286 M. Barnett and R. Duvall, 'Power in Global Governance', in M. Barnett and R. Duval (eds.), *Power in Global Governance* (2005) 15.

287 Ibid., 16.

288 A. Von Bogdandy, P. Dann and M. Goldmann, 'Developing the Publicness of Public International Law: Towards a Legal Framework for Global Governance Activities', in A. Von Bogdandy, R. Wolfrum, J. V. Bernstorff, P. Dann and M. Goldmann (eds.), op. cit. *supra* note 50, 11, define authority as the 'legal capacity to *determine* others and to reduce their freedom, i.e., to unilaterally shape their legal or factual situation' (emphasis in original).

289 See, inter alia: F. Seyersted, *supra* note 96, 73, 74.

290 The expression is used in M. Zürn, 'Global Governance as Multi-Level Governance', in D. Levi-Faur (ed.), op. cit. *supra* note 38, 735, to generally characterise the role played by States in global governance. See, in a similar vein: R. Sadurska and C. Chinkin, 'The Collapse of the International Tin Council: A Case of State Responsibility?', 30 Va J Int'l L (1989–1990) 845, 873, referring to the 'managerial control' functions of the shareholders of domestic companies, and establishing an analogy with the member States of international organisations; and T. Weiss and R. Wilkinson, 'International Organization and Global Governance: What Matters and Why', in T. Weiss and R. Wilkinson (eds.), op. cit. *supra* note 207, 4, claiming that 'states have taken on the role of managers of global interdependence'.

291 This is so if one approaches the topic from the perspective of the sovereign equality of States, as held by E. De Wet, 'Holding International Institutions Accountable: The Complementary Role of Non-Judicial Oversight Mechanisms and Judicial Review', in A. Von Bogdandy, R. Wolfrum, J. V. Bernstorff, P. Dann and M. Goldmann (eds.), op. cit. *supra* note 50, 857, 858. De Wet differentiates between vertical, intermediate and horizontal oversight mechanisms, noting that member States play a central role in relation to the first ones (see: 863–8).

292 J. A. Scholte, *supra* note 89, 25–8, even if acknowledging important limitations in this regard.

It is here where member State representatives interact and political authorities give legitimacy to the technical judgements of staff.[293] As sketched by Martinez-Diaz, it is possible to identify four main models of governance when it comes to Executive Boards: as political counterweight, as performance police, as democratic forum and as strategic thinker.[294] In a study involving the Executive Boards of the IMF, the WB, the IDB, the AfDB, the AsDB and the EBRD, the author concludes that these organisations are based on a delegate-and-control model whereby their Executive Boards are best equipped to perform the role of political counterweight to the technical decisions made by the organisation's management and staff.[295] As concluded by the author, Executive Boards exercise close control over the activities of these institutions,[296] and thereby come forth as a 'political check by member governments on the organization's actions and polices'.[297]

Approaching member States as 'authority managers' in a way gives expression to Kuper's proposal that sovereignty be plurarchic; notably, that sovereignty be 'dispersed horizontally and vertically, to multiple levels and loci of authority, each exercising distinct and determinate power over kinds of human practice and resources'.[298] In this scheme, and as underlined in the current chapter, it is important to keep in mind that international organisations are also 'living bodies',[299] which must be granted the space to develop a life of their own. Accordingly, there is only so much that member States can *control* in a given institutional setting, as they are caught in between the obligation to diligently *monitor* and *oversee* the organisation's operations, on the one hand, and the need to preserve their proper functioning, under a functional necessity rationale, on the other hand. At the end of the day, the structuring of plurarchic sovereignty cannot but be 'limited on functional grounds by needs for efficacious coordinated action and democratic inclusion'.[300] In an institutional context, sovereignty as exercised by member States will thus manifest itself on a 'macro' level of political management, strategy formulation and oversight over policy implementation, alongside the technical decisions of management and staff. As managers of authority in international organisations, member States thus find a concrete role to play in global governance.

293 L. Martinez-Diaz, *supra* note 252, 83.

294 Ibid., 82. For a detailed discussion of what all four roles of Executive Boards entail, see further pp. 86–90.

295 Ibid., 104.

296 Ibid.

297 Ibid., 86.

298 A. Kuper, *supra* note 283, 197.

299 H. Schermers and N. Blokker, *supra* note 152, 728.

300 A. Kuper, *supra* note 283, 197. Driven by such kinds of concerns, ICJ Judge Kenneth Keith has asserted that, '[g]iven the almost unlimited power of the Security Council and the very limited power, if any, of the Court review of its exercise, those involved in Security Council decision-making, it seems to me, have a special responsibility to see that that power is exercised in a principled and fair way' (K. Keith, 'The International Rule of Law', 28 LJIL (2015) 403, 412).

1.4 CONCLUSION OF CHAPTER I

The international legal personality of international organisations singles them out as independent actors in the international scene, capable of responding for their wrongs under the regime of international responsibility. While the legal status of international organisations is generally well understood, that of member States is far less clear. Hence, the present chapter explored the intricacies of the relationship between international organisations and their member States, keeping in mind the inherent conflict between law and politics that characterises the latter's participation in institutional operations. Its purpose was to clarify the normative presuppositions on the basis of which the borderline between both subjects of international law can be delineated. Chapter I was thus intended to set the stage for the subsequent analysis: in exploring the terms in which member States are continuously engaged in the exercise of the powers that they transferred to international organisations, it shed light onto the elements that define member State conduct as subjects of international law. Needless to say, it is in the latter capacity that States' acts can be directly addressed by international (human rights) law.

While it is true that nowadays political authority is diffused – as other actors (ranging from transnational corporations to NGOs and indigenous people's groups) increasingly play a role, through formal and informal networks, in setting authoritative standards[301] – the State remains a fundamental actor in the realm of global governance, including when it acts within the framework of international (financial) institutions. The notion that the latter are *used* by States to pursue national interests was advanced in the first section, where the focus was placed on the mobilisation of national legislative and judicial mechanisms to monitor the creation and participation of government representatives in international organisations. Subsequently, this notion was addressed from an international law perspective to capture the legal visibility of member States underneath the institutional veil. Perceived as government action on foreign affairs, membership was therefore mainly addressed through the lens of inter-State cooperation. Without questioning the collective identity of international organisations, the autonomy of their staff, and the fiduciary responsibilities owed to them by member States (imposed within the organisations' internal legal order), the analysis developed on the margin that is left for member States' sovereign preferences to be represented. This margin runs in parallel with the life that international organisations lead on their own as independent international legal persons, and is entrenched in the idea of membership – so much so that it has even been embraced by the WB Code of Conduct for Board Officials, wherein, as mentioned in Section 1.2.3.2, member State representatives are granted the space to act in the interests of their respective constituencies.

The dynamics of the institutional veil thus reveal that the relationship between international organisations and their members points to diverse potential loci of

301 R. Keohane and J. Nye, 'Introduction', in J. S. Nye and J. D. Donnahue (eds.), *Governance in a Globalizing World* (2000) 1–42.

international responsibility. When an institutional wrong is committed, the usual premise is that the international organisation, as an international legal person, will be responsible for it. The contours of member State *involvement* in said wrong are typically overshadowed however. For this reason, it was asserted that the legal personality of international organisations and their *volonté distincte* should not dominate the discussion as powerful legal tropes, as they sometimes are,[302] since they impede an analytical account of member State conduct beyond the veil of institutional operations.

Truth be told, when it comes to assessing responsibility, it may be hard to establish a link between member States and the concrete conduct performed by international organisation officials on the ground: for instance, IMF Executive Directors do not participate directly in missions to countries or the negotiation of programmes (for the sake of preserving the integrity of negotiations).[303] As emphasized in Sections 1.2.1 and 1.2.2, the crucial need to preserve institutional autonomy brings with it a non-negligible limitation on what member States can *control* in a given institutional setting. As 'authority managers', member States are thus more likely to become visible, and their acts legally relevant for responsibility purposes, on a 'macro' level: at the level of the governance mechanisms and procedures they establish and conduct – and in which, by implication, they play the role of leading actors.

302 D. Bederman, *supra* note 161, 331.
303 R. Stone, *supra* note 58, 57. They can, however, be kept informed about them (see Chapter III).

II

Accounting for the Governance Role of Member States of International Financial Institutions in the Regime of International Responsibility

Chapter I discussed the normative presuppositions on the basis of which the frontier between member States and international organisations can be determined. As clarified, member States remain legally visible actors in the international scene owing to their role as governors of international organisations. How, then, is this governance role perceived when it comes to issues of international responsibility? To answer this question, Chapter II critically analyses the contours of secondary rules of international law,[304] with the main purpose of applying them to the concrete context of member State participation in the representative bodies of international financial institutions.

As will be seen, the conceptualisation of a regime of member State responsibility essentially entails an answer to the question of how to place, in international law, the power that member States wield through their involvement in the functioning of international organisations. Relational as it is, this power has for a long time steered legal debates towards the assertion of member State responsibility *for* the consequences of the organisation's wrongful acts, while the question can be addressed as well from the viewpoint of member States' *own* wrongful acts performed in institutional settings. The present chapter aims to substantiate the latter perspective, but it cannot do so without first exploring the former.

Section 2.1 analyses the conceptual underpinnings of the regime of member State responsibility as they have been appraised in the past decades by the legal epistemic community. In so doing, it pays particular attention to the terms in which member States' governance role has been approached across the various debates. Section 2.1.1 explains how initial doctrinal and jurisprudential inquiries revolved around whether member States bore concurrent or secondary responsibility for institutional wrongs. It then notes that this discussion was subsequently discarded by the IDI in the 1990s, and that the ILC ultimately cemented the principle of non-responsibility of the member States in the ARIO.

304 Recall *supra* note 46, for a distinction between primary and secondary rules of international law.

While member States' control over institutional affairs through their participation in decision-making processes has been acknowledged all along, the question of how to legally frame this form of control and subsume it in a coherent set of secondary rules of international law remained uncertain. Section 2.1.2.1 evaluates how the ILC dealt with the topic in Part V of the ARIO, which foresees a number of exceptional cases where the institutional veil may be pierced for responsibility purposes. Given the insufficiencies of this regime when it comes to determining the responsibility of member States as governors of international organisations, Section 2.1.2.2 examines whether the matter may entail, instead, member States' responsibility for their own wrongful acts performed in an institutional setting. It thus concentrates on attribution rules. Importantly, as will be seen in Section 2.1.3, significant – even if occasional – indications exist in case-law towards the finding of member State responsibility along these lines.

Discussions on attribution have so far mostly dealt with contexts where member States emerge as implementers of institutional decisions and as troop contributors. It is important to retrieve these discussions, however, in that they enable the identification of common benchmarks that can be applied in the far less debated setting of member State participation in institutional decision-making. Here, as before, at the heart of the analysis lie elementary questions which, as put by Hoffmeister, may be articulated in terms of 'who is the factual actor of the alleged breach?; who has the legal power to bring an end to the alleged breach?; and who bears the international obligation invoked concerning the alleged breach?'[305]

To respond to such query in the concrete context of international financial institutions, Section 2.2.1 begins by identifying the actor, i.e., the (member) State. To that end, it explores the international legal status of Executive Directors and the terms in which the legal conundrum brought about by the duality inherent in their role may be overcome. Grounded on the conclusion that Executive Directors are (as well) State organs, Section 2.2.2 brings attention to the internal dynamics of decision-making in international financial institutions. These attest to the notion that voting emerges as a corollary of the power of sovereign representation, and should therefore be deemed conduct attributable to the State. This is so, also in the context of multi-party constituencies.

All Chapter II sections are seen as crucial steps towards the concrete delineation of the boundaries between member States and international financial institutions for responsibility purposes. The chapter thus provides a solid understanding of what exactly is the conduct that is to be judged against member States' human rights obligations.

305 F. Hoffmeister, *supra* note 146, 745.

2.1 SETTING IN PLACE A REGIME OF MEMBER STATE RESPONSIBILITY: APPROACHES WITHIN THE LEGAL EPISTEMIC COMMUNITY

If, for long, international organisations were broadly seen as benign cooperative endeavours (paving the way, according to some, towards the 'salvation of mankind'),[306] both the dissolution, in the 1970s, of the Arab Organization for Industrialization (AOI) and the fall, in the 1980s, of the International Tin Council (ITC) heralded some changes in perception. These events notably led to the acknowledgement that institutional and member State activity too could bring about 'grave injustice[s]'[307] and ethical difficulties,[308] thereby vigorously steering the – already existing – legal debate as to what sort of regime could be set in place to account for such conduct.

As this section intends to demonstrate, current loopholes in the treatment of member States in terms of their responsibility for their governance role in international organisations and, notably, their participation in decision-making bodies are mostly owed to the way in which the topic of member State responsibility in general was addressed since its inception. Indeed, while the power exercised by member States over international organisations has always been acknowledged, it was quickly overshadowed by concerns with the organisations' legal personality. The latter became – understandably in any case – the viewpoint from which member State responsibility was to be addressed, which implied its consideration only at a residual level. This conceptual mindset was dogmatically kept in the ILC's ARIO.

2.1.1 *Evolution of Legal Debates regarding Member State Responsibility*

The formative period for the recognition of the legal personality of international organisations gained pace with the emergence, in the nineteenth century, of the first international public unions and international commissions.[309] Naturally, legal texts at the turn of the century were concerned with how best to fit these creatures into existing categories of legal thought,[310] notably in terms of their character and status under international

306 J. Klabbers, 'The EJIL Foreword: The Transformation of International Organizations Law', 26(1) EJIL (2015) 9, 29.

307 *J H Rayner (Mincing Lane) Ltd* v. *Department of Trade and Industry and Other* and Related Appeals *Maclaine Watson & Co Ltd* v. *Department of Trade and Industry* and *Maclaine Watson & Co Ltd* v. *International Tin Council*, United Kingdom House of Lords, 26 October 1989, 81 ILR 670, 683 (per Lord Griffiths) (hereinafter *ITC* case).

308 R. Higgins, 'The Responsibility of States Members for the Defaults of International Organizations: Continuing the Dialogue', in *Themes and Theories: Selected Essays, Speeches and Writings in International Law* (2009) 920.

309 D. Bederman, *supra* note 161, 278.

310 J. Klabbers, *supra* note 134, 290–2.

and private law,[311] their powers,[312] as well as the question of privileges and immunities – most prominently of their officials.[313]

If, by the mid-1920s, various legal scholars would readily discard the view that States were the only subjects of international law,[314] the ICJ *Reparations* case[315] was in any event of paramount importance for its vindication of the international legal personality of international organisations. While the legal implications thereof were unclear at the time, for commentators such as Eagleton, the capacity of possessing international rights and duties served already as evidence that international organisations could incur responsibility for their own wrongful acts.[316]

An appropriate comparator for international organisations – and, more accurately, their international legal personality – was found in the idea of a 'body corporate'.[317] This was only logical, as limited liability corporations had become nearly universally recognised in municipal law.[318] Sir John Fischer Williams, for instance, in discussing the status of the League of Nations in 1926, referred to it as 'a thing in international law analogous to the body corporate in municipal law',[319] coming closer to the *Société anonyme* rather than to the *Société en nom collectif* or the *Société en commandite*, as the former would more markedly explain the autonomy of the League of Nations from its member States.[320]

311 Discussions about the legal status of entities such as the International Commission of the Cape Spartel Lighthouse, one of the first international organisations ever created, are quite illustrative in this respect. See: D. Bederman, *supra* note 161, 319–32. Moreover, for an overview of the debate surrounding the status of the League of Nations, see Sir J. F. Williams's address to the International Law Association in 1926, reprinted in: J. F. Williams, 'The Status of the League of Nations in International Law', in *Chapters on Current International Law and the Law of Nations* (1929) 477–80.

312 See how the PCIJ dealt with the question of institutional powers in: *Case of the SS Lotus*, Publ. PCIJ, Series A, No. 10 (1927) (marking the origins of the doctrine of attributed powers) and *Interpretation of the Greco-Turkish Agreement of December 1st, 1926*, Publ. PCIJ, Series B, No. 16 (1928) (marking the origins of the doctrine of implied powers).

313 For an extended account of the historical development of the privileges and immunities of international officials, as well as those of international organisations (which were only developed at a later stage), see: J. L. Kunz, 'Privileges and Immunities of International Organizations', 41 Am J Int'l L (1947) 828, especially 828–32, and the bibliography references contained therein.

314 D. Bederman, *supra* note 161, 335.

315 *Supra* note 167.

316 C. Eagleton, 'International Organization and the Law of Responsibility', 76 RCADI 1950/I, 319, 323, 385–404.

317 D. Bederman, *supra* note 161, 356.

318 Ibid., 356, 357.

319 J. F. Williams, *supra* note 311, 480.

320 Ibid., 483. The image of international organisations as an international body corporate endured over time, which is reflected, for instance, in the writings of Jenks (see: C. W. Jenks, *The Proper Law of International Organisations* (1962)) and Mann (see: F. A. Mann, 'International Corporations and National Law', 42 BYIL (1967) 145, especially 148–9).

Against this backdrop, member States would play the role of 'corporators of the new corporate entity'.[321] Throughout the years, opinions were put forward whereby, based on analogies with certain corporations in municipal legal systems whose rules prescribed the concurrent or secondary responsibility of the shareholders for the obligations of the corporation, member States could be seen to be similarly liable for the acts of international organisations.[322] Notably, debates revolved around whether:[323] a) third parties, having a legal claim against an international organisation, could bring their claim, at their choice, against either the organisation or its members (i.e., concurrent responsibility);[324] or b) third parties, having a legal claim against an international organisation, had a remedy against member States in the event of default by the former (i.e., subsidiary responsibility).[325] Naturally, others would advocate the impossibility of finding in general international law a concrete rule in either direction.[326] The debate did not reach very far, however, as in the 1990s the use of domestic corporate law analogies slowly began to wane.[327]

Early case-law reflected the abovementioned divergences. The first case where member State responsibility was addressed was the Westland Helicopters arbitration,[328] which involved a claim for damages, by Westland Helicopters Ltd (WHL), stemming from the dissolution of the AOI. This claim was directed against the AOI, its four member States and a joint stock company, created by the WHL and the Higher Committee of the AOI, which was composed of the entire membership. In its decision, the arbitral tribunal acknowledged the international legal personality of the AOI; however, it found member State liability to subsist since, 'as a general rule, those who engage in transactions of an economic nature are deemed liable for the obligations which flow therefrom'.[329] As noted by the tribunal, the member States, 'in forming the AOI, did not intend wholly to disappear behind it, but rather to participate in the AOI as "members with liability"'.[330] Closely connected to this was the tribunal's appreciation of the AOI's Higher Committee as playing a 'double

321 J. F. Williams, *supra* note 311, 481. Referring to the League of Nations, the author further explains (482): 'The League resembles a company all of whose shareholders are themselves bodies corporate, whose board of directors is composed of nominees of certain shareholders.'

322 For an extended overview of earlier doctrinal positions, see: M. Hirsch, *supra* note 76, 137–46.

323 The following definitions derive from Article 2(b) of the IDI Resolution on Member State Responsibility, *supra* note 64.

324 E.g.: I. Seidl-Hohenveldern, *supra* note 137, 119–21.

325 E.g.: H. T. Adam, *Les Organismes Internationaux Spécialisés: Contribution a la Théorie Générale des Établissements Publics Internationaux* (1965) 127–30.

326 E.g.: F. A. Mann, *supra* note 320, 160, 161; I. Shihata, 'Role of Law in Economic Development: The Legal Problems of International Public Ventures', 25 *Revue Egyptienne de Droit International* (1969) 125.

327 See: R. Higgins, Preliminary Exposé, *supra* note 74, 263.

328 *Westland Helicopters Ltd* v. *Arab Organization for Industrialization, United Arab Emirates, Kingdom of Saudi Arabia, State of Qatar, Arab Republic of Egypt and Arab British Helicopter Company*, Arbitration, 5 March 1984, 23 ILM (1984) 1071 (hereinafter *Westland Helicopters* arbitration).

329 Ibid., 1084.

330 Ibid.

role, both as organ of the AOI and as a grouping of States'.[331] Hence, on the basis of member States' guaranteeing role, as well as considerations of equity, justice and third party protection, the arbitral tribunal concluded for the rightness of directing the claim against the AOI's member States, ultimately asserting that 'the AOI [was] one with the States'.[332] This assertion has been rightly criticised for dismissing the AOI's legal personality[333] and, unsurprisingly, the award was later annulled on appeal by the Swiss Federal Supreme Court.[334]

The legal personality of international organisations played a rather prominent role in the (in)famous *ITC* cases,[335] decided one year later by the UK House of Lords. The ITC litigation was triggered by the insolvency of the ITC in 1985, and its consequent default on numerous contracts for the purchase of tin and bank loans. The question to be answered was whether the institutional veil of the ITC could be lifted so as to hold the member States responsible for its defaults.

Quite straightforwardly, the House of Lords asserted that the ITC was a 'legal personality distinct in law from its membership',[336] which meant that '[t]he only parties to the contracts between the appellants and the I.T.C. were the appellants and [that] the I.T.C. Members of a body corporate are not liable for the debts of a body corporate because the members are not parties to the corporation's contracts'.[337] Moreover, the alleged existence of a rule of general international law prescribing the joint and several responsibility of the member States was likewise dismissed by the Lords, given the insufficiency of elements to establish such a rule.[338]

It is of note that the claimants did raise several pertinent arguments relating to the governance role played by ITC member States in the council. Yet, they fell short in extracting from said role convincing grounds to establish member State responsibility. They maintained, for instance, that the organisation, 'through the buffer stock manager, did what its members wanted it to do' and should thereby be regarded as the agent of the latter as undisclosed principals.[339] However, Lord Oliver dismissed the suggestion of constitutional agency by noting that 'whether a corporation acts directly on the instructions of its members, who constitute the directorate, or indirectly because of the members' control in general meeting, makes no difference in principle'.[340] Next to this, the claimants noted that 'the members acting in council did in fact know and approve of, and authorise the actions of the I.T.C. officers

331 Ibid., 1085.
332 Ibid.
333 See, inter alia: R. Higgins, *supra* note 74.
334 *Arab Organization for Industrialization and others* v. *Westland Helicopters Ltd*, Swiss Federal Supreme Court (First Civil Court), 19 July 1988, 80 ILR 652, especially 658.
335 *ITC* case, *supra* note 307.
336 Ibid., 678.
337 Ibid., 679 (per Lord Templeman). See also 708 (per Lord Oliver).
338 Ibid., 679–81 (per Lord Templeman) and 710–15 (per Lord Oliver).
339 ILDC 1733 (UK 1990), para. 47. See also paras. 49, 50.
340 *ITC* case, *supra* note 307, 717.

including the making of contracts for the purchase of tin'.[341] Besides, as argued by the claimants, the precariousness of the ITC's financial position was known to the members and, despite such awareness, they allowed it to continue to trade.[342] While the claimants could have argued for a lack of due care on the part of ITC member States in supervising the organisation's operations,[343] they rather found in said elements a duty of the member States to indemnify the ITC.

The obligation to assist the organisation for reparation purposes has indeed been mentioned as an intermediate solution between unlimited member State responsibility and its general exclusion.[344] This obligation, in any event, is generally seen to exist solely within the spectrum of the internal rules of the organisation, as was later set forth in Article 40(2) ARIO.[345] From the perspective of third parties, then, it arguably does not provide a real guarantee of reparation from the wrongdoing international organisation, inasmuch as the latter will often lack effective means to enforce the obligation of its members to put it in funds.[346] Lord Griffiths touched upon the matter, noting that it would be 'the obvious just solution'.[347] He cautioned, nonetheless, that 'this end must be pursued through diplomacy and an international solution must be found to an international problem; it cannot be solved through English domestic law'.[348] Ultimately, this and all the other claims were dismissed by the House of Lords.

Discussions on member State responsibility grew exponentially in the aftermath of the *Westland* and *ITC* cases, largely owing to the contribution of the IDI to the topic during the 1990s. As admitted by Rapporteur Higgins, who led the IDI's work, domestic law considerations, such as the operation of immunity (of international organisations from domestic jurisdiction) or the concept of non-justiciability (as institutional matters bring to the fore relations that occur between international

341 Ibid., 720 (emphasis in original).

342 Ibid.

343 In the two ITC cases put before the Court of Justice of the European Communities, the discussions drew on whether the European Community had been negligent in allowing the ITC to continue its activity while being aware that it was unable to meet its obligations. See: Case C-241/87, *Maclaine Watson* v. *Council and Commission of the European Communities*, 30 O.J.E.C. (No. C 262) 5 (1987) and Case C-19/89, *AMT (Tin Recoveries)* v. *Council and Commission of the European Communities*, 32 O.J.E.C. (No. C 62) 7 (1989).

344 C. Brölmann, 'Member States and International Legal Responsibility: Developments of the Institutional Veil', 12(2) IOLR (2015) 358, 366.

345 Para. 5 of the commentaries to Article 40(2) ARIO notes that where the rules of the organisation do not so provide, this obligation can be seen as a corollary of member States' general duty to cooperate with the organisation and contribute to its expenses, as implied under the organisation's constituent instrument.

346 P. Palchetti, 'Exploring Alternative Routes: The Obligation of Members to Enable the Organization to Make Reparation', in M. Ragazzi (ed.), *The Responsibility of International Organizations: Essays in Memory of Sir Ian Brownlie* (2013), 309–12.

347 *ITC* case, *supra* note 307, 684.

348 Ibid.

actors), were constantly in the background of the debate.[349] Accordingly, it was felt that the difficulties inherent in the establishment of international organisation responsibility entailed, in practice, that victims would be left without a remedy, were it not for the possibility of holding member States responsible as well.[350] All these issues considered, the solution advanced by the IDI was in any event to endorse a residual rule of non-responsibility of the member States for institutional wrongs.[351] This was steered by Higgins's understanding that '[w]here the organization has a volonté distincte the continuing role of states members qua organs should be regarded as neutral as regards the issue of members' liability for the acts of the international organization'.[352]

The IDI's 'organization-centred approach'[353] was mainly justified on policy grounds and was deemed to strike a proper balance between the independent functioning of international organisations and the need to protect third parties dealing with the latter.[354] This comes as a logical corollary of Higgins's understanding that 'if members know that they are potentially liable for contractual damages or tortious harm caused by the acts of an international organization, they will necessarily intervene in virtually all decision-making by international organizations'.[355]

Concerns with the legal personality and independent functioning of international organisations were later given considerable weight in the work of the ILC[356] and in numerous texts addressing member State responsibility[357] – so much so that they obtained almost axiomatic status.[358] The international legal personality of international organisations thus became the main vantage point from which responsibility issues in an institutional context were addressed. It should be noted that the power (i.e., control or influence) exercised by member States over international

349 Even if, as warned by Higgins, these elements were ultimately irrelevant for the question of member State responsibility. See: Preliminary Exposé, *supra* note 74, 251.

350 P. Klein, *La Responsabilité des Organisations Internationales dans les Ordres Juridiques Internes et des Droit des Gens* (1998) 426.

351 See: Articles 5 and 6 IDI Resolution, *supra* note 64.

352 Preliminary Exposé, *supra* note 74, 261.

353 I. Brownlie, 'The Responsibility of States for the Acts of International Organizations', in M. Ragazzi (ed.), op. cit. *supra* note 48, 362.

354 Preamble and Article 8 of the IDI Resolution on Member State Responsibility, *supra* note 64.

355 R. Higgins, Preliminary Exposé, *supra* note 74, 288. Similarly: C. F. Amerasinghe, 'Liability to Third Parties of Member States of International Organizations: Practice, Principle and Judicial Precedent', 85 Am J Int'l L (1991) 259, 278.

356 ILC, Special Rapporteur Gaja, *Fourth Report on Responsibility of International Organizations*, UN Doc. A/CN.4/564/Add.1-2 (2006) para. 94 and UN Doc. A/CN.4/2891, YILC, 2006, Vol. I, 153, para. 53.

357 This is visible still today. See, inter alia: N. Blokker, *supra* note 37, 39.

358 A. Stumer, 'Liability of Member States for Acts of International Organizations: Reconsidering the Policy Objections', 48(2) Harv Int'l LJ (2007) 553, 554. Stumer undertakes to demystify the assumption that the concurrent or secondary responsibility of member States endangers the legal personality of international organisations by noting how, on the contrary, such a responsibility regime actually assumes it – and, *a fortiori*, the responsibility of international organisations for their own wrongful acts (see: 570–4).

organisations was not overlooked.[359] However, debates revolved (and still revolve) around the extent to which such control could lead to a finding of member States' responsibility *for* institutional conduct, and not for their own acts performed in an institutional context.[360]

2.1.2 *The Responsibility Framework Devised by the International Law Commission: What Scope to Accommodate Member States' Governance Role?*

Early in its work on State responsibility, the ILC acknowledged the need to conduct a complete and systematic analysis of the rules governing the responsibility of international organisations and their members.[361] Yet, several decades later, by the time the ASR were adopted, the ILC still felt unprepared to respond to the 'controversial substantive questions as to the functioning of international organizations and the relations between their members'.[362] The matter was thus purposefully left unattended. With the adoption of the ARIO in 2011, the ILC attempted to fill this gap by delineating the criteria on the basis of which member States may be found responsible in connection with the acts of international organisations (in Part V).

The ILC debates preceding the adoption of the ARIO will be surveyed, with a view to shedding light on the choices behind the current regime of member State responsibility (Section 2.1.2.1). In so doing, due consideration will be paid to the views and concerns expressed with regard to member States' governance role. It will be clarified that the provisions prescribing derived member State responsibility do not cover the creation and participation of member States in the decision-making processes of international organisations. Hence, in Section 2.1.2.2, an analysis will be undertaken of whether these cases may instead give rise to member State responsibility for their own conduct performed in an institutional setting.

359 For example, in the ITC Court of Appeal's decision, *Maclaine Watson & Co Ltd* v. *Department of Trade & Industry*, [1988] 80 ILR 47, 144, Judge Nourse did note that member States' extensive participation and control in the affairs of the organisation should be taken as a factor pointing strongly towards their responsibility.

360 Sadurska and Chinkin arise as an exception, as they discussed member State responsibility for failure to exercise due care in the supervision of international organisation activities. See: R. Sadurska and C. Chinkin, *supra* note 290, especially 880–7. Hirsch also briefly noted that, because member States retained control over institutional activities, the former could not shield behind the latter, and, thus, should be held responsible 'for obligations engendered by *their activities* through these organizations' (emphasis added). See: M. Hirsch, *supra* note 76, 136. The bulk of the author's monograph, however, focuses on the contours of member State responsibility *for* the acts of international organisations. As he contends, member States should be held indirectly responsible for the defaults of international organisations in their dealings with creditors. Yet, when it comes to non-voluntary third parties, the law should be more protective of them, and, thus, provide for the secondary responsibility of member States, under certain conditions (see: 164–9).

361 ILC, Special Rapporteur García-Amador, *State Responsibility*, UN Doc. A/CN.4/96, YILC, 1956, Vol. II, 189, 190.

362 Para. 4 of the commentaries to Article 57 ASR.

The latter intent justifies delving into rules on attribution, as the need is certainly there to elucidate what, after all, is to be considered member State conduct. While debates on attribution have so far focused on contexts other than member State participation in the representative organs of international organisations, important assumptions regarding the former may be transposed to the latter contexts. As will be seen, these relate to the margin that is left for member State discretion in institutional settings, and the notion that conduct should be attributed to the entity that is at the origin of the infringement of an obligation, which is also the entity that can best defend and remedy the measure concerned.

2.1.2.1 The Institutional Veil and Member State Responsibility

A CARVING IN STONE THE PRINCIPLE OF NON-RESPONSIBILITY OF THE MEMBER STATES. In conceptualising a responsibility regime for international organisations and their member States, the ILC had before it two main options: full acceptance of the dependence of international organisations on their members, in which case the latter would be held responsible for most institutional acts; or treatment of international organisations as autonomous creatures operating on the international plane, which would entail holding them generally responsible for their own conduct.[363] According to Special Rapporteur Gaja, precedents such as those discussed in Section 2.1.1 provided clear enough grounds to sustain the principle of independent responsibility of international organisations, with member State responsibility for institutional conduct being defensible only in exceptional circumstances.[364] This view was not shared by all, however. Opposition was particularly voiced by Brownlie, who did not find the principle of independent responsibility to apply to the exclusion of the member States. Accordingly, such principle 'could allow States to circumvent their obligations by concluding a multilateral treaty establishing an international organization'.[365]

Backed by wide support from States and international organisations,[366] and steered by the majority of its members (among whom Pellet was particularly forceful),[367] the ILC ultimately endorsed the principle of non-responsibility of the member States.[368] The ARIO thus consecrate international organisations and their

363 M. Hirsch, *supra* note 76, 176, 177. For an extended (critical) overview of the ILC debates, see: F. Bordin, *The Analogy between States and International Organizations: Legal Reasoning and the Development of the Law of International Organizations*, Doctoral Dissertation defended at the University of Cambridge, 2014, 172–91.

364 UN Doc. A/CN.4/2891, YILC, 2006, Vol. I, 152, 153.

365 UN Doc. A/CN.4/2892, YILC, 2006, Vol. I, 157, para. 16.

366 ILC, Special Rapporteur Gaja, *Seventh Report on Responsibility of International Organizations*, UN Doc. A/CN.4/610 (2009) 29, para. 60.

367 UN Doc. A/CN.4/2892, YILC, 2006, Vol. I., 156, para. 12.

368 This rule is not expressly stated in the ARIO but, as explained in the commentaries, it is deemed to be 'clearly implied' in Article 62. See: para. 2 of the commentaries to Article 62 ARIO, and also para. 2 of the commentaries to Article 40.

member States as legally autonomous entities with independent responsibility.[369] As a result, 'membership does not as such entail for member States international responsibility when the organization commits an internationally wrongful act'.[370] This means that conduct beyond mere membership must be identified for States to fall within the categories set out in Part V ARIO.

B TAMING MEMBER STATES' GOVERNANCE ROLE THROUGH THE PROSCRIPTION OF CIRCUMVENTION. The ILC was not oblivious to the concerns raised in the doctrine and jurisprudence (particularly in the human rights field, as will be discussed in Chapter III) as to the danger that States would hide behind the institutional veil in order to sidestep their international law obligations. The principle of non-responsibility being established, member State power vis-à-vis international organisations was still to be legally accounted for, through the delineation of criteria that would somehow enable the piercing of the institutional veil. Article 61(1) on circumvention was included to perform such a function. It prescribes member State responsibility in cases where 'by taking advantage of the fact that the organization has competence in relation to the subject-matter of one of the State's international obligations, it circumvents that obligation by causing the organization to commit an act that, if committed by the State, would have constituted a breach of the obligation'.

The provision was not met without controversy, notably for the lack of clarity around its normative underpinnings.[371] Still, it can be read as encompassing the principle of good faith, prohibiting an abuse of rights by member States, both in creating and in participating in institutional affairs.[372] Circumvention, notwithstanding, seems to go beyond this,[373] but not much more is explained in the commentaries as to what it exactly entails.

369 Just as Article 1 ASR stipulates that '[e]very internationally wrongful act of a State entails the international responsibility of that State', Article 3 ARIO prescribes that '[e]very internationally wrongful act of an international organization entails the international responsibility of that organization'.

370 Ibid. Cf.: S. Yee, *supra* note 48, 435–56, who exceptionally upholds member State responsibility by virtue of membership or the normal conduct associated with membership, notably, for 'bringing to life' international organisations and for the power they hold (be it through control, influence or the power to veto) as participants in their decision-making processes. Yee's concern with the imposition of limits upon member State power is certainly valid. However, it will be contended in Section 2.2 that this power does not translate into unlimited member State responsibility for institutional conduct, but, rather, to member States' responsibility for their own conduct performed in an institutional context.

371 For a thorough and critical account of the debates within the ILC, see: O. Murray, 'Piercing the Corporate Veil: The Responsibility of Member States of an International Organization', 8 IOLR (2011) 291, 313–26, and F. Bordin, *supra* note 363, 183–6.

372 Generally upholding such reading, see, e.g.: A. Pellet, UN Doc. A/CN.4/2892, YILC, 2006, Vol. I, 156, para. 10. This case, then, seems to be one of application of primary rules rather than secondary ones. See also: E. Paasivirta, 'Responsibility of a Member State of an International Organization: Where Will It End?: Comments on Article 60 of the ILC Draft on the Responsibility of International Organizations', 7 IOLR (2010) 49.

373 Para. 2 of the commentaries to Article 61 ARIO.

The commentaries specify that there must be a 'significant link between the conduct of the circumventing member State and that of the international organization'.[374] The question could thus be asked as to whether member State participation in institutional decision-making processes could constitute such a significant link: does, for instance, unanimous decision-making determining institutional action in circumvention of the obligations of the member States constitute a means by which the collectivity of States *causes* the organisation to act? This kind of hypothesis is arguable inasmuch as, unlike Articles 58 and 59 (on aid and assistance and direction and control, respectively), Article 61 does not expressly exclude member State responsibility for conduct done in accordance with the rules of the organisation (see Section 2.1.2.1, C). Indeed, De Schutter and Salomon have recently invoked Article 61 to discuss the responsibility of euro area member States as participants in the Council of the EU, for the design and approval of macroeconomic adjustment programmes in Greece (recall Introduction).[375] However, previous drafts of the provision refer to situations where the member State *prompts* the organisation to act,[376] and thus, point to a level of control that seems higher than mere participation in decision-making.[377]

Moreover, the provision is solely applicable where member States *intended* to avoid compliance.[378] During the ILC debates, some members had noted that the requirement of intent was too high and worked to the detriment of third parties.[379] Others disagreed.[380] These differences of opinion were reflected in the shifting approaches contained in the various versions of the draft article. Indeed, just two years before the adoption of its final version, the commentaries specified that the existence of a specific intention of circumvention was not required.[381]

Here, as elsewhere, a choice had to be made between diverging policy options, and the end result was the construction of a provision that is, at the end of the day, difficult to apply. Arguably, the inverse option of eliminating intention as a link between the conduct of the circumventing member State and that of the international organisation would lead to the invocation of member State responsibility in too broad terms.[382] Be that as it may, the provision as it now stands does not respond

374 Para. 7 of the commentaries to Article 61 ARIO.

375 Legal Brief on the Case of Greece, *supra* note 28, 4, 5.

376 *Report of the ILC on the work of Its Sixty-first Session*, Official Records of the General Assembly, 64th Session, Supp. 10, UN Doc. A/64/10 (2009) Article 60(1) and also para. 7 of the corresponding commentaries.

377 E. Paasivirta, *supra* note 372, 59.

378 According to the ILC, member State responsibility will thus 'not arise when the act of the international organization ... has to be regarded as the unintended result of the member State's conduct'. See: para. 2 of the commentaries to Article 61 ARIO.

379 UN Doc. A/CN.4/2902, YILC, 2006, Vol. I, 245, para. 51.

380 ILC, Special Rapporteur Gaja, *Seventh Report on Responsibility of International Organizations*, *supra* note 366, 17. See also, e.g.: Comments of Germany in ILC, Sixty-third session, *Responsibility of International Organizations: Comments and Observations Received from Governments*, UN Doc. A/CN.4/636 (2011) 37–9.

381 UN Doc. A/64/10, *supra* note 376, para. 2 of the commentaries to Article 60.

382 E. Paasivirta, *supra* note 372, 53.

appropriately to the ends it was meant to pursue, notably, the invocation of member States' responsibility when they fail to ensure compliance with their international law obligations. As has rightly been noted, 'below conscious circumvention of obligations there is a vast and important space in which responsibility can and should arise for a member State'.[383]

C MEMBER STATE POWER OVER INSTITUTIONAL DECISION-MAKING AS A FORM OF COMPLICITY? OR DIRECTION AND CONTROL?. During the ILC debates preceding the adoption of the ARIO, the Chinese delegation appealed to the fact that 'since the decisions and actions of an international organization were, as a rule, under the control, or reliant on the support, of member States, those member States that voted in favour of the decision in question ... should incur a corresponding international responsibility'.[384] The bases for the establishment of such responsibility were not explored by the delegation. Notwithstanding, its references to both the notion of support and control call to mind the possibility of establishing member State responsibility for complicity (i.e., for aiding and assisting) or directing and controlling the international organisation in the commission of an internationally wrongful act, as foreseen by the ILC in Articles 58 and 59 ARIO, respectively.

Scholars have pondered whether the financial backing of an international financial institution's activity which results in human rights violations, with knowledge of the circumstances surrounding such conduct, could amount to aid or assistance.[385] Similarly, and more elaborately, it has been contended that the exercise of voting rights by a member State leading to the adoption of an internationally wrongful decision by the organisation in terms contrary to the former's international obligations could bring about its international responsibility as an accomplice.[386] In light of the criteria set out in Article 16 ASR, which were replicated in Article 58,[387] for the vote to amount to aid or assistance, the member State must have had knowledge of the circumstances of the internationally wrongful act and the intention of facilitating its commission.[388] Moreover, since the aiding and assisting conduct must contribute significantly to the wrongful act, it follows that the decision of the international organisation could not have been adopted without the State's vote.[389] In such instances,

383 S. Yee, '"Member Responsibility" and the ILC Articles on the Responsibility of International Organizations: Some Observations', in M. Ragazzi (ed.), op. cit. *supra* note 346, 332.

384 Comments of China, UNGA Sixth Committee, 60th Session, Summary Record of the 11th meeting, UN Doc. A/C.6/60/SR.11 (2005) para. 53 (emphasis added). This aspect was later echoed by members of the ILC, such as, Paula Escarameia, in UN Doc. A/CN.4/2892, YILC, 2006, Vol. I., 155, para. 5.

385 C. Ryngaert and H. Buchanan, *supra* note 37, 143.

386 P. Klein, *supra* note 350, 469.

387 See: para. 1 of the commentaries to Article 58 ARIO.

388 See: para. 5 of the commentaries to Article 16 ASR.

389 P. Klein, 'The Attribution of Acts to International Organizations', in J. Crawford, A. Pellet, S. Olleson and K. Parlett (eds.), *The Law of International Responsibility* (2010) 308.

member States would be found responsible for their own conduct[390] as performed *in connection with* the internationally wrongful act of the organisation.

Next to this, the power exerted by member States in the management of the organisation, or as participants in the adoption of a decision leading to a wrongful act, could be seen as a form of direction and control over the organisation under Article 59 ARIO, provided that a certain degree of influence is exercised in fact by the States.[391] This would lead to a finding of member State responsibility *for* the wrongful act of the international organisation. 'Direction' and 'control' have nonetheless been interpreted by the ILC in a rather narrow sense, implying a degree of subordination that would very rarely apply to the relationship between international organisations and their members.[392] To be sure, 'direction' is not to be understood as mere incitement or suggestion, whereas for 'control' to be established, domination is required and not simply the exercise of oversight.[393]

Be that as it may, member States' contribution to the adoption of internationally wrongful institutional acts through their participation in decision-making processes was discarded by the ILC as possible grounds for the establishment of derived member State responsibility. Notably, the ARIO specify that '[an] act by a State member of an international organization done in accordance with the rules of the organization does not as such engage the international responsibility of that State'.[394] Hence, Articles 58 and 59 apply where States act as legal entities that are separate from the international organisation beyond what is required from them by the latter's rules.[395]

The ARIO do note, however, that there may be borderline cases giving rise to derived member State responsibility on grounds of 'conduct taken by the State within the framework of the organization', i.e., as a member.[396] Hence, while, according to the ARIO, it is not possible to find member States responsible in their normal exercise of voting rights, there could still be instances where they actually exercise decisive influence over the organisation's behaviour prior to the decision-making process: the member State could have, for example, (informally)

390 As explained in ILC, Special Rapporteur Ago, *Seventh Report on State Responsibility*, UN Doc. A/CN.4/307 and Add.1 and 2 (1978) 58, para. 72, this conduct, in itself, will normally not be of a wrongful character.

391 See: O. De Schutter, 'Human Rights and the Rise of International Organisations: The Logic of Sliding Scales in the Law of International Responsibility', in J. Wouters, E. Brems, S. Smis and P. Schmitt (eds.), *Accountability for Human Rights Violations by International Organisations* (2010) 51, 87; and P. Klein, *supra* note 389, 309.

392 P. Klein, ibid.

393 See: para. 7 of the commentaries to Article 17 ASR. As clarified in para. 2 of the commentaries to Article 59 ARIO, this article was based on the requirements of Article 17 ASR.

394 See: Articles 58(2) and 59(2) ARIO.

395 See: ILC, Special Rapporteur Gaja, *Fourth Report on Responsibility of International Organizations*, *supra* note 356, para. 62; and *Eighth Report on Responsibility of International Organizations*, UN Doc. A/CN.4/640 (2011) 33, para. 103.

396 See: para. 4 of the commentaries to Article 58 ARIO and para. 2 of the commentaries to Article 59 ARIO.

controlled the proceedings that led to the (formal) adoption of the wrongful decision. As already discussed, this is far from being a theoretical abstraction in the context of, e.g., the Bretton Woods institutions, given that, prior to Board meetings, informal backstage negotiations are quite pervasive. Here, member State responsibility under Article 59 ARIO could thus be pondered.

It is certainly a positive development to acknowledge that the principle of independent responsibility is not the end of the story, and therefore to advance instances of derived member State responsibility. However, the stringency of the framework devised in the ARIO is conspicuous. 'Intention', 'significant contribution' or 'domination' by member States constitute elements that occur only exceptionally and that are, in any case, difficult for victims of institutional wrongs to prove. Moreover, the ILC's construction makes member State responsibility depend on the commission of an internationally wrongful act by the international organisation. This of course reduces the chances of invoking it, as the international law obligations of international organisations are far less extended than those of States. In particular, the terms of their subjection to international human rights law remain quite unclear.

D PART V ARIO AS AN INSUFFICIENT FRAMEWORK TO ACCOUNT FOR MEMBER STATE GOVERNANCE AND THE SWITCH TO THE ATTRIBUTION DEBATE. If one judges Part V ARIO against the findings of Chapter I (concerning the power of member States vis-à-vis international organisations) and the notion (to be explored in Chapter III) that member States do not leave their human rights obligations behind once they adhere to international organisations, it is possible to conclude that the regime devised by the ILC does not sufficiently account for such concerns. Although Part V is important for expressing the general notion that member States cannot help, push or force international organisations to commit an act that is internationally wrongful,[397] the criteria enabling the piercing of the institutional veil are, as was seen, quite limited in their application.[398] The problem is thus twofold. On the one hand, as warned by NATO, 'the draft articles and associated commentary do not always appear fully to contemplate the specific situation of [the organization] in which, owing to the nature of the activity in which it is engaged or other factors, the member States retain virtually all decision-making authority and participate on a daily basis in the governance and functioning of the organization'.[399] This is an interesting remark, which appeals to the importance of taking into account member States' governance role. On the other hand, there is

397 P. J. Kuijper, 'Introduction to the Symposium on Responsibility of International Organizations and of (Member) States: Attributed or Direct Responsibility or Both?', 7(2) IOLR 2010 9, 22.

398 See, however: C. Ryngaert and H. Buchanan, *supra* note 37, 145, 146, supporting a strict interpretation of the exceptions contained in the ARIO.

399 See: *Responsibility of International Organizations: Comments and Observations Received from International Organizations*, UN Doc. A/CN.4/637, 14 February 2011, 11, para. 1.

a significant gap between the ARIO and the way the question of member State responsibility is treated under certain human rights regimes.[400]

Part of the predicament lies in the fact that Part V ARIO is centred on excesses of power that member States may exert over international organisations, while power is also particularly relevant to determine when a given agent fails to perform.[401] This question was raised, albeit sparingly, during the ILC debates. Referring to the ICJ Legality of Use of Force cases and the European Court of Human Rights (ECtHR) *Banković* case,[402] Austria contended that the responsibility of NATO member States could be explored from the perspective of their failure to secure ECHR rights;[403] and in the same vein, that the earlier *ITC* and *Westland* cases[404] could be examined through the lens of member State responsibility for their negligent supervision of these organisations.[405] Switzerland, in turn, noted that member States 'should not be allowed simply to remain passive in the face of flagrant violations of international law by the organization. If a member consciously ignored such violations in circumstances in which it might reasonably be expected to try to stop them, that member might incur responsibility in situations other than those envisaged in [then] draft articles 25 to 29.'[406] While Special Rapporteur Gaja did not address this issue in his Seventh Report,[407] he did mention in an earlier report that 'States often are under an obligation to invigilate the conduct of individuals or other entities'.[408] The matter, however, is seen to pertain more to the realm of primary international law than to secondary rules, and, thus, just as it was left out of the ASR,[409] it did not find any place in the ARIO (see Chapter III).

400 O. De Schutter, *supra* note 391, 92.

401 See: A. Nollkaemper, *supra* note 88, 28. See also: S. Lukes, *supra* note 86, 67, according to whom: 'politicians and others in "strategic positions", who individually or in alliance could make a difference, can be viewed as powerful to the extent that they *fail* to address remediable problems'.

402 See Section 3.3.1.2.

403 Comments of Austria, UN Doc. A/C.6/60/SR.11, *supra* note 384, 12, para. 65.

404 Discussed in Section 2.1.1.

405 Comments of Austria, UN Doc. A/C.6/60/SR.11, *supra* note 384, 12, para. 65.

406 Comments of Switzerland, UNGA Sixth Committee, 61st Session, Summary Record of the 15th meeting UN Doc. A/C.6/61/SR.15, 15 November 2006, 3, para. 7.

407 In his *Seventh Report on Responsibility of International Organizations*, *supra* note 366, 24 et seq., the Special Rapporteur had the opportunity to answer most of the comments previously raised by States.

408 ILC, Special Rapporteur Gaja, *Third Report on Responsibility of International Organizations*, UN Doc. A/CN.4/553 (2005) 6, para. 15.

409 The topic of due diligence had already been addressed by the ILC in 1957 and it was contended then that as long as the future ASR would not exclude such type of responsibility, the inclusion of a clause to cover the rule of due diligence would be redundant. See: ILC, Special Rapporteur García-Amador, *Second Report on State Responsibility*, UN. Doc. A/CN.4/106 (1957) 106, 122, 123, especially, 106, para. 7. At a later stage, the discussion on due diligence was somewhat enmeshed in that of the obligation of prevention, which was initially envisaged in draft article 23. See: YILC 1978, Vol. II, Part Two, 81, 82. For further discussion on this provision, as well as draft articles 20–1 addressing obligations of conduct and of result, and an explanation of the reasons for their deletion, see: ILC, Special Rapporteur Crawford, *Second Report on State Responsibility*, UN Doc. A/CN.4/498 and Add.1–4 (1999) 20–9.

All in all, the ARIO may be remarked for giving too much weight to the legal personality of international organisations, to the detriment of the realities of international life (recall Chapter I) and the systemic values of the international community (see Chapter III).[410] However, a different perspective could be adopted, notably, that of member States' responsibility for their own wrongful conduct performed within the framework of international organisations. As was indeed noted in the ARIO (without further specification), '[n]ot all the questions that may affect the responsibility of a State in connection with the act of an international organization are examined in the present draft articles'.[411] If the issue is not anymore one of residual member State responsibility, but one which calls for the application of the ASR, then it turns into an inquiry about how to identify legally relevant State conduct in an institutional context, i.e., into a question of attribution.

In this vein, Brownlie is right when he claims that '[t]he appropriate analysis is to treat the organization (or the joint agency of States) simply as a part of the factual elements, which, upon analysis, may lead to the responsibility of the member States, or some of them, to a third State. On this view the applicable legal category is that of State responsibility, and not the law of international organizations.'[412] While the author does not explore further the terms under which State responsibility could be established,[413] the remainder of this book will attempt to answer this question, with an obvious focus on the role played by member State representatives in international financial institutions. For now, Section 2.1.2.2 will generally explore the terms in which conduct may be attributed to States when they act in institutional settings.

2.1.2.2 Attribution of Conduct to (Member) States: Turning the Spotlight on Member State Organs

While the ARIO carved in stone the principle of non-responsibility of member States for institutional wrongs, they are far less elucidating when it comes to the *problématique* of attribution. This matter is indeed complex and has become the centrepiece of legal debates addressing the question of member State responsibility, for it requires disentangling in every case the intricate relationship between international organisations and their member States. More concretely, it requires attaching an agent or organ's action or omission to either the member State or the international organisation – a 'legal connecting operation'[414] in which the sole determinant is the control that the member State or the international organisation

[410] S. Yee, *supra* note 383, 332.

[411] See: para. 2 of the introductory commentaries to Part V ARIO.

[412] I. Brownlie, *supra* note 353, 360.

[413] Brownlie himself admitted during the ILC debates that the weakness in his position lay in the fact that he could not find a readily identifiable principle for establishing attribution. See: UN Doc. A/CN.4/2893, YILC, 2006, Vol. I, 168, para. 56.

[414] ILC, Special Rapporteur Ago, *Third report on State Responsibility*, UN Doc. A/CN.4/246 and ADD. 1–3 (1972 and 1973) 218, para. 58. Since States and international organisations, as legal persons, are not

exercised over said agent or organ.[415] As different forms of control come into play in this scheme, determining which one takes precedence over the other is often far from evident, and may even lead to cases of dual (or multiple) attribution, as will be seen below.

The role played by member States in the representative organs of international organisations has barely merited attention in attribution discussions. However, some useful insights can still be derived from the attribution framework devised by the ILC and reactions thereto within academic and judicial circles. Section A will focus on member States' role as implementers of institutional obligations and the notions of organic and normative control. Section B, in turn, will draw on member State participation in military operations and the notion of preventive capacity. The findings of both sections will then feed into the analysis reserved for Section 2.2, which is centred on the attribution of conduct to member States as participants in international financial institutions. As will be seen, in all these instances, although the conduct of member States is inextricably linked to that of the organisation, there is still a significant margin of sovereign discretion enabling the identification of State subjectivity, and, thereby, the attribution of conduct to the State. It is this margin that must be identified in institutional decision-making in order to establish member States' responsibility for their own wrongful behaviour.

A MEMBER STATES AS IMPLEMENTERS OF INSTITUTIONAL DECISIONS AND THE INTERPLAY BETWEEN ORGANIC AND NORMATIVE CONTROL. In an institutional context, the starting point for the attribution of conduct to either the member State or the international organisation is to resort to what has been termed the 'organic model':[416] just as 'the conduct of any State organ shall be considered an act of that State' (Article 4(1) ASR), the 'conduct of an organ or agent of an international organization in the performance of functions of that organ or agent shall be considered an act of that organization' (Article 6(1) ARIO). Such a black-and-white scenario of independent attribution of conduct fits nicely with the principle of exclusive responsibility so dear to the ILC[417] (recall Article 3 ARIO and Article 1 ASR). Things become more complicated, however, when considering that international organisations also carry out conduct *through* their member States, either because the latter are responsible for implementing their decisions, or because they are placed at the organisation's disposal to help it achieve its activities (see below).

physically capable of conduct, only the actions or omissions of an individual or group of individuals may be attributable to them (para. 57). Attribution, as a connecting operation, is therefore legal, in that it is unrelated to any link of natural causality or of 'material' or 'psychological' character (para. 58).

415 See: ILC commentaries to Articles 6 (para. 2) and 8 (paras. 3–8) ASR and 7 ARIO (para. 4).

416 P. J. Kuijper and E. Paasivirta, *supra* note 61, 49.

417 A. Nollkaemper and D. Jacobs, *supra* note 72, 381–3.

During the ILC debates preceding the adoption of the ARIO, concerns had been raised as to the difficulty of differentiating between situations where States act qua sovereigns and situations where they act as integral components of the international organisation.[418] With some simplification, the ARIO provide an answer to this concern in assuming that there are circumstances where a State organ may be fully seconded to an international organisation, in which case the conduct of that organ is to be *de jure* attributed, exclusively and directly, to the international organisation in accordance with Article 6 ARIO.[419] Such a construction, however, has tinctures of artificiality in that, as noted by Wessel and Sari, '[a] state will always retain a substantial degree of authority over any organs it makes available to an international organization, otherwise they would cease to be state organs by definition'.[420] State organs, then, inevitably maintain a dual institutional status.[421]

It has been contended that the implementation of institutional obligations by member States falls under Article 6 ARIO, and should thereby be attributed to the international organisation. The European Commission was the main supporter of this view during the ILC debates.[422] It sustained the applicability of special rules of attribution in said context by appealing to the vertical dimension of the EU's relationship with the member States, notably, the fact that (with a few exceptions) the practical implementation of EU law, even in areas of exclusive competence, is carried out by the authorities of the member States, rather than the EU institutions themselves.[423] Paasivirta and Kuijper later classified this as the 'competence model', a configuration which essentially prescribes that responsibility should lie where the competence is.[424] Hence, if competence is exclusive to the EU, then it logically follows that responsibility should lie with the EU, even if the implementing acts are carried out by the member States. As further explained by Hoffmeister, the logic of normative control applies as well to member State action that falls within the scope of EU law: even if said action involves a discretionary judgement,

418 See, e.g.: Xue, UN Doc. A/CN.4/2893, YILC, 2006, Vol. I, 162, 163, paras. 8–12.

419 See: para. 1 of the commentaries to Article 7 ARIO. Article 6(1) ARIO determines that '[t]he conduct of an organ or agent of an international organization in the performance of functions of that organ or agent shall be considered an act of that organization under international law, whatever position the organ or agent holds in respect of the organization'.

420 A. Sari and R. Wessel, *supra* note 61, 132.

421 Ibid., 131, 132.

422 See, inter alia: *Responsibility of International Organizations: Comments and Observations Received from International Organizations*, UN Doc. A/CN.4/545 (2004) 29, 30 and UN Doc. A/CN.4/556 (2005) 31, 32.

423 UN Doc. A/CN.4/545 (2004) 29.
Interestingly, still, Article 1(4) of the *Draft revised agreement on the accession of the European Union to the Convention for the Protection of Human Rights and Fundamental Freedoms*, Council of Europe Final Report to the CDDH, Appendix 1 (2013), (subsequently rejected by the CJEU in *Opinion* 2/13, *supra* note 191) sets out that 'an act, measure or omission of organs of a member State of the European Union or of persons acting on its behalf shall be attributed to that State, even if such act, measure or omission occurs when the State implements the law of the European Union'.

424 P. J. Kuijper and E. Paasivirta, *supra* note 61, 54–63.

it is Union law that determines its substantive legality and governs final judicial authority over it.[425]

Contrary to this view, it is submitted that the implementation of EU law by member State authorities does not justify their assimilation to institutional organs under Article 6 ARIO. Despite the argument that EU action is necessarily carried out via national authorities, the latter do not lose their character as State organs when implementing EU law.[426] Importantly, States' legal existence pertains to innumerable legal regimes (see *infra* Section 3.1), and, thus, however constrained by their membership obligations, the conduct performed by (EU) member States might also be relevant in the eyes of a different legal framework.

The European human rights regime so demonstrates. Here, member State actions as implementers of secondary EU law have been attributed without hesitation to States. For example, in the *Bosphorus* case,[427] where the implementation of a directly applicable regulation by Irish authorities was at issue, the Court asserted that 'a Contracting Party is responsible under Article 1 of the Convention for all acts and omissions of its organs regardless of whether the act or omission in question was a consequence of domestic law or of the necessity to comply with international legal obligations'.[428] Such line of thought was followed by the Court in the similar context of the implementation of UNSC sanctions, notably, in *Nada*[429] and *Al-Dulimi*.[430]

WTO dispute settlement practice, in contrast, points to the acceptance of the 'verticality' of the EU's *modus operandi* via the member States. For example, in the *EC–Geographic Indications* case,[431] also referred to in the ARIO,[432] the Panel accepted the view that when implementing Community law, member States 'act

425 F. Hoffmeister, *supra* note 146, 741, 742.

426 As an alternative, Talmon proposes picking up on the idea that the implementing State organ qualifies as an 'agent' of the international organisation through whom the latter acts. This would imply the simultaneous application of Article 4 ASR and Article 6 ARIO, and, thus, the dual attribution of the implementing conduct to both the State and the international organisation. See: S. Talmon, 'Responsibility of International Organizations: Does the European Community Require Special Treatment?', in M. Ragazzi (ed.), op. cit. *supra* note 48, 412–14. Tzanakopoulos follows a very similar line of thought, in: A. Tzanakopoulos, *Disobeying the Security Council: Countermeasures against Wrongful Sanctions* (2011) 34–6; and A. Tzanakopoulos, 'Sharing Responsibility for UN Targeted Sanctions', 12(2) IOLR (2015) 427, 438, 439.

427 *Bosphorus Hava Yollari Turizm veTicaret Anonim Sirketi* v. *Ireland*, App. No. 45036/98, 30 June 2005.

428 Ibid., para. 153.

429 *Nada* v. *Switzerland*, App. No. 10593/08, 12 September 2012, paras. 120–3.

430 *Al-Dulimi and Montana Management Inc* v. *Switzerland*, App No 5809/08, 26 November 2013, paras. 90–2. The grounds under which the Chamber found the implementing conduct of Switzerland to be susceptible of engaging its responsibility were fully endorsed by the Grand Chamber Court decision of 21 June 2016 (see: paras. 93–5).

431 *European Communities – Protection of Trademarks and Geographical Indications for Agricultural Products and Foodstuffs*, WT/DS174/R, 15 March 2005.

432 See: para. 4 of the commentaries to Article 64 ARIO.

de facto as organs of the Community, for which the Community would be responsible under WTO law and international law in general'.[433] Notwithstanding, the matter was approached differently in the later *Airbus* case.[434] Here, the WTO Panel asserted that 'whatever responsibility the European Community bears for the actions of its member States does not diminish their rights and obligations as WTO Members'.[435] Membership of the European Community therefore 'does not affect their individual status as Members of the WTO' and the possibility that, in such capacity, they perform conduct in violation of WTO Agreements.[436]

In balancing the judicial precedents set out above (except for the last one), Special Rapporteur Gaja resolutely maintained throughout his reports that, generally, the conduct of the implementing member State is to be attributed to the State under Article 4 ASR.[437] In his Second Report he noted: 'The fact that a member State may be bound towards an international organization to conduct itself in a certain manner does not imply that under international law conduct should be attributed to the organization and not to the State.'[438] Also, in his Seventh Report, the point was clearly made that 'the act of a State implementing a binding act of an organization is attributable to that State and represents an internationally wrongful act of the same State'.[439]

The Special Rapporteur's approach seems to rely mainly on the notion that '[m] ember States are generally free to provide for implementation in the way they prefer, through State organs that remain under the State's control'.[440] This, however, seems too light an assumption to make, in that the margin of discretion left to member States might not always be as wide. To the contrary, it might even be strictly conditioned. The UNSC targeted sanctions regimes provide a good background to discuss this question. In *Kadi I*, the CJEU based its reasoning on the understanding that UN member States, and through them the EU, had discretion in relation to the implementation of UNSC sanctions resolutions, as these allowed for a 'free choice among the various possible models for transposition'.[441] Such line of thought was

433 *EC–Geographic Indications* case, para. 7.725. For other cases decided along similar lines, see: P. J. Kuijper and E. Paasivirta, *supra* note 61, 60–2.

434 *European Communities and certain Member States: Measures Affecting Trade in Large Civil Aircraft*, Report of the Panel, WT/DS316/R, 30 June 2010.

435 Ibid., para. 7.175.

436 Ibid., para. 7.174.

437 The ARIO, however, concede that a special rule on the attribution of conduct to the EU might exist when it comes to the implementation of its binding acts by member States. See: para. 2 of the commentaries to Article 64, on *lex specialis*.

438 ILC, Special Rapporteur Gaja, *Second Report on Responsibility of International Organizations*, UN Doc. A/CN.4/541 (2004) 6, para. 13.

439 ILC, Special Rapporteur Gaja, *Seventh Report on Responsibility of International Organizations*, *supra* note 366, 25, para. 74. The Special Rapporteur invoked examples such as the *Bosphorus* and *Kadi* cases to support his view.

440 ILC, Special Rapporteur Gaja, *Third Report on Responsibility of International Organizations*, *supra* note 752, 5, para. 12.

441 ECJ, *Kadi I*, *supra* note 229, para. 298. See also: para. 286.

likewise accepted by the ECtHR in *Nada*.[442] However, the Swiss Federal Tribunal, in its earlier assessment of the *Nada* case,[443] considered that Switzerland had been strictly conditioned when it came to the implementation of the sanctions envisaged in UNSC Resolution 1267 (1999), and subsequent resolutions affecting al-Qaeda and the Taliban.[444] This led the Tribunal to determine its lack of jurisdiction *ratione personae* to hear the case.[445]

The distinction between strictly conditioned conduct and conduct performed with a certain margin of discretion is thus an important one. To be sure, some UNSC resolutions imposing sanctions may only set general aims or results to be achieved, leaving member States with a wide margin to determine how best to reach those ends.[446] In these cases, the application of Article 4 ASR does not seem to raise much controversy. Other UNSC resolutions, however, may condition member State conduct in more absolute terms. Even UNSC Resolution 1267 (1999), one of the resolutions at stake in *Kadi* (which the CJEU interpreted as leaving some freedom of implementation), could be said to constitute one such example: as noted by Tzanakopoulos, 'when the obligation is to freeze the assets of a specific person (in the instance Mr Kadi), it is hard to imagine how the EC could comply with it in any other way but through the freezing of the assets of that person'.[447]

According to Hirsch, the crucial factor for the purposes of attribution of acts implementing decisions of international organisations, and thereby for the determination of responsibility, lies precisely on the margin of discretion that is left to the acting State.[448] As seen above, however, even in cases where such a margin comes close to being non-existent, it is still not justified to assimilate State organs to organs of the

442 *Nada* case, *supra* note 429, paras. 176–80.

443 *Youssef Nada* v. *State Secretariat for Economic Affairs and Federal Department of Economic Affairs*, Swiss Federal Tribunal, Administrative Appeal Judgment, Case No. 1A 45/2007, 14 November 2007.

444 Ibid., para. 8.1.

445 The danger of reviewing an act of the State that merely implements a UNSC resolution leaving no leeway for manoeuvre resides in the fact that it necessarily entails an indirect review of the legality of that very resolution, which clearly lies outside the jurisdiction of the court. See references to this point in para. 116 of EGC, *Kadi II*, *supra* note 229.
In *Al-Dulimi*, the ECtHR Chamber asserted as well that the UNSC resolutions at stake 'did not confer on the States concerned any discretion in the implementation of the obligations arising thereunder' (*Al-Dulimi*, *supra* note 430, para. 117). Notwithstanding, the Court was able to assess the implementing conduct of Switzerland by resorting to the 'equivalent protection' test, which allows for a presumption of compliance with the ECHR to be made, provided that the international organisation in question (*in casu*, the 'focal point' system of the UNSC Resolution 1370 (2006) applicable to the Iraqi sanctions regime) is seen to protect human rights in terms that are at least equivalent to the protection offered by the Convention (see *infra* Section 3.3.1.1). A differing approach was followed by the ECtHR's Grand Chamber, however. Notably, it did identify a margin of State discretion in the fact that Swiss courts had enough leeway to scrutinise the measures taken at national level for the implementation of the UNSC sanctions at issue, and thereby avoid any arbitrariness in that context (see: paras. 143–9).

446 A. Tzanakopoulos, *supra* note 426, 39–41, including footnotes.

447 Ibid., 41.

448 M. Hirsch, *supra* note 76, 82–8.

international organisation under Article 6 ARIO. The State acts in its own name when it implements UNSC resolutions at the national level[449] and, ultimately, it may always choose not to implement a given institutional decision[450] if it finds itself running the risk of perpetrating a wrongful act under a different regime. The choice to implement thus constitutes, as such, conduct performed by an organ of the State. Furthermore, although this organ may be strictly conditioned in its conduct, the question is also one of *how* it implements, notably, of whether it complies with certain obligations under international law, *in casu*, guarantees of fair trial.

Yet, it is undeniable that apart from the organic control that links the implementing authority to its State, other forms of control, notably exerted by the international organisation, come into play: Hirsch refers to the latter as legal control,[451] while Tzanakopoulos prefers the term normative control.[452] This begs the question of whether the ARIO provide for any other attribution rule that takes into account such additional forms of control.

Authors have discussed the possibility of applying Article 7 ARIO in such contexts. This article presupposes that, rather than being fully seconded to the international organisation, a State organ can also be placed at the disposal of the international organisation for a given purpose, and thereby still act, to a certain extent, in a national capacity during its secondment. In these cases, State conduct can still be attributed to the international organisation when the latter exercises effective control over the former.[453] When it comes to the implementation of strictly binding UNSC resolutions or EU regulations, can these organisations be said to exert effective normative control over their member States? And what implications arise therefrom in terms of attribution?

The commentary to Article 7 suggests that the purpose of the effective control criteria is to determine 'whether a specific conduct of the seconded organ or agent is to be attributed to the receiving organization or to the seconding State'.[454] If the attribution of conduct is seen as an exclusive operation, as Special Rapporteur Ago appeared to suggest in his approach to Article 6 ASR,[455] then it would entail

449 *Nada* case, *supra* note 443, para. 90.

450 See: D. Sarooshi, *supra* note 44, 63, 103, referring to the responsibility of a State when it *chooses* to implement domestically an internationally wrongful act committed by an international organisation. The author's views are reproduced in D. Sarooshi, 'International Organizations and State Responsibility', in M. Ragazzi (ed.), op. cit. *supra* note 346, 83, 86.

451 Ibid., 87.

452 A. Tzanakopoulos, *supra* note 426, 39.

453 Article 7 ARIO reads: '[t]he conduct of an organ of a State . . . that is placed at the disposal of another international organization shall be considered under international law an act of the latter organization if the organization exercises effective control over that conduct'.

454 See: para. 2 of the commentaries to Article 7 ARIO.

455 While admitting that a given State organ placed at the disposal of another State could act simultaneously, though independently, as an organ of its own State, Special Rapporteur Ago asserted that it would be necessary 'to ascertain in each particular instance on whose behalf and by whose authority a specific act or omission has been committed' (ILC, Special Rapporteur Ago, *Third Report on State Responsibility*, *supra* note 414, 268, para. 201). See also: A. Nollkaemper and D. Jacobs, 'Introduction:

attributing the implementing act of the State exclusively to the international organisation when the latter is seen to condition this conduct in terms that amount to effective control. Yet, the ARIO do not rule out the possibility of dual (and even multiple) attribution of conduct,[456] which, in some instances such as the current one, might indeed be the better approach. This would lead to the attribution of the implementing conduct of the member State to both the State (based on organic control) and the international organisation (based on effective normative control).

Notwithstanding, Article 7 does not seem to follow such understanding, as it prescribes a control test that is based on effective factual control[457] and is rather tailored for military operations.[458] The discussion is in any case useful, inasmuch as it introduces pertinent forms of control beyond those envisaged in the ARIO, which may more appropriately apply in controversial cases such as those when member States are strictly conditioned in the implementation of institutional decisions.

B MEMBER STATES AS TROOP-CONTRIBUTING STATES AND THE NOTION OF 'ABILITY TO PREVENT'. The attribution of conduct in contexts where States place their troops at the disposal of international organisations falls under Article 7 ARIO. The uncertainty around this provision and, notably, the contours of effective control have brought about intense debates, particularly in the aftermath of the ECtHR's decisions in *Behrami* and *Saramati*.[459] In these cases, where the responsibility of NATO member States that had contributed forces to KFOR and UNMIK was at issue, the Court asserted that the involvement of member States did not undermine the 'effectiveness of NATO's operational control' regarding KFOR.[460] Based on the fact that 'KFOR was exercising lawfully delegated Chapter VII powers of the UNSC', the Court determined that the 'UNSC retained ultimate authority and control' in that case,[461] and thereby, that 'the impugned action was in principle "attributable" to the UN'.[462] This, according to the Court, entailed the non-attributability of said conduct to the member States.

The Court seems to have relied on a formal and abstract understanding of control, notably, on the political control exerted by the UN, to arrive at its conclusion. However, such a low threshold of control contradicts the understanding that is typically associated with the control test contained in Article 7, that is, of effective, de facto (operational)

Mapping the Normative Framework for the Distribution of Shared Responsibility', in A. Nollkaemper and D. Jacobs (eds.), op. cit. *supra* note 21, 35–40.

456 See: para. 4 of the introductory commentaries to Chapter II ARIO.

457 See: para. 4 of the commentaries to Article 7 ARIO.

458 ILC, Special Rapporteur Gaja, *Seventh Report on Responsibility of International Organizations*, *supra* note 366, 9, para. 25.

459 *Agim Behrami and Bekir Behrami* v *France*, App. No. 71412/01 and *Ruzhdi Saramati* v *France, Germany and Norway*, App. No. 78166/01, 2 May 2007.

460 Ibid., 40, para. 139.

461 Ibid., 41, paras. 141 and 140, respectively.

462 Ibid., 41, para. 141.

control, as mentioned in Section 2.1.2.2, A.[463] In any event, the ECtHR followed closely the latter criterion in its subsequent *Al-Jedda* decision,[464] which involved the detention of a terrorist suspect by UK forces operating as part of a multinational force. Although the conduct of UK soldiers had at some point been authorised under a UNSC resolution, the Court set aside the possibility of attributing said conduct to the UN as the latter was seen to exercise 'neither effective control nor ultimate authority and control' thereof.[465] Rather, it found such a form of control to lie exclusively in the hands of British forces.[466]

Different grounds of attribution of conduct in the context of military operations may thus come into play. The complexity here lies in the fact that among the member States and the international organisations involved, it is possible to identify 'merged and redistributed systems of authorization, strategic leadership, operational control, command, and discipline'.[467] Against this backdrop, some authors deem Article 7 to prescribe, as point of departure, the prima facie attribution of conduct to the lending entity, i.e., the member State;[468] others rather favour the legal and institutional ties that may exist between national contingents and the receiving organisation over factual control elements;[469] still others reject a presumptive institutional line of attribution and – while acknowledging that *de jure* institutional links operate both ways – rather espouse a bifocal, conduct-specific analysis to determine which entity, if not both, exercised effective control over the conduct at issue.[470]

In the well-known *Nuhanović* and *Mustafić* decisions against the Netherlands,[471] regarding the conduct of Dutch soldiers under the command of the UN peacekeeping force in Srebrenica, the criterion of effective control was praised by the Dutch Court of Appeal (and reiterated by the Dutch Supreme Court)[472] as the only applicable test to determine attribution. Importantly, effective control was interpreted to denote not solely factual control but also normative

463 See: para. 4 of the commentaries to Article 7 ARIO. In the literature see, inter alia: K. M. Larsen, 'Attribution of Conduct in Peace Operations: The "Ultimate Control and Authority" Test', 19(3) EJIL (2008) 509, 521, 522, noting that the ECtHR uses the 'ultimate authority and control' test in *Behrami* without providing the legal basis for it, thereby going against its own case-law, that of the ICJ, the work of the ILC on international responsibility and UN practice.

464 *Al-Jedda* v. *United Kingdom*, App. No. 27021/08, 7 July 2011.

465 Ibid., para. 84.

466 Ibid., para. 85.

467 T. Dannenbaum, 'Dual Attribution in the Context of Military Operations', 12(2) IOLR (2015) 401, 403.

468 K. Boon, 'Are Control Tests Fit for the Future? The Slippage Problem in Attribution Doctrines', 15 Melb J Int'l L (2014) 330, 353.

469 A. Sari and R. Wessel, *supra* note 61, 132, 133.

470 T. Dannenbaum, *supra* note 467, especially 406–8.

471 *Nuhanović* v. *Netherlands*, Gerechtshof's-Gravenhage, Appellate Judgment, LJN: BR 5388, 5 July 2011, and *Mustafić* v. *Netherlands*, Gerechtshof's-Gravenhage, Appellate Judgment, LJN: BR 5386, 5 July 2011.

472 *Nuhanović* and *Mustafić* cases, *supra* note 82.

control, inasmuch as it was deemed to require an assessment of whether the 'UN or the State had the *power to prevent* the conduct concerned' (emphasis added).[473] As warned by Nollkaemper, 'ability to prevent' should not stand on its own as the relevant benchmark, as it would open a 'door rather wide . . . If one accepts "ability to control" as the relevant standard, the conduct of peacekeeping forces by definition can be attributed to the state (whether or not in parallel to the UN), since there is always the possibility for that state to exercise control in a way that prevents the impugned conduct from occurring.'[474] Such a purely normative understanding was not upheld by the Court, however. Rather, for the conduct of Dutchbat to be attributable to the Netherlands, the Court had to satisfy itself that, in the specific factual situation at issue, the State had both the ability to prevent said conduct and the legal (or normative) power to do so, through the adoption of disciplinary measures.[475]

The decisions proffered by Dutch courts put forward the general notion that the entity to be held responsible is the one that is most capable of preventing the wrongful conduct, or of remedying it.[476] As has rightly been noted, such a conception of power suggests a diverse function for secondary rules from that intended by the ILC:[477] while the ARIO mostly centre on the manifestation of power as a form of control, the prevention and remediation elements referred to bring about the manifestation of power as capacity.[478] This approach to power, as will shortly be discussed, is most useful to understand the links that tie member States to their representatives while participating in the decision-making bodies of international organisations.

C LESSONS LEARNED FROM THE ATTRIBUTION DEBATE. The operation of attribution rules in the contexts analysed in Section 2.1.2.1, B finds a common ground in the idea of capacity to prevent. Coming back to the acts of member States as implementers of institutional obligations, it is possibly on the basis of the notion of capacity to prevent (and to remedy) that WTO dispute settlement bodies tend to attribute member State conduct to the EU,[479] while the ECtHR does not: in the

473 *Nuhanović* case, *supra* note 471, para. 5.9.

474 A. Nollkaemper, 'Dual Attribution: Liability of the Netherlands for Conduct of Dutchbat in Srebrenica', 9 JICJ (2011) 1143, 1148.

475 *Nuhanović* case, *supra* note 471, paras. 5.10–5.18. The concept of effective control was also interpreted along similar lines in the District Court of The Hague's decision *Mothers of Srebrenica* v. *Netherlands*, Rechtbank's-Gravenhage, LJN: 8748/c/09/295247, 16 July 2014, paras. 4.33, 4.34, 4.46.

476 T. Dannenbaum, 'Translating the Standard of Effective Control into a System of Effective Accountability: How Liability Should Be Apportioned for Violations of Human Rights by Member State Troop Contingents Serving as United Nations Peacekeepers', 51(1) Harv Int'l LJ (2010) 113, 158. See also: M. Hirsch, *supra* note 76, 77.

477 K. Boon, *supra* note 468, 369.

478 That power assumes such different connotations is referred to in: A. Nollkaemper and D. Jacobs, *supra* note 455, 29, 30.

479 P. J. Kuijper and E. Paasivirta, *supra* note 61, 63.

former case, the EU is prepared to show up as respondent and has the legal power to undertake certain measures in accordance with its obligations;[480] in the latter context, this is not possible, inasmuch as the EU is not a signatory to the ECHR. In contrast with the military operations context, however, in implementation cases attribution cannot be determined on the basis of effective, factual control over the particular conduct of the agent, in that the organisation will normally not possess such control.[481] Still, in these cases it is useful to reminisce the underlying postulation of effective control tests, notably, that it is significant to consider where the 'root cause' of the wrongful act lies, and whether it can best be removed there.[482] As will be discussed in Section 2.2, this holds equally true in the context of member State participation in the representative organs of international organisations.

Important to retain from this debate is that different types of control – be they political, operational, economic or normative, factual or ultimate – may come into play in the attribution of conduct to the member State and the international organisation. In reality, the same act may even be attributed to both, or more, actors. Owing to the flexibility of control tests, their interplay has the advantage of permitting differentiated burdens on international legal subjects, in that they 'may confer greater obligations on entities with a strong nexus to the act or omission in question'.[483] As shown by the judicial cases discussed in Sections 2.1.2.1, A and B, solutions in this sphere are not unequivocal, and every situation begs for an independent inquiry in order to determine the precise scope and legal relevance of the attributive links identified.[484] What is sure is that, within the existing power relationships between member States and international organisations, attribution rules cannot overlook the margin that is left for States to act as subjects of international law underneath the institutional veil, in that the degree of 'voluntariness' that comes with it is undoubtedly of relevance for responsibility purposes. This holds true whether States play the role of implementers, troop contributors or, as will be seen below, decision-makers.

Important lessons can thus be drawn from the ILC's work on international responsibility, and accompanying debates within judicial and academic circles. Still, their importance lies more in providing a general theoretical background to the discussion on member States' responsibility for their participation in the representative organs of international organisations, than in setting out clear

480 F. Hoffmeister, *supra* note 146, 738, 739.

481 S. Talmon, *supra* note 426, 414.

482 F. Hoffmeister, *supra* note 146, 737. Similarly, Gaja noted that 'only the entity which is at the origin of the alleged infringement of an obligation ... would be held responsible and could defend the measure concerned'. See: G. Gaja, 'Accession to the ECHR', in A. Biondi, P. Eeckhout and S. Ripley (eds.), *EU Law after Lisbon* (2012) 190.

483 K. Boon, *supra* note 468, 334.

484 P. Klein, *supra* note 350, 384.

criteria to establish such responsibility. A significant step towards understanding how to apply responsibility rules to member States in said contexts is to examine the treatment of the matter in judicial fora. The subsequent section will take this task on board. In so doing, it will recall, whenever pertinent, the rules devised by the ILC in the ARIO and the ASR.

2.1.3 *Judicial Treatment of Member States' Governance: A Focus on Their Participation in Institutional Decision-Making Processes*

The question of member States' responsibility for their participation in the representative organs of international organisations has been put to the test in international courts. A few cases have involved the member States of international financial institutions, such as the WB, the IDB and the European Investment Bank (EIB), but still, they were all ultimately left undecided. More conclusive findings can be derived from judicial proceedings dealing with member State participation in organisations such as the EU, the UN and NATO. All these cases will be discussed in the following sections, which are organised according to the function of the Court that adjudicated the dispute in order to provide a clear overview of each body's jurisprudence on the matter.

As will be seen, courts have shown their readiness to accept that member States can be held responsible for their own conduct performed in institutional settings, without it being seen as a threat to the international legal personality of the international organisation. It transpires from various cases, however, that the contours of attribution of conduct to member States are insufficiently explored, either by the claimant, or by the court. This undermines the success of the claim, for as soon as the contentious conduct at issue is suspected to have been performed by the international organisation rather than the member State, courts will easily be tempted to affirm the inadmissibility of the case for lack of jurisdiction *ratione personae*.

2.1.3.1 A Lost Opportunity by the Inter-American Commission on Human Rights

In 2005, a petition was filed before the IACHR against the member States of the WB and the IDB (together with the institutions themselves and the Guatemalan Government), for alleged human rights violations stemming from the construction, throughout the 1970s, of the Chixoy hydroelectric dam in Guatemala.[485] As the petition was rejected in 2009, an appeal was submitted in 2011[486] solely against the member States, notably, the 'Directors on the Boards of Executive Directors of the World Bank and the IDB'.[487]

[485] See *supra* note 48.
[486] Ibid.
[487] Ibid., para. 3.

Despite the aim of targeting the member States, the appeal mostly centred on the financial institutions' gross negligence in performing their supervisory roles throughout project appraisal, approval and implementation.[488] It seemed to assume that, as participants in these institutions' decision-making bodies, member States were necessarily implicated in the human rights violations at issue. Yet, the grounds to invoke member State responsibility were quite unclear. In one passage, the petition seems to point to a relationship of agency when it claims that the member States 'should not be able to ignore, or indeed violate [human rights] obligations simply by organizing themselves into the IDB or by using the Bank as an agent to carry out policies or practices that violate their respective international human rights obligations'.[489] In this case, Article 4 ASR would apply. Yet, such a determination is not specifically made. Another passage rather suggests responsibility for complicity, when it is noted that 'the World Bank, along with its Member States and in particular its Board of Executive Directors, is complicit in [Guatemala's] human rights violations'.[490] Finally, special attention is paid to the role of the US, which would be 'particularly liable for the human rights violations' at stake as 'the principal member of Boards of Executive Directors of the IDB and the World Bank, essentially with veto power over all decisions of both entities'[491] – a 'veto power' which it did not use. In asserting that, instead, the US granted 'support and funding, both for the Chixoy project specifically and for the Government of Guatemala's military campaign, both directly and indirectly through the World Bank and IDB',[492] the appeal furthermore seems to suggest the US's responsibility for circumvention.

In 2009, the secretariat of the IACHR summarily rejected the petition and never got to respond to the 2011 appeal. An opportunity was thus lost to clarify why the petition did not satisfy admissibility criteria. Apparently, the secretariat was left with the impression that it was directed against the international financial institutions themselves, as opposed to their member States.[493] Giving credit where credit is due, the outcome is not terribly surprising, in that, as was described, the grounds to differentiate the responsibility of member States from that of the WB and the IDB were not presented in sufficiently clear terms.

2.1.3.2 A Matter Left Unanswered by the WTO Panel

In the field of WTO law, an example of litigation involving the responsibility of member States of international financial institutions is the *Airbus* case.[494] The case

488 Ibid., especially: paras. 29, 35, 36, 48–61 and 68–73.
489 Ibid., para. 46 (emphasis added). See also para. 47, similarly suggesting the role of the international organisation as an agent of the member States.
490 Ibid., para. 68.
491 Ibid., para. 75.
492 Ibid., para. 79.
493 Information on file with the author.
494 Mentioned *supra* note 434.

was filed by the US against, inter alia, four EU member States for the alleged provision of subsidies to large civil aircraft in breach of the Agreement on Subsidies and Countervailing Measures (SCM Agreement). Among the violations invoked, the US included the provision of financing 'by the EC and the member States, *through the European Investment Bank*'.[495]

The US was thereby compelled to justify why EIB loans fell under the remit of application of Article 1 of the SCM Agreement, which defined a subsidy as a 'financial contribution by a government or any public body within the territory of a Member'.[496] It did so by taking particular note of the role of the Board of Governors and the Board of Directors as the main governing bodies of the EIB, composed of member State representatives, which had among their responsibilities the appointment of the bank's management committee.[497] In the view of the EU, however, '[t]he US attempts to imply that EIB [was] controlled by member State governments through the Board of Governors and the Board of Directors [were] simplistic and misleading'.[498]

Ultimately, the WTO Panel did not devote much attention to the issue, other than to state that, as a general matter, it was not entirely clear whether such entities as the EIB could be properly considered to fall under said Article 1 of the SCM Agreement.[499] As a matter of fact, the question did not even beg for an answer, as the EU would in any case respond for EIB loans. Here, as before, an opportunity was missed to clarify the legal relevance of member State participation in the governance bodies of international financial institutions.

2.1.3.3 Indications of Attribution of Conduct to States within the European Human Rights Regime

The participation of member States in EU institutions has merited considerable judicial scrutiny by the ECtHR. A prominent case thereof is *Matthews*.[500] This case involved the 1994 elections for the European Parliament, with regard to which the residents of Gibraltar, a dependent territory of the UK, had been denied their right to vote under an EC Act from 1976, which did not include Gibraltar in the franchise for the said elections. The 1976 Act had been adopted by the UK, together with the member States of the European Community, following the requirements of Article

495 *European Communities and certain Member States: Measures Affecting Trade in Large Civil Aircraft*, Request for the Establishment of a Panel by the United States, WT/DS316/R, 3 June 2005, 2 (emphasis added).

496 Article 1.1(a)(1) of the Agreement on Subsidies and Countervailing Measures.

497 *European Communities and certain Member States: Measures Affecting Trade in Large Civil Aircraft*, First Submission of the United States, WT/DS316, 15 November 2006, 100.

498 *European Communities and certain Member States: Measures Affecting Trade in Large Civil Aircraft*, First Written Submission by the European Communities, WT/DS316, 5 April 2007, 287.

499 *Airbus* case, *supra* note 434, para. 7.888.

500 *Matthews* v. *United Kingdom*, App. No. 24833/94, 18 February 1999.

138(3) EEC Treaty and of Council Decision 76/787.[501] The first question to solve was whether the contention at hand – regarding a matter of Community 'nature' and 'character' – could actually be subjected to the Court's review. Essentially, this would entail categorising the adoption of the 1976 Act and its Annex II (determining the absence of elections to the European Parliament in Gibraltar), allegedly incompatible with the ECHR, as State – and not institutional – conduct.

Mindful of this prerequisite, both the Applicant and the Respondent centred part of their argumentation on the classification and attribution of the contentious acts at stake. The Applicant maintained that the 1976 Act constituted an international treaty, and that Annex II to the Act had been included therein under the unilateral will of the Respondent.[502] Since the conclusion of the 1976 Act had disabled the Respondent from complying with its obligations under the ECHR, the latter's responsibility could be invoked.[503] The Respondent, in turn, insisted that the 1976 Act and Annex II could not be subjected to the ECtHR's review on grounds that they fell within the EC legal order.[504] Despite its status as an international treaty, the Respondent reckoned, the 1976 Act was not an ordinary treaty but one of a 'special nature', operationalising Article 138(3) EEC Treaty and Council Decision 76/787.[505] Moreover, responsibility for Annex II could not fall upon the Respondent as it could not have been revoked or unilaterally amended by the latter.[506] Hence, arguing that the acts had been adopted by the Community or consequent to its requirements, and thus formed part of a distinct legal order, the Respondent underlined that they could not be imputed to the member States, together or individually.[507]

On the basis of the understanding that member State responsibility persists after the transfer of powers to an international organisation, the ECtHR endorsed the Applicant's approach and vindicated – quite audaciously to some[508] – that the adoption of EC primary law qualified as State conduct. Indeed, as noted by the Court, 'the alleged violation of the Convention flows from an annex to the 1976 Act, entered into by the United Kingdom, together with the extension to the European Parliament's competences brought about by the Maastricht Treaty.

501 Ibid., paras. 7–18.

502 European Commission of Human Rights Report, adopted on 29 October 1997, paras. 43, 44 (hereinafter 'Report of the European Commission') and *Matthews* case, para. 27.

503 Ibid.

504 Report of the European Commission, para. 28.

505 Ibid., para. 30.

506 Ibid., para. 29.

507 *Matthews* case, para. 26.

508 The ECtHR's stance is not uncontroversial. Already in its concurring opinion with the European Commission of Human Rights, M. F. Martinez had expressed his strong disagreement with such an understanding (see: Report of the European Commission). Cori and Kauff-Gazin view the ECtHR's approach as having been driven, to a great extent, by a purely internationalist intent and the desire to ensure the protection of fundamental rights in Europe, without taking sufficient account of the specificities of the EC legal order. See: G. Cori and F. Kauff-Gazin, 'L'arrêt Matthews: Une Protection Globale des Droits de L'Homme par une Vision Réductrice de L'Ordre Juridique Communautaire?', 1 *Europe* (2000) 2, 4.

The Council Decision and the 1976 Act ... and the Maastricht Treaty ... all constituted international instruments which were *freely entered into* by the United Kingdom.'[509] Such reference to the State's freedom of action is in consonance with the above-made assertion that attribution is inextricably linked to the margin that is left for member State discretion in institutional settings.[510]

Whether the ECtHR would apply the same reasoning to member State participation in the adoption of 'normal' Community acts, i.e., secondary EU law, is not certain. In commenting on the decision, Lawson and Schermers pointed to the possibility of extending the ECtHR's reasoning to genuine Community acts, noting that '[s]ince the Member States enabled the Community institutions to adopt these binding measures, they should bear the consequences if violations of the Convention occur'.[511]

This particular question was at stake in the earlier *CFDT* case.[512] After negating its jurisdiction *ratione personae* to consider the complaint against the EC Council's decision not to designate the French trade union as a representative organisation to submit a list of candidates for the Consultative Committee of the ECSC,[513] the European Commission of Human Rights examined the question of whether the member States could be found individually responsible with relation to such act.[514] It easily dispensed with the argument that France had unlawfully omitted to include the applicant's name in the abovementioned list by ascertaining that France had not yet recognised the right to individual petition under Article 25 ECHR.[515] It did not, however, discard the possibility of establishing France's responsibility if that were not the case. With respect to the other member States, the Commission deemed the matter to lie outside its jurisdiction *ratione personae* in that 'these States by taking part in the decision of the Council of the European Communities had not in the circumstances of the instant case exercised their "jurisdiction" within the meaning of Article 1 of the Convention'.[516]

In contrast, in the field of the EU's Common Foreign and Security Policy (CFSP) – where, according to Articles 24 and 31 TEU,[517] the adoption of

509 *Matthews* case, para. 33 (emphasis added).

510 Recall *supra* Section 2.1.2.2.

511 R. A. Lawson and H. Schermers, *Leading Cases of the European Court of Human Rights* (1999) 677, 679. Similarly, Gori and Kauff-Gazin note that '[p]oussé jusqu'à ses ultimes consequences, le raisonnement de la Cour pourrait conduire à une extension ultérieure de sa compétence à l'égard des actes communautaires. En effet ... ces derniers, au moins les actes adoptés à l'unanimité, pourraient être considérés comme des actes pour lesquels les Etats membres restent les ultimes responsables, même s'ils les adoptent dans l'enceinte communautaire' (see: G. Cori and F. Kauff-Gazin, *supra* note 508, 4).

512 *Confedération Française Démocratique du Travail* v. *The European Communities*, App. No. 8030/77, 10 July 1978, 240.

513 Ibid., 239, 240, paras. 1–3.

514 Ibid., 240, para. 5.

515 Ibid., para. 6.

516 Ibid., para. 7.

517 *Supra* note 152.

legislative acts is excluded and States decide under the unanimity rule, and exceptionally under a qualified majority rule – member State participation in decision-making was clearly demarcated by the ECtHR for responsibility purposes. Indeed, in the *Segi* case,[518] the court took due account of the role of member State representatives in the adoption of CFSP decisions and asserted that, in such an area with a strong intergovernmental character, '[b]y taking part in their preparation and adoption each State engages its responsibility. That responsibility is assumed jointly by the States when they adopt a CFSP decision.'[519]

The ECtHR's deference to the representative nature of institutional decision-making processes might constitute an indication that the court is prepared to transpose the understanding espoused in *Segi* to other institutional contexts. It is true that in the *Behrami* case[520] – which, as seen in Section 2.1.2.2, B, involved military operations undertaken under a UNSC Resolution – the Court denied its competence to review member State voting behaviour in the UNSC. It notably affirmed that 'the Convention cannot be interpreted in a manner which would subject the acts and omissions of Contracting Parties which are covered by UNSC Resolutions and occur prior to or in the course of such missions, to the scrutiny of the Court ... This reasoning equally applies to voluntary acts of the respondent States such as the vote of a permanent member of the UNSC in favour of the relevant Chapter VII Resolution.'[521] In the Court's view, non-attribution in this context was justified since, even if the acts of member States 'may not have amounted to obligations flowing from membership of the UN ... they remained crucial to the effective fulfilment by the UNSC of its Chapter VII mandate and, consequently, by the UN of its imperative peace and security aim'.[522]

Such a formal construction can, however, be criticised for shielding through a forced attribution criterion what actually lay behind the Court's intent, that is, the safeguarding of the primacy of UN substantive values.[523] Broad assumptions regarding the UN system of collective security do not justify the Court's assertion that the voting behaviour of member States of the UNSC cannot be judged for its conformity with the ECHR. In sum, the ECtHR's statement can be said to be misleading.[524]

[518] *Segi and others & Gestoras Pro-Amnistia and others* V. 15 *States Of The European Union*, App. No. 6422/02 and App. No. 9916/02, 23 May 2002, 3, 4.

[519] Ibid. See: F. Naert, 'Binding International Organisations to Member State Treaties or Responsibility of Member States for Their Own Actions in the Framework of International Organisations', in J. Wouters, E. Brems, S. Smis and P. Schmitt (eds.), op. cit. *supra* note 391, 164–6.

[520] *Supra* note 459.

[521] Ibid., para. 149.

[522] Ibid.

[523] P. De Sena and M. C. Vitucci, 'The European Courts and the Security Council: Between *Dédoublement Fonctionnel* and Balancing of Values', 20(1) EJIL (2009) 193, 205, 206, 218.

[524] A. Zimmermann, 'Article 27', in B. Simma, D. Khan, G. Nolte and A. Paulus (eds.), op. cit. *supra* note 212, 887.

That the Court's approach in *Behrami* to voting in the UN can be deemed an isolated case[525] finds support in the later *Gasparini* decision,[526] where the representative role of member States in the decision-making bodies of NATO was touched upon. Here, the participation of Italy and Belgium in NATO's decision-making was judged in its own right against the States' obligations under the ECHR, as the following passage demonstrates: 'la Cour estime que les deux Etats mis en cause ont pu à bon droit considérer, au moment où ils ont approuvé le règlement sur le personnel civil et ses annexes par l'intermédiaire de leurs représentants permanents siégeant au Conseil de l'Atlantique Nord, que les dispositions régissant la procédure devant la CROTAN satisfaisaient aux exigences du procès équitable'.[527]

The above precedents show that the ECtHR is open to isolating member State participation in institutional decision-making for responsibility purposes in, at least, some institutional contexts – ranging from the EU CFSP to NATO's operational framework. However, it is hard to extrapolate the ECtHR's jurisprudence to international financial institutions, as there is the risk that the Court will assert its lack of jurisdiction *ratione personae* to hear the case. Importantly, then, a strong case must be made before the Court with regard to the categorisation of member State voting behaviour as conduct that falls within its jurisdiction in the sense of Article 1 ECHR.

2.1.3.4 The ICJ's Assertive Take on Member State Participation in Institutional Decision-Making As Conduct Attributable to the State

The ICJ had the opportunity to address the responsibility of States for their own conduct throughout institutional decision-making in the *FYROM* case.[528] The origins of the contention may be found in NATO's public announcement, on 3 April 2008, that FYROM would not be invited to begin accession talks to join the Alliance. In its press release, it stated: '[W]e agreed that an invitation to the former Yugoslav Republic of Macedonia will be extended as soon as a mutually acceptable solution to the name issue has been reached.'[529] Such a statement could be viewed as

[525] J. Klabbers, *supra* note 149, 321. The decision in general seems to be an isolated one. Recall *supra* Section 2.1.2.2, B, where mention is made of the vast criticism with which the *Behrami* decision was received and of the fact that later ECtHR decisions brought about, to some extent, a reversion in the court's reasoning.

[526] *Gasparini* v. *Italy and Belgium*, App. No. 10750/03, 12 May 2009.

[527] Ibid., 10.

[528] *Application of the Interim Accord of 13 September 1995 (The Former Yugoslav Republic of Macedonia* v. *Greece)*, Judgment, [2011], ICJ Reports 644. The ensuing discussion derives from: A. S. Barros, 'Application of the Interim Accord of 13 September 1995 (The Former Yugoslav Republic of Macedonia *v.* Greece), Judgment, [2011], ICJ Reports 644', in C. Ryngaert, I. Dekker, R. Wessel and J. Wouters (eds.), op. cit. *supra* 101, 56–65.

[529] NATO Press Release, *Bucharest Summit Declaration Issued by the Heads of State and Government Participating in the Meeting of the North Atlantic Council in Bucharest on 3 April 2008*, para. 20 (emphasis added), available at: www.nato.int/cps/en/natolive/official_texts_8443.htm, last consulted 15 October 2018.

the corollary of a legal decision taken by NATO as a whole, expressing the will of the organisation. Yet, understanding that it was rather Greece, in its capacity as a member of NATO, that had objected and acted to prevent FYROM from receiving an invitation to proceed to NATO membership, FYROM instituted proceedings solely against Greece. To be sure, FYROM was backed by an Interim Accord adopted on 13 September 1995 (Interim Accord), whereby Greece had agreed 'not to object to the application by or the membership of [FYROM] in international, multilateral and regional organizations and institutions of which [Greece] is a member',[530] unless the Parties' divergences regarding the name would be at issue.

Unsurprisingly, Greece objected to the ICJ's jurisdiction and the admissibility of FYROM's application by claiming, among other reasons, that the conduct at issue was a 'collective decision taken by NATO and its organs',[531] wherein 'Greece had no individual or autonomous role to play'.[532] Alluding to the 'veil effect',[533] Greece attempted to demonstrate that a consensus-based decision-making process such as that of NATO reflected the 'will of the organisation and not the will of a given Member State'.[534] Accordingly, in Greece's view, 'it is not possible and it is legally irrelevant . . . to try to search out and individualise the ("real") author of the proposal on which the consensus is based. Such decisions are, by definition, not attributable to any individual State.'[535] Hypothetically, under this institutionalist approach, FYROM could have attempted to assert Greece's responsibility for having exercised, through its dissent, direction or control over the act formally performed by NATO, in accordance with Article 59 ARIO. However, the stringent conditions of this article, already discussed in Section 2.1.2.1, C, would significantly reduce the chances of piercing the institutional veil and engaging Greece's responsibility for NATO's conduct.

Against this backdrop, FYROM assessed responsibility by concentrating on the individual conduct of Greece, which, through its State organs and agents,[536] had made clear – before, during, and after the Bucharest Summit – that it objected to FYROM's admission to NATO. As clarified by FYROM, the dispute did 'not require the Court to address the actions of any third states or any international organizations',[537] and, thus, the action in question was attributable solely to Greece, 'within the meaning of Article 4 and the other provisions of Chapter II' of the ASR.[538]

530 Article 11, para. 1 of the Interim Accord.
531 *FYROM* case, Counter-Memorial, 109.
532 Ibid., 112.
533 Ibid., 117. Greece employed the metaphor of the 'veil' to assert that it prevented the member States from being held responsible for the conduct of NATO. This constitutes, however, a misplacement of the facts that formed the subject-matter of the Court's decision, as the contention regarded FYROM's responsibility for its own conduct and not for the decision of NATO.
534 Ibid., 119.
535 Ibid., 120.
536 *FYROM* case, Memorial, 123.
537 Ibid., 69, 70.
538 Ibid., 87.

It was this understanding that was eventually embraced by the ICJ. Indeed, the Court did not find it problematic to set a clear distinction between NATO's decision taken at the end of the Bucharest Summit and Greece's behaviour prior to that moment. As clarified by the ICJ, the issue before it did 'not concern . . . the conduct of NATO or the member States of NATO, but rather solely the conduct of the Respondent'.[539] It was thus not necessary to 'determine the responsibility of NATO or of its member States in order to assess the conduct of the Respondent'.[540] Greece's conduct – one should add, as a sovereign State – would rather have to be assessed in light of its obligations under the Interim Accord, 'irrespective of NATO's final decision on the Applicant's membership application'.[541] Along these lines, it can be asserted that the *Monetary Gold* principle – in light of which courts do not possess jurisdiction to decide on a given matter on grounds that a third party's legal interests (in this case, those of the international organisation or of other member States) would form the very subject-matter of the ruling – does not apply in cases where the responsibility of the member State is being invoked for its own conduct performed in an institutional setting.[542]

The ICJ's straightforward stance is in contrast with its hesitating tone in the 1948 *Admissions* case,[543] when it came to deciding upon the separateness between the UNSC and its member States in the framework of their refusal of certain membership applications to the UN. Although the request for the ICJ's advisory opinion did not regard the responsibility of member States for their actual votes, the question of the border between an international organisation and its members in decision-making was still an underlying one. When admission is refused because of a veto, is this refusal an institutional act or rather an act of the vetoing member State? The Court seems to have dithered between these two conceptions, which is notably reflected in the following passage regarding the conditions for admission required by para. 1 of Article 4 UN Charter: 'All these conditions are subject to the judgment of the Organization. The judgment of the Organization means the judgment of the two organs mentioned in paragraph 2 of Article 4, and, in the last analysis, that of its Members. The question put is concerned with the individual attitude of each Member called upon to pronounce itself on the question of admission.'[544]

Coming back to the *FYROM* case, it is of note that the unfolding of the ICJ's reasoning was facilitated by the Court's wide understanding of participation in

539 *FYROM* case, Judgment, paras. 42 and 43.

540 Ibid.

541 Cfr: Dissenting Opinion of Judge Ad Hoc Roucounas.

542 Greece attempted to apply this principle in the *FYROM* case (Counter-Memorial, 122–3). For a discussion of the application of the *Monetary Gold* principle to cases where member State responsibility is invoked *for* international organisation conduct, see: P. Palchetti, 'Litigating Member State Responsibility: The Monetary Gold Principle and the Protection of Absent Organizations', in A. S. Barros, C. Ryngaert and J. Wouters (eds.), op. cit. *supra* note 37, 178–90.

543 *Supra* note 204.

544 Ibid., 62.

decision-making. Contrary to Greece's submission that the non-objection clause could only be interpreted as requiring 'a specific, negative act', 'to the point of outright opposition',[545] such as a veto,[546] the ICJ observed that 'nothing in the text of that clause limits the Respondent's obligation not to object to organizations that use a voting procedure to decide on the admission of new members'.[547] Hence, based on the evidence submitted by both Parties, namely, diplomatic correspondence and official statements produced before, during and after the adoption of the final decision by NATO, the ICJ concluded that the acts of Greece were more than mere 'observations' (as claimed by FYROM),[548] and were therefore tantamount to an 'objection'.[549] It is important to keep the Court's assertion in mind, as cases regarding member States' responsibility for their participation in institutional decisions might well include situations where, despite the existence of voting rules, a formal vote has not taken place. In this vein, also in instances of consensual decision-making, which, as will be seen below, is the default case in international financial institutions, the position adopted by member States can be legally relevant for responsibility purposes.

The question could be asked whether the ICJ's reasoning is solely applicable to situations where, through its voting behaviour, the member State actually impedes institutional action –on the basis of either a power of dissent in consensus decision-making or a power to veto in unanimity decision-making. In the *FYROM* case, it was clear that the sole reason why NATO did not invite FYROM to begin accession talks pertained to Greece's objection thereof. Ultimately, the answer lies in the scope of the State's primary obligations. As suggested by FYROM, the obligation 'not to object' did not solely cover situations where Greece's conduct would 'have the effect of preventing membership (where unanimity is . . . required for membership decisions). In other words . . . it is the act of objection itself that is prohibited, irrespective of its consequences.'[550] Following this line of thought, the ICJ did not find it relevant to establish 'whether the decision taken by NATO at the Bucharest Summit with respect to the Applicant's candidacy was due exclusively, principally, or marginally to the Respondent's objection'.[551] It is thus possible to conclude that where the obligation at issue is one of conduct and not of result,[552] the institutional outcome flowing from the State's voting behaviour is not a necessary element to consider for responsibility purposes.

545 *FYROM* case, Counter-Memorial, 129.
546 Ibid., 138.
547 *FYROM* case, Judgment, para. 70.
548 *FYROM* case, Counter-Memorial, 141.
549 *FYROM* case, Judgment, paras. 81–3.
550 *FYROM* case, Memorial, 81, 82.
551 *FYROM* case, Judgment, para. 70.
552 As noted by the ICJ, and agreed by both Parties, the obligation under the first clause of Article 11, para. 1 of the Interim Accord was an obligation of conduct (see para. 70 of the judgment).

In the present case, FYROM was bound by a specific duty determining the contours of its participation in institutional settings and was thereby held responsible regardless of the final decision adopted by the organisation as a whole. In general, therefore, any international legal regime can constitute a basis upon which to assess member State participation in institutional decision-making, as long as it entails obligations clearly conditioning the State's behaviour. Chapter III will be entirely devoted to exploring this matter in the particular context of member State participation in the decision-making processes of international financial institutions. First, however, a discussion will be undertaken in Section 2.2 of the application of attribution rules in such settings, in an attempt to test whether the sort of reasoning employed in the *FYROM* case can be generalised to member State participation in international financial institutions.

2.2 MEMBER STATE PARTICIPATION IN INTERNATIONAL FINANCIAL INSTITUTIONS AS LEGALLY RELEVANT STATE CONDUCT

2.2.1 *Executive Directors As Member State Representatives*

2.2.1.1 Preliminary Remarks on Representative Organs

Writing in 1945 about constitutional problems of international organisations, Jenks made interesting comments regarding the composition of representative organs which are worth reproducing here. In Jenks's view:

> [I]t is essential that the representative organs of [international] organizations should ... be composed of persons who can speak with the full authority of their governments. Such persons should, however, be encouraged ... to regard themselves as being simultaneously representatives of the nations appointing them and members of an international representative organ with a collective responsibility as such. Their duties should be regarded as including both the defence of national interests and the collective formulation of international policies, the establishment of a proper equilibrium between these elements in their duties being left for adjustment from time to time in the light of prevailing conditions. If a constitutional foundation can be laid for the gradual acceptance of the conception that the responsibility of persons discharging such duties to their constituencies – the individual nations – is paralleled by a responsibility as members of an international organ with a collective international responsibility, a sound basis will be available for long-term institutional development.[553]

[553] See: C. W. Jenks, 'Some Constitutional Problems of International Organizations', 22 BYIL (1945) 11, 27, 28.

Jenks's formulation provides rich insights into the dual role that member States play in international organisations (recall Section 1.2.3.1). In a simple fashion, it denotes the fundamental differences that exist between inter-State diplomacy and *institutional* inter-State diplomacy. Moreover, it makes the important point that whilst member States partake in the affairs of representative organs, their responsibility runs in parallel with that of the international organisation. A similar contention had been made twenty years earlier by the PCIJ with regard to the Council of the League of Nations, which the court characterised as being 'composed of representatives of Members, that is to say, of persons delegated by their respective Governments, from whom they receive instructions and whose responsibility they engage'.[554]

The topicality of such assertions is conspicuous. For example, in 2011, during the final stages of the ARIO debates, NATO itself conveyed a similar message to the ILC with regard to the North Atlantic Council, the principal policy and decision-making institution of NATO, by noting that 'NATO decisions are taken on the basis of consensus, after discussion and consultation among the representatives of member States ... Each member State retains full responsibility for its decisions.'[555]

Notwithstanding, when it comes to subsuming the above views into international responsibility rules, the incompleteness of the current framework looms on the horizon. Here as elsewhere, it becomes evident that the combination of, on the one hand, representational and, on the other hand, functional (i.e., international organisation-related) features in the role of those who participate in 'organes interétatiques' sits uneasily with the one-dimensional character of the international legal system.[556] In other words, it contrasts with the assumption under which international law normally operates, i.e., that its subjects are unitary and indivisible. In the present context, this means that international rights and obligations would apply either to the organisation or to the member State: 'it cannot be half or both at the same time, unless both are bound independently', as put by Brölmann.[557]

It has been contended that the notion of *dédoublement fonctionnel* cannot properly be said to constitute an attribution tool; as an image deprived of legal effects, it blurs the fundamental distinction that must be made between the institutional organ and the member States.[558] While, indeed, the said duality is not per se an attribution rule, one can hardly agree that it falls short of legal implications. It points, at the very minimum, to the existence of organic attributive links that tie the individual to both the member State he/she represents and the institutional organ he/she integrates, all of which cannot certainly be ignored.

554 *Interpretation of Article 3 para 2 of the Treaty of Lausanne*, Series B, No. 12 (1925) 29 (emphasis added).
555 *Responsibility of International Organizations: Comments and Observations Received from International Organizations*, UN Doc. A/CN.4/637 (2011) 11, 12, paras. 3, 4 (emphasis added).
556 C. Brölmann, *supra* note 57, 256, 257.
557 Ibid., 256.
558 E. Lagrange, *supra* note 93, 30, 31.

It is clear that representative organs are part – the name so indicates – of the organic structure of international organisations. They 'act on behalf of the international entity, and are not to be equated with the (collectivity of) the states'.[559] This entails that these organs' acts (i.e., final institutional decisions) are attributable to the international organisation. The crux of the question, however, lies in ascertaining whether said cooperative action can be unpacked into independent actions, by disentangling the individual contribution of each member State representative to the outcome, in which case they would be held responsible as separate actors.[560] The above-discussed ICJ *FYROM* case[561] attests to the pertinence of the question. After all, as has been noted, 'adding another "degree of separation" between the natural persons and the collective' is unproblematic for responsibility purposes, inasmuch as 'the agency of the collective is not derived directly from the agency of their constitutive persons'.[562]

It is true that when States act qua members of the international organisation, they act within its internal legal order, which entails that their conduct is not primarily governed by general international law. However, the constituent instruments of international organisations – on the basis of which States are entitled to act – do not pertain solely to the internal legal order of the organisation, but are also contracts celebrated between sovereign States.[563] Necessarily, then, member States coexist side by side with the international organisation. It is in that capacity (i.e., as legal subjects exposed to international law) that the opposability of their action towards third parties comes into play.[564]

As may already be suspected, the position that member State representatives occupy in international organisations does not fit easily with the framework of secondary rules devised by the ILC. Notably, the duality inherent in their role entails that neither Article 6 ARIO nor Article 4 ASR is entirely applicable: on the one hand, if they are to speak with the full authority of their governments (recall Jenks's depiction at the beginning of this section), they cannot be deemed State organs fully seconded to the international organisation; on the other hand, the exclusive application of Article 4 ASR would be tantamount to denying (incorrectly) their fiduciary responsibilities towards the organisation.

Along the lines of the debate on attribution in the context of military operations (recall Section B), it could be asked whether Article 7 ARIO applies in these cases as well: would it prescribe the prima facie attribution of conduct to the member State, or,

559 R. Wessel, 'International Governmental Organizations As Non-State Actors', in M. Noortmann, A. Reinisch and C. Ryngaert (eds.), *Non-State Actors in International Law* (2015) 197.

560 Lagrange answers this question in the negative. See: E. Lagrange, *supra* note 93, 55.

561 *Supra* note 528.

562 R. Pierik, *supra* note 63, 54.

563 On this distinction, see: C. Ahlborn, *supra* note 141.

564 As noted by Skogly, in their operations through the UN and its specialised agencies, member States 'are legally bound to carry out the mandate of the organization, and at the same [time] to do this within the general framework of international law' (see: S. Skogly, *Beyond International Borders: States' Human Rights Obligations in International Cooperation* (2006) 195).

rather, should a presumptive institutional line of attribution (which, as seen, can operate in both directions) be rejected, in favour of a bifocal, conduct-specific analysis to determine which entity, if not both, exercised effective control over the conduct at issue? It should be noted, however, that Article 7 ARIO does not appositely cover the conduct of member State representatives: firstly, their link to the organisation is of a permanent institutional character; secondly, the commentaries to Article 6 ASR, on which Article 7 ARIO is based, exclude from the notion of an organ 'placed at the disposal' of the organisation the case of 'State organs, sent to another State for the purposes of the former State or even for shared purposes, which retain their own autonomy and status'.[565] As will be seen below, member State representatives can be said to maintain, to a large extent, an autonomous role when they participate in the decision-making processes of international financial institutions.

In any event, in order to claim member State responsibility in said settings, an attributive link to the member State must necessarily be established. To that end, delving into the sort of doctrinal debates presented in Section 2.1.2.2 concerning control tests might prove to be a useful exercise. As was seen, control is not solely a factual element, but is also present in institutional (and functional) attribution criteria.[566] The following sections will test these varied forms of control in the particular context of international financial institutions.

2.2.1.2 The International Legal Status of Executive Directors

A GOVERNANCE ARRANGEMENTS WITHIN INTERNATIONAL FINANCIAL INSTITUTIONS: A SNAPSHOT OF THE BRETTON WOODS INSTITUTIONS. As seen in the previous section, international organisations typically comprise an organ wherein their members are represented. In the case of the Bretton Woods institutions – an exemplar of institutional design subsequently followed by regional financial institutions[567] – such a role is vested in the Board of Governors, the highest governing body of the organisations. Each member State[568] is represented therein by one Governor and one Alternate,

565 See: para. 4 of the commentaries to Article 6 ASR.

566 K. Boon, *supra* note 468, 342.

567 As mentioned in the introduction to this book, the regional financial institutions that were created in the post–World War II era followed closely the institutional set-up of the Bretton Woods institutions, with the Boards of Governors and Executive Directors assuming the governance and representative functions of these organisations. See, inter alia: Article 26 of the Agreement Establishing the Asian Development Bank, 22 August 1966 (Agreement Establishing the AsDB); Article 21 of the Articles of Agreement of the Asian Infrastructure Investment Bank, 25 December 2015 (AIIB Articles of Agreement); Section 13 of the Agreement Establishing the Nordic Investment Bank, 4 December 1975 (Agreement Establishing the NIB); Article 22 of the Agreement Establishing the European Bank for Reconstruction and Development, 29 May 1990 (Agreement Establishing the EBRD); and Article 4 of the Agreement Establishing the African Development Bank, 4 August 1963 (Agreement Establishing the AfDB).

568 Currently, both the IMF and the IBRD count with 189 member States. For more information on the governance structure of these institutions see, regarding the IMF: www.imf.org/external/about/

usually the minister of finance, head of the central bank or a senior of similar rank. The Boards of Governors normally meet once a year, during the IMF-WB Spring and Annual Meetings, to discuss the work of their respective institutions. Both Boards are advised by the Development Committee, a ministerial-level forum composed of twenty-five members who together represent the full membership of the institutions.[569]

While all powers of the IMF and the WB are vested in the Boards of Governors, who serve 'at the pleasure' of the member States that appointed them, most powers have been delegated to the Executive Boards.[570] These, as Jenks put it, are limited representative organs.[571] Both institutions' Articles of Agreement contain arrangements regarding the selection of Executive Directors which are designed to ensure that all members are represented.[572] The Executive Board of the IMF is composed of twenty-four Directors, who are all elected by the members, and the WB's Board is composed of twenty-five, among which five are directly appointed by the member States holding the five largest quotas, while the other Directors are elected every two years by the remaining members. Executive Directors are organised in single and mostly multi-party constituencies.[573] Member States are free to choose the constituency to which they belong, taking into account certain factors such as regional distribution. Each constituency has autonomy to decide how and from which country its Executive Director will be selected, as well as which rotation scheme will be used to fill other positions. Generally, such schemes reflect the relative quota of each member State in the constituency, although practice can vary considerably (see below).[574]

Executive Directors are responsible for the conduct of the general operations of the institutions.[575] Under their direction, the President (or Managing Director in the IMF)

govstruct.htm; and with regard to the WB: www.worldbank.org/en/about/leadership/members, last consulted 15 October 2018.

569 More information on the Development Committee may be found at: http://www.devcommittee.org/, last consulted 15 October 2018. The IMF Board of Governors is further advised by the International Monetary and Financial Committee (IMFC) on matters related to the management of the international monetary and financial system. For further information, see: https://www.imf.org/en/About/Factsheets/A-Guide-to-Committees-Groups-and-Clubs#IC, last consulted 15 October 2018.

570 See: IMF Articles of Agreement, Article XII(3) and IBRD Articles of Agreement, Article V(2), *supra* note 4. This is also the case in other financial institutions. See, inter alia: Articles 24 and 27 of the Agreement Establishing the EBRD, Articles 23 and 26 of the AIIB Articles of Agreement, and Articles 29(2) and 32 of the Agreement Establishing the AfDB, *supra* note 567; Article VIII(2)(b) and (3)(a) of the Agreement Establishing the Inter-American Development Bank, 30 December 1959 (Agreement Establishing the IDB); and Articles 23 and 26 of the Agreement Establishing the BSTDB, *supra* note 263.

571 C. W. Jenks, *supra* note 553, 28–30.

572 See: IMF Articles of Agreement, Article XII(2) and IBRD Articles of Agreement, Article V(4), *supra* note 4.

573 Further information is available at: www.imf.org/external/np/exr/facts/govern.htm and www.worldbank.org/en/about/leadership/directors, last consulted 15 October 2018.

574 Annex I to the IEO Report on IMF Governance, *supra* note 58, 24.

575 See: IMF Articles of Agreement, Article XII(3)(a) and (4)(a) and IBRD Articles of Agreement, Article V(4)(a) and (5)(b), *supra* note 4.

and the staff carry out the 'ordinary business'. Apart from being involved in most aspects of the organisations' operations, both formally through Board meetings and informally through interactions with management and staff, Executive Directors also play a significant role in informing and advising their constituent governments on the organisations' activities.[576]

With regard to the IMF, its Directors' role has been described by the IEO as including the following functions: 'setting strategy and monitoring strategy implementation, conducting bilateral surveillance (i.e., Article IV consultations) and surveillance of the international monetary system as a whole, approving the use of Fund resources by members, appointing the [Managing Director], providing institutional oversight, and setting administrative policy'.[577] As to the WB, according to a manual prepared by its Corporate Secretariat, Executive Directors are required to: 'provide overall guidance to Management on strategic directions and on corporate, regional, country-level and thematic issues; exercise oversight over operational, financial, and institutional matters, selection and [accountability] of senior management, and risk management functions; approve the use of financial resources by all World Bank Group entities . . . and decide on policies presented by management that impact the organization's general operations and use of resources'.[578] In performing all such functions, the manual reckons, 'Executive Directors have a dual responsibility, as they represent the interests and concerns of their constituency countries to the Boards and the Bank's management, as well as the fiduciary responsibility to act in the best interests of the organization as a whole.'[579]

B INDICATIONS OF THE LEGAL STATUS OF EXECUTIVE DIRECTORS IN THE INSTITUTIONS' INTERNAL RULES. The main question to be answered is whether Executive Directors can be considered State organs, for the purposes of the application of Article 4 ASR. When this matter is addressed in terms of self-perception, research on IMF Governance undertaken by the IEO in 2008 shows that 'all Directors clearly understand their representational role, [while] their status as officers of the Fund is less clear',[580] as already mentioned in Chapter I. On the basis of qualitative research conducted by the author, it is possible to claim that, customarily, Executive Directors' representational functions are strongly felt in international financial institutions. Representatives of both powerful and less powerful member States of the IMF, the WB, the EBRD and the IDB, as well as senior advisors of their constituencies, so

576 A. Mountford, 'Governance of the International Monetary Fund', in R. Lamdany and L. Martinez-Diaz (eds.), op. cit. *supra* note 252, 27.
577 Annex I to the IEO Report on IMF Governance, *supra* note 58, 23.
578 WBG Corporate Secretariat, *Board Operations and Administration Manual* (2014) 1 (on file with author).
579 Ibid.
580 IEO Report on IMF Governance, *supra* note 58, 16.

confirmed.[581] To some, the representational role of Executive Directors in single-party constituencies is so evident that the duality issue should not even be raised.[582]

Admittedly, these observations are not immediately relevant for international law, for the attribution of conduct is, as seen in Section 2.1.2.2, 'a legal connecting operation which as such has nothing to do ... with a link of ... "psychological" character'.[583] However, they indicate at least that whatever the degree of integration of Executive Directors in the organic structure of international financial institutions is, it will certainly be far from absolute. Rather, the above observations suggest that strong links must exist between Executive Directors and their member States (see below).

It is of note that the determination of the legal status of Executive Directors has long been a matter fraught with controversy. At the time of the Bretton Woods meetings, substantial opposition persisted between the US and the UK Treasuries, and notably between Harry Dexter White, representing the former, and John Maynard Keynes, representing the latter, as to whether the IMF and the WB should be run by member State representatives or by international civil servants.[584] White's stance was that control of the institutions should be centred in a Board of Directors whose members represented their governments. With regard to the IMF, they would be continuously involved in the adoption of decisions on exchange rates and other matters concerning the institution's relations with member States.[585] Permanent high-level supervision by the Directors was thus White's proposition.[586] Keynes, in turn, defended the setting up of an efficient technical international secretariat responsible for conducting research and for the institutions' day-to-day operations – with the Board meeting only

581 Interview #IV, 3 June 2014; Interview #VI, 23 March 2015; Interview #XII, 5 June 2015; Interview #XIII, 5 June 2015; Interview #XIV, 8 June 2015; Interview #XV, 11 June 2015; Interview #XVI, 11 June 2015; Interview #XVII, 12 June 2015; Interview #XVIII, 12 June 2015; Interview #XXI, 17 June 2015; Interview #XXIV, 19 June 2015; Interview #XXV, 22 June 2015; Interview #XXVI, 22 June 2015; Interview #XXVII, 25 June 2015; Interview #XXIX, 26 June 2015; Interview #XXX, 26 June 2015; Interview #XXXI, 29 June 2015; and Interview #XXXIII, 31 June 2015.

Among the legal advisors of the NIB, the WB, the IMF and the EBRD interviewed for this research, one was particularly forceful in affirming the representational role of Executive Directors. Legal advisors tend not to affirm upfront the duality inherent in the role of Executive Directors out of fear that it might open the door to more easily bypassing the institutions' interests. Without denying such duality, they in any case emphasize the official nature of the role of the Executive Boards. Interview #II, 3 October 2013; Interview #III, 2 June 2014; Interview #V, 23 March 2015; Interview #XX, 15 June 2015.

582 Interview #XXVIII, 25 June 2015.

583 YILC, 1971, Vol. II, Part one, 218, para. 58.

584 See R. Mikesel, *supra* note 250, 52.

585 Ibid. As described by the author: 'White's position, and that of the U.S. administration generally, reflected a desire to have the Fund heavily influenced by the United States in order to promote the U.S. economic objectives of stable exchange rates, non-discrimination in trade, and international financial equilibrium.'

586 F. Harrod, *The Life of John Maynard Keynes* (1951) 634.

occasionally on general institutional policies.[587] Ultimately, the difficulty in reaching a compromise is reflected in the vagueness of the references to the Executive Board's functioning contained in the IMF's and the WB's Articles of Agreement.[588]

Be that as it may, the need to come to grips with this dissension and define the international legal status of Executive Directors was soon felt, as the question of determining their privileges and immunities came to the fore. In the *travaux préparatoires* of the 1947 UN Convention on the Privileges and Immunities of the Specialized Agencies, it was outright admitted that 'it is not always possible to classify certain functionaries of international organizations clearly either as "representatives of governments" or as "officials" because their status and function combine characteristic features of both categories'.[589] Ultimately, although it was acknowledged that while, *sensu stricto*, Executive Directors did not come within the category of officials, they were so considered for the purposes of the Convention.[590]

Nonetheless, the solution was far from being watertight, inasmuch as the Headquarters Agreement between the UN and the US envisages the possibility of granting diplomatic privileges and immunities to Executive Directors.[591] Notably, such privileges and immunities are accorded to 'every person designated by a Member of a specialized agency ... as its principal resident representative, with the rank of ambassador or minister plenipotentiary'.[592] To be sure, it is the practice of the US State Department to routinely accept designations of Executive Directors (and, until the 1980s, their Alternates as well) as 'principal resident representatives', whenever requested by member States.[593]

587 Ibid. As expressed by Keynes: 'I should like to see the Board of the Fund composed of cautious bankers, and the Board of the Bank of imaginative expansionists ... Some of us ... had been hoping that the officials of the two bodies [Fund and Bank] would, in the course of time, come to regard themselves as primarily international officials, taking a world objective outlook, and only where clearly necessary grinding their own national axes. So one would have wished to minimize rather than maximize, their national representative character and their position as delegates from outside authorities'; quoted in E. Hexner, 'The Executive Board of the International Monetary Fund: A Decision-Making Instrument', 18(1) *International Organization* (1964) 74, 84. See also, for a more extended account of Keyne's views: F. Harrod, *supra* note 586, especially 632-634.

588 See: Article XII(3)(g) of the IMF Articles of Agreement (and the equivalent Article V(4)(e) of the WB Articles of Agreement, *supra* note 4), which prescribes: 'The Executive Board shall function in continuous session at the principal office of the Fund and shall meet as often as the business of the Fund may require.'

589 UNGA Final Report of Subcommittee 1 of the Sixth Committee, *Co-Ordination of the Privileges and Immunities of the United Nations and of the Specialized Agencies*, UN Doc. A/C.6/191 (1947) 8, para. 21.

590 Ibid.

591 See: Agreement between the United Nations and the United States of America regarding the Headquarters of the United Nations, 11 UNTS 11, 1947, Article V(15).

592 Ibid., Article V(15)(3). The granting of diplomatic privileges and immunities to Executive Directors has also been grounded in Article V(15)(4), referring to 'such other principal resident representatives of members to a specialized agency and such resident members of the staffs of representatives to a specialized agency as may be agreed upon between the principal executive officer of the specialized agency, the Government of the United States and the Government of the Member concerned'.

593 Communication with the WB, on file with the author.

A similar debate regarding the status of Executive Directors occurred in the framework of the ILC's work on relations between States and international organisations, which eventually led to the adoption of the 1975 Vienna Convention on the Representation of States in their Relations with International Organizations.[594] As outlined in one of the reports of Special Rapporteur E-Erian,[595] the IMF had made attempts to exclude the application of the draft articles to the institution. Its main contention was that 'questions relating to permanent representatives or member delegations to international organizations are not applicable to the Fund in the light of the Fund's organizational structure'.[596] The Special Rapporteur was not convinced by this argument, however, asserting that 'a great deal of the draft articles have their field of application to the Fund and the other financial specialized agencies'.[597]

In order to better understand the role of Executive Directors for attribution purposes, consideration of the internal division of competences between international financial institutions and their member States may prove quite useful. Article 6(2) ARIO suggests, indeed, taking into account the 'rules of the organization' to that end. First and foremost, a conclusion must be reached as to whether Executive Directors actually fit the notion of 'official' of the international financial institution. This implies looking at the institutions' constituent instruments and the secondary law emanating therefrom, such as, their by-laws, rules, regulations, standards or codes of conduct.[598]

It is true that the internal law of international financial institutions is not opposable to third parties, as it is *res inter alios acta* for the latter (unless they consent thereto).[599] From the standpoint of international law and any legal claims that individuals may have (in the present case, for alleged human rights violations), the internal division of competences is of a factual character.[600] It must thus be treated as part of the facts and as necessary

594 Vienna Convention on the Representation of States in their Relations with International Organizations of a Universal Character, UN Doc. A/CONF. 67/16 (1975). The Convention never entered into force as it has not met the minimum number of required ratifications.

595 ILC, Special Rapporteur El-Erian, *Sixth Report on Relations between States and International Organizations*, UN Doc. A/CN.4/241 and Add.1–6 (1971).

596 Ibid., 25, para. 100. To support its claim, the IMF invoked a 1967 study prepared by the UN Secretariat (UN Doc. A/CN.4/L.118 and Add. 1 and 2 (1967)), where it was considered that the IBRD, the IFC, the IDA and the IMF had a 'particular organizational structure' when compared to the other UN Specialized Agencies (see: 191, ftn 84). After inquiring into the *modus operandi* of Executive Directors, the study considered that 'the variety of posts held by Executive Directors from time to time and the different ways in which individual Directors perform their duties make it inappropriate to treat them as being exclusively "representatives" or the opposite' (205, para. 71).

597 ILC, Special Rapporteur El-Erian, *Sixth Report on Relations between States and International Organizations*, *supra* note 595, 25, para. 103.

598 Article 2(b) ARIO defines 'rules of the organization' as: 'the constituent instruments, decisions, resolutions and other acts of the international organization adopted in accordance with those instruments, and established practice of the organization'.

599 See Article 34 of the Vienna Convention on the Law of Treaties, *supra* note 152.

600 The PCIJ's decision *Certain German Interests in Polish Upper Silesia (Germany* v. *Poland)*, PCIJ Series A, No. 7 (1926) 19, consolidates the view that, from the standpoint of international law, the

background material to the case. This, in any case, is only a supplementary consideration,[601] for the internal rules of international financial institutions are certainly useful to better understand the relationship they hold with their member States and the application of attribution rules to both subjects of international law.[602]

As previously discussed, Article 6 ARIO determines that both the acts of organs and those of the agents of an international organisation are attributable to the latter. An 'organ' is understood as 'any person or entity which has that status in accordance with the rules of the organization', whereas the term 'agent' comprises 'an official or other person or entity, other than an organ, who is charged by the organization with carrying out, or helping to carry out, one of its functions, and thus through whom the organization acts'.[603] The notion of 'agent' is interpreted in quite broad terms, and is seen to derive from the case-law of the ICJ, as noted by the ILC in its commentaries.[604] The broadness of the ILC's definitions, however, is not very useful for the understanding of the idiosyncrasies of Executive Directors' role: although the latter do integrate an institutional organ, this organ is a representative one, and, thus, merely focusing on how Executive Directors contribute to the pursuit of the organisation's functions forces the said representational element into oblivion. After all, 'representatives of members ... can very well be parts of an international organ'.[605]

Two additional elements could be usefully analysed in this context: the appointment of Executive Directors and their exercise of functions under institutional control.[606] Regarding the former, and as already mentioned, IMF Executive Directors are all elected by the members, while WB Executive Directors are either directly appointed by the member States holding the five largest quotas, or elected every two years by the remaining members. In both cases, they are subdivided into single and multi-party constituencies.[607] In multi-party constituencies, the process of election is varied. In the Office of Executive

internal law of the State is of a factual nature. The same holds true for the internal law of international organisations.

601 Y. Chen, 'Attribution, Causation and Responsibility of International Organizations', in D. Sarooshi (ed.), *Remedies and Responsibility for the Actions of International Organizations/Mesures de Réparation et Responsabilité à Raison des Actes des Organisations Internationales* (2014) 57.

602 Similarly, in cases involving member State responsibility in the context of military operations, reference is made to status of forces agreements celebrated between international organisations and troop contributing States to determine attribution.

603 See: Article 2(c)(d) ARIO.

604 See: paras. 23–5 of the commentaries to Article 2 ARIO and paras. 2–5 of the commentaries to Article 6 ARIO.

605 J. L. Kunz, *supra* note 313, 854.

606 See: Suzanne Basdevant's definition of official contained in J. L. Kunz, ibid.

607 See: Article V(4)(b) of the IBRD Articles of Agreement and Article XII(3)(b)–(e) of the IMF Articles of Agreement, *supra* note 4. The terms used in some constituent instruments of international financial institutions are that each member State is entitled to appoint one Director and one Alternate. See, inter alia: Section 15 of the Statutes of the NIB, *supra* note 567; Articles 25(1)(4) of the Agreement Establishing the BSTDB, *supra* note 263. In others, it is specified that it is the Governors who elect the Executive Directors. See, inter alia: Article 26 of the Agreement Establishing the EBRD, Article 33(1) of the AfDB Articles of Agreement, and Article 25 of the

Director of the Nordic and Baltic Countries of the WB (EDS20), for example, the position of Executive Director rotates among the larger countries in the constituency.[608] An alternative model is that of the Office of Executive Director of Albania, Greece, Italy, Malta, Portugal, San Marino and Timor-Leste (EDS21), wherein the standing arrangement is that the Executive Director is always Italian, and the Alternate Executive Director is always Portuguese.[609] Importantly, Italy's indication of the person who will occupy the position of Executive Director and Portugal's recommendation of the person who will occupy the place of Alternate Executive Director are seen as proposals, which are circulated to the relevant ministries of all the remaining members of the constituency. The election process is complete only once all the member States of the constituency have sent their positive vote and thereby delegated representational authority to the Executive Director and his or her Alternate.[610] A final noteworthy example is that of the Office of Executive Director of the Africa Group 1 (EDS14),[611] which has a system of full rotation that is aimed at providing member States equal opportunity to serve the constituency. Executive Directors are elected for a period of two years. In the constituency's rotation scheme, the member State next in line is eligible to nominate three candidates for the position of Alternate Executive Director. In case none of the candidates qualifies, a second chance to present an additional three candidates is given, failing which the member State is skipped in favour of the member next in the line of rotation. Successful candidates are then recommended to the full constituency for endorsement.[612]

Interestingly, although the schemes just described already enable all member States to choose their representatives through election, the need to safeguard the effectiveness of representation in these institutions led to the setting up of additional mechanisms that account for the interests of member States not allowed to appoint an Executive Director. Notably, said members are entitled to send a representative to attend any meeting of the

AIIB Articles of Agreement, *supra* note 567. For an extended – even if partially outdated – explanation of the procedures for the election and appointment of Executive Directors in the IMF, see: J. Gold, *Voting and Decisions in the International Monetary Fund: An Essay on the Law and Practice of the Fund* (1972) 55–73.

608 Regeringskansliet, Ministry for Foreign Affairs Sweden, *Swedish Assessment of Multilateral Organisations: The World Bank* (2008) 2.

609 In the corresponding constituency in the IMF (in which, however, Timor-Leste is not included), the Alternate Executive Director is always Greek. Other constituencies follow this sort of arrangement of 'permanent' elected Executive Directors: in EDS08, the Executive Director is always from Argentina; in EDS10, the Director is always a Belgian; and in EDS15 it is always a Brazilian occupying the place.

610 Interview #XVIII, 12 June 2015; Interview #XXV, 22 June 2015.

611 EDS14 is composed of: Botswana, Burundi, Eritrea, Eswatini, Ethiopia, Gambia, Kenya, Lesotho, Liberia, Malawi, Mozambique, Namibia, Rwanda, Seychelles, Sierra Leone, Somalia, South Sudan, Sudan, Tanzania, Uganda, Zambia and Zimbabwe.

612 Africa Group I Constituency World Bank Group, Rules, Guidelines and Procedures, adopted in August 2010 and amended in October 2012, paras. 12–16.

Executive Directors when a request made by, or a matter particularly affecting, that member is under consideration.[613]

Secondly, it is important to clarify that Executive Directors do not exercise their functions 'under the control' of the international financial institutions. Various elements could be resorted to in an attempt to identify institutional control: to start with, by looking at the institutions' constituent instruments and the terms in which they define the role of Executive Directors within the organisation. However, and as already mentioned, the articles of agreement of the Bretton Woods institutions were purposefully left elusive in this respect. They merely state that the Executive Directors are responsible for the conduct of the general operations of the institutions and that they shall function in continuous session at their principal offices, meeting as often as business requires.[614] Agreements establishing other regional financial institutions, even if incidentally more detailed, remain similarly indefinite in this respect.[615] Relevantly, constituent instruments typically contain provisions specifying that the institutions' executive heads and the staff, in the discharge of their functions, 'owe their duty entirely to the [institutions] and to no other authority', whereas there is no such requirement with regard to Executive Directors.[616]

In any event, apart from the abovementioned discussion on Executive Directors' privileges and immunities, two aspects deriving from the organisations' constituent instruments are usually raised by legal practitioners – François Gianviti, a former IMF General Counsel, lying amongst the most vocal[617] – to support the official character of Executive Directors' position.[618] One relates to the fact that their remuneration is

613 See: Article V(4)(h) of the IBRD Articles of Agreement and Article XII(3)(j) of the IMF Articles of Agreement, *supra* note 4, as well as Section 19(1)(a)(b) of the IMF By-Laws, Rules and Regulations, Sixty-Third Issue, April 2016. This scheme is likewise applied in other international financial institutions. See, e.g.: Article 27(2) of the AIIB Articles of Agreement, *supra* note 567.

614 See: Article XII(3)(a)(g) of the IMF Articles of Agreement and Article V(4)(a)(e) of the IBRD Articles of Agreement, *supra* note 4.

615 See, inter alia: Article VIII(3) of the Agreement Establishing the IDB, *supra* note 570; Articles 26 and 27 of the Agreement Establishing the BSTDB, Articles 32 and 34 of the Agreement Establishing the AfDB, and Articles 31 and 32 of the Agreement Establishing the AsDB, *supra* note 567.

616 See, inter alia: Article XII(4)(c) of the IMF Articles of Agreement and Article V(5)(c) of the IBRD Articles of Agreement, *supra* note 4; Article VIII(5)(d) of the Agreement Establishing the IDB, *supra* note 570; Article 38(3) of the Agreement Establishing the AfDB and Article 31(3) of the AIIB Articles of Agreement, *supra* note 567; and Article 31(3) of the Agreement Establishing the BSTDB, *supra* note 263. The last exceptionally establishes in Article 31(2) that the 'Bank, its President, Vice President(s), Directors, officers, and staff shall, in their decisions, take into account only considerations relevant to the Bank's purpose, functions, and operation'.

617 F. François Gianviti, 'Decision-Making in the International Monetary Fund', 1 *Current Developments in Monetary and Financial Law* (1999) 31. Gianviti puts excessive emphasis on the fiduciary responsibilities of Executive Directors towards the IMF, almost as if the overall organic integrity of the institution would be threatened by affirming member State subjectivity in its decision-making body.

618 Another argument that has been raised – which is, in any event, unrelated to the constituent instruments – is that the email addresses of Executive Directors indicate their allegiance to the international financial institutions rather than national authorities. IMF Executive Directors' email

provided by the institutions, although it is determined by the Board of Governors.[619] The other argument regards elected Directors and the fact that they remain quite 'untouchable' by the members of their constituency while serving in office.[620] This is so, it is argued, because even if members wish to replace elected Executive Directors, they cannot (legally) do so before the term of his or her service, and also because the Executive Director's vote is still valid even if cast against member State instructions.[621]

These arguments, however, do not outweigh the fact that 'a large number of elected directors share with the appointed ones immediate dependence on the governments which have supported them. Even an executive director elected by a number of small states will do his best to accommodate the views and suggestions of all of his constituents (in addition to the one which nominated him).'[622] The abovementioned IEO Report on IMF Governance further clarifies that '[a]ppointed Directors can be recalled at will by their capitals' and that while 'Directors who are elected by a single-country constituency face similar scrutiny from their authorities … Directors elected by multi-country constituencies face different scrutiny and incentives … In any case, for most Directors, the impact on their future careers in their home countries provide[s] an incentive to listen to their authorities' guidance.'[623]

Finally, the subsisting validity of Executive Directors' votes (second argument) may be counteracted, if the need is felt, by subsequent member State action: in 2013, for example, a new IMF-backed rescue programme for Greece was submitted to the Board's approval, and while the Brazilian Executive Director decided to abstain from voting, Brazil was very quick in subsequently igniting a *démarche* to distance itself from the Director's decision.[624] Notably, Brazil's Minister of Finance made

addresses, for instance, end with 'imf.org' and those of WB Executive Directors end with 'world bank .org'. It should be noted that, as Executive Directors have permanent residency in these organisations, it can only be logical to have such an email address, which, as such, does not say much about their *real* allegiances in the performance of their functions.

619 See, inter alia: Article V(2)(h) of the IBRD Articles of Agreement, *supra* note 4, and Section 13(e)(i)(ii) of the IBRD By-laws, 26 September 1980; Article XII(2)(i) of the IMF Articles of Agreement, *supra* note 4, and Section 14(e)(i)(ii) of the IMF By-laws, Rules and Regulations, *supra* note 613; Article 28(2)(vii) of the Agreement Establishing the AsDB, *supra* note 567; and Section 4(B) of the By-laws of the European Bank for Reconstruction and Development, 15 April 1991 (EBRD By-laws). It is of note that in the recently established AIIB, Executive Directors and Alternate Directors in principle serve without remuneration from the Bank, as prescribed in Article 25(6) of the AIIB Articles of Agreement, *supra* note 567.

620 Interview #XXIII, 19 June 2015.

621 Ibid.

622 E. Hexner, *supra* note 587, 86.

623 IEO Report on IMF Governance, *supra* note 58, 16. When that is not the case, bitter consequences may ensue: during the Argentinian crisis, owing to a Government change in Argentina, the IMF Executive Director was requested to resign, but refused to do so. In reaction to this, Argentinian authorities contacted directly the management of the IMF, to inform them that the Director in question was not representing the country, and to provide the contact details of someone in the Argentinian Embassy who would thenceforth perform such a role (Interview #XXXII, 30 June 2015).

624 Financial Times news article, 'Brazil Calls for IMF Eurozone Rescue Programmes Revision', 8 August 2013, available at: https://next.ft.com/content/8fb83f5c-004b-11e3-9c40-00144feab7de, last consulted 15 October 2018.

public that it had recalled the Executive Director to Brasília to 'explain himself',[625] and directly contacted the IMF Managing Director to express support for the organisation's decision, thereby managing to 'rectify' and 'clarify' Brazil's position, to use Lagarde's words.[626]

It can be concluded from the above that the constituent instruments of international financial institutions are not entirely clear as to which entity ultimately has 'authority and control' over Executive Directors. But, in the presence of two relevant institutional links, if they are to point somewhere, they surely point less to the role of Directors as officials than as member State representatives. In addition to the organisations' constituent instruments, other formal sources may help in better grasping the levers of organic control exercised over Executive Directors, such as the institutions' codes of conduct. To which entity do Directors owe their loyalty? And which entity has the final say over disciplinary matters?

With regard to the IMF's by-laws, what is known is that they (and their Alternates) are required to devote 'all the time and attention to the business of the Fund that its interest require[s]'.[627] As is the case with other international financial institutions, there are separate codes of conduct in the IMF: one concerns the members of the Executive Board, including Alternates and Advisors,[628] and the other code, the staff.[629] This aspect alone, as has been rightly noted, reflects the different expectations lying on the Executive Board, Management and staff,[630] and ultimately serves as an expression of the role of Directors as representatives of the member States.[631]

A look into the disciplinary arrangements of the IMF codes of conduct reveals that the Fund 'can exercise no "ultimate" enforcement authority over executive directors for violations of ethics principles'.[632] Indeed, if a majority of the Ethics Committee concludes that misconduct has been committed, the kind of consequences envisaged are the following: '[T]he members of the Committee shall make recommendations to the Committee of the Whole of the Executive Board regarding whether a warning should be issued to an Executive Director, and whether such warning

625 Ibid.

626 See: Bloomberg news article, 'Brazil Summons IMF Rep Home after Abstention on Greece Vote', 1 August 2013, available at: www.bloomberg.com/news/articles/2013-08-01/brazil-summons-imf-rep-home-after-abstention-on-greece-debt-vote, last consulted 15 October 2018.

627 See: Section 14(d) of the IMF By-laws, Rules and Regulations, *supra* note 613. This is also the case in other international financial institutions. See, inter alia: Section 7(A)(a)(b) of the By-Laws of the Asian Development Bank, August 1966; and Section 4(A)(a)(b) of the EBRD By-Laws, *supra* note 619.

628 Code of Conduct for the Members of the Executive Board of the International Monetary Fund, adopted on 14 July 2000, revised on 12 December 2003 and 1 August 2012.

629 IMF Code of Conduct for Staff, adopted on 31 July 1998.

630 K. Campbell, 'Managing Conflicts of Interest and Other Ethics Issues at the IMF", in R. Lamdany and L. Martinez-Diaz, op. cit. *supra* note 252, 257.

631 A. Mountford, 'The Formal Governance Structure of the International Monetary Fund', IEO Background Paper, BP/08/01 (2008) 12.

632 K. Campbell, *supra* note 630, 263.

should be conveyed to the Governor(s) of the member country (or countries) that appointed, elected or designated the Executive Director.'[633]

As mentioned, other international financial institutions have likewise adopted a separate code of conduct for their Executive Directors. These include, inter alia, the WB,[634] the AsDB,[635] the EBRD[636] and the IDB.[637] The latter two codes interestingly contain introductory provisions wherein the duality inherent in the fiduciary responsibilities of Executive Directors is manifest.[638] When it comes to the Ethics Committees' – or Conduct Committee, in the case of the IDB – procedures envisaged in the codes of conduct of the WB, the AsDB and the IDB, they all similarly prescribe measures that go as far as the issuance of a written censure by the Executive Directors and the provision of notice of such censure to the Governor(s) of the member State(s) that appointed or elected the Executive Director.[639] With regard to the EBRD, member State involvement is even more explicit, in that it is the Director's Governor or the Director's Authorities that decide what action, if any, is to be taken.[640]

It is thus possible to conclude that international financial institutions are not equipped to exert coercive power over Executive Directors. It is the member States that put them in office and it is the member States that have a final say in cases where they misbehave.[641] To be sure, in interviews carried out for this research, when

633 Para. 26 of the Code of Conduct for the Members of the Executive Board of the International Monetary Fund, *supra* note 628.

634 World Bank Code of Conduct for Board Officials, adopted on 1 November 2007.

635 Asian Development Bank Code of Conduct for Directors, Alternates and the President, June 2011.

636 Code of Conduct for Officials of the Board of Directors of the EBRD, revised in February 2012 (Code of Conduct for the EBRD Board of Directors).

637 Code of Ethics for the Boards of Executive Directors of the Inter-American Development Bank, the Inter-American Investment Corporation and the Donors Committee of the Multilateral Investment Fund, adopted on 2003, amended on 2009 (Code of Ethics for IDB Executive Directors).

638 In the Code of Ethics for IDB Executive Directors, ibid., 3, it is prescribed that 'Executive Directors are entrusted with the conduct of the operations of their respective Institution and shall exercise their fiduciary responsibility with objectivity and impartiality. At the same time, Executive Directors are the representatives to their respective Institution of the country or countries that have appointed or elected them'; and Rule 2(a) of the Code of Conduct for the EBRD Board of Directors, *supra* note 636, determines: 'Board Officials shall discharge their duties to the Bank with the interests and objectives of the Bank in view and consistent with their obligations to their Authorities.' Again, this contrasts with Rule 2(b), which prescribes that Bank Personnel 'owe their duty entirely to the Bank'.

639 See: Article 19(e)(i) of the WB Code of Conduct for Board Officials, *supra* note 634; Article 7(d) of the Asian Development Bank Code of Conduct for Directors, Alternates and the President, *supra* note 635; and Article 8(e) of the Operating Guidelines for the Conduct Committee of the Board of Executive Directors of the Inter-American Development Bank, the Inter-American Investment Corporation and the Donors Committee of the Multilateral Investment Fund, adopted on June 2004, amended on April 2009.

640 See: Rule 17(b) of the Code of Conduct for the EBRD Board of Directors, *supra* note 636.

641 By way of comparison, in the abovementioned *Nuhanović* decision of the Dutch Supreme Court, *supra* note 82, the organic link between the Netherlands as a troop-contributing State and the military personnel was relevantly kept inasmuch as 'the Netherlands, as the troop-contributing State, retained control over the personnel affairs of the military personnel concerned, who had remained in the

confronted with the question of which entity they were ultimately accountable to, all member State representatives (and their advisors) responded that it was the national authorities.[642] Next to this, it is highly significant to note that throughout their mandate, and especially when they participate in institutional decision-making processes, Executive Directors have clear reporting lines to their member States,[643] as will be discussed in Section 2.2.2. It comes as no surprise, then, that in the case of both single-party and multi-party constituencies of the WB, the official websites of the various Executive Director offices introduce the office as serving the purpose of representing the country(ies) of the constituency(ies).[644]

C CONCLUDING REMARKS: EXECUTIVE DIRECTORS AS STATE ORGANS. From Sections 2.2.1.2, A and B, it follows that Executive Directors can be considered, in their individuality, as State organs. This does not negate the fact that, within the international financial institutions' legal order, they also owe fiduciary duties to the organisation. The institutions' constituent instruments do exert a form of normative control over their conduct, inasmuch as, internally, the validity of the acts of Executive Directors depends on whether they follow the rules prescribed by the organisations' constitution.[645] In any case, these rules are, as seen, quite vague, and limit themselves to imposing upon Executive Directors the duty of taking into account the interests and purposes of the institutions in their work.[646]

The control exerted by member States over Executive Directors is also not absolute. But even if States do not in fact exercise control over all their organs all the time, they will still be responsible for their organs' acts since they have control over the way they set up their organic apparatus.[647] Accordingly, the essence of government relates to the possession of 'effective power to regulate, control or

service of the Netherlands, and retained the power to punish these military personnel under disciplinary and criminal law' (see: para. 3.10.2).

642 Interview #IV, 3 June 2014 (Alternate Executive Director); Interview #XIII, 5 June 2015 (Advisor); Interview #XV, 11 June 2015 (Advisor); Interview #XVI, 11 June 2015 (Executive Director); Interview #XVII, 12 June 2015 (Advisor); Interview #XVIII, 12 June 2015 (Executive Director); Interview #XXI, 17 June 2015 (Executive Director); Interview #XXIV, 19 June 2015 (Alternate Executive Director); Interview #XXVII, 25 June 2015 (Senior Advisor); Interview #XXVIII, 25 June 2015 (Senior Advisor); Interview #XXIX, 26 June 2015 (Executive Director); Interview #XXX, 26 June 2015 (Alternate Executive Director); Interview #XXXI, 29 June 2015 (Alternate Executive Director); and Interview #XXXIII, 31 June 2015 (Alternate Executive Director).

643 This was the conclusion of the IEO Report on IMF Governance, *supra* note 58, 11.

644 See, e.g., the website of EDS06, whereby: 'The Office of the Executive Director (EDS06) represents Afghanistan, Algeria, Ghana, Iran, Morocco, Pakistan and Tunisia.' Available at: www.worldbank.org/en/about/leadership/directors/eds06, last consulted 15 October 2018.

645 To name one example, the voting rights of member States may be suspended in case of non-compliance with the obligations imposed by the institution's constituent instrument. See, e.g.: Article XXVI(2)(b) of the IMF Articles of Agreement, *supra* note 4.

646 Anecdotal evidence gathered at the time of this research indicates that concerns were being raised by the staff of an international financial institution with regard to an Executive Director's intrusion in their sphere of independence.

647 A. Tzanakopoulos, *supra* note 426, 38.

supervise individuals, or otherwise restrain their conduct, through the exercise of lawful authority'.[648] As will be further clarified in the following section, the possibility to regulate or otherwise restrain the conduct of Executive Directors becomes more visible when considering their participation in institutional decision-making processes.

In sum, member State representation in international financial institutions is ensured through the Boards of Governors and the Boards of Executive Directors. With regard to the former, the fact that these organs are composed of ministers or governors of central banks brings with it the indisputability of their representational role. In delegating most of their powers to Executive Directors, what is thus ultimately transferred is the power to represent.[649] Remarkably, in the WB at least, all Executive Director offices proudly hoist at the entrance the flag of each and every member State of the constituency.[650] One cannot but defer to the value of symbolism and wonder what is it other than a powerful epitome of sovereign representation.

While the Executive Director can therefore be deemed a State organ, further analysis is called for concerning the terms in which his or her participation in institutional decision-making processes constitutes conduct that can be attributed to the State. This chapter's final section will explore the matter, firstly by providing a generic account of how the qualification of the vote as an act of the State has been treated in the doctrine; and secondly by developing the findings thereof in the context of international financial institutions. An important step is thus made to demystify the notion that the relationship between international organisations and their member States is a 'schizophrenic' one.[651]

2.2.2 *Member State Participation in Institutional Decision-Making As Conduct Attributable to the State*

2.2.2.1 The Vote As a Corollary of the Power of Representation

The question posed in this section relates to whether or not voting defines (member) State participation in the international plane.[652] What is the nature of the vote? To use White's terms, is it tantamount to the exercise of a sovereign right under

648 Appellate Body Report, *Canada – Measures Affecting the Importation of Milk and the Exportation of Dairy Products*, WTO Doc. WT/DS103/AB/R, AB-1999-4, 13 October 1999, para. 97.

649 This does not, in any event, release Governors from their overall responsibility for the institutions' direction and performance, as well as for overseeing the Executive Boards' performance, as noted in the IEO Report on IMF Governance, *supra* note 58, 7.

650 It is of note that in the abovementioned Vienna Convention on the Representation of States in their Relations with International Organizations, *supra* note 594, the use of the flag by sending States in their permanent missions to international organisations is seen as a right (see Article 19).

651 J. Klabbers, *supra* note 75, 227.

652 The term is borrowed from ILC, Special Rapporteur Cedeño, *First Report on Unilateral Acts of States*, UN Doc. A/CN.4/486 (1998) para. 48.

international law (i.e., a prerogative of membership)?[653] Or does it rather correspond to the exercise of a procedural right, which is solely relevant within the internal legal order of the organisation?[654]

Some authors would agree with Amerasinghe's contention that holding member States responsible for the exercise of voting rights 'involve[s] a fictitious assumption of participation in decision making'.[655] Admittedly, one could simply state that the adoption of a decision by the international organisation, which concludes the decision-making process, renders it unnecessary to consider the member State's prior contribution to the institutional decision: whatever the State's imprint was would ultimately become diluted in the collective will informing the decision adopted.[656] In other words, a member State's vote would constitute but a moment integrated in a complex procedure leading to the collective decision.[657]

According to such line of thought, if any legal effects are to stem from the vote, they are internal to the international organisation's order. For example, in discussing the use of veto power by member States in the UNSC, White analyses the question of responsibility through the lens of the obligations of States qua members of the international organisation, and therefore appeals to the performance of their duties in accordance with the purposes and principles of the organisation's constituent instrument.[658] Similarly, '[le] but essentiel des Nations Unies' was in Scelle's mind when he claimed before the ICJ in the 1948 *Admissions* case that member States' exercise of voting power for the admission of new members 'qui ne serait pas dicté par cette préoccupation

653 It is interesting to note that in the French version of Article 5 UN Charter reference is made to 'droits et privilèges *inhérents* à la qualité de Membre' (emphasis added), while the English version only refers to 'rights and privileges of membership'. If admissibility or the rights to vote and participate in institutional affairs are *inherent* in the quality of member State, then State representatives with the capacity to exercise them could even be said to solely act on behalf of sovereign States, and not in a dual capacity. See: E. Lagrange, *supra* note 93, 30.

654 N. White, *supra* note 276, 150.

655 C. F. Amerasinghe, *supra* note 355, 278. In a 'Draft Questionnaire', from June 1989, and 'Questionnaire', from September 1990, prepared in the framework of IDI's work on member State responsibility, *supra* note 74, 289 (hereinafter IDI Questionnaire on member State responsibility), one of the questions addressed to the institute's members was the following: 'So far as the legal consequences for member states are concerned, what is the significance of their participation in the decisions of the organization *qua* constituent elements of the relevant organs?' (301). While some members found member State participation in decision-making processes to be relevant for the purposes of the law of international responsibility (see further in this section), others, such as M. Daniel Vignes (305) and James Crawford (333, 334), advanced the opposite.

656 According to N. White, *supra* note 276, 30, 31, the international legal personality of international organisations and the existence of a separate will imply that States either transferred their will to the organisation or gave it the elements required to develop a will of its own. See, similarly: G. Marchegiano, 'The Juristic Character of the International Commission of Cape Spartel Lighthouse', 25 Am J Int'l L (1931) 339, 342.

657 E. Lagrange, *supra* note 93, 308.

658 N. White, *supra* note 276, 149–51.

essentielle doit être considéré comme entaché d'illégalité'.[659] In general, as noted by Blokker, when participating in international organisations, member States are required to pursue their goals in good faith.[660]

Based on the doctrine of unilateral act (see below), Lagrange quite forcefully denies that the will expressed by member States within institutional decision-making processes has any international legal relevance. According to the author, 'les effets de l'origine et de la dépendance nationales des représentants permanents se dilueraient dans la permanence de l'institution'.[661] In this vein, 'la volonté exprimée ... dans l'ordre institutionnel n'a pas l'efficacité d'un acte juridique unilatéral; elle se ramène à un simple concours à une procédure collective qui n'engage pas la responsabilité des auteurs'.[662] Lagrange's position is understandable if one considers the premises upon which it is based: in order to qualify the vote as a legally relevant act, the author resorts to elements (such as the unequivocal heteronormativity of the act, i.e., the intended creation of a new legal relationship with a third party)[663] that come close to the stringent definition of unilateral legal act adopted by the ILC in its work on Unilateral Acts of States.[664] A strictly unilateral act constitutes, according to the ILC, an 'unequivocal expression of will which is formulated by a State with the intention of producing legal effects in relation to one or more other States or international organizations, and which is known to that State or international organization'.[665] Hence, a unilateral legal act can only be so qualified when

659 ICJ *Admissions* case, *supra* note 204, *Mémoires, Plaidoiries et Documents, Part II*, Exposé de M. le Professeur Georges Scelle, 22 Avril 1948, 76. Scelle makes the case that when member States' motivations underlying their votes are formally expressed during the debates held among their representatives, these can be subjected to legal scrutiny.

660 N. Blokker, *supra* note 235, 147, 148. See also H. Schermers and N. Blokker, *supra* note 152, 121–3, specifying that the systematic blocking of decisions requiring unanimity voting amounts to a violation of member States' good faith obligation towards the international organisation.
In the 1948 *Admissions* case, *supra* note 204, Judges Basdevant, Winiarski, McNAir and Read analysed, in their Dissenting Opinion, States' behaviour in their capacity as members of the UN, and invoked the duty of States to use their voting power in accordance with general principles of international law, namely, that of good faith (see: 83, para 4, 91, para. 20 and 92, para. 21). For an account of the application of the principle of good faith in UN practice, see: R. Kolb, *supra* note 212, 174–8.

661 E. Lagrange, *supra* note 93, 144.

662 Ibid., 41.

663 References to the heteronormative effect of legal acts can be found in, inter alia: paras. 25, 37, 79 and 121 of ILC, Special Rapporteur Cedeño, *First Report on Unilateral Acts of States*, UN Doc. A/CN.4/486 (1998).

664 E. Lagrange, *supra* note 93, especially 34–45 and 310–57. The author does not refer much to the work of the ILC (which was only starting at the time of her monograph's publication), but, rather, to authors such as Suy, Jacqué, Cahier or Combacau, who clearly inspired the ILC's understanding of unilateral legal act.

665 ILC, Special Rapporteur Cedeño, *Fifth Report on Unilateral Acts of States*, UN Doc. A/CN.4/525 and 1 and 2 (2002) 102, para. 81.

the State understands that it assumes a legal commitment in formulating it,[666] and this expression of will is formulated 'unequivocally'.[667] Furthermore, it is essential that the act is given publicity.[668]

Applied to the vote, said criteria are difficult to meet. While voting certainly constitutes a manifestation of will imputable to the State, it is doubtful that it produces heteronormative effects[669] – and that, for example, the approval of a WB loan expresses the State's unequivocal intention of acquiring legal obligations towards third parties with regard to the project at issue. Next to this, when it comes to publicity, whilst extensive information regarding public roll calls and recorded votes can be found with regard to the UN or the EU, international financial institutions tend to be much more secretive in this respect – also because, as seen in Chapter I, decision-making is mostly done by consensus.

Lagrange is thus right in denying the application of these criteria to the act of voting. However, the qualifier used by the author to ground her position does not seem to be the most appropriate one. Indeed, at the initial stages of the ILC's work on Unilateral Acts of States, the decision was made to exclude from its scope acts that could engage the international responsibility of States, inasmuch as the topic was already being considered by the Commission elsewhere.[670] When looking at the ASR, the reality is that the ILC seems to apply a rather wide definition of conduct attributable to the State: it is simply, 'an "act of the State" [which] must involve some action or omission by a human being or group'.[671] No reference is made to the intention of the author of the act, and thus, what matters is that international law attaches certain effects to it.

For the vote to be qualified as an act attributable to the State in light of secondary rules of international law, the sole requirement is that it produces legal effects beyond the internal legal order of the organisation.[672] It is submitted here that it does. As a corollary of the power of representation,[673] the act of voting corresponds to the exercise of governmental powers in the external

666 ILC, Special Rapporteur Cedeño, *Third Report on Unilateral Acts of States*, UN Doc. A/CN.4/505 (2000) 252, para. 35.

667 Ibid., paras. 70 et seq.

668 Ibid., paras. 78–9.

669 M. Gounelle, *La Motivation des Actes Juridiques en Droit International Public: Contribution à Une Théorie de L'acte Juridique en Droit International Public* (1979) 218.

670 ILC, Special Rapporteur Cedeño, *First Report on Unilateral Acts of States*, *supra* note 132, 324, para. 29 and *Second Report on Unilateral Acts of States*, UN Doc. A/CN.4/500 and Add.1 (1999) 196, 197, paras. 3–10.

671 See: para. 5 of the commentaries to Article 2 ASR.

672 As noted by Gounelle, *supra* note 669, 217, 218: '[i]l faut remarquer que tout vote d'un Etat peut être un acte juridique dès lors qu'il crée une règle qui n'est pas purement intérieure à l'organisation. Dans le cas où la règle créée a au contraire un destination purement interne, la qualité du vote en tant qu'acte juridique international peut être discutée.'

673 F. Guérin, *La Qualité de Membre d'une Organisation Internationale*, Paris II (1998) t.2, 410, quoted in E. Lagrange, *supra* note 93, 145.

domain.[674] Votes thereby project themselves in member States' relations with third parties – notably, with the individuals affected by the institutional decisions and operations deriving from those very votes.

In early writings, Lindeiner-Wildau characterised the participation of member States in institutional decision-making as a 'participation quasi-directe des Etats',[675] and distinguished such cases from what a (truly) supranational institutional setting would look like, notably, one where 'les personnes constituant l'organe supranational et prenant part à la formation de sa volonté ne soient pas liées par des instructions, et que l'organe en tant que tel soit indépendant vis à vis des Etats, surtout vis à vis des gouvernements nationaux'.[676] Accordingly, the fact that the individuals composing representative organs are not independent from national authorities and (may) receive instructions therefrom brings about two fundamental elements that justify attributing their conduct to the States they represent. Such is the essence of the legal principle of representation, notably, '[l]e «représentant» exprime ... non pas sa propre volonté mais la volonté du «représenté» ... c'est-à-dire l'Etat'.[677]

Along these lines, Seidl-Hohenveldern asserted that the decision of a member of an institutional organ acting under instructions from his home State, 'whose interest he has to represent in the organ concerned ... will be held to be an act of his home State'.[678] In the framework of the IDI's work on member State responsibility, Shihata posited that when States act in international organisations through official representatives, their responsibility can 'conceivably' be invoked.[679] More straightforwardly, Salomon upheld the view that 'chaque Etat participant à la décision par son vote positif ou négatif, voire par son abstention s'engage personnellement devant son opinion publique nationale comme devant l'opinion publique mondiale qui peuvent lui demander de rendre compte de son vote ... la position prise par un Etat dans une organisation internationale est susceptible d'engager sa responsabilité'.[680] Recently, various authors have reaffirmed these premises, be it in somewhat brief terms,[681] or in more comprehensive studies addressing the responsibility of

674 The French Conseil d'Etat regarded the participation of France in the adoption of the European Communities supplementary budget for 1983 along such lines in the case *Association Les Verts Parti Ecologiste*, Case N° 54359 54360, CLI:FR:CEASS:1984:54359.19841123, 23 November 1984.

675 K. Von Lindeiner-Wildau, *La Supranationalité en tant que Principe de Droit* (1970) 50.

676 Ibid.

677 Ibid.

678 I. Seidl-Hohenveldern, 'Responsibility of Member States of an International Organization for Acts of that Organization', in P. Lamberti Zanardi et al. (eds.), *International Law at the Time of Its Codification: Essays in Honour of Roberto Ago* (1987) 419.

679 IDI Questionnaire on member State responsibility, *supra* note 655, 311, 312.

680 Ibid., 344.

681 See, inter alia: M. Salomon, 'International Economic Governance and Human Rights Accountability', in M. Salomon, A. Tostensen and W. Vandenhole (eds.), *Casting the Net Wider: Human Rights, Development and New Duty-Bearers* (2007) 178–81, reiterated in a recent publication, mentioned *supra* note 26; Center for International Environmental Law, Legal Analysis on

member States for their participation in institutional decision-making processes.[682]

It has been well documented that the votes cast, or the positions taken, within the representative organs of international organisations emerge as an accurate reflection of the pursuit of national preferences all the way through the decision-making process in contexts such as the Council of the EU[683] or the UNSC.[684] Beyond their voting behaviour, member States' stance towards the subject at hand may even be further specified inasmuch as diverging States that opt to vote in favour of a proposal can always present a 'declaration of vote' (in the EU), also termed 'explanation of vote' (in the UN),[685] whereby their dissenting position or precise interpretation of a certain norm is avowed.[686]

That votes and attendant explanations imbue the conduct of State representatives with a sense of sovereign identity has also been acknowledged in other contexts and served other international law purposes. Notably, the ICJ has already looked underneath (the veil of) UN conduct in order to deduce *opinio juris* for purposes of the formation of customary international law from member State voting behaviour, namely, from the 'attitude of the Parties and the attitude of States towards certain

'International Financial Institutions & Human Rights Law', Public Hearing of the Inter-American Commission of Human Rights on Human rights violations and responsibility of international financial institutions, 127th Regular Period of Sessions (2007) 4–6 (hereinafter 'CIEL Legal Analysis on International Financial Institutions & Human Rights Law'); A. Khalfan and I. Seiderman, 'Extraterritorial Human Rights Obligations: Wider Implications of the Maastricht Principles and the Continuing Accountability Challenge', in W. Vandenhole (ed.), *Challenging Territoriality in Human Rights Law: Building Blocks for a Plural and Diverse Duty-Bearer Regime*, Routledge (2015) 30, 31; and F. Naert, *supra* note 519, 162–6.

682 See: P. Palchetti, 'Sulla Responsabilità di uno Stato per il Voto Espresso in Seno ad Un'Organizzazione Internazionale', XCV *Rivista di Diritto Internazionale* (2012) 352, 352–73; O. Murray, *supra* note 371, 291–347; and A. S. Barros and C. Ryngaert, *supra* note 58.

683 See W. Van Aken, 'Voting in the Council of the European Union: Contested Decision-Making in the EU Council of Ministers (1995–2010)', Report published by the Swedish Institute for European Policy Studies, 2012, in particular 12–20. This information was confirmed in interviews held with officials from an EU member States' permanent representation (Interview #1, 16 April 2013). Cf. Blokker, describing the dual role of States in COREPER, in N. Blokker, *supra* note 235, 147 and 148.

684 See, inter alia: N. White, *supra* note 276, 146–50, noting, amongst various examples on the historical use of the veto in the UNSC, how it represents 'a realist core in the midst of an institutional framework' and a 'political expression of power'. For an account of how the US has consistently used its veto power on questions regarding Israel, see: D. Held, 'The Diffusion of Authority', in T. Weiss and R. Wilkinson (eds.), *supra* note 207, 63; and how China has systematically vetoed (or abstained in) matters that brought about sensitivities similar to those pertaining to the legal status of Taiwan, see: P. Chan, 'A Keen Observer of the International Rule of Law? International Law in China's Voting Behaviour and Argumentation in the United Nations Security Council', 26 LJIL (2013) 875, 889–91.

685 The term 'explanation of vote' can be found in Rule 88 of the Rules of Procedure of the General Assembly, UN. Doc. A/520/Rev.17 (2007).

686 As explained with regard to the Council of the EU, the positive vote of the diverging member State may still be cast either for strategic reasons, particularly if the member State either is the next to hold the Presidency of the Council or integrates the Trio Presidency, or because a blocking minority is absent. See W. Van Aken, *supra* note 683, 12–14.

General Assembly resolutions'.[687] Accordingly, '[t]he effect of consent to the text of such resolutions . . . may be understood as an acceptance of the validity of the rule or set of rules declared by the resolution by themselves'.[688] Various voices in the doctrine have shown support for the notion that the position taken by a member State through its vote in favour of a recommendation could subsequently be opposed to that state.[689] The ILC has likewise endorsed this view in its work on Identification of Customary International Law, and has asserted in its conclusions that '[f]orms of State practice include ... conduct in connection with resolutions adopted by an international organization'.[690]

At this stage, it is essential to recall the findings of the ICJ in the *FYROM* case[691] and note that, in this analytical scheme, while the vote (or position), as such, is to be considered as State conduct, it should be distinguished from the final decision adopted by the institutional organ, the latter constituting an expression of the international organisation's will.[692] Accordingly, the final decision is attributable to the international organisation, under Article 6 ARIO, whereas the vote still refers to the member State's own discretionary action and is thus attributable to it, under Article 4 ASR.[693]

Despite the interconnectedness of these actors' roles (which brings with it the difficulty of pinpointing which is the relevant contentious act at issue), two different spheres of conduct may thus be identified. It is against member States' voting behaviour (or position) that their international law obligations conditioning their participation in institutional decision-making may be judged. While Chapter III will explore the terms in which international human rights law conditions member State conduct in international financial institutions, attention will now be paid to the contours of attribution to States of the votes cast, or positions adopted, by their representatives in such frameworks.

687 *Case Concerning Military and Paramilitary Activities in and against Nicaragua (Nicaragua V. United States of America)*, Merits, Judgment, ICJ Reports 1986, para. 188. This line of reasoning is forwarded in paras. 203 and 204.

688 Ibid.

689 See, inter alia: P. Sands and P. Klein, *Bowett's Law of International Institutions* (2009) 294, 295; R. Higgins, *The Development of International Law through the Political Organs of the United Nations* (1963) 2. An extensive account of legal writings in this respect can be found in ILC, Special Rapporteur Wood, *Third Report on Identification of Customary International Law*, UN Doc. A/CN.4/682, 27 March 2015, paras. 45–53.

690 ILC, *Identification of Customary International Law*, Text of the draft conclusions as adopted by the Drafting Committee on second reading, UN Doc. A/CN.4/L.908 (2018), Conclusion 6 on forms of practice.

691 Mentioned *supra* note 528.

692 See: P. Palchetti, *supra* note 682, 354, 355. See also: CIEL Legal Analysis on International Financial Institutions & Human Rights Law, *supra* note 681, 4.

693 Yet another question relates to the relevance of member State voting behaviour and the effect of the way in which decisions are adopted upon the legally binding nature of the institutional decision. As explained by Schermers and Blokker, member State voting behaviour in this regard does not bear any legal relevance in terms of limiting the effect of the decision adopted. See H. Schermers and N. Blokker, *supra* note 152, 591.

2.2.2.2 The Dynamics of Decision-Making in International Financial Institutions

The notion espoused in Section 2.2.2.1 that the position advanced by State representatives in institutional decision-making constitutes an expression of the exercise of governmental powers in the external domain is conspicuous in international financial institutions.[694] It is true that the governance dynamics and practices of these organisations, as they relate to voting procedures, present variations.[695] Nevertheless, the aim of the current section is less to scrutinize each organisation's distinctive features, than to generally make the case for the existence of clear, legally relevant links between Executive Directors and their member States in both formal and informal decision-making processes. Said links constitute, after all, the baseline justification for attributing their voting behaviour to States.

A THE GUIDANCE PROVIDED BY MEMBER STATES TO THEIR EXECUTIVE DIRECTORS. This section's focus will be placed on existing reporting lines between Executive Directors and their national authorities. Yet, it should be noted at the outset that overall guidance of their work does not stem solely from government departments. With regard to the IMF (and similarly the WB), a good overview of its governance structure can be found in Figure 1.

In what particularly relates to the work of Executive Directors, it is possible to extract from Figure I that various bodies play a significant role in influencing their conduct. While the IMF Articles of Agreement solely refer to the Board of Governors, the reality is that the IMFC, the Development Committee (which is missing in the image as it is more WB-oriented) and informal bodies such as the various 'Gs' definitely come forth as important actors in the governance of the institution. Formally, guidance from the Board of Governors is provided in the framework of the IMF-WB Annual Meetings, where they adopt statements on, inter alia, the policies of the IMF and the WB.[696] Said meetings have become quite ceremonial, however, and high-level negotiation has shifted to the IMFC and the Development Committee.[697] These forums have in fact become the main source of ministerial-political-level guidance, advice and feedback to the Executive Boards of the Bretton Woods institutions.[698] The IMF's IMFC meets twice a year, during the IMF-WB Spring and Annual Meetings, to discuss the management of the

694 Cf. J. Gold, *supra* note 607, 99, who, referring to the IMF, is of the view that '[w]hen governors or directors take decisions as the Board of Governors or as the Executive Directors, they decide as a body consisting of officers of the Fund and not as the "representatives" of the members that appointed or elected them'.

695 Interview #XXXII, 30 June 2015.

696 A. Mountford, *supra* note 631, 18.

697 Ibid., 34.

698 Ibid., 20–2. The influence of these bodies in policy-making was confirmed by member State representatives of the WB and the IMF (Interview #XXI, 17 June 2015 and Interview #XXV, 22 June 2015; Interview #XXVIII, 25 June 2015).

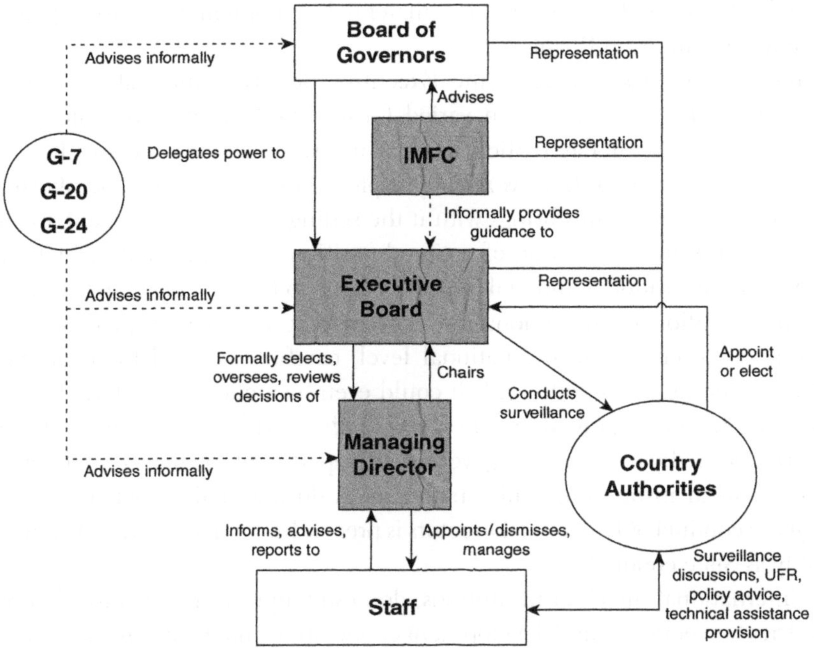

FIGURE 1: IMF Governance Structure
Source: IEO Report on IMF Governance, 2008

international monetary and financial system, the conduct of the IMF, and even policy changes. It then issues *communiqués* summarising its views, which play an important role in the delineation of the Fund's future work programme. In its turn, the joint IMF-WB Development Committee advises the Boards of both institutions on critical development issues and makes suggestions on the implementation of its conclusions.[699]

Beyond the IMF's and the WB's formal governance structures, the 'Gs' play a significant role in global macroeconomic coordination.[700] Their influence over the conduct of the Boards is beyond doubt, although it is hard to measure given the informal fashion, intermittent and ad hoc,[701] in which it is normally exerted (see below). At times, however, the 'Gs' may condition decision-making processes in international financial institutions quite straightforwardly – suffice it to recall the G7's approval in 2014 of sanctions against Russia for its illegal annexation of Crimea (subsequently renewed in 2015 and 2016),[702] which brought with it the request,

699 A. Mountford, *supra* note 631, 20–2, 34.

700 See: R. Stone, *supra* note 58, 6, 7, noting that the G20 took the lead in coordinating international responses, including that of the IMF, to the 2008 international crisis.

701 IEO Report on IMF Governance, *supra* note 58, 7.

702 See, e.g.: The Moscow Times news article, 'G7 Leaders Agree to Prolong Anti-Russian Sanctions', 27 May 2016, available at: www.themoscowtimes.com/news/article/g7-leaders-agree-to-prolong-anti-russian-sanctions/570670.html, last consulted 15 October 2018.

directed at the Executive Boards of multilateral development banks, to suspend new financing operations in Russia.[703]

While high-level guidance of the Executive Boards of international financial institutions may thus come from varied forums, both formal and informal, the steering of their day-to-day participation in decision-making processes lies in the hands of country authorities. As already explored in Section 1.1.1, membership in international organisations brings with it the setting up of a government apparatus responsible for the formulation of national positions to be pursued by State representatives in institutional undertakings. According to Plantey, inasmuch as member State participation in institutional decision-making is generally preceded by the formulation of choices at the national level, carefully tailored to accommodate national interests and ambitions, '[i]t could even be argued that external organisational negotiation begins at national level'.[704] As will be seen, more powerful countries normally have specific government departments dedicated to the international financial institution, while smaller ones do not. This affects the extent to which the conduct of Executive Directors is preconditioned domestically, but not its identity as State conduct.

In international financial institutions, domestic input is mainly provided by the ministries for economic and development cooperation and the ministries of finance. Along the lines of Plantey, Hexner has noted with regard to the IMF that 'the source of the large power of the Executive Board rests in reality ... with the monetary authorities of the member states'.[705] As explained by the author, continuous liaison with the latter, through a communication system based on a daily flow of reports and advice, lies among the main factors securing the ready acceptance of the authority of the Executive Board by the member States.[706]

Instructions from national authorities come in varied forms. Whether technical, legal or political, these may include ideal and fall-back positions, red lines, expertise and arguments related to the specific item on the agenda, and can be more general in character, indicating the broad position of the State regarding a given policy area.[707] The extent to which Executive Directors are subject to such instructions is dependent on a number of factors, such as the nature of the matter at hand, the

703 Interview #XVIII, 12 June 2015.

704 A. Plantey, *supra* note 144, 281.

705 E. Hexner, *supra* note 587, 77.

706 Ibid., 78, 81, 88. In multi-party constituencies, liaison between an Executive Director office and national authorities is ensured by all the officials integrating the office. To the extent possible, the various advisors to the Executive Director and the Alternate have the nationalities of the different members of the constituency, so that effective communication channels with national authorities are ensured and clear messages are conveyed to the Executive Director, their foremost representative (Interview #XVI, 11 June 2015).

707 D. Panke, *supra* note 104, 30, 32. For example, when it comes to the IMF Annual Report, prior to its approval by the Executive Board, it is subjected to comments by the treasuries and central banks of the member States. See: E. Hexner, *supra* note 587, 83.

capacity of the administrative machinery of the respective government(s) or the position and prestige of the Director vis-à-vis his or her member State authorities.[708] What is sure, in any event, is that whenever Executive Directors (including from less powerful States) feel the need to back up a certain position, they reach out to their State authorities with a view to obtaining concrete instructions on how to proceed.[709]

US representatives are known to receive swift and detailed instructions on which positions to follow in the Boards of international financial institutions. According to the Bretton Woods Agreements Act,[710] various actors at the national level play a role in devising general policy directives for the guidance of Executive Directors, including the President of the US and the National Advisory Council on International Monetary and Financial Problems (the Council), where the Secretary of the Treasury (as Chair), the Secretary of State and the Secretary of Commerce, among others, take part.[711] With particular regard to decision-making on financial matters, the Act prescribes: 'Whenever, under the Articles of Agreement of the Fund or the Articles of Agreement of the Bank, the approval, consent or agreement of the United States is required before an act may be done by the respective institutions, the decision as to whether such approval, consent, or agreement shall be given or refused shall ... be made by the Council, under the general direction of the President.'[712]

Similarly, and as already mentioned in Chapter I, the UK's participation in WB decision-making processes is comprehensively steered at the domestic level. The positions adopted by the UK Executive Director are formally decided by the UK Delegation to the WB with close guidance of the Department for International Development (DFID), sitting in London. On the basis of analytical support from country offices and policy division teams, DFID provides its own input on policy/project-related questions and often delineates concrete instructions to be followed by the UK's representative.[713] When it comes to the general policy framework of the

708 E. Hexner, *supra* note 587, 86.

709 Interview #XIII, 5 June 2015; Interview #XIV, 8 June 2015; Interview #XVIII, 12 June 2015; Interview #XXI, 17 June 2015; Interview #XXIV, 19 June 2015; Interview #XXVI, 22 June 2015.
Interestingly, one WB Executive Director gave as an example of domestic consultation for concrete instructions the approval of the construction of pulp mills in the Uruguay River, financed by the IFC and MIGA. That this matter was controversial became even more evident when Argentina initiated proceedings against Uruguay before the ICJ, leading to the well-known decision *Case Concerning Pulp Mills on the River Uruguay (Argentina* v. *Uruguay)*, Judgment, ICJ Reports 2010.

710 Bretton Woods Agreements Act, as amended through P.L. 114–113, Enacted 18 December 2015, in 22 US Code § 286.

711 Ibid., Sec. 4(a)(b)(1).

712 Ibid., Sec. 4(4).

713 This information was provided by officials of both the UK Delegation to the WB and the DFID (Interview #X, 27 May 2015; Interview #XIII, 5 June 2015). See also: Bretton Woods Project, 'The UK's Role in the World Bank and IMF Department for International Development and HM Treasury', 13 March 2013, available at: www.brettonwoodsproject.org/2013/03/ukinbwi/, last consulted 15 October 2018.

Bank or particularly contentious issues raised in the context of project appraisal, the Secretary of State has the final word, which is to be followed by the UK Executive Director.

The governmental apparatus in nearby Germany is likewise set up to efficiently follow and steer the country's participation in international financial institutions. The BMZ is structured along several units, among which some specifically deal with multilateral development banks such as the WB or the EBRD. As explained by a BMZ official with regard to Germany's participation in WB decision-making, the process is channelled through Executive Director Office EDS05. Once a project is in the pipeline, EDS05 sends the draft proposal to all relevant units of the BMZ, including the unit specifically dealing with the WB, and all others that can have a say on the matter at issue, from human rights to environment-related aspects. Regional units may likewise play a role in this regard. In the end, a compilation of – mostly technical – comments from the various units involved is sent back to EDS05, which can include specific suggestions to agree, abstain or vote against the project at hand. These are normally followed. The interaction is an ongoing one, inasmuch as the Executive Director can always get back to whichever unit when in need of further information, data or advice. Next to the normal procedure just described, the German Bundestag can also be engaged when critical and politically sensitive projects (e.g., the construction of dams in India) are at stake.[714]

In financial institutions where States are represented in multi-party constituencies, communication flows between Executive Directors and their national authorities can also be quite intense.[715] An EBRD member State representative noted that he had his phone permanently connected to his capital during decision-making processes – not without underlining, at the same time, the margin of *manouevre* for discussion that he was granted in such contexts.[716] Practices for developing coordination on negotiation positions are in any case varied. They depend on several factors, including the number and diversity of the States integrating the constituency, its 'culture' (i.e., the formal and informal consultation mechanisms that have developed among members) and the way voting power is distributed therein.[717] As will shortly be seen, differences among States boil down to a question of institutional availability.[718] This, in any case, does not affect the way attribution rules apply.

With regard to the WB Executive Director Office EDS20 (representing Denmark, Estonia, Finland, Iceland, Latvia, Lithuania, Norway and Sweden), for example, decision-making processes were described by a document prepared by the Swedish Ministry for Foreign Affairs as follows: 'Before board meetings, capitals normally negotiate a joint instruction to the constituency office. The Ministry for Foreign

714 Interview #VIII, 23 April 2015.
715 Interview #III, 2 June 2014.
716 Interview #VI, 23 March 2015.
717 L. Martinez-Diaz, *supra* note 252, 100.
718 D. Panke, *supra* note 104, 26, summarising such differences in the UN context.

Affairs and the Ministry of Finance handle matters concerning Sweden's involvement in the WB jointly, with the support of Sida and Swedish missions abroad.'[719] As further explained by an advisor of EDS20, capitals are sent the office's assessment of a given proposal mostly when it comes to sensitive issues or when national interests are at stake. The input received in such cases comes forth in the form of instructions.[720]

Compared to the former, representatives of developing States may be less able to comprehensively engage with institutional affairs and maintain strong communication channels with their capitals.[721] Owing to capacity constraints, the latter have less time to acquire project-related information beyond reading the staff reports, and institutional back-up from capitals does not always arrive.[722] National authorities thus tend to be more selective, by formulating concrete positions when the matter is of particular interest to them.[723] Such a state of affairs has not, in any event, detracted an advisor of a multi-party constituency representing African countries from claiming that the vote represents first of all the constituency's members; in second degree Africa; and only in third degree the international financial institution.[724]

Issues of national political calibration evince the representative character of the vote, as discussions held in 2015 on the increase of staff salaries in various international financial institutions demonstrated: while, in general, member States agreed that employee satisfaction was important and that international civil service called for high remunerations, countries like Portugal, Spain, Greece and Italy, enduring economic hardship, could not coherently vote in favour of staff salary increases, and were thus instructed accordingly.[725] It is of note that, while negative votes may be cast for emphasis in particular situations, abstention is the means normally used to show opposition.[726] As confirmed by various member State representatives (including from single-party constituencies, for that matter), it comes forth as an important political statement.[727]

Cases of opposition may also arise within the multi-party constituency itself. For this reason, the constituent instruments of some international financial institutions

719 *Swedish Assessment of Multilateral Organisations: The World Bank*, *supra* note 608, 2.

720 Interview #XII, 5 June 2015.

721 The IDB constitutes an exception to this, as it is an organisation where borrowers have considerable leeway to exert influence over institutional affairs (Interview #XVI, 11 June 2015; Interview #XXXIII, 31 June 2015).

722 In the absence of a concrete position on a certain matter, member State representatives may always choose to align themselves with a certain State or group of States – which is ultimately tantamount to assuming a position.

723 R. Stone, *supra* note 58, 59; Interview #XIV, 8 June 2015.

724 Interview #XVII, 12 June 2015.

725 Interview #V, 23 March 2015.

726 R. M. Nelson and M. A. Weiss, *supra* note 119, 9.

727 Interview #IV, 3 June 2014; Interview #XII, 5 June 2015; Interview #XIII, 5 June 2015; Interview #XVIII, 12 June 2015; Interview #XXI, 17 June 2015; Interview XXIX, 26 June 2015; Interview #XXIX, 26 June 2015; Interview #XXXIII, 31 June 2015.

such as the EBRD provide for the possibility of vote splitting.[728] In contrast, in the Bretton Woods institutions, each Executive Director is required to cast all his or her votes as a single unit,[729] and, thus, any action to be undertaken is left entirely to his or her own discretion.[730] In practice, dissenting positions are made known informally, through the issuing of 'greys', which, as already mentioned, are written statements that circulate among member State representatives prior to formal Board meetings, usually by electronic means (see below). It is, for instance, possible that, owing to particular national instructions, the Alternate Director will not co-sign with the Executive Director the 'grey' that their constituency sends to the Board.[731] In exceptional circumstances, the Executive Director may even request that the Governors of the respective members of the constituency meet in an attempt to find a common understanding.[732] Still, internal consensus is always sought and, most of the times, achieved.[733]

Executive Directors representing multiple States thus tend to have more margin of manoeuvre in their work, when compared to the *modus operandi* of representatives of a single State.[734] In any event, also in multi-party constituencies, the political direction and main policy lines of all member States are known, and must therefore be respected and pursued by their representatives.[735]

Even if some member States may be less vocal when it comes to steering the conduct of Executive Directors, the reality is that, in both single- and multi-party constituencies, whenever needed, member States may regulate, or otherwise restrain, their representatives' participation in decision-making processes.[736] This calls to mind the notion of 'capacity to prevent' discussed in Sections 2.1.2.2, B and C,[737] which entails that the entity to which the act is to be attributed is the one that is most capable of preventing the wrongful conduct, or of remedying it.

While in single-party constituencies the operation of attribution rules is more straightforward, in multi-party ones the question could be raised whether the

728 Article 29(3) of the Agreement Establishing the EBRD, *supra* note 567.

729 Article XII(3)(i) of the IMF Articles of Agreement and Article V(4)(g) of the IBRD Articles of Agreement, *supra* note 4.

730 E. Hexner, *supra* note 587, 76.

731 Interview #XXX, 26 June 2015.

732 Interview #XVII, 12 June 2015, p. 61; Interview #XXX, 26 June 2015.

733 Interview #XXI, 17 June 2015.

In his response to a parliamentary inquiry regarding Belgium's participation in the WB, the Belgian Minister of Development and Cooperation described the *modus operandi* of the country's representative in the following terms: 'En tant que *executive director* de la circonscription à laquelle appartient la Belgique, notre représentant cherche toujours à obtenir un consensus entre ses membres, avec des conclusions qui peuvent être défendues par l'ensemble des membres de notre circonscription.' See: Commission des Relations Extérieures, *supra* note 115, para. 04.04.

734 Interview #XII, 5 June 2015.

735 Interview #XII, 5 June 2015; Interview #XVII, 12 June 2015; Interview #XVIII, 12 June 2015.

736 Recall what was said in Section 2.2.1.2, C, regarding the essence of government and the qualification of State organs.

737 See: Section 2.1.2.2, C.

Executive Director's act is to be attributed to each individual State, or, rather, to the aggregation of States. As seen in Section 2.2.1.2, B, in multi-party constituencies all member States are separately involved in the election of *their* representative, which means that the latter exercises elements of governmental authority from each and every member of the constituency. The Executive Director – as an organ of a given State – can thus be seen to act 'on the joint instructions of its own and another State, or . . . [as] a single entity which is a joint organ of several States', a situation that is foreseen by the ILC in the ASR.[738] The vote of – or the position adopted by – the Executive Director is thus cast in representation of the various members of the constituency, and should thereby be attributed to each individual member State. This should not be the case, however, if a given member State specifically expresses its dissenting will through the issuing of a 'grey' or 'statement', and, naturally, in cases of vote splitting (when this is possible).

B INFORMAL GOVERNANCE PROCEDURES AS EFFECTIVE MEANS OF REPRESENTATION. The bonds that link Executive Directors to their member States are quite notorious in the informal governance procedures of institutions such as the WB and the IMF. Indeed, procedures within and outside the meetings of Executive Boards are governed by an unwritten system of standards, conventions and obligations.[739] Informal meetings customarily precede the formal meetings of the Boards (held twice a week at the WB and three times a week at the IMF). They provide a forum for Executive Directors to explore organisational, administrative and operational problems among themselves, as well as with management, and thereby play a decisive role in influencing final Board action.[740] Along these lines, an advisor of an Executive Director has even affirmed that 'the real work is done out of the Board, with 95 per cent of the time being spent in discussions with give and take from all sides'.[741]

Informal meetings are, for example, held between the members of certain blocks of States across the Executive Boards of different international financial institutions, which exist for geopolitical reasons, or because of particular interests.[742] In the IMF, one could point to the ECOFIN,[743] in the IDB to the Pacific Alliance,[744] and in the WB to the G11 or, with particular regard to African members, the African Union.[745]

738 See: para. 3 of the commentaries to Article 6 ASR, noting that in such cases, other attribution rules apply.
739 E. Hexner, *supra* note 587, 81.
740 Ibid., 89.
741 Interview #XV, 11 June 2015. The idea was similarly expressed by other member State representatives and advisors (Interview #IV, 3 June 2014; Interview #XXIX, 26 June 2015; Interview #XXX, 26 June 2015).
742 Interview #III, 2 June 2014. A brief, general account of caucuses and negotiating groups in international organisations is provided in: H. Schermers and N. Blokker, *supra* note 152, 530, 531.
743 Interview #XXVII, 25 June 2015.
744 Interview #XXXIII, 31 June 2015.
745 Interview #XXIX, 26 June 2015; Interview #XVII, 12 June 2015.

Member State representatives partaking in such blocks normally meet before formal Board meetings in order to coordinate their positions and, if possible, issue joint statements on given points in the agenda. Here, as elsewhere, the sovereign links grounding Executive Directors' votes, or imparted positions, become patent.

A crucial feature of informal 'negotiation' lies in the exchange of the already mentioned 'greys' (in the case of the IMF) or 'statements' (in the case of the WB) among Executive Directors.[746] As has been signalled, said statements constitute, in a way, a form of voting,[747] or at least complement the votes cast when formal decision-making procedures are followed. Importantly, national authorities have full access to such statements,[748] and may thereby obtain information about the sensitivities underlying Executive Board diplomacy,[749] as well as provide more direct input to their representatives.[750]

Informal governance procedures thus constitute effective means to accommodate member States' interests.[751] While this is mostly so for powerful States, less powerful ones also make use of informality to lobby the former when in need of support.[752] An example of a powerful State that routinely resorts to informal mechanisms with the aim of influencing the development of IMF conditionality decisions is that of France in matters concerning francophone Africa, where significant economic, political and military interests come into play. With particular regard to IMF operations in these countries, while French Executive Directors, like any other Executive Directors, do not participate in the Fund's missions or in negotiations to programmes, they can request special briefings with staff.[753] What is more, member State influence is even exerted directly in these contexts, as both IMF missions to Africa and African Governors often stop in Paris in order to brief the French Treasury.[754]

Formal rules are further bypassed in the IMF when lending occurs in the course of a crisis, particularly when the country at issue is a systemically important one.[755] Here, decision-making authority is centralised on a small network of senior government officials, generally the G7, with whom IMF management and staff endeavour to work out strategies, raise financing or allocate burdens. It is only when a tentative agreement is reached that the proposed package will be submitted for Board review and approval.[756]

746 A. Mountford, *supra* note 631, 16.
747 Interview #XXXII, 30 June 2015.
748 Interview #III, 2 June 2014; Interview #XXI, 17 June 2015; Interview #XXV, 22 June 2015; Interview #XXXI, 29 June 2015.
749 The expression is used in E. Hexner, *supra* note 587, 88.
750 IEO Report on IMF Governance, *supra* note 58, 13.
751 R. Stone, *supra* note 58, 1, 13–15, 33–48.
752 Interview #XXX, 26 June 2015.
753 R. Stone, *supra* note 58, 57. As noted by the author, US representatives similarly hold routine meetings with chiefs of mission prior, and subsequent to, missions to Latin American countries.
754 Ibid., 61, 175; Interview #XXVII, 25 June 2015.
755 R. Stone, *supra* note 58, 55.
756 IEO Report on IMF Governance, *supra* note 58, 6.

In order to provide a tangible image of decision-making in systemic crisis, it is instructive to quote excerpts of Boughton's comprehensive description of the 1995 Mexican Peso Crisis and how it was dealt with in IMF circles.[757] At stake was Camdessus's (IMF Managing Director at the time) proposal for a stand-by arrangement of $17.8 billion, a figure arrived at while negotiations were being held in parallel with the US Government, an additional lender to Mexico. Since disbursement would have to be urgently approved by the Board, Camdessus summoned up an exceptional Board meeting in restricted session. As Boughton reports:

> When he sketched out his request, some Directors reacted bitterly ... It appeared to them that the Managing Director had effectively committed the Fund to this course of action after discussions with the U.S. authorities but without any consultation with the rest of the Executive Board ... The IMF Executive Board approved the arrangement the next day, February 1, but only after a very long and contentious series of meetings. To give Directors time to seek advice from their national authorities, Camdessus scheduled the Board meeting for the afternoon ... The German authorities were especially upset ... [and] instructed [their Executive Director] to abstain in protest ... The G7 finance deputies conferred through a protracted conference call while the Executive Board was in session, but they failed to reach a consensus. When the Board meeting finally adjourned ... seven European chairs ... appeared to be opposed to the stand-by arrangement. Subsequently, five of those asked to be recorded formally as abstaining from the Board decision.[758]

In a story-telling way, Boughton unveils several of the elements already referred to in this chapter. Notably, he brings to view the decisive influence that the US exerted over the Fund – which, in any event, does not seem to be of a magnitude amounting to direction and control over the IMF, under Article 59 ARIO: not only did the Managing Director play an important influencing role, but also the proposed package still had to be approved by the Executive Board, which, to a certain extent, attenuates the impact of the control initially exercised. Next to this, Boughton's narration draws attention to the block of G7 negotiations (even if exceptionally unsuccessful), and, very importantly, to the omnipresence of national authorities, with whom the Executive Directors were in permanent contact. As similarly reported by Stone, during the 1 February meeting 'there was constant activity in the anteroom as directors called their capitals for instructions'.[759] Several Executive Directors, including the German Director, were instructed to abstain, which, as previously mentioned, transpires as an important political statement; so much so that, as also described by Boughton, 'Camdessus, furious at what he considered to be pointless and even hypocritical objections ... appeared "to have adrenalin coming out of his ears," but he failed to convince anyone to withdraw the abstention'.[760]

757 J. M. Boughton, *Tearing Down Walls: The International Monetary Fund 1990–1999* (2012) 455–96.
758 Ibid., 476–8.
759 R. Stone, *supra* note 58, 149.
760 J. M. Boughton, *supra* note 757, 479.

Informal governance can thus be said to play a decisive role in influencing the action of the Executive Board. As demonstrated, it constitutes an effective means to accommodate member State interests and brings to mind, once again, how pervasive member States are, as actors in their own right, in the decision-making processes of international financial institutions.

2.3 CONCLUSION OF CHAPTER II

In order to conceptualise the contours of a member State responsibility regime, it is fundamental to answer the question of how far the regime should go, and for what type of reasons.[761] In the past decades, different views within the legal epistemic community have been expressed in this respect. Section 2.1.1 undertook to retrieve them, as they shed light on the conceptual underpinnings of the current regime devised by the ILC in the ARIO and help understand why certain gaps endure in the field. As discussed, some of the latter can be explained by the fact that, since their inception, debates praised the international legal personality of international organisations as the main vantage point from which responsibility issues in an institutional context were to be addressed. An overzealous attitude towards the organisation's legal personality brought with it an insufficient exploration of the terms in which the responsibility of the State could be established for its own conduct performed in institutional settings. This issue was taken up later, in the second part of the chapter.

It was seen that policy considerations permeated the initial debates all along, which paid deference either to the independent functioning of international organisations, or to the interests of third parties. While concerns with the former would more readily lead to defending a regime of limited liability, the need to protect third parties was not unacknowledged. Accordingly, it could justify the piercing of the corporate veil under certain circumstances in order to hold member States responsible.[762]

As explained in Section 2.1.2.1, although the ILC endorsed the principle of independent responsibility of the international organisation, it did envisage a few exceptions thereof. In light of Part V, it could for instance be asked whether the influence that the G7 exerts over informal decision-making at the IMF (discussed in Section 2.2.2.2, B) could amount to direction and control as prescribed in Article 59 ARIO; or whether unanimous decision-making determining institutional action in contravention of member States' human rights obligations could constitute a means by which said States incur responsibility for circumvention, as foreseen in Article 61 ARIO.

It was concluded that member State participation in the governance bodies of international organisations could not be understood by resorting to Part V. The ARIO mainly (and correctly) treat international organisations as a unitary

761 E. Paasivirta, *supra* note 372, 51.
762 See: R. Sadurska and C. Chinkin, *supra* note 290, 873.

whole for responsibility purposes. This is problematic, however, when it comes to decision-making, as the presence of member States, in their sovereign individuality, is too strong to claim that representative organs act as a 'single unified agent'.[763] There remains no doubt as to the legal status of the acts emerging from decision-making processes as institutional decisions per se, reflecting the *volonté distincte* of the organisation. However, this autonomy of the organisation, which brings about its international responsibility for its own decisions, should not dematerialise the participation of member States in those processes. Such parallel participation could, in its own right, entail legal consequences. As demonstrated by judicial disputes such as the ICJ *FYROM* case,[764] this becomes clear when the exercise of voting rights is qualified as an act of the State, distinct from the final decision adopted, and is thereby judged in light of international law rules prescribing specific courses of State action in an institutional setting.

The participation of member States in the decision-making processes of international financial institutions was thoroughly discussed in Section 2.2. First, the international legal status of Executive Directors was scrutinised, in order to clarify the propriety of qualifying them as State organs as opposed to officials of the organisation (Section 2.2.1.2). It was seen, with regard to both single-party and multi-party contituencies, that Executive Directors have clear reporting lines to their member States and that, even when concrete instructions are not given by national authorities, there is anyhow tacit endorsement of the Executive Directors' behaviour, for these are the individuals that member States appointed to represent their interests in said multilateral cooperative forums. Here, just as in contexts where States act as implementers of institutional decisions, or as troop contributors (Section 2.1.2.2), attributing the conduct of Executive Directors (notably their exercise of voting rights) to the States they represent is the most appropriate formula to account for the margin that is left for States to act as subjects of international law underneath the institutional veil.

Observers have even argued, with regard to IMF Executive Directors, that they do better in being member States' representatives and performing an oversight role, than in delving into matters such as the technical details of negotiations, which are the functions foreseen for staff.[765] This calls to mind the question, already addressed in Section 1.3, of the (re)-allocation of sites of governance in the framework of the binary member States–international financial institution relationship. There, it was concluded that the most important manifestation of member States' power comes forth in their role as 'authority managers', which brings with it the responsibility of overseeing the operations of the organisation in order to make sure that these do not run counter to human rights protection.

763 The expression is used by V. Pettit, 'Responsibility Incorporated', 117 *Ethics* (2007) 171, 179.
764 Mentioned *supra* note 528.
765 Interview #XXXII, 30 June 2015.

To recall Brownlie, writing about the problem of delegation for international responsibility purposes,[766] '[i]n the final analysis the question is one of a duty to control and to prevent violations of particular principles or legal standards. A State cannot by delegation (even if this be genuine) avoid responsibility for breaches of its duties under international law.'[767] The discussion held in Chapter II shows that the ARIO and the ASR combined provide ways to account for Brownlie's concerns. Apart from the default responsibility of the international organisation for wrongful conduct attributable to it, two additional – even if more limited – circumstances of member State responsibility can be envisaged: the member State may be held responsible for/in connection with institutional conduct, for which it is necessary to prove the wrongfulness of the organisation's acts (except in the case of Articles 60 and 61 ARIO); and the member State may be held responsible for its own wrongful behaviour performed in an institutional setting, which solely entails proof of wrongfulness on the side of the State. The second scenario goes beyond the ARIO, which focus on excesses of power exerted by member States over international organisations, since it also enquires into power to determine whether a given agent, that is, the member State, failed to perform.

Chapter III will draw on the latter hypothesis, by focusing on the prescriptions imposed by human rights due diligence. In so doing, it provides an answer to the introductory statement of this section, i.e., it shows that the regime of member State responsibility should go as far as to hold member States responsible for failure to exercise due diligence, for reasons related to the role they play as 'authority managers' in international financial institutions.

766 Albeit in a different context, notably, that of State responsibility for setting up, or permitting the creation of, forms of local administration.

767 Emphasis in original. I. Brownlie, 'State Responsibility: The Problem of Delegation', in K. Ginther, G. Hafner, W. Lang, H. Neuhold and L. Sucharipa-Behrmann (eds.), *Völkerrecht zwischen normativem Anspruch und politischer Realität: Festschrift für Karl Zemanek zum 65. Geburtstag* (1994) 300.

III

Member States As Human Rights Protectors in International Financial Institutions: Matching Governance with Responsibility

In Chapter II, an analysis was made of the functioning of attribution in the governance bodies of international financial institutions. Drawing on such findings, Chapter III explores the terms in which international human rights law steers the conduct of Executive Directors as member State representatives in said settings and how their responsibility may ultimately be engaged when things go wrong. It does so under the fundamental premise that their actions ought to conform with the interests of the beneficiaries of multilateral cooperation.[768] The question then arises of how to substantiate these individuals' true *droit au Droit*,[769] when member State governance functions are at issue?

Driven by rule of law requirements of legality, Section 3.1 begins by emphasizing that member States preserve their international legal obligations after adhering to international organisations – a postulation that often came to the fore in debates regarding the contours of a member State responsibility regime (recall Chapter II). Section 3.2 brings the notion of the rule of law closer to a constitutionalist reading of the exercise of public power by member States. It does so under the firm belief that the determination of an individual's fate is incompatible with unfettered exercises of power, and, thus, that member State governance may only find constitutional justification where it is juxtaposed by enforceable rights of procedural fairness and due process.[770] The constitutional values of representation and responsiveness are thus discussed, with particular attention to the terms in which they proactively and retrospectively frame and tame member State governance.

Drawing on said values, and the procedural requirements they entail, Section 3.3 examines how these elements have been incorporated in the human rights regime. Based on the authoritative interpretations of human rights bodies, this section advances the view that member States have a due diligence duty to ensure that human rights are respected and protected throughout the operations of international

[768] A discussion of how to circumscribe the notion of 'beneficiaries of multilateral cooperation' will be undertaken in Section 3.4.2.1, B.

[769] A. A. Cançado Trindade, 'Prologue: An Overview of the Contribution of International Tribunals to the Rule of Law', in G. De Baere and J. Wouters (eds.), *The Contribution of International and Supranational Courts to the Rule of Law* (2015) 8.

[770] See: T. Allan, *Constitutional Justice: A Liberal Theory of the Rule of Law* (2001) 174.

organisations, owing to their *power* or *capacity to influence* institutional behaviour. As will be argued, this entails the extension of the scope of member States' human rights obligations extraterritorially (Section 2.3.1.2).

The discharge of member States' human rights due diligence duties in the particular context of international financial institutions is further explored in Section 3.4. Alive to the role that due diligence has played in international law (discussed in Section 3.4.1), Section 3.4.2 examines the terms in which it particularly conditions member States' behaviour in two instances, notably, in their participation in institutional decision-making processes, as well as in the design of the organisation's structure, procedures and operational framework. These instances constitute crucial 'case-studies', in that they are possibly the main means by which member States shape and influence institutional conduct, and, thus, where their role as 'authority managers' assumes pride of place.

As will be seen, public participation rights, such as the rights of access to information, participation in decision-making and access to justice (which have been incorporated in human rights law) bring with them important procedural requirements of conduct that affect member States' use of their voting power, as well as their behaviour prior to the adoption of a decision (Section 3.4.2.1). Furthermore, when it comes to their role in setting up the organisation's operational framework, the right of access to justice assumes the crucial function of demanding upon member States the assurance that adequate dispute settlement mechanisms are provided to individuals impacted by institutional operations (Section 3.4.2.2).

Section 3.5 finally explores the terms in which member States' failure to act diligently in the performance of their governance functions brings about their international responsibility. Placing itself on the side of the claimant, and the various elements that must be demonstrated before a court, it begins with a discussion of how to determine the wrongfulness of member State conduct (Section 3.5.1). It then proceeds to an analysis of various aspects concerning the provision of remedies to victims. The latter subject is not without its difficulties, and calls for important judgements as to what objectives are to be assigned to a system of international responsibility.[771] Notably, it entails a judgement concerning the addressees of such a system: who, among those impacted by institutional operations, is to be granted standing before a court (Section 3.5.2.1); and his or her claim is to be directed at which member States (Section 3.5.2.3)? Likewise, it entails a judgement with regard to the functions of such system: what sort of remedial claims are victims entitled to make (Section 3.5.2.2)? These questions will be answered with the stated goal in mind of ascertaining how the regime of member State responsibility can broadly serve the normative interest of ensuring an effective human rights protection.

[771] See: A. Nollkaemper and D. Jacobs, *supra* note 455, 16–19.

3.1 FRAMING THE ISSUE: THE PRESERVATION OF LEGALITY AS A CONDITION FOR MEMBERSHIP IN INTERNATIONAL ORGANISATIONS

It is almost an axiomatic truth that, as members of international organisations, States are not exonerated from their previous duties under general international law.[772] The fact that member States' legal existence pertains to numerous legal regimes necessarily implies that States' margin of manoeuvre within institutional settings is subjected to limitations. Moreover, it entails that the space is created, regardless of the model of institutional design adopted, for States not to act against their prior obligations. Essentially, States should not achieve, through the organisation, a result that is precluded under international law.[773]

This is at times explicitly embraced by international instruments, even if in somewhat generic terms.[774] In addition, the interpretative work undertaken by international and regional tribunals as diversified as the ECtHR, the International Criminal Tribunal for the Former Yugoslavia (ICTY) and the WTO Panel has also contributed to buttressing the requirement of preservation of legality.[775] The ECtHR's case-law, which will be more thoroughly discussed below, includes indeed a string of cases where the analysis of member State responsibility essentially drew on such a premise.

Generally, through an extensive interpretation of international legal rules, it has been observed that member States have an obligation to not tolerate, encourage or incite certain conduct within institutional contexts.[776] Moreover, legal provisions requiring States to undertake all necessary measures to prevent a certain event can be said to apply as well in an institutional context. This is, for instance, the case of the obligation to 'undertake to prevent' genocide, prescribed by Article I of the Genocide Convention,[777] as straightforwardly advanced by various legal scholars[778]

772 See, e.g.: the understanding espoused already in 1961 with regard to the member States of the then European Communities by P. Pescatore, 'Les Relations Extérieures des Communautés Européennes', 103 RCADI 1961/II, 1, 217. See also: para. 5 of the commentaries to Article 58 and para. 9 of the commentaries to Article 61 ARIO.

773 ILC, Special Rapporteur Gaja, *Fourth Report on Responsibility of International Organizations, supra* note 356, para. 67.

774 See, inter alia: Article 3(7) Convention on Access to Information, Public Participation in Decision-Making and Access to Justice in Environmental Matters, 2161 UNTS 450, 25 June 1998 (Aarhus Convention); and Article 139(3) of the United Nations Convention on the Law of the Sea 10 December 1982, 1833 UNTS 397.

775 With regard to the ICTY, see: *Prosecutor* v. *Simic et al., Decision on Motion for Judicial Assistance to be Provided by SFOR and Others*, Trial Chamber, International Criminal Tribunal for the Former Yugoslavia, 18 October 2000, paras. 46 and 47. Turning to the WTO, see: *Airbus* case, *supra* note 434, paras. 7.169–7.175.

776 See: F. Naert, *supra* note 519, 164.

777 Convention on the Prevention and Punishment of the Crime of Genocide, 78 UNTS 277, 9 December 1948.

778 See, inter alia: G. Gaja, 'The Role of the United Nations in Preventing and Suppressing Genocide', in *The UN Genocide Convention: A Commentary* (2009) 405; A. Zimmermann, *supra* note 524,

and the ICJ.[779] As will be further explored in this chapter, the most tangible implication of these obligations in an institutional context is their conditioning of the exercise of voting rights by member states.

It is of note that legal constraints upon member State conduct in the framework of international organisations may at times give rise to conflicts of authority, i.e., to conflicting obligations binding upon States under different legal orders, notably, the internal legal order of the organisation and the international treaty to which the State is also a party.[780] In such instances, member States must undertake a proportionality test[781] and find a compromise within their own margin of appreciation and action. Importantly, there must always be some space for member States to accommodate legality (i.e., the general framework of international law). The crux of the question thus lies on what member States *do* or *omit to do* in a given institutional context in light of their subsisting international legal commitments.

Beyond member State compliance with international legal rules, there are still significant questions to be asked if one is to espouse a thick rule of law perspective[782] to assess member State governance. These questions have to do with the legitimacy of the exercise of public power[783] by member States and the level of protection that is afforded thereof to the individual – notably, to

885–8; A. Peters, 'The Security Council's Responsibility to Protect', 8 IOLR (2011) 15, 38–40; P. Palchetti, *supra* note 682, 352, 359, 360; and F. Naert, *supra* note 519, 164.

779 *Case Concerning Application of the Convention on the Prevention and Punishment of the Crime of Genocide (Bosnia and Herzegovina* v. *Serbia and Montenegro)*, Judgment, ICJ Reports 2007, para. 427.

780 These conflicts may of course also arise with regard to member State obligations flowing from their membership in other international organisations. For an example of a conflict of authority between State obligations as members of the EBRD and the EU, see: A. S. Barros, 'EBRD Statement on Operational Approach in Russia', in Oxford International Organizations Database (OXIO) (2017).

781 P. De Sena and M. C. Vitucci, *supra* note 523, 216 et seq.

782 The distinction is often made in the literature between 'thin' (i.e., formalist) and 'thick' (i.e., substantive) approaches to the rule of law, including the international rule of law. While the former is rather formalist and finds contentment in the observance of legality (which in itself entails respect for certain requirements such as certainty and predictability), the latter appeals to substantive standards, notably democracy and respect for human rights, as necessary to achieve the rule of law ideal. The UN has paid increased attention to the rule of law in recent years and, to higher or lower degrees, has publicly supported a 'thick' rule of law perspective, as demonstrated by the UNGA *Declaration of the High-Level Meeting of the General Assembly on the Rule of Law at the National and International Levels*, UNGA Resolution A/RES/67/1 (2012) (see especially paras. 5, 7 and 14). For a more detailed account of the distinction between 'thin' and 'thick' conceptions of the rule of law, see: N. Hachez, 'What Elements of the Rule of Law Can Be Put to Use at International Level?', 2 RBDI (2013) 307, 310–14.

783 See, inter alia: T. Gemkow and M. Zürn, 'Constraining International Authority through the Rule of Law: Legitimatory Potential and Political Dynamics', in M. Zürn, A. Nollkaemper and R. Peerenboom (eds.), *Rule of Law Dynamics – In an Era of International and Transnational Governance* (2012) 68–89, inquiring whether it is possible to improve the legitimacy of international public authority through the enactment of institutional procedures that introduce, at the international level, components of the rule of law, in particular human rights protection, and whether such procedures actually exist.

individual dignity.[784] A thin rule of law approach would not sufficiently account for the latter concerns. Here, then, the rule of law is brought close to a constitutionalist understanding of (global) governance,[785] as will be further discussed in the subsequent section.

3.2 A CONSTITUTIONALIST READING OF STATE PARTICIPATION IN INTERNATIONAL ORGANISATIONS

Earlier in this book it was highlighted that the conduct performed by States in international organisations is conditioned by domestic legal restraints, and is thereby subjected, to varied extents, to domestic checks and balances (see Section 1.1.1). It was then noted that governmental action, including in foreign affairs, must be undertaken within the limits of law and the requirements of political legitimacy. Against this backdrop, the present section analyses how these notions are to be carried over, in some form, to the global realm.[786] If the aim of global governance is to achieve 'normatively laden political goals when handling common problems',[787] and if the exercise of public power, including at the global level, carries with it certain constitutional conditions,[788] then it should be asked whether there are fundamental norms governing the performance, by member States, of governmental functions through international organisations, as well as the relationship between member States and the individuals affected by institutional operations.[789]

3.2.1 *Ensuring Representation and Responsiveness towards the Interests of the Beneficiaries of Multilateral Cooperation*

The idea of checks and balances at the global level must be read in generic terms, in that otherwise one runs the risk of 'mythologising' national democratic governance

784 R. Dworkin, 'The Rule of Law', 4 Law Ukr. Legal J (2013) 7, 11.

785 See: M. Loughlin, 'The Rule of Law: A Theme in Five Variations', 10 FLC (2015) 437, 444, 445, explaining the rule of law as a principle of constitutionalism, although focusing solely on its separation of powers dimension.

786 Cf. N. Tsagourias, 'Introduction – Constitutionalism: A Theoretical Roadmap', in N. Tsagourias (ed.), *Transnational Constitutionalism: International and European Perspectives* (2010) 5, noting that the restraints posed by constitutionalism at the international level are of a different kind and degree from those at the domestic level, where powers are separated.

787 M. Zürn, *supra* note 290, 731.

788 P. Allott, 'Intergovernmental Societies and the Idea of Constitutionalism', in J. M. Coicaud and V. Heiskanen (eds.), *The Legitimacy of International Organisations* (2001) 91, 92.

789 In the remainder of this section, some level of generalisation is unavoidable. The claim that it is possible to identify certain constitutional values as pillars of the international legal order bypasses, to a certain extent, the fact that power relations between States are unequal, as well as the fact that it may be hard to reach a truly common understanding of what such values should be – issues, in sum, that call to mind what Hedley Bull once termed 'premature global solidarism'. See: A. Hurrel, *On Global Order: Power, Values and the Constitution of International Society* (2007) 55.

as a model for international governance.[790] For one, the notion of reflexive identity that is inherent in a constituent power (in the sense of collective self-rule) does not apply at the global level, as the individuals affected by member States' actions, performed in plenary and non-plenary organs, do not normally correspond to those that put them in power.[791] Accordingly, one can hardly link the idea of international constitutional order with self-government.[792] The crux of the analysis is thus not on how those who are represented control the exercise of power by their representatives in institutional settings, but, rather, on how this power is controlled by those who are affected by it.[793]

Questioning the relevance of originalist assumptions for an assessment of the legitimacy of constitutional arrangements, Walker talks about 'post-constituent constitutionalism' (with reference to the EU), a dynamic concept that draws attention to the various ways in which different constitutional forms may interact over time, thereby allowing for the subsequent development of an initially absent supranational constituent power.[794] Constitutional demands thus also have a bearing upon the responsiveness, towards individuals, of State participation in international organisations – 'the individuals' being the circle of persons that are *affected* by State action or inaction, i.e., the various 'stakeholders' whose lives are shaped by the situation in question.[795]

The present query is not aimed at devising the contours of a core international value system against which the conduct of member States may be judged – even if it is assumed that human rights norms integrate such a system (see Section 3.2.2). The discussion herein raised rather refers to the purpose and functions of governance along the lines of 'functionalist constitutionalism',[796] which essentially calls for an analysis of how to discipline the exercise of public authority by member States in order to comply with rule of law prescriptions. Recognisably, constitutionalism also

790 E. De Wet, 'The International Constitutional Order', 55 Int'l & Comp LQ (2006) 51, 71–4.

791 See: H. Lindahl, 'Constituent Power and Reflexive Identity: Towards an Ontology of Collective Selfhood', in M. Loughlin and N. Walker (eds.), op. cit. *supra* note 50, 15, who uses the concept of reflexive identity in the sense of self-constitution and discusses the terms in which the notion of 'self' may be defined.

792 Interestingly, however, Fassbender has contended that the UN Charter could be treated as a constitution, 'the people' being the authorising agent. See: B. Fassbender, *supra* note 50, especially 281–90.

793 The scope of representation at the global level must thus be widened, as discussed by A. Kuper, *supra* note 283, 126, 127.

794 N. Walker, 'Post-Constituent Constitutionalism? The Case of the European Union', in M. Loughlin and N. Walker (eds.), op. cit. *supra* note 50, especially 261–4.

795 See: J. A. Scholte, 'Reconstructing Contemporary Democracy', 15 Ind J Global Legal Stud (2008) 305, especially 309, 329, 336 and 340.
A discussion of who can be considered 'affected' by institutional and member State conduct will be undertaken in Sections 3.4.2.1 and 3.5.2.1.

796 The term is used by Klabbers, drawing inspiration from Martin Loughlin's work on 'The Functionalist Style in International Law'. See J. Klabbers, 'Setting the Scene', in J. Klabbers, A. Peters and G. Ulfstein (eds.), *The Constitutionalization of International Law* (2009) 9, 10, 26, 27.

serves the aim of organising the global public space, by structuring relations in society between States, and between them and international organisations. As has been contended, what is necessary in order to grasp these relationships is to look into the rationale behind the restraining function of constitutionalism, that is, to protect people against exercises of political power by a given entity.[797]

With constitutionalism, the individual (i.e., his/her well-being, interests, needs and rights) comes forth as the ultimate unit of legal concern.[798] Such humanistic principle has led Peters to proclaim the 'humanization of sovereignty',[799] which brings with it States' obligation to protect human rights and, especially, to meet their core protection responsibilities.[800] Following this line of thought, the interests of the beneficiaries of international cooperation become the main reference point to determine how member State governance is to be constrained in constitutionalist terms. In essence, what is required of the international legal order is that it frames and tames member State power in terms that are both representative of, and responsive to, said interests through some form of institutionalized protection.

The understanding that the exercise of power in the global realm must be representative and responsive to the interests of individuals has been commonly advanced by authors endorsing a constitutionalist approach to international law.[801] Often, the discussion unfolds through a proceduralist lens, by invoking rule of law-based procedural standards, guarantees of fair trial, and mechanisms of review.[802] Ultimately, it is assumed, proceduralisation increases the likelihood of fair and acceptable outcomes.[803] This resonates with writings of Global Administrative Law (GAL) scholars, who also emphasize the need to discipline the exercise of public power through constitution-like principles such as participation, transparency and accountability[804] – principles which have already been tested in the framework of international institutional law.[805]

Global multilevel governance thus calls for a two-stage legitimation process.[806] In its participatory dimension, constitutionalism boasts a prospective tone, requiring

797 N. Tsagourias, *supra* note 786, 5.

798 A. Peters, 'Membership in the Global Constitutional Community', in J. Klabbers, A. Peters and G. Ulfstein (eds.), op. cit. *supra* note 796, 155, 179. See also: J. Waldron, 'The Rule of International Law', 30 Harv JL & Pub Pol'y (2008) 15, 25.

799 A. Peters, 'Humanity As the A and of Sovereignty', 20(3) EJIL (2009).

800 B. Fassbender, 'Article 2(1)', in B. Simma, D. Khan, G. Nolte and A. Paulus (eds.), op. cit. *supra* note 212, 156.

801 See: J. Klabbers, *supra* note 796, 26, 27.

802 See the observations made by Peters on the discussions led by academics and practitioners regarding the UNSC practice of listing and delisting terrorism suspects in: A. Peters, *supra* note 798, 164, 165.

803 Ibid., 177, 178.

804 See: S. Cassese, 'Administrative Law without the State? The Challenge of Global Regulation', 37 JILP (2006) 663, 685.

805 For an application of these broadly defined principles to international organisations, see: B. Kingsbury and L. Casini, 'Global Administrative Law Dimensions of International Organizations Law', 6 IOLR (2009) 319, 325, 333 et seq.

806 See: M. Zürn, *supra* note 290, 736, 737.

that those who are governed by rules and decisions somehow participate in the process of elaboration of such rules and decisions. Certainly, individuals need not cause or generate every decision for governance to be representative, but they must be afforded some leeway to have an impact on governance[807] and shape its outcome.[808] Pragmatically put, this requires the institutional conditions necessary for good judgments about interests to be made, by adequately informed and capable officials, who are empowered and constrained to act on such judgments responsibly.[809] Moreover, constitutionalism brings with it a retrospective dimension: it requires that the governed are granted the opportunity to exert some sort of *control* over the actions and omissions of those that govern, and, eventually, to seek redress for whichever wrong arises therefrom.

Doctrinal attempts to introduce elements of the rule of law tradition in international institutional contexts have mainly drawn on the exercise of governmental power by international organisations. To illustrate this, mention could be made of the ILA 2004 Report on the Accountability of International Organisations, which applies a set of procedural principles to international organisations, such as that of stating the reasons for their decisions and the principle of participatory decision-making, with the aim of constitutionalising their operations.[810] Still, to the extent that member States *share* the exercise of sovereign powers with international organisations, such as in the context of decision-making processes (recall Chapter I), it can only be apposite to apply (*mutatis mutandis*) this sort of procedural rules to member State conduct as well.[811] Indeed, as has been noted by Klabbers, contemporary calls for constitutionallism are partly misdirected inasmuch as they focus single-mindedly on organisations as separate entities, in isolation from their member States.[812]

Ultimately, in framing and taming exercises of sovereign power, by both member States and international organisations, constitutionalism emerges as an important means to (re-)organise and (re-)allocate competences among the subjects of the international legal order, rendering them more understandable to all stakeholders.[813] What is more, it certainly responds to States' interests (and those of international organisations for that matter) of living together in a predictable manner.[814]

807 A. Kuper, *supra* note 283, 79.

808 J. A. Scholte, *supra* note 795, 336.

809 Such are the main elements that are necessary to examine whether political representation can be said to serve the best interests of the public, as can be deduced from Kuper's study on representation as responsiveness, in A. Kuper, *supra* note 283, 77 et seq.

810 *Supra* note 50, 8–15.

811 As warned by Bogdandy, an equal application of general principles of public international law to all exercises of public power is hardly conceivable. See: A. Von Bogdandy, 'General Principles of International Public Authority: Sketching a Research Filed', in A. Von Bogdandy, R. Wolfrum, J. V. Bernstorff, P. Dann and M. Goldmann (eds.), op. cit. *supra* note 50, 747.

812 J. Klabbers, 'Constitutionalism Lite', 1 IOLR (2004) 31, 44.

813 E. De Wet, *supra* note 790, 51.

814 N. Tsagourias, 'The Constitutional Role of General Principles of Law in International and European Jurisprudence', in N. Tsagourias (ed.), op. cit. *supra* note 786, 104.

3.2.2 *The Constitutionalist Traits of International Human Rights Law*

International human rights law, which presents obvious constitutional traits,[815] emerges as a crucial yardstick to judge member State performance. It is, by its very nature, permeated by the values of representation and responsiveness; here, too, procedural concerns take up a fundamental role, to ensure that human rights are duly respected (i.e., not directly interfered with by the State) and protected (i.e., requiring the State to take positive action to prevent third parties from interfering with human rights). Mention can for instance be made of the due process guarantees contained in Articles 8 and 10 of the Universal Declaration of Human Rights (UDHR);[816] Articles 2(3) and 14 of the International Covenant on Civil and Political Rights;[817] Articles 6 and 13 of the ECHR;[818] Articles 8 and 25 of the American Convention on Human Rights (ACHR);[819] Article 7 of the African Charter on Human and Peoples' Rights (Banjul Charter);[820] and Article 9 of the Arab Charter on Human Rights.[821] Based on an analysis of these provisions, together with constitutional and statutory rules and practices common to a great variety of States, Fassbender defined 'fair and clear procedures' as requiring a number of

815 De Wet, for instance, espouses the existence of an international value system informed by human rights norms. According to the author, this system is a layered one, wherein *jus cogens* norms assume a normatively superior character, followed by *erga omnes* human rights obligations of a customary character, and a third layer of *erga omnes* norms with increased – but not unanimous – recognition in international law. See: De Wet, *supra* note 790, 57–63.

816 UDHR, UN Doc. A/810 at 71, 10 December 1948.

817 International Covenant on Civil and Political Rights, 999 UNTS 171, 16 December 1966. See also: UN Human Rights Committee, General Comment 29, States of Emergency (article 4), UN Doc. CCPR/C/21/Rev.1/Add.11 (2001) paras. 15 and 16.

818 The ECtHR had the opportunity to dissect Article 6(1) of the Convention in the *Golder* case (*Case of Golder* v. *The United Kingdom*, App. No. 4451/70, 21 February 1975), where the question was raised as to whether the right of access to courts or tribunals could be read into the right to an effective remedy. Noting the reference to the rule of law contained in the Preamble of the Convention, the Court asserted that 'one can scarcely conceive of the rule of law without there being a possibility of having access to the courts' (para. 34). Furthermore, it characterised this right as 'one of the universally "recognised" fundamental principles of law', the same being true with regard to 'the principle of international law which forbids the denial of justice' (para. 35).

819 In a similar way to its European counterpart, the IACtHR has determined that States Parties to the ACHR, 9 ILM 673, 22 November 1969, 'have an obligation to provide effective judicial remedies to victims of human rights violations (Art. 25), remedies that must be substantiated in accordance with the rules of due process of law (Art. 8(1)), all in keeping with the general obligation of such States to guarantee the free and full exercise of the rights recognized by the Convention to all persons subject to their jurisdiction (Art. 1)', in: *Velasquez Rodriguez*, Preliminary Objections, Judgment of 26 June 1987, Series C No. 1, para. 91.

820 African Charter on Human and Peoples' Rights, 1520 UNTS 217, 27 June 1981.

821 999 UNTS 171, 22 May 2004. It has moreover been contended that, beyond the human rights regime, it is possible to argue for the existence of universal principles of procedural due process (even if conceding that there may be well-founded arguments against such a universalist perspective). See: G. della Cananea, 'Procedural Due Process of Law beyond the State', in A. Von Bogdandy, R. Wolfrum, J. V. Bernstorff, P. Dann and M. Goldmann (eds.), op. cit. *supra* note 50, 965–99.

minimum standards including the right to be informed, the right to be heard and the right to an effective review mechanism.[822]

Importantly, for international responsibility to be invoked, the exact scope and intensity of said rights must be determined in accordance with the specific circumstances of the situation at stake.[823] Hence, member States' legal obligations acquire particular configurations when they act as creators or as participants in international organisations. As will shortly be seen, human rights bodies have not provided for comprehensive normative guidance on how the human rights obligations of States apply in institutional contexts, but have consistently advanced the fundamental notion that State adherence to international organisations implies the setting up of (procedural) guarantees to ensure an effective human rights protection.

While such guarantees of protection can easily be seen to derive from the rights enunciated above (such as the right to an effective remedy), they have also been considered as integral components of human rights in general, through extensive interpretations of the latter.[824] Which specific rights are to be protected will of course depend on the field of activity of the international organisation at stake: while economic and social rights might be easily precipitated by the IMF, the WB or the World Intellectual Property Organization, the latter two institutions will likely bring attention to other rights in addition to these, such as, respectively, cultural and environmental rights and intellectual property rights. When discussing the authoritative interpretations of human rights bodies on human rights protection requisites, the following section will thus focus on their application in the context of international financial institutions.

Important to retain from the constitutionalist discourse is that if the international value system is to be seen as a layered one, it places certain values and principles, such as representation and responsiveness, in a normatively higher position. These values provide the necessary framework to interpret member States' human rights obligations. Seen from this perspective, constitutionalism translates into a 'mindset',[825] that is, into an 'ideal' that guides legal (in this case, human rights) reasoning towards 'fidelity to that idea of law'.[826]

822 B. Fassbender, 'Targeted Sanctions Imposed by the UN Security Council and Due Process Rights: A Study Commissioned by the UN Office of Legal Affairs and Follow-Up Action by the United Nations', reprinted 3 IOLR (2006) 437.

823 Ibid., 447, 476.

824 See Section 3.4.2.

825 M. Koskenniemi, *supra* note 79.

826 G. De Baere, 'European Integration and the Rule of Law in Foreign Policy', in J. Dickson and P. Eleftheriadis (eds.), *Philosophical Foundations of European Union Law* (2012) 372, 373.

3.3 MEMBER STATES OF INTERNATIONAL (FINANCIAL) INSTITUTIONS AS GUARANTORS OF HUMAN RIGHTS PROTECTION

In 2000, Heads of State and Government gathered at the UN to adopt the Millennium Declaration, whereby they committed to an ambitious set of collective responsibilities and a duty 'to all peoples of the world'.[827] They also affirmed their strong support for international cooperation in solving international problems of an economic, social and cultural character.[828] Despite the absence of clear human rights language in the Millennium Development Goals framework, the outcome document of the 2010 Millennium Summit does acknowledge the fundamentality of respecting, promoting and protecting human rights in international development cooperation.[829] Importantly, the new global development framework designed five years later, with the adoption of the 2030 Agenda for Sustainable Development and the Addis Ababa Action Agenda, strongly endorses human rights principles and standards.[830]

Notwithstanding such developments, the discharge of the human rights responsibilities of member States of international financial institutions remains underdeveloped, which is hardly understandable considering that some States already apply a human-rights-based approach to development in their own policies or advocate human rights in their foreign affairs.[831] There is no need for new law, but, rather, to build on existing human rights norms and to clarify their scope of application in institutional frameworks. It is important to note that, with regard to IBRD member States for example, more than 82 per cent of the voting shares are held by States which have ratified at least five of the ten core international human rights treaties. The percentage rises up to 97 per cent in the case of the AIIB.[832]

827 United Nations Millennium Declaration, UNGA Resolution A/RES/55/2, UN Doc. A/55/L.2 (2000) para. 2.

828 Ibid., para. 4.

829 *Keeping the promise: united to achieve the Millennium Development Goals*, UN Doc. A/65/L.1 (2010).

830 See, respectively: 'Transforming our World: the 2030 Agenda for Sustainable Development', endorsed by UNGA Resolution A/RES/70/1 (2015); and 'Addis Ababa Action Agenda of the Third International Conference on Financing for Development' (2015), endorsed by UNGA 69/313 (2015). See also: 'Busan Partnership for Effective Development Co-Operation, Fourth High Level Forum on Aid Effectiveness, Busan, Republic of Korea' (2011), which, by 2014, had been endorsed by 161 states, according to the OECD, 'Towards more effective development co-operation: Overview of monitoring findings', in *Making Development Co-operation More Effective: 2014 Progress Report* (2014).

831 The question is thus also one of international policy coherence. See, e.g.: the Human Rights Action Plan of the Foreign Service of Finland 2013–2015, whereby the Ministry of Foreign Affairs is responsible for 'actively work[ing] to strengthen the universality of human rights through both bilateral cooperation and multilateral cooperation'. For other examples, see: S. McInerney-Lankford, 'International Development Actors and Human Rights', in M. Langford, A. Sumner and A. E. Yamin (eds.), *The Millennium Development Goals and Human Rights: Past, Present and Future* (2013) 176–8, 182, 183 and 186.

832 See: German Institut for Human Rights, 'Submission for the Review of the World Bank's Environmental and Social Framework (ESF): Comments on the Draft Environmental and Social Framework as Published in July 2014', 27 February 2015 (available at: https://consultations.worldbank.org/Data/hub/

Interestingly, the IDB's Operational Policy on Gender Equality makes explicit reference in its opening paragraph to the existing human rights obligations of the Bank's member States (including those stemming from the UDHR and CEDAW), as if justifying its adoption.[833] As was already noted, the persisting human rights obligations of member States do have a bearing upon the ways in which international financial institutions come to operate. They play a conditioning role in institutional design, in the setting up of the institutions' policy framework and in the monitoring of institutional activity. Human rights courts and bodies have not fallen short of conveying this message, as the following sections will demonstrate.

3.3.1 *The European Human Rights Regime As a Point of Departure*

Since the 1990s, the ECtHR has pronounced a significant number of decisions dealing with the human rights responsibility of member States of international organisations.[834] The jurisprudential developments advanced by the Court are in reality unprecedented when compared to the practically inexistent treatment of the subject in other regional human rights regimes.[835] Despite its regional mandate, it is worth noting that the ECtHR's authoritative interpretations apply to forty-seven States,[836] all of which are for instance also members of the Bretton Woods institutions (except Andorra, Liechtenstein and Monaco) and the EBRD (except Andorra

files/20150227_gihr_wb_sg_submission_esp_-_ess_1-2-7-10_commentary_-_gesamt.pdf, last consulted 15 October 2018); and German Institute for Human Rights, 'Consultation on AIIB Environmental and Social Framework (ESF): Comments on the AIIB's Draft Environmental and Social Framework dated 3rd August 2015' (available at: www.institut-fuer-menschenrechte.de/fileadmin/user_upload/Publikationen/Stellungnahmen/Comments_on_the_AIIBs_Draft_Environmental_and_Social_Framework_23_October_2015.pdf, last consulted 15 October 2018).

833 Inter-American Development Bank, Operational Policy on Gender Equality in Development, 3 November 2010, para. 1.1.

834 Already in the 1970s, given the (then) European Commission of Human Rights' prompt assertions of lack of jurisdiction *ratione personae* to examine complaints directed against international organisations such as the EC, the inquiry quickly turned into whether member States could be found responsible for acts performed in an institutional framework allegedly in violation of the ECHR. In the cases put before the supervisory bodies of the convention, the legal analysis has drawn on the terms in which the ECHR applies following the transfer of portions of sovereignty to an international body. Applications have dealt with member State responsibility for the violation of ECHR rights in the context of the adoption and mostly of the implementation of EC measures, be it the execution of a decision of the ECJ or the implementation of a directive or regulation. For an overview of early case-law, see: R. Lawson and H. Schermers, *supra* note 511, 678; for an account of subsequent ECtHR decisions, see: C. Ryngaert, 'The European Court of Human Rights' Approach to the Responsibility of Member States in Connection with Acts of International Organizations', 60(4) Int'l & Comp LQ (2011) 997.

835 Within the Inter-American human rights regime, to the author's knowledge only one petition has so far been filed before the Inter-American Commission on Human Rights, notably, the *Chixoy Dam* petition, *supra* note 48.

836 See: www.coe.int/en/web/conventions/full-list/-/conventions/treaty/005/signatures, last consulted 15 October 2018.

and Monaco) – institutions where EU member States undoubtedly play a prominent and influential role.

The present section will focus on the terms in which the duty of States to preserve legality under the ECHR has been delineated.[837] As will be seen, the ECtHR has assertively advanced the understanding that the transfer of competences to international organisations does not exclude member States' responsibility under the ECHR. The Court has developed less on how this premise relates to the extraterritoriality of member States' human rights obligations, yet, based on the duty of due diligence, it becomes clearer what the scope of the regime is.

3.3.1.1 The Transfer of the Exercise of Powers to International Organisations and the Principle of 'Equivalent Protection'

The contribution of the ECtHR to the general understanding of member State obligations following their adherence to international organisations cannot be examined without first taking note of the impact that the then European Commission of Human Rights had on the Court's case-law. In *M. & Co.* v. *Germany*,[838] where it dealt with the responsibility of Germany for having given effect to a decision of the then EC Court of Justice, the Commission put forward a principled approach that would highly influence the unfolding of subsequent jurisprudence: the understanding that the transfer of powers to an international organisation 'does not necessarily exclude a State's responsibility under the Convention with regard to the exercise of the transferred powers'.[839] In this vein, such transfer is not prohibited, provided that, within the organisation, fundamental rights receive an 'equivalent protection'.[840]

The well-known *Matthews*[841] and *Waite and Kennedy*[842] decisions of the ECtHR were construed along these lines. As already discussed in Section 2.1.3.3, *Matthews* involved the responsibility of the UK for not having ensured that within the legal

837 While it is true that the ECHR mostly prescribes civil and political rights, elements of ESC rights can also be found thereof – the Court's vast environmental jurisprudence being a case in point. Through an evolutionary interpretation of the convention, the Court has considered environmental rights as contained in, derived from or implied in certain human rights. See, e.g.: *Lopez Ostra* v. *Spain*, App. No. 16798/90, 9 December 1994, paras. 51–60, and *Guerra and Others* v. *Italy* (App. No. 116/1996/735/932, 19 February 1998, paras. 56–60. As will be discussed below, all such findings are of pertinence when judging the performance of States as members of international financial institutions.

838 *M. & Co.* v. *the Federal Republic of Germany*, App. No. 13258/87, Decision of 9 February 1990, Decisions and Reports, Vol. 64, 138.

839 Ibid., 145.

840 Ibid. See: M. Milanovic, 'Norm Conflict in International Law: Whither Human Rights?', 20(1) Duke J Comp & Int'l L (2009) 69, 113, referring to the use of the principle of equivalent protection as a method of conflict avoidance (between the ECHR and the founding treaty of an international organisation) through harmonious interpretation.

841 *Supra* note 500.

842 *Waite and Kennedy* v. *Germany*, App. No. 26083/94, 18 February 1999.

system of the (then) European Community laws would not be passed that were incompatible with the State's obligations under the Convention.[843] More concretely, the case regarded the 1994 elections for the European Parliament and the fact that residents of Gibraltar, a dependent territory of the UK, had been denied their right to vote under the terms of an EC Act from 1976.[844] Against this backdrop, the applicant argued that the UK had failed to comply with Article 3 of Protocol 1 to the ECHR, a provision that secured her right to free elections.[845] In response, the UK mainly based its argumentation on imputability questions[846] and the non-applicability of Article 3 of Protocol 1 to the facts under discussion, on grounds that the ECHR did not impose, upon States, obligations relating to the undertakings of a supranational organisation, in respect of which the former had limited their own sovereignty.[847]

The ECtHR thus had before it the question of whether and in what terms the UK was responsible for 'securing' the rights contained in Article 3 of Protocol No. 1.[848] In order to answer this question, the Court would have to clearly delineate a principled basis for its analysis. It was in this context that it famously held that '[t]he Convention does not exclude the transfer of competences to international organisations provided that Convention rights continue to be "secured". Member States' responsibility therefore continues even after such a transfer.'[849] From such an assertion it follows that it is not solely the initial act of establishing an international organisation and drawing up its operational framework that matters to the Court, but also the *continued* participation of member States in institutional affairs. A balance would thus have to be sought between the general interest of States in cooperating within the framework of the EC and the protection of the rights enshrined in the ECHR.[850]

843 For an in-depth analysis of this case, see: A. S. Barros, 'Matthews v. The United Kingdom', in C. Ryngaert, I. Dekker, R. Wessel and J. Wouters (eds.), op. cit. *supra* note 101, 286–99.

844 EC Act Concerning the Election of the Representatives of the European Parliament by Direct Universal Suffrage of 1976, *OJ* L 278, 8 October 1976.

845 Article 3 of Protocol 1 to the ECHR reads as follows: 'The High Contracting Parties undertake to hold free elections at reasonable intervals by secret ballot, under conditions which will ensure the free expression of the opinion of the people in the choice of the legislature.'

846 Already dealt with in Section 2.1.3.3.

847 *Matthews* case, para. 36.

848 As a matter of fact, examining whether the 1976 Act entered into by the UK would not detract it from guaranteeing its ECHR obligations entailed a judgement on the compatibility of a provision pertaining to the EC legal system with the ECHR. This was the first case where an analysis of the sort was undertaken within the European human rights system, and, thus, constitutes a turning point in the jurisprudence of the ECtHR.

849 *Matthews* case, para. 32.

850 It is important to note that, although the Court did not explicitly refer to the 'equivalent protection' requirement espoused by the Commission in earlier case-law (recall the *M. & Co.* case referred to above), it presupposed such an approach in its reasoning. In fact, the ECtHR observed at the outset (para. 33) that the 1976 Act, while a treaty within the Community legal order, could not be challenged before the then ECJ, which essentially meant that the Community legal system did not offer protection for the right to free elections equivalent to that required of States under Article 3 of Protocol No. 1 of the ECHR. See also para. 42, where the ECtHR noted that there had been 'no submission that there exist alternative means of providing for electoral representation of the population of Gibraltar in the European Parliament, and the Court finds no indication of any'.

Underlying the ECtHR's willingness to examine the UK's compliance with its guaranteeing duties was the Court's realisation that 'legislation emanating from the legislative process of the European Community affects the population of Gibraltar in the same way as legislation which enters the domestic legal order exclusively via the House of Assembly [of Gibraltar]'.[851] Accordingly, inasmuch as the ECHR was intended to guarantee practical and effective rights, the UK's responsibility could be engaged regardless of whether the source of the violation was to be found in domestic or European legislation.[852]

In order to eventually establish responsibility in this case, the ECHR would have to be interpreted as imposing upon State Parties obligations extending to the legal system of a supranational representative organ. 'Legislature', in the sense of Article 3 of Protocol No. 1, would thus have to encompass elections to the European Parliament. It is of note that, according to the European Commission of Human Rights, such an understanding implied extending the scope of Article 3 'beyond what was intended by the drafters of the Convention and beyond the object and purpose of the provision'.[853] The ECtHR concluded the opposite. Based on the character of the ECHR as a living instrument and an interpretation of the obligations prescribed therein in light of present day conditions, the ECtHR found Article 3 to encompass electoral representation in the European Parliament.[854]

The Court's reasoning brings to the fore an important message: it proves that, although human rights provisions may not readily seem to apply to institutional contexts, they are still susceptible to extensive interpretation and thereby account for the new ways in which States endeavour to cooperate internationally. As observed by the ECtHR, '[t]o the extent that Contracting States organise common constitutional or parliamentary structures by international treaties, the Court must take these mutually agreed structural changes into account in interpreting the Convention and its Protocols'.[855] Eventually, the UK was found responsible for failing to ensure respect for the right to vote of the residents of Gibraltar, as this right had been deprived of its essence and effectiveness.[856]

For an interpretation of para. 33 of the decision as being based on the principle of 'equivalent protection', see, inter alia: R. Lawson and H. Schermers, *supra* note 511, 679 and P. Klein, *supra* note 389, 313. In contrast, Ciampi contends that the application of the 'equivalent protection' criteria in the present case would be redundant. This is explained by the fact that the author views the adoption of the acts under contention as not constituting conduct performed by the UK in light of its obligations flowing from membership of the EC. See: A. Ciampi, 'L'Union Européenne et le Respect des Droits de L'Homme Dans la Mise en Ouvre des Sanctions Devant la Cour Européenne des Droits de L'Homme', RGDIP (2006) 85, 91.

851 *Matthews* case, para. 34.

852 Ibid.

853 European Commission of Human Rights Report, Application No. 24833/94, 29 October 1997, para. 63.

854 *Matthews* case, para. 39.

855 Ibid.

856 Ibid., paras. 63–5.

The line of argument advanced in the case-law prior to *Matthews*, and further developed in this case, has been used as a benchmark in various cases subsequently decided by the ECtHR, such as the well-known *Bosphorus*[857] and *Gasparini*[858] cases. Most of these cases involve member State responsibility for the implementation of institutional decisions (recall Chapter II) and not for the transfer of powers to an international organisation proper. In any event, the *Bosphorus* decision, which involved the impoundment of an aircraft by the Irish authorities on the basis of an EU Regulation (in itself implementing UNSC sanctions against the FRY) importantly contributed to expanding the meaning of 'equivalent protection'. It clarified that States' action taken in compliance with their obligations flowing from membership of an international organisation is justified provided that the organisation is seen to protect fundamental rights in a 'manner which can be considered at least equivalent to that for which the Convention provides'.[859] 'Equivalent protection' therefore leads to a presumption of compliance with the ECHR, which in any event may be rebutted if the circumstances so demand.[860]

In the later *Gasparini* case, these findings were applied in the framework of NATO operations, particularly the procedures of its Appeal Board, which had allegedly violated guarantees of fair trial.[861] *Gasparini* approximates us to the kinds of question that emerge once the role of States as governors of international organisations is at issue. One such question pertains to the terms in which States set up the operational framework of international organisations – and in *Gasparini* the ECtHR showed its readiness to scrutinise this matter with regard to NATO.[862] It did so in a somewhat unclear fashion, however, as it went straight to a substantive assessment of whether NATO procedures passed the 'equivalent protection' test without first looking into the requirement that the individual falls within the jurisdiction of the State (cf. Article 1 ECHR), as supported by an intervening act of the latter.[863] Be that as it may, in *Gasparini* (although the application was declared inadmissible) one finds the

857 *Supra* note 427.
858 *Supra* note 526.
859 *Bosphorus* case, para. 155.
860 Ibid., para. 156.
861 *Gasparini* case, 4, 5. Other cases where the 'equivalent protection' criterion was used include: *Galić* v. *the Netherlands*, App. No. 22617/07, 9 June 2009, paras. 43–6, and *Rambus Inc.* v. *Germany*, App. No. 40382/04, 16 June 2009, 7, 8. In the recent *Avotiņš* v. *Latvia*, App. No. 17502/07, 23 May 2016, decided along the lines of *Michaud* v. *France*, App. No. 12323/11, 6 December 2012, the ECtHR particularly examined the 'equivalent protection' presumption under the premises that it only applies where a margin of manoeuvre on the part of the State's authorities is absent and where the full potential of the supervisory mechanism provided for by EU law has been deployed (see: paras. 105–12).
862 *Gasparini* case, 7–10.
863 C. Ryngaert, 'Oscillating between Embracing and Avoiding Bosphorus: The European Court of Human Rights on Member State Responsibility for Acts of International Organisations and the Case of the EU', 39(2) EL Rev (2014) 176, 179, 180.
Criticising the Court's inconsistency in its case-law when it comes to the requirement of State involvement for a finding of responsibility, see: T. Lock, 'Gasparini v. Italy and Belgium', in C. Ryngaert, I. Dekker, R. Wessel and J. Wouters (eds.), op. cit. *supra* note 101, 333–5.

important lesson that, under the ECHR, the responsibility of member States may be engaged for not bringing sufficient pressure to bear on international organisations to provide for adequate dispute settlement mechanisms[864] (see Section 3.4.2.2).

3.3.1.2 The Extraterritorial Scope of Member States' Human Rights (Protection) Duties

In its acknowledgement of member States' protection duties under the ECHR, the ECtHR cannot but be confronted with the question of the extraterritorial application of convention rights. Indeed, discussions on member State responsibility will more often than not concern individuals that fall outside the territorial jurisdiction of the State at issue: in international financial institutions, this sort of problem will normally involve, on the one hand, individuals that were affected by a given project/ programme in the borrower country and, on the other hand, the borrowing States which participated in the institutional decision-making process. In such cases, do said individuals belong to the pool of persons for whom (member) States ought to secure human rights?[865]

In *Matthews*, the ECtHR did not have to tackle this matter inasmuch as the question put before it involved the responsibility of the UK as a member State of the EC vis-à-vis a citizen of Gibraltar, which is a dependent territory of that country. Extraterritoriality, then, would have only been at stake in case the responsibility of another EC member State had been invoked. The ECtHR seemed prepared to accept it when it referred to the collective responsibility of EC member States for the consequences of primary EU law upon the residents of Gibraltar. Notably, the ECtHR claimed that the 'United Kingdom, *together with all the other parties to the Maastricht Treaty*, is responsible *ratione materiae* under Article 1 of the Convention … for the consequences of that Treaty'.[866] Yet, two years later, in the *Banković* case,[867] where the Court dealt with a different form of State participation in international organisations, notably, as troop-contributing States in military operations conducted under the auspices of NATO, it advanced a quite restrictive[868] interpretation of jurisdiction. Here, it saw jurisdiction as 'primarily' and 'essentially' a territorial concept,[869] allowing for the extraterritorial application of the

[864] C. Ryngaert and H. Buchanan, *supra* note 37, 146.

[865] See: M. Heijer and R. Lawson, 'Extraterritorial Human Rights and the Concept of "Jurisdiction"', in M. Langford, W. Vandenhole, M. Scheinin and W. V. Genugten (eds.), op. cit. *supra* note 55, 163, noting that, in comparison with international law, 'jurisdiction under human rights law is not about whether a State is entitled to act, but primarily about delineating as appropriately as possible the pool of persons to which a State ought to secure human rights'.

[866] *Matthews* case, para. 33 (emphasis added).

[867] *Banković and Others* v. *Belgium and 16 other Contracting States*, App. No. 52207/99, 12 December 2001.

[868] Not to say wrong, as put by: T. Scovazzi, '*Banković and Others v. Belgium and 16 other Contracting States*', in C. Ryngaert, I. Dekker, R. Wessel and J. Wouters (eds.), op. cit. *supra* note 101, 303, 304.

[869] *Banković* case, *supra* note 867, paras. 59, 61 and 63.

Convention only in exceptional cases where the State 'through the *effective control of the relevant territory and its inhabitants abroad* … exercises all or some of the public powers normally to be exercised by that Government'.[870]

To some extent, the ECtHR's approach was broadened in subsequent case-law – which, despite not dealing with questions of member State responsibility, is in any event worth revisiting for present purposes. In the *Ilascu* case, the Court asserted that even when a Contracting State is prevented from exercising authority over a certain part of its territory, it is still bound to take all the appropriate measures within its power to secure the rights of individuals.[871] Next to this, when it comes to 'jurisdiction' resulting from control over persons, the ECtHR held in *Al-Skeini* – which involved the operations of British security personnel in Iraq – that *physical power* and *control* over a person constitute a decisive factor determining the application of the European Convention.[872] Such an understanding was recently reiterated in the *Hassan*[873] and *Jaloud* cases,[874] likewise dealing with the presence of foreign security forces in Iraq.

The ECtHR's jurisprudence dealing with extraterritoriality presents various similarities with that of the IACHR. Accordingly, in *Coard et al.* v. *United States*, a case regarding the occupation of Grenada by US forces and the detention of several members of the military junta by the latter, the IACHR noted that '[i]n principle, the inquiry turns not on the presumed victim's nationality or presence within a particular geographic area, but on whether, under the specific circumstances, the State observed the rights of a person subject to its *authority and control*'.[875] In *Alejandre et al.* v. *Cuba*, where Cuban agents had shot down an unarmed plane over international waters killing all four pilots, the IACHR found 'conclusive evidence' that the agents of the Cuban State 'placed the civilian pilots … under their authority',[876] thereby satisfying the jurisdictional requirement of the ACHR.[877] Recently, the Commission's *authority* and *control* test has been applied in several cases involving the apprehension and detention of persons in Guantanamo.[878]

870 Ibid., para. 71 (emphasis added). The ECtHR thus rejected that the NATO bombing of Radio Television Servia during the Kosovo intervention amounted to a de facto control of the air space, stating that 'the applicants' submission is tantamount to arguing that anyone adversely affected by an act imputable to a Contracting State, wherever in the world that act may have been committed or its consequences felt, is thereby brought within the jurisdiction of the State' (para. 75).

871 *Ilascu and others* v. *Moldova and Russia*, App. No. 48787/99, 8 July 2004, paras. 331 and 333.

872 *Al-Skeini and others* v. *United Kingdom*, App No. 55721/07, 7 July 2011, paras. 136 and 137.

873 *Hassan* v. *United Kingdom*, App. no. 29750/09, 16 September, 2014, paras. 75–80.

874 *Jaloud* v. *Netherlands*, App. No. 47708/08, 20 November, 2014, paras. 140–53.

875 *Coard et al.* v. *United States*, Case No. 10.951, 29 September 1999, para. 37 (emphasis added).

876 *Armando Alejandre Jr. et al.* v. *Cuba*, Case No. 11.589, 29 September 1999, para. 25.

877 ACHR, *supra* note 819.

878 See, inter alia, the IACHR's Report No. 17/12, Petition P-900-08, Admissibility, Djamel Ameziane, United States, 20 March 2012, paras. 29–35. For various decisions regarding the US Detention Center in Guantanamo, see: www.oas.org/en/iachr/pdl/decisions/Guantanamo.asp#Medidas, last consulted 15 October 2018.

From the above incursion into the European and Inter-American human rights regimes, a concluding observation is in order. The doctrine of State authority and control as applied in the cases of occupation, military or administrative control may be too restrictive a test to apply in the context of ESC rights violations involving the member States of international financial institutions.[879] Typically, the extraterritorial applicability of ESC rights emerges in situations where State involvement is less direct,[880] as the elements of direct control or effect are often not required for a State to produce a negative impact.[881] Indeed, it can hardly be asserted that through their participation in the WB, for example, member States are able to exercise (even overall) control over, say, indigenous communities that have been forcibly displaced to make way for the construction of a dam.

All in all, as will be further explored in the following section, 'it is not the fact of the affected person having earlier been subjected to the authority of a State, but rather the relationship of the State with a particular set of circumstances being of such a special nature, which is decisive in considering the State to be under a duty to use its influence, knowledge or other resources at its disposal to prevent the manifestation of human rights violations, provided that the State is indeed legally and factually capable to do so'.[882] A more fruitful approach, as argued by Narula, is thus to focus on the vehicles through which extraterritorial violations occur, notably, the international organisations wherein States participate, and to ensure that States' international human rights obligations extend to their relationships with these actors.[883]

Coming back to the case-law of the ECtHR, it is possible to find in the Court's reasoning an approach that is open to a wider stance towards extraterritoriality. This is fundamental, if ECHR obligations are to be 'divided and tailored', as put by the Court in *Al-Skeini*, in terms that are reflective of the power that is held by member States.[884] When it comes to State participation in international organisations, the jurisdictional link between the individuals (extraterritorially) affected by institutional activity and member States can precisely be established because of the particular position of power held by the latter vis-à-vis the international organisation.

879 S. Narula, *supra* note 53, 124, 125.

880 M. Heijer and R. Lawson, *supra* note 865, 186.

881 W. Vandenhole, 'Extraterritorial Human Rights Obligations: Taking Stock, Looking Forward', 5 JEDH (2013) 804, 819.

882 M. Heijer and R. Lawson, *supra* note 865, 190.
In a quest for more lenient jurisdictional tests in the context of economic, social and cultural rights, concepts such as *reasonableness* have been advanced in legal doctrine, requiring an assessment of whether there is a sufficiently proximate link between the individual and the act of the State, and thus, whether it is *reasonable* to bring the individual within the human rights jurisdiction of that State. See: C. Ryngaert, 'Jurisdiction: Towards a Reasonableness Test', in M. Langford, W. Vandenhole, M. Scheinin and W. V. Genugten (eds.), op. cit. *supra* note 53, 192–211.

883 S. Narula, *supra* note 53, 128, referring to the extraterritorial application of ESC rights to States both as members of international financial institutions and as home States of transnational corporations.

884 *Al-Skeini*, *supra* note 872, para. 137.

This relational power thereby becomes a key element in determining the extraterritorial applicability and scope of ECHR obligations.[885]

Hence, in the ECtHR's recurrent appeal to States' positive duty to secure and protect convention rights in institutional settings (recall *M&CO*; *Matthews*; *Bosphorus*; or *Gasparini*) what the jurisprudence of the Court suggests is that States Parties to the ECHR are bound by a duty of due diligence, according to which they must ensure that while entrusting an international organisation with certain competences, they will still have at their disposal sufficient tools to monitor and respond to the impacts of the organisation's activities on human rights.[886] In this vein, applying the ECtHR's principled assertions to member State participation in international financial institutions would generally entail that the formulation of policies, the definition of project-specific standards and the design of inspection mechanisms ensure, at a minimum, that human rights are respected and protected throughout the activities of the organisation (see Section 3.4.2).[887]

Such an understanding can be viewed, to some extent, as substantiating the transposition, to the realm of international institutional law, of the Court's own assessments with regard to States' positive obligation to protect human rights from private conduct. To name one example, in *Osman* v. *United Kingdom*,[888] although the ECtHR did not specifically use the term due diligence,[889] it did appeal to the State's positive obligation to ensure the 'practical and effective protection of the rights and freedoms' enshrined in the ECHR.[890] According to the Court, a violation of such an obligation would arise if, in light of the circumstances of the particular case, it could be established that the State's 'authorities did not do all that could be reasonably expected of them to avoid a real and immediate risk to life of which they have or ought to have knowledge'.[891] Here, again, the State assumes a particular position of power that enables it to somehow act upon the independent entity. Coming back to the context of international organisations, the fact that the ECtHR imposes duties of protection and oversight upon member States shows that it considers their role to be significantly connected to institutional operations, and, thereby, their extraterritorial impacts – just as States are significantly connected to the operations of private entities within their jurisdiction.

885 A. Nollkaemper, *supra* note 88, 28.

886 This interpretation is upheld by, inter alia: P. Klein, *supra* note 389, 310–12; P. Sands and P. Klein, *supra* note 689, 530; O. De Schutter, *supra* note 391; and A. Stumer, *supra* note 358, 563.

887 M. Salomon, *supra* note 681, 181.

888 *Osman* v. *United Kingdom*, 87/1997/871/1083, Judgment, 28 October 1998, para. 116.

889 The term was rather used by the Inter-American Court of Human Rights in the landmark *Velasquez Rodriguez* case, *supra* note 819, judgment of July 29, 1988 (merits), paras. 172–5, where the State's duty to protect individuals from acts of third parties was clearly upheld, and was interpreted as requiring a standard of due diligence to guard against and to provide adequate remedies for the consequences of such conduct.

890 *Osman* case, *supra* note 888, para. 116.

891 Ibid.

To sum up, the ECtHR's imposition of human rights protection duties upon member States – which is based, as was seen, on the power they wield vis-à-vis international (financial) institutions – necessarily entails that the individuals affected by a given project/programme in the borrower country belong to the pool of persons with regard to which member States set out to diligently secure human rights. Such an extension of the scope of member States' human rights obligations extraterritorially is certainly justified in view of the need, highlighted in *Matthews*, *Bosphorus* or *Osman*, to ensure the practical and effective nature of the safeguards prescribed by the ECHR.

3.3.2 *The Duty of International Cooperation and the Requirements Imposed by the Economic, Social and Cultural Rights Regime*

The duty of States to cooperate internationally constitutes a defining element of the UN Charter. As stated in Article 1(3), one of the purposes of the UN is to 'achieve international co-operation in solving international problems of an economic, social, cultural, or humanitarian character, and in promoting and encouraging respect for human rights and for fundamental freedoms for all'. In what regards the promotion of human rights, the Charter further reiterates that the achievement of 'universal respect for, and observance of, human rights and fundamental freedoms' (Article 55 (c)) requires States to 'take joint and separate action in co-operation with the Organization' (Article 56).

Even though the legally binding character of this duty, as prescribed in the UN Charter, remained – and still remains – controversial, it did contribute to a move from an international law of coexistence to one of cooperative engagement.[892] Within the realm of international human rights law, the essential role of international cooperation in the realisation of human rights was further recognised in the UDHR,[893] although the meaning and practical implications of the concept were still to be clarified. Advances in this regard came about with the International Covenant on Economic, Social and Cultural Rights[894] (ICESCR), and corresponding interpretations by the CESCR. In fact, the duty is referred to in various articles throughout the treaty,[895] particularly prominently in Article 2(1), under which: 'Each State Party … undertakes to take steps, individually and through international assistance and co-operation, especially economic and technical, to the maximum of

892 See: M. Langford, F. Coomans and F. Gómez Isa, 'Extraterritorial Duties in International Law', in M. Langford, W. Vandenhole, M. Scheinin and W. V. Genugten (eds.), op. cit. *supra* note 53, 54, 55.

893 See Articles 22 and 28, *supra* note 816.

894 International Covenant on Economic, Social and Cultural Rights, 993 UNTS 3, 3 January 1976 (ICESCR). Other human rights instruments praising the importance of international cooperation include the Convention on the Rights of the Child, 1577 UNTS 3, 20 November 1989 (Articles 4, 17, 23(4), 24(4) and 28(3)) and the Convention on the Rights of Persons with Disabilities, 2515 UNTS 3, 13 December 2006 (Articles 4(2) and 32).

895 See Articles 11(1)(2), 15(4) and 23.

its available resources, with a view to achieving progressively the full realization of the rights recognized in the present Covenant.'

Undoubtedly, the materialisation of international cooperation often occurs through the phenomenon of international organisations. This begs the question: what are the legal implications of States' commitment to 'take joint action' towards the progressive achievement of common goals? Necessarily, the participation of States in a given institutional framework is conditioned upon their respect for the individual interests that their cooperative engagements are purported to serve. In this way, international cooperation can be seen as a central element in determining the scope of necessary member State conduct: it serves as a vehicle and is part of the duty of States to take steps towards the progressive realisation of ESC rights.[896] International cooperation fits nicely with the idea of process and proactivity in global governance, and thereby favours obligations of conduct over obligations of result.[897] According to Salomon, it 'both precludes obstructive international endeavours that would undermine the realization of economic, social and cultural rights, and requires proactive measures by states acting both individually and collectively'.[898]

Given the realm of international human rights law in which the CESCR dwells, this body has paid particular attention to the role of States as members of international financial institutions. Notably, the Committee has asserted that State participation thereof should be exercised in conformity with human rights norms,[899] with particular emphasis being placed on the States' obligation of international assistance and cooperation. Throughout the years, the CESCR has advised several State Parties, as a 'member of international organizations, including international financial institutions such as the International Monetary Fund and the World Bank, *to do all it can to ensure* that the policies and decisions of those organizations are in conformity with the obligations of States parties under the Covenant, in particular

896 M. Langford, F. Coomans and F. Gómez Isa, *supra* note 892, 63.

897 The idea is pervasive in M. Salomon's monograph *Global Responsibility for Human Rights: World Poverty and the Development of International Law* (2007).

898 Ibid., 64. In 92–9, Salomon provides an overview of how international cooperation has been praised in various world conferences as necessary to addressing human rights concerns.

899 See General Comment No. 19 on the Right to Social Security, *supra* note 236, para. 58, whereby 'States parties should *ensure* that their actions as members of international organizations *take due account* of the right to social security. Accordingly, States parties that are members of international financial institutions, notably the International Monetary Fund, the World Bank, and regional development banks, should take steps to ensure that the right to social security is taken into account in their lending policies, credit agreements and other international measures.' Moreover, 'States parties should ensure that the policies and practices of international and regional financial institutions, in particular those concerning their role in structural adjustment and in the design and implementation of social security systems, promote and do not interfere with the right to social security'. See also: General Comment No. 18 on the Right to Work, UN Doc. E/C.12/GC/18 (2005) para. 30; General Comment No. 15 on the Right to Water, UN Doc. E/C.12/2002/11 (2002) para. 36; and General Comment No. 14 on the Right to the Highest Attainable Standard of Health, UN Doc. E/C.12/2000/4 (2000) para. 39.

the obligations … concerning international assistance and cooperation'.[900] Essentially, State Parties to the Covenant are required to 'take due account' of the rights prescribed therein, and to proactively 'ensure' that the operations of international financial institutions 'promote and do not interfere with' those rights.[901] As much was recently reiterated in a statement of the CESCR on the topic of public debt and austerity measures.[902]

Albeit short in specific normative guidance, the CESCR's interpretations are in any case significant to keep in mind, inasmuch as they assume the extraterritorial reach of the rights contained in the Covenant and blend them with the notion of diligent State conduct. Similarly to the ECtHR, the CESCR has systematically appealed to member States' duty to respect and protect human rights,[903] notably by highlighting the role of States as guarantors of the human rights conformity of the policies and practices of international financial institutions.

Hence, it can be stated that individuals affected by the operations of an international financial institution may fall under the (extraterritorial) jurisdiction of their member States, depending on the power of the latter to steer the organisation's performance.[904] Accordingly, the due diligence standard, with its emphasis on

900 See, e.g.: Concluding observations of the Committee on Economic, Social, and Cultural Rights on the Fourth Report of the U.K., UN Doc. E/C.12/1/Add.79 (2002) para. 26; Concluding observations of the Committee on Economic, Social, and Cultural Rights on the Fourth Periodic Report of Germany, UN Doc. E/C.12/1/Add.68 (2001) para. 31 (emphasis added). It is interesting to note that, in its subsequent report to the CESCR, Germany took care to demonstrate that it had 'used its influence with the World Bank to ensure that its decisions and commitments were in tune with the undertakings entered into by the States parties' (see: UN Doc. E/C.12/DEU/5 (2010) para. 16).
While the CESCR's observations were mainly made between 2000 and 2002, in the latest version of its Reporting Guidelines (UN Doc. E/C.12/2008/2, Annex (2009)), States are explicitly requested to indicate '[m]echanisms in place to ensure that a State party's obligations under the Covenant are fully taken into account in its actions as a member of international organizations and international financial institutions … in order to ensure that economic, social and cultural rights, particularly of the most disadvantaged and marginalized groups, are not undermined' (para. 3(c)).

901 General Comment No. 19 on the Right to Social Security, *supra* note 236.

902 CESCR, 'Public debt, austerity measures and the International Covenant on Economic, Social and Cultural Rights', UN Doc. E/C.12/2016/1 (2016) para. 9.

903 Khalfan and Seiderman argue that, in addition to respect and protect obligations, member States are also bound by an obligation to fulfil human rights, when the mandate or primary activity of an international organisation substantially addresses human rights areas, such as the case of the WB. See: A. Khalfan and I. Seiderman, *supra* note 681, 31. See also: E. De Sena, *supra* note 55, arguing that, under Article 2(1) ICESCR, member States are required to ensure, through the policies and lending operations (notably, the conditionality clauses imposed therein) they approve in international financial institutions, that a portion of the financial aid supplied by these organisations is used for achieving ESC rights.

904 In this regard, reference can be made to the Maastricht Principles, *supra* note 53, where the jurisdictional scope of States' obligations to respect, protect and fulfil economic, social and cultural rights is defined in Principle 9(c) by reference to, among others, 'situations in which the State, *acting separately or jointly*, whether through its executive, legislative or judicial branches, *is in a position to exercise decisive influence* or to take measures to realize economic, social, and cultural rights extraterritorially, in accordance with international law' (emphasis added). Further, in Principle 15, it is asserted that, '[a]s a member of an international organization, the State remains responsible for

capacity to influence, becomes a useful means to determine, and at the same time limit, the jurisdictional scope of States' human rights obligations. Next to this, and as will be further explored in Section 3.4.2, due diligence emerges as an allocation principle: the obligation is imposed upon States precisely owing to the particular position of power they assume within a given institutional setting.[905] Responsibility, then, relates to how member States use their *power* or *capacity to influence* the behaviour of the international financial institution and, therefrom, the impact of the organisation's operations in peoples' lives.

3.4 HUMAN RIGHTS DUE DILIGENCE IN THE CONTEXT OF INTERNATIONAL FINANCIAL INSTITUTIONS

As seen in the previous sections, both the ECtHR and the CESCR impose upon member States the duty to positively protect human rights in terms that bring to mind the concept of due diligence. Said bodies have not expanded much on how this duty is to be discharged in practice, however. The duty to protect entails two core obligations of a differing nature: one consists of an obligation to prevent harmful conduct and the other of an obligation to punish it.[906] The aim of the current section is to clarify the role of due diligence with regard to both elements of the positive duty to protect and the terms in which member States are thereby conditioned, in terms of their conduct, as creators of, and participants in, international financial institutions.

In order to clarify the normative content and implications of the international law duty of due diligence, Section 3.4.1 starts by briefly portraying its nature, notion and scope as it has evolved in international practice. Section 3.4.2 subsequently embarks on an exploratory discussion of how to 'operationalise' this standard of conduct in the context of member State participation in international financial institutions. Implying a standard of care aimed at both preventing and punishing harm, due diligence prescriptions add an important procedural dimension to the human rights regime, which is particularly relevant in the latter institutional contexts. As will be seen, human rights due diligence conditions not only the participation of member States in institutional decision-making processes, but also the way in which use is made of the institutional and policy apparatus they set up to provide individuals with access to justice.

its own conduct in relation to its human rights obligations within its territory and extraterritorially. A State that transfers competences to, or participates in, an international organization *must take all reasonable steps to ensure* that the relevant organization acts consistently with the international human rights obligations of that State' (emphasis added).

905 See R. Pisillo-Mazzeschi, *supra* note 56, 402–4, where the author explains that due diligence constitutes not only a means to determine the content of primary norms but also a criteria for the evaluation of wrongfulness and, *a fortiori*, the establishment of responsibility.

906 See, inter alia: R. Pisillo-Mazzeschi, 'The Due Diligence Rule and the Nature of the International Responsibility of States', 35 GYIL (1992) 9, 26–30.

3.4.1 *Due Diligence As a Framework to Evaluate Member State Behaviour*

3.4.1.1 Preliminary Remarks on Due Diligence

The concept of due diligence has played a role in international practice since the second half of the nineteenth century.[907] In its traditional meaning, due diligence relates to the principle of *sic utere tuo ut alienum non laedas*, i.e., the State's general international legal obligation of not allowing its territory to be used against the interests of another State.[908] In older arbitral awards,[909] this notion translated into instances of State responsibility for an 'implied, tacit or constructive approval in the negligent failure' to prevent, investigate and punish, or to enable victims to pursue civil remedies against the offender.[910]

Owing to its preventive role, a failure to exercise due diligence entails an omission of the required conduct.[911] From this, it follows that it is not the conduct of the private entity that is attributed to the State; it is, rather, the State's own omission to exercise due diligence in the fulfilment of a given obligation that is directly attributable to it. The case-law of the ICJ so confirms. In the early *Corfu Channel* case,[912] the ICJ found Albania responsible on such grounds, for damage inflicted upon two British warships (and concomitant loss of life) which had collided with mines located in Albania's territorial waters. Albania's responsibility was notably asserted for having omitted to take all the necessary steps to prevent harm, while it knew, or should have known (due to its close surveillance of the area), about the dangers posed in its territorial waters.[913]

The due diligence rule was later applied by the ICJ in the well-known 2007 *Genocide* case,[914] where the Court examined Serbia and Montenegro (FRY)'s responsibility for failure to prevent genocide in Bosnia and Herzegovina, under Article 1 of the Genocide Convention. Understanding that the obligation to prevent genocide brings with it due diligence requirements, the ICJ made important comments regarding the contours of the latter that are worth reproducing here.[915]

907 ILA Due Diligence Report, *supra* note 56, 2.

908 M. Sornarajah, 'Linking State Responsibility for Certain Harms Caused by Corporate Nationals Abroad to Civil Recourse in the Legal Systems of Home States', in C. Scott (ed.), *Torture As Tort: Comparative Perspectives on the Development of Transnational Human Rights Litigation* (2001) 499.

909 Such as *Alabama Claims of the United States of America against Great Britain*, 14 September 1872, where the UK was found responsible for not having controlled the private activity of building a vessel for use in war, which resulted in extraterritorial harm being inflicted upon the US.

910 See: Borchard, 1970, 217, as quoted by Sornarajah, *supra* note 908, 499.

911 As warned by Mazzeschi, due diligence does not play a role with respect to all wrongful State omissions. See: R. Pisillo-Mazzeschi, *supra* note 56, 388.

912 *Corfu Channel Case (United Kingdom* v. *Albania)*, Merits, ICJ Reports 4 (1949).

913 Ibid., 23.

914 *Supra* note 779.

915 Despite the Court's reluctance to establish a general jurisprudence applicable to all cases where States are bound by obligations of prevention (*Genocide* case, para. 429), the analysis it made can be considered as having a general nature. See: J. Dugard and A. Vermeer-Künzli, 'The Elusive

Similarly to the *Corfu Channel* decision, the ICJ reiterated that the breach of the obligation of due diligence results from a 'failure to adopt and implement suitable measures to prevent',[916] thus translating into an omission.[917] The Court characterised due diligence as a 'best efforts' obligation,[918] which means that the question of whether the State has duly discharged its obligations is essentially one of whether it has acted to the best of its ability in the given context. Due diligence thus imports an element of flexibility that must be tested in light of the circumstances of each situation. In the *Genocide* case, the ICJ interpreted the duty as requiring an assessment of the State's 'capacity to influence effectively the action of persons likely to commit, or already committing' the violation, clarifying that such capacity could be determined only *in concreto*.[919] It is this capacity to influence, combined with the State's constructive awareness of the serious danger that acts of genocide could be committed, that triggers the duty to perform with due diligence.[920]

Various objective elements have been advanced to measure the degree of diligence that is due, such as the relevance of the interest calling for protection and the extent of predictability of harm.[921] In addition, in the *Alabama Claims* Arbitration, the Tribunal advanced a criterion whereby diligence would be required in proportion to the risks at stake. Although the yardstick proposed by the Tribunal did not attract many followers then,[922] it was, for instance, later endorsed by the ILC in the field of international environmental law.[923]

To sum up, although the duty of due diligence lacks a concrete normative content that is applicable to every substantive area of international law, it does introduce a general framework whereby States are required to adopt positive measures on the basis of an implied duty of vigilance and prevention of harm.[924] Such duty will then

Allocation of Responsibility to Informal Organizations: The Case of the Quartet of the Middle East', in M. Ragazzi (ed.), op. cit. *supra* note 346, 265.

916 *Genocide* case, para. 432.

917 Ibid.

918 Ibid., para. 438.

919 Ibid., para. 430.

920 Ibid., para. 432. The requirements of 'factual capability' and awareness also derive from the ICJ's decision in *United States Diplomatic and Consular Staff in Tehran (United States of America* v. *Iran)*, Judgment, ICJ Reports 1980, 3 (hereinafter *Tehran Hostages* case), where the Court established the responsibility of Iran on the basis of various elements including the fact that Iranian authorities 'had the means at their disposal to perform their obligations' and that they 'were fully aware ... of the urgent need for action on their part' (para. 68).

921 R. P. Mazzeschi, *supra* note 906, 44.

922 M. Blomeyer-Bartenstein, 'Due Diligence', in R. Bernhardt (ed.), *Encyclopaedia of Public International Law* (1987) 140.

923 See: Commentary to Article 3, para. (11) of the Articles on Prevention of Transboundary Harm from Hazardous Activities, in Report of the International Law Commission, Fifty-Third session, Official Record of the General Assembly, Fifty-Sixth session, Supplement n. 10, UN Doc. A/56/10 (2001).

924 See: *Pulp Mills* case, *supra* note 709, para. 204.
As noted by Barnidge, it is misleading to claim that the duty of due diligence is not informed by a specified content, given that 'the due diligence principle's definition, as a flexible reasonableness standard adaptable to particular facts and circumstances, provides the underlying legal framework',

feed into relevant regimes of international law according to their specificities. Inasmuch as it entails procedural requirements of conduct, the duty of due diligence brings with it the expansion of the effect of primary international legal rules.[925]

In the field of international human rights law, based on the findings of the ECtHR and the CESCR, due diligence is to be linked to States' obligation to monitor and oversee the activities of international organisations, to make sure that these do not occur to the detriment of human rights requirements. Before discussing the legal implications of due diligence in the specific context of member State participation in international financial institutions (Section 3.4.2), it is deemed appropriate to briefly go through the contours of due diligence as applied in institutional contexts.

3.4.1.2 Operationalising Due Diligence in Institutional Settings

Discussions on due diligence as a framework to evaluate member State responsibility have only seldom been raised in academia. What is more, references to the matter tend to be insufficiently comprehensive to understand the real implications of due diligence in institutional settings. To be sure, the problem does not lie in the lack of support for the idea that member States are generally bound by due diligence obligations. Rather, the dearth of attention devoted to the topic may be partially explained by enduring uncertainties as to whether international law provides for a common standard of due diligence,[926] which could then be easily transposed to institutional contexts.

Generic references to due diligence can be traced back to Seyersted who advanced the idea that member State responsibility could arise 'if they, by delegating their powers to the Organization ... have enabled it to cause the violation or have cut themselves off from preventing it or from taking other necessary measures to secure fulfillment of their obligations'.[927] A few decades later, the matter was touched upon in the framework of the IDI's Questionnaire on member State responsibility.[928] While Amerasinghe invoked, in passing, a 'special duty of care placed upon members',[929] Salmon referred more explicitly to an 'obligation des Etats membres d'exercer une *due diligence*, une vigilance, pour que l'organisation n'accomplisse pas des actes illicites s'il y a la possibilité de les prévenir. Cette obligation est particulièrement précise pour l'Etat hôte des activités de l'organisation, mais peut

which relates to the care that is due in the given context. See R. Barnidge, 'The Due Diligence Principle under International Law', 8 Int'l Comm L Rev (2006) 81, 118.

925 V. Tzevelekos, 'In Search of Alternative Solutions: Can the State of Origin Be Held Internationally Responsible for Investors' Human Rights Abuses That Are Not Attributable to It?', 35 Brook J Int'l L (2010) 155, 179.

926 See: ILA Due Diligence Report, *supra* note 56, where, following an appraisal of the application of due diligence in various fields of international law, the question of its overall utility as a standard of conduct is still raised in the conclusions.

927 F. Seyersted, *supra* note 96, 74.

928 *Supra* note 655.

929 Ibid., 360.

s'étendre à tout membre de l'organisation.'[930] According to the latter author, the vigilance that is due is one that is 'raisonnable', and failure to observe it could lead to member States' responsibility for their own conduct, in parallel with the responsibility of the organisation.[931] Along similar lines, the 2004 ILA Report on Accountability of International Organisations referred to member States' fundamental obligation to ensure the lawfulness of institutional actions and decisions and to exercise adequate supervision of the organisation so as to protect the interests of third parties.[932]

A significant – if more contextualised – contribution to the discussion is undoubtedly that of Sadurska and Chinkin, who made use of due diligence to examine the responsibility of ITC member States for the organisation's collapse[933] (recall the *ITC* litigation). Based on the premise that the member States held sufficiently broad powers within the ITC to be able to exert control over its feeble activities,[934] the authors advanced the position that member States' deliberate choice not to exercise their supervisory powers (e.g., by intervening in the actions of the buffer stock manager) constituted a failure to act to prevent a foreseeable outcome, and thereby gave rise to their responsibility under international law.[935]

In institutional contexts, as elsewhere, due diligence has an important preventive function. To borrow from the terms of the UN Business and Human Rights framework, it translates into an 'ongoing management process that a reasonable and prudent [entity] needs to undertake',[936] thereby emerging as an *ex ante* tool that regulates and at the same time deters institutional actions that impose risks.[937]

Member States, as seen in Section 1.3, are responsible for performing their 'authority management' role under such a preventive due diligence framework. As a standard to evaluate member State behaviour, responsibility for failure to exercise due diligence is thus brought forth not simply because an act or omission might be at stake but, more accurately, because of the performance or non-performance of a

930 Ibid., 340.

931 Ibid., 339, 344. The caveat in Salmon's exposition lies in deeming member State due diligence obligations as being of a non-directly applicable character, meaning that they can be invoked solely by other member States and not third parties. This is contrary to the understanding herein espoused that due diligence provides a framework to assess member State responsibility towards third parties under international (human rights) law.

932 ILA Report on Accountability of International Organisations, *supra* note 50, p. 15. See also: P. Klein, *supra* note 389, 311, according to whom 'due diligence would require that States ensure that the rights and interests of third parties are not violated in the course of activities of the organizations which they have created'; and E. David, *Droit des Organisations Internationales* (2016) 599–605, focusing specifically on UN member State obligations regarding the Rwandan genocide.

933 R. Sadurska and C. Chinkin, *supra* note 290.

934 Ibid., 860, 861, 872.

935 Ibid., 880–8, especially 885.

936 UN Human Rights Office of the High Commissioner, 'The Corporate Responsibility to Respect Human Rights: An Interpretive Guide' (2012) 6.

937 L. A. Kornhauser, *supra* note 21, 121.

certain action, as a result of a particular role in which the member State representative has been placed within the governance set-up of the organisation.[938]

At this point it is worth briefly recalling Section 1.1's assertions regarding the transfer of the exercise of sovereign powers to international organisations. It was namely asserted that this transfer, rather than freezing at the moment of adoption of the international organisation's constituent instrument, brings about a process of interaction between the institution and its members that unfolds in a 'continuum'. Undoubtedly, the apportionment of the exercise of sovereign powers between both international legal subjects is most visible in the context of institutional decision-making processes, where member States' role is indispensable for the effectiveness of institutional operations. After all, as Schermers and Blokker note, 'governments are the most important initiators of decisions of international organizations'.[939] From this perspective, member State approval of a loan or programme in international financial institutions is tantamount to an authorisation of institutional conduct, and thereby constitutes the source of legitimacy of the latter.[940] For this reason, it is only logical that human rights due diligence, as applied in an institutional context, be observed right from the inception of the exercise of sovereign powers, i.e., the moment when 'decision-making negotiation' begins.

It should, however, be recalled that such a State-centred *indirect* responsibility approach has its limitations. As observed by Ryngaert (with regard to States' duty to protect against the conduct of multinational corporations), 'reliance on the state, backed up by a state responsibility regime, does not, in itself, guarantee that individuals and communities will be protected from non-state actor activities' adverse effects on human rights'.[941] One such limitation may reside in a weakened supervisory capacity on the side of the State.[942] Hence, apart from member States' human rights protection duties, it is of utmost importance to keep in mind the regime of international organisations' responsibility for their own harmful conduct, which runs in parallel with that of member State responsibility.

938 A. F. Lang, 'Shared Political Responsibility', in A. Nollkaemper and D. Jacobs (eds.), op. cit. *supra* note 21, 65.

939 An exception being the EU, in which the Commission has an exclusive right of initiative for almost all legislative acts. See: H. Schermers and N. Blokker, *supra* note 152, 505.

940 In the case of the WB, and as already mentioned in Chapter I, some projects (the AOBs) are processed on an absence-of-objection basis, which means that they are not included by management in the Executive Board meetings' agendas and are therefore considered approved if none of the Executive Directors raises an objection. While the act of member State approval is less tangible here, it can be seen as a tacit one.

941 C. Ryngaert, 'State Responsibility and Non-State Actors', in M. Noortmann, A. Reinisch and C. Ryngaert (eds.), *Non-State Actors in International* Law, op. cit. *supra* note 559, 179.

942 Ibid., 180.

3.4.2 *The Human Rights Due Diligence Obligations of the Member States of International Financial Institutions*

3.4.2.1 Member State Participation in Decision-Making Processes

As participants in the decision-making processes of international financial institutions, member States employing 'all means reasonably available to them'[943] may signify various things. Importantly, it is not solely about requiring member States to abstain or vote against certain projects or programmes in more extreme situations of foreseeable harm; it is also, and mostly so, about compelling member States to adopt a diligent attitude prior to deciding whether to approve or reject a proposal for a loan (and in the follow-up to that very same decision), by making sure that the human rights impacts of the project or programme at hand are appropriately accounted for. Failure to observe the required standard of care in human rights protection may give rise to the invocation of member State responsibility, in terms that will be discussed later in the chapter.

A INTERNATIONAL LEGAL CONSTRAINTS UPON THE VOTING BEHAVIOUR OF MEMBER STATES: SOME DOCTRINAL VIEWS. The existence of international legal constraints upon the voting behaviour of member States has been upheld by several scholars.[944] Often, discussions addressing this matter draw on the voting power of the member States of the UNSC and, in particular, on the question of whether the duty to prevent genocide or other R2P crimes[945] implies exercising the right to vote (or veto) in a certain manner. Peters has advanced the view that the obligation of UNSC members to 'cooperate in bringing to an end the commission of core crimes takes the form of an obligation to vote positively on a resolution authorising a robust intervention if this is the only means to bring an end to R2P crimes and violations'.[946] With particular regard to the permanent members of the UNSC, the author argues that the use of the veto is intrinsically correlated with a special responsibility not to

943 The terms are used by the ICJ in the *Genocide* case, *supra* note 779, para. 430.

944 Sarooshi, for example, has contended: 'It is even arguable that States should take action within the organization – e.g., by voting against a decision – to try and ensure that the international organization does not commit an internationally wrongful act.' See: D. Sarooshi, *supra* note 346, 84.

945 The 'World Summit Outcome Document', adopted by UN General Assembly Resolution A/RES/60/1 (2005), lists, in para. 138, the following crimes as R2P (or 'responsibility to protect') crimes: genocide, war crimes, ethnic cleansing and crimes against humanity. See further paras. 138 and 139, providing an explanation of the concept and implications of R2P.

946 A. Peters, *supra* note 778, 38. Along similar lines, see: J. Heieck, 'The Responsibility Not to Veto Revisited: How the Duty to Prevent Genocide As a *Jus Cogens* Norm Imposes a Legal Duty Not to Veto on the Five Permanent Members of the Security Council', in R. Barnes and V. Tzevelekos (eds.), *Beyond Responsibility to Protect: Generating Change in International Law* (2016) especially 119–21, arguing that the duty to prevent genocide, as a *jus cogens* norm, compels, through its due diligence standard, permanent UNSC members to cast positive votes for, and not to veto, Council resolutions aimed at preventing genocide; *Contra*: P. Palchetti, *supra* note 682, 359–62, arguing that in these cases it is not possible to claim that member States are required to vote in a specific manner.

impede collective action when it is necessary to prevent or respond to genocide.[947] Along similar lines, Zimmermann contends that a member State of the UNSC incurs responsibility in cases where it 'manifestly fails to support [by vetoing] or even delays possible SC measures aimed at preventing genocide and ensuring respect for the Geneva Conventions, which might have contributed to preventing such acts'.[948]

Apart from the specific duty to prevent genocide, international human rights law has also been said to condition the voting behaviour of member States – not only of the UNSC,[949] but also of other international organisations and, most importantly for present purposes, international financial institutions. The views commonly advanced in this respect assume, as a standpoint for discussion, a human-rights-based approach to development cooperation, and, thereby, to member States' participation in multilateral institutional undertakings in the field. The human rights regime thus emerges as a framework to guide member States in policy construction and in the appraisal, approval and supervision of projects, in terms that allow for the identification of human rights concerns and the adoption of measures to ensure that they are effectively protected.[950] In sum, and to recall the constitutionalist terms used in Section 3.2, what is essentially called for is that human rights be *represented* in institutional decision-making, by shaping the contours of these processes.

B MEMBER STATES' ROLE IN ENSURING THE REPRESENTATION OF HUMAN RIGHTS CONCERNS. According to the 2015 G20/OECD Principles of Corporate Governance, which may be used as a source of inspiration, a fundamental element inherent in the monitoring role of (corporate) boards is that their members act 'on a fully informed basis'.[951] As applied to Executive Directors, this entails that prior to taking a decision, they must be well informed about the human rights – and, when

947 A. Peters, *supra* note 778, 39, 40, where the author quotes various UN documents to corroborate her contention.

948 A. Zimmermann, *supra* note 524, 887.

949 O. De Schutter, for example, has made the point with regard to UNSC member States' obligations when it comes to the imposition of economic sanctions. See: O. De Schutter, *supra* note 391, 90–2.

950 See, inter alia: Legal Brief on the Case of Greece, *supra* note 28, especially 5–8, 14, 15; M. Salomon, *supra* note 681, 174–9 and also M. Salomon, *supra* note 26, 536, 539, 540; S. McInerney-Lankford, 'International Financial Institutions and Human Rights: Select Perspectives on Legal Obligations', in D. Bradlow and D. Hunter (eds.), op. cit. *supra* note 1, 264–9; W. Van Genugten, *The World Bank Group, the IMF and Human Rights: A Contextualised Way Forward* (2015) 21–3; CIEL Legal Analysis on International Financial Institutions & Human Rights Law, *supra* note 681, 4–6. Various UN Special Rapporteurs have likewise alerted to member States' human rights obligations when participating in the decision-making processes of international financial institutions. See, inter alia: UN Human Rights Council Report 'Mission to the World Bank', *supra* note 26, para. 9; *UN Guiding Principles on Foreign Debt and Human Rights, supra* note 4, paras. 6 and 22; and the letter sent to the WB President Jim Yong Kim by 28 Special Rapporteurs mentioned *supra* note 26.

951 G20/OECD Principles of Corporate Governance, OECD Report to G20 Finance Ministers and Central Bank Governors (2015), Chapter VI, 51, available at: www.oecd.org/daf/ca/Corporate-Governance-Principles-ENG.pdf; last consulted 15 October 2018.

relevant, environmental – impacts of the project or programme subject to their approval, with particular attention being paid to the needs of the most marginalised and vulnerable groups, such as people with disabilities or children.[952] Constructive knowledge can normally be obtained by resorting to the preparatory work and project- or programme-specific information that is gathered by the staff: it is this information that will then feed into the Executive Directors' decisions (see Section 3.5.1.1 on Executive Directors' access to knowledge).

In order to tangibly gauge the human rights risks of a given project, the undertaking of proper impact assessments is essential. To use the WB as an example, as part of its 'Environmental and Social Due Diligence', the organisation is committed to monitoring the environmental and social impact assessments of all projects proposed for support through Investment Project Financing.[953] Its operational policies are bereft of human rights language, however: they do not refer to human rights impact assessments (HRIAs) but to 'social assessments'.[954] Social impact assessments form, in any event, a basic expectation of international human rights law.[955] Importantly, and regardless of the nomenclature used, the extent of the human rights impacts of projects subject to the Board's approval must be properly understood by Executive Directors.[956] That being said, while it is *unreasonable* to require member States to undertake said assessments themselves, it is clear that State representatives must satisfy themselves that the Bank's own policy prescriptions, interpreted in light of the human rights regime, have been met throughout the identification, preparation and appraisal phases of projects and

952 See: UN Committee on the Rights of the Child (CRC) General Comment No. 16 on State obligations regarding the impact of the business sector on children's rights, UN Doc. CRC/C/GC/16 (2013) para. 48.

953 World Bank Environmental and Social Policy for Investment Project Financing, contained in its ESF, *supra* note 187, paras. 30–5.

954 A description of what the WB understands by 'social risks and impacts' is contained in para. 4(b), ibid.

955 M. Salomon, *supra* note 26, 534, 535.

956 In contexts where the activity at stake presents a risk of producing significant adverse environmental impacts, the practice of carrying out environmental impact assessments (EIAs) was considered by the ICJ in the *Pulp Mills* case (*supra* note 709) as 'a requirement under general international law'. The ICJ moreover asserted that the failure to undertake an EIA in such conditions would constitute a violation of 'due diligence, and the duty of vigilance and prevention which it implies' (para. 204). While it is true that HRIAs are less well-established than EIAs, it is noteworthy that in recent years a growing interest in their use has emerged. For instance, various UN human rights mechanisms such as the CRC, the CESCR and the UN Special Rapporteurs have upheld the need to undertake HRIAs, as described in a report prepared by the Nordic Trust Fund – the World Bank, 'Study on Human Rights Impact Assessments: A Review of the Literature, Differences with other Forms of Assessments and Relevance for Development' (2013) 4–6. Finally, Principle 14 of the Maastricht Principles, *supra* note 53, also refers to States' duty to undertake HRIAs in extraterritorial contexts, as means to evaluate the potential impacts of their policies, laws and practices and as a basis for preventive decision-making. The abovementioned Principle 15 extends this duty to States as members of international organisations (see: ETO Consortium, Handbook, 'For Human Rights beyond Borders: How to Hold States Accountable for Extraterritorial Obligations' (2017) 28).

programmes.[957] Needless to say, these due diligence requirements apply to international financial institutions in general.

Another element that is fundamental to ensure an effective representation of human rights concerns is the involvement of stakeholders throughout the whole project cycle. As will shortly be seen, this entails the undertaking of meaningful consultations,[958] timely dissemination of information, and engagement with potentially affected individuals, so that these last have a part in the project's design and implementation.[959] All such requirements have important implications for the understanding of member States' 'authority management' role in institutional decision-making: essentially, they impose upon member States the duty to ensure that all those involved in the development process have a say in the decisions that impact upon their lives.[960]

Albeit not explicitly mentioned in human rights instruments such as the ACHR, the Banjul Charter or the ECHR, public participation rights have been widely interpreted by human rights courts as being contained or implied in several human rights provisions. Litigation involving environmental matters constitutes a prime example of case-law where courts normally undertake a procedural examination of whether individual interests were duly considered in national decision-making proceedings. The ECtHR has, for instance, derived the duties to inform and to undertake consultations with affected parties from the right to life (Article 2)[961] and the right to respect for private and family life (Article 8).[962] The African Commission on Human & Peoples' Rights has done so with regard to the right to healthy environment,[963] and so too have the IACHR and the IACtHR, under the *chapeaux* of the right to property.[964]

957 M. Salomon, *supra* note 681, 181.

958 Consultation is embraced as a major element of human rights due diligence in Principles 17 and 18 of the UN Human Rights Council, Report of the Special Representative of the Secretary-General on the Issue of Human Rights and Transnational Corporations and Other Business Enterprises, John Ruggie, *Guiding Principles on Business and Human Rights: Implementing the United Nations 'Protect, Respect and Remedy' Framework*, UN Doc. A/HRC/17/31 (2011).

959 See, e.g.: UN Human Rights Council, Report of the Independent Expert on the Issue of Human Rights Obligations Relating to the Enjoyment of a Safe, Clean, Healthy and Sustainable Environment, John H. Knox, UN Doc. A/HRC/25/53 (2013) 8–12; and HRW Abuse Free Development Report, *supra* note 25, especially 53, 54 and the bibliographical references to UN documents contained therein.

960 UN Human Rights Council, Report of the Special Rapporteur on Extreme Poverty and Human Rights, Magdalena Sepúlveda Carmona, Mission to Timor-Leste, UN Doc. A/HRC/20/25/Add.1 (2012) para. 24.

961 See, inter alia: *Öneryildiz* v. *Turkey*, App. No. 48939/99, 30 November 2004, paras. 89–91, referring to States' positive duty to undertake adequate measures to protect individuals, including setting up both preventive and remedial mechanisms and ensuring individuals' access to information.

962 See, inter alia: *Tatar* v. *Romania*, App. No. 67021/01, 27 January 2009, paras. 87, 88, 118, 119, restating the findings of the Court in *Öneryildiz*, and referring as well to the participation of individuals in decision-making procedures.

963 See: *Social and Economic Rights Action Center & the Center for Economic and Social Rights* v. *Nigeria*, Communication No. 155/96, 27 May 2002, especially para. 53 (also known as the *Ogoniland* case).

964 See: *Kichwa Indigenous People of Sarayaku* v. *Ecuador*, IACtHR, Judgment of 28 November 2007, Series C No. 245, paras. 161–7. Here, the Court drew on the obligation to guarantee the right to

An important question arising in this context regards the identification of the rights holders vis-à-vis the member States. To answer this, inspiration may be drawn from the Aarhus Convention,[965] also because it requires States Parties to promote its application in institutional settings.[966] It constitutes an environmental and human rights treaty entirely devoted to granting public participation rights to individuals, notably, to the 'public affected or likely to be affected by, or having an interest in, the environmental decision-making' (Article 2(5)). Moreover, the 2005 Almathy Guidelines, which were adopted to concretise the application of the Aarhus Convention in, inter alia, the decision-making processes of international organisations,[967] deem as relevant stakeholders: '(a) The members of the public who are, or are likely to be, most directly affected; (b) Representatives of public-interest organizations; (c) Representatives of other interests that might cause, contribute to, be affected by or be in a position to alleviate the problems under discussion.'[968]

Taking the case-law of the ECtHR as an example, it is true that the court has been remarkable in incorporating procedural duties linked to public participation rights into the human rights domain. However, a close comparison between its case-law and the philosophy behind the Aarhus Convention reveals the individualistic perspective through which human rights have been used in environmental litigation.[969] To name but one example, in the *Taskin* case,[970] which involved the environmentally noxious operations of a mine, the ECtHR confirmed that the right to participation in decision-making processes under Article 8 ECHR does not apply to decisions regarding the environment in general, and only benefits those whose rights are somehow affected.[971] It follows that the scope of this provision

consultation of indigenous peoples and provided an extensive account of the various elements contained in this duty, by reference to legislation and case-law of numerous OAS member States.

965 Mentioned *supra* note 774.

966 Ibid., Article 3(7).

967 See: Report of the Second Meeting of the Parties to the Convention on Access to Information, Public Participation in Decision-making and Access to Justice in Environmental Matters, *Promoting the Application of the Principles of the Aarhus Convention in International Forums*, UN Doc ECE/MP.PP/2005/2/Add.5 (2005).

968 UNECE, *Almaty Guidelines on Promoting the Application of the Principles of the Aarhus Convention in International Forums* (2005) para. 30.

969 By contrast, the African Commission on Human & Peoples' Rights and, to a certain extent, the IACHR have showed their openness to embracing a communitarian approach to human rights. This is natural with regard to the former, as the whole philosophy behind the African Charter is informed by the collective-social dimension of human rights as Peoples' Rights. Also, as seen above, the Charter includes a right to a healthy environment. In what concerns the IACHR, mention could be made to *Maya Indigenous Communities of the Toledo District* v. *Belize*, Case 12.053, Report N° 40/04, 12 October 2004, where the court interpreted the right to property (notably, the entitlement of indigenous peoples to use their ancestral land for agriculture and hunting) as affording protection from environmental devastation and unsustainable development.

970 *Taskin* v. *Turkey*, App. No. 46117/99, 10 November 2004.

971 Ibid., para. 118. See also: *Kyrtatos* v. *Greece*, App. No. 41666/98, 22 May 2003. For a comparison between human rights adjudication, including in the *Taskin* case, and the Aarhus Convention, see: A. Boyle, 'Human Rights and the Environment: Where Next?', 23 EJIL (2012) 613, 624–6.

is significantly narrower than Article 6 Aarhus Convention, which accords said right to anyone 'having an interest in' the environmental decision-making process.[972] A similar observation can be made with regard to the right of access to information. Although its importance has been re-stated in numerous ECtHR cases,[973] once again, it is only recognised in relation to those personally affected by an environmental matter. With a wider scope, the Aarhus Convention endorses such right as an entitlement of anyone: since it does not require an interest to be stated,[974] it ensures States' duty to inform in light of a broader concern for environmental governance, transparency of decision-making and public participation.[975]

Interestingly, public participation rights are widely acknowledged across the operational policies of international financial institutions, in terms that resonate with the Aarhus Convention. To use the WB as an example, its recently adopted ESF[976] so confirms. It emphasizes that the borrower is required to 'engage with stakeholders ... through information disclosure, consultation, and informed participation in a manner proportionate to the risks to and impacts on affected communities' and acknowledges the Bank's duty to diligently monitor the process.[977] Importantly, policy ESS10 on 'Stakeholder Engagement and Information Disclosure'[978] defines stakeholders as individuals or groups who are 'affected or likely to be affected by the project' and 'may have an interest in the project'.[979]

Both the Aarhus Convention and the operational policies of international financial institutions such as the WB emerge as important benchmarks to understand the scope of member States' human rights due diligence obligations. They contextualise the latter by taking into account the framework under which said institutions operate. In this vein, they allow for a wider interpretation of member State obligations to ensure that meaningful consultations and timely dissemination of information take place throughout the operations of the organisation. These are notably extended to a broad range of stakeholders: not only those affected, but also those likely to be affected, or having an interest in, said operations.

972 Article 6 Aarhus Convention, *supra* note 774, read in conjunction with Article 2(5), where the 'public concerned' is defined.
973 Recall, for example, the cases mentioned *supra* note 962.
974 See: Article 4(1)(a) Aarhus Convention, *supra* note 774.
975 A. Boyle, 'Human Rights or Environmental Rights? A Reassessment', 18 Fordham Envtl L Rev (2007) 471, 491.
976 *Supra* note 187.
977 World Bank Environmental and Social Policy for Investment Project Financing, ibid., para. 53.
978 *Supra* note 187, 131–7.
979 Ibid., para. 5. Similar wording is used in the EBRD Performance Requirement 10 on Information Disclosure and Stakeholder Engagement, May 2014, para. 9, 55. It particularly notes (54) that it is guided by the spirit, principles and ultimate goals of the Aarhus Convention. The AfDB's Handbook on Stakeholder Consultation and Participation in ADB Operations, 2001, 2, speaks of 'people/communities who may – directly or indirectly, positively or negatively – affect or be affected by the outcomes of projects or programs'; finally, both the AIIB and the AsDB refer throughout their safeguard policies to affected persons and, generally, to 'other stakeholders' (see, respectively: AIIB Environmental and Social Framework, February 2016, and Safeguard Policy Statement, June 2009).

C MEMBER STATES AS GUARANTORS OF THE PROPORTIONALITY OF HUMAN RIGHTS INTERFERENCE. The operations of international financial institutions – almost unavoidably – produce certain negative impacts in the lives of individuals, thereby interfering with the enjoyment of human rights. This interference, then, must be outweighed by other considerations, such as the economic or environmental benefits that come with a given project. The question will, more often than not, be one of guaranteeing the necessity and proportionality of human rights impacts. Arguably, the WB, for instance, rightly postponed a loan aimed at strengthening the healthcare sector in Uganda in 2014, after the adoption of a law by President Museveni imposing harsh penalties for homosexuality.[980] Here, the high likelihood of discrimination and endangerment of members of the LGBT community weighed too strongly against any other possible considerations in the proportionality test. As has been noted, while the provision of public benefits might impose external costs, if these exceed the former then it is socially better that the provision of benefits does not occur.[981]

The quest for economic development must therefore be measured against the particular rights of individuals, as well as the needs of society in general. As much has been repeatedly emphasized by human rights bodies, for instance, in cases involving the impacts of economic activity upon human rights and the environment.[982] Hence, in the minds of Executive Directors, prior to the approval of a loan must generally lie the question of whether the human rights restriction that comes with the project or programme at hand is in accordance with human rights standards, compatible with the nature of these rights and in the interest of legitimate aims, and whether the interference is proportional and necessary for the promotion of the general welfare in a democratic society.[983]

A more concrete account in this respect has been advanced by the CESCR. In addressing the use of retrogressive measures by States, the Committee has usefully asserted that it must be demonstrated that 'the adoption of retrogressive measures was based on the most careful consideration of alternatives, that disadvantaged groups have been prioritized and that the measures can be justified by reference to the totality of the rights and by the fact that full use was made of available resource'.[984]

980 See Reuters news article, available at: www.reuters.com/article/us-uganda-gay-idUSKBNO G6oZX20140806, last consulted 15 October 2018.

981 L. A. Kornhauser, *supra* note 21, 142.

982 Emblematic cases in this respect include: the *Hatton* case, decided by the ECtHR (see: *Hatton and others* v. *United Kingdom*, App. No. 36022/97, 8 July 2003, para. 99 et seq.); the *Ogoniland* case, decided by the African Commission on Human & Peoples' Rights (*supra* note 963, paras. 51–8) and the *Maya Indigenous Community of Toledo* v. *Belize* case, decided by the IACHR (*supra* note 969, paras. 148–54).

983 See: Articles 4 and 5(1) of the ICESCR, *supra* note 894, and interpretations thereof contained in CESCR, General Commment No. 14, *supra* note 899, paras. 28 and 29. Very similar language is used by the ECtHR, e.g., in the *Nada* case, *supra* note 429, para. 181.

984 CESCR, 'An Evaluation of the Obligation to Take Steps to the "Maximum of Available Resources" under an Optional Protocol to the Covenant', UN Doc. E/C.12/2007/1 (2007) para. 46. The

From the above, it is possible to draw some inspiration as to what Executive Directors are required to do. Notably, they are required to ensure that the project or programme at hand will not result in a disproportional interference with the enjoyment of human rights in the borrowing country. Where injurious interference is unavoidable, they must confirm, when assessing project-related documentation, that mitigation measures have been envisaged in the programme/project design, such as compensation to victims and other sorts of 'safety nets'.[985] For example, following the requirements of the WB's ESS7 on Indigenous Peoples, Executive Directors must be able to verify that 'the Borrower will minimize and/or compensate for [unavoidable] impacts in a culturally appropriate manner proportionate to the nature and scale of such impacts and the form and degree of vulnerability of the affected Indigenous Peoples'.[986] Importantly, in performing their monitoring role, Executive Directors are required to observe a higher standard of care in cases where the risk of harm is also particularly higher, as in, for instance, infrastructure project lending.[987] Part of the solution here lies in urging management to pay particular attention to a given aspect of the project, and duly following up on the management's initiatives.[988]

The principles that apply to the Executive Boards of multilateral development banks are similarly relevant, *mutatis mutandis*, in the context of IMF operations. Here, Executive Directors' role in guaranteeing the proportionality of human rights interference is key when it comes to the imposition of macroeconomic adjustment conditionality upon borrower States. It is widely known that IMF-imposed limitations on government expenditure for the purposes of debt restructuring are often pursued at the expense of social investment. This significantly reduces the capacity of debtor countries, particularly the poorest, to establish the necessary conditions for the realisation of human rights.[989]

While the involvement of IMF Executive Directors in loan negotiations with borrowers is less direct when compared to that of WB Executive Directors,[990] the former

Committee moreover emphasized that 'the human rights framework obliges States to act with care and deliberation, to assess the impacts of their actions and omissions, and to adjust their policies and measures as soon as they become aware that current policies might lead to unsustainable results. States' failure to meet this obligation may result in human rights violations.' Ibid.

985 S. Skogly, 'The Human Rights Obligations of the World Bank and the IMF', in W. V. Genugten, P. Hunt and S. Mathews (eds.), *World Bank, IMF and Human Rights* (2003) 51. With regard to the IMF's PRGT-supported programmes (recall *supra* note 4), for instance, it is explicitly mentioned in its 'Revised Operational Guidance to IMF Staff on the 2002 Conditionality Guidelines' (23 July 2014, para. 7) that, '[w]here feasible and appropriate, policy measures to mitigate adverse impacts on the most vulnerable should be included in program design'.

986 ESS7 on Indigenous Peoples/Sub-Saharan African Historically Underserved Traditional Local Communities, *supra* note 187, para. 18.

987 Recall Section 3.4.1.1.

988 Interview #XVIII, 12 June 2015.

989 *UN Guiding Principles on Foreign Debt and Human Rights*, *supra* note 4, 3, 4, 9.

990 As explained by R. Stone, *supra* note 58, 57, Executive Directors do not normally participate in missions to countries or the negotiation of programmes, and do not have access to confidential documents produced throughout the negotiation phase. This, however, does not prevent Executive

are certainly well aware of the general terms of such negotiations (see Section 3.5.1.1). In the IMF, too, human rights due diligence requires Executive Directors to screen the negotiation process – and related documents[991] – through a human rights lens and to orient their votes accordingly. As recently stated by the CESCR, the member States of international financial institutions, and the IMF in particular, who grant loans against certain conditionalities are required 'to carry out a human rights impact assessment prior to the provision of the loan concerned, in order to ensure that the conditionalities do not disproportionately affect economic, social and cultural rights, and do not lead to discrimination'.[992] Executive Directors should moreover ensure, among other things: that the programme at hand contains a debt sustainability analysis,[993] incorporating inequality as an essential element;[994] that whichever restrictions come with the loan, they do not impact negatively on domestic policies aimed at improving social well-being;[995] and that the policy or programme furthers the delivery of basic services which are essential for the enjoyment of human rights, in an equal and non-discriminatory fashion.[996] In sum, Executive Directors must make sure that the loan subject to their approval maintains a satisfactory level of human rights protection[997] and does not undermine the existence of conditions in which rights can be fully exercised in the borrower country.[998]

As a final note, it should be highlighted that, apart from the diligence that is due prior to the approval of a project or programme, the role of member States in monitoring and following up their implementation is likewise fundamental. Weaknesses in this respect have been acknowledged by the WB, for example.[999] While the Bank's ESF attempts to respond to this matter from the viewpoint of the institution's supervisory role,[1000] that of

Directors from being informed (even fully informed, in the case of the US, France or the UK), as they can always request special briefings with staff.

991 Three types of document are subjected to the Board's scrutiny: the staff report, the 'buff' (i.e., a statement issued by the potential borrower regarding the staff report) and the 'greys' (Interview #XXV, 22 June 2015).

992 CESCR, 'Public debt, austerity measures and the International Covenant on Economic, Social and Cultural Rights', *supra* note 902, paras. 9 and 11. See also: *UN Guiding Principles on Foreign Debt and Human Rights, supra* note 4, para. 40.

993 States themselves acknowledged this in the Addis Ababa Action Agenda of the Third International Conference on Financing for Development, *supra* note 830.

994 UN Human Rights Council 2016 Report on Foreign Debt, *supra* note 7, para. 57.

995 *UN Guiding Principles on Foreign Debt and Human Rights, supra* note 4, para. 8. See also: M. Salomon, *supra* note 681, 165.

996 *UN Guiding Principles on Foreign Debt and Human Rights, supra* note 4, para. 11 et seq.

997 *IKA-ETAM* v. *Greece, supra* note 30, paras. 69–82, where the European Committee of Social Rights found Greece responsible for violating the right to social security under the European Social Charter on the basis of the adoption of retrogressive measures.

998 UN Human Rights Council 2016 Report on Foreign Debt, *supra* note 7, para. 9.

999 The World Bank, 'The World Bank's Safeguard Policies: Proposed Review and Update', Approach Paper (2012).

1000 This is referred to several times in, e.g.: The World Bank, 'Review and Update of the World Bank's Safeguard Policies: Environmental and Social Framework (Proposed Second Draft)', Consultation Paper (2015).

the member States should not be overlooked. As noted by an Executive Director, there is no institutionalised form of supervision by the Board regarding the social and environmental risks of projects or programmes.[1001] Yet, throughout the whole project cycle, Executive Directors have all the leeway (both formally and informally) to request clarifications from the staff regarding human-rights-related concerns.[1002] Given their 'authority management' role, member States are required to account for problems that emerge during the institution's operations in a timely manner, and to ensure that the organisation mitigates any unintended or unanticipated adverse consequences stemming from said operations. Ultimately, to monitor is also to understand the impacts of what is approved and when these impacts are seen to interfere disproportionately with human rights, a lesson can be learned for future decision-making.

D FINAL REMARKS ON THE CONTOURS OF DUE DILIGENCE AS A STANDARD OF CARE IN INSTITUTIONAL DECISION-MAKING. All the above being said, it should be noted that human rights due diligence does not require member States to take all possible measures to protect individuals against institutional harm. Too stringent a framework would otherwise demotivate States to engage in multilateral institutional undertakings.[1003] In fact, the standard to understand what diligence is due is commonly perceived as one of reasonableness.[1004] For instance, according to the ILC Articles on Prevention of Transboundary Harm,[1005] due diligence manifests itself 'in reasonable efforts by a State to inform itself of factual and legal components that relate foreseeably to a contemplated procedure and to take appropriate measures, in timely fashion, to address them'.[1006] The ICJ moreover hinted at this in the *Genocide* case, when referring to due diligence as an obligation of States 'to employ all means reasonably available to them'.[1007]

Reasonableness thus seems to point to a subjective standard,[1008] whereby the means at the disposal of the member State should be taken into account when examining whether it has observed the required standard of care. It has generally been noted that lack of economic or administrative capacity may mitigate the

1001 Interview #XXIX, 26 June 2015.

1002 Interview #III, 2 June 2014; Interview #XIII, 5 June 2015; Interview #XV, 11 June 2015; Interview #XVII, 12 June 2015.

1003 A. Kämpf, 'Human Rights Require Accountability: Why German Development Cooperation Needs a Human Rights Complaints Mechanism', German Institute for Human Rights Policy Paper, 2015, 17.

1004 See, inter alia: R. Barnidge, *supra* note 924, 107, 108, 116–20; Maastricht Principles, *supra* note 53, Principle 15. For an overview of international investment law jurisprudence applying the reasonableness standard, see: ILA Due Diligence Report, *supra* note 56, 8, 9.

1005 *Supra* note 923.

1006 Ibid., para. 10 of the commentaries to Article 3.

1007 *Genocide* case, *supra* note 779, para. 430. See also Article 8(4) of the Optional Protocol to the ICESCR, UNGA Resolution A/RES/63/117 (2008), where the reasonableness test is used as the standard by which communications may be examined by the Committee.

1008 For a brief discussion about whether due diligence implies an objective or subjective assessment, see: ILA Due Diligence Report, *supra* note 56, 10.

attendant obligations for developing countries,[1009] and this remains no less true when it comes to their participation in international financial institutions. But even for member States in such position, a minimum degree of vigilance is called for.[1010] Next to this, it is important to note that member States with a stronger voice in international financial institutions will probably have more means at their disposal to actually effect change when compared to those with little power. Such differences may entail that, in the end, not all the member States that were involved in a given decision-making process are found responsible for a breach of due diligence.

Ultimately, where the member State has taken all reasonable measures vis-à-vis the staff and other members to eliminate or mitigate foreseeable human rights harm in project or programme design, and the latter is still included in the Board's agenda for approval, the only option that remains available to the member State is to abstain or vote against the project. The same philosophy applies when the approval of a second tranche release is at stake. As has generally been noted, 'failing to prohibit wrongful conduct is one way of failing to prevent it; it is simply a passive form of authorization'.[1011]

US representatives have, for example, opposed loans on environmental[1012] and human rights grounds. In fact, domestic legislation requires US representatives to oppose many other kinds of loan.[1013] With regard to their *domestic* human rights obligations, US Executive Directors are called upon to 'advance the cause of human rights' when acting within international financial institutions and to oppose any loan, financial or technical assistance which runs counter to 'the basic human needs' of the recipients of such assistance.[1014] This example serves as a valid interpretative reference of what (international) human rights law would require in these contexts.

A WB-financed land-titling project in Cambodia, approved by the Executive Board in 2002, constitutes an interesting 'case-study' in this respect. Serious human rights violations linked to the project's implementation led to the submission of a Request for Inspection to the Bank's Inspection Panel in 2009, on behalf of more

1009 T. Koivura, 'Due Diligence', in *Max Planck Encyclopedia of Public International Law*, February 2010, paras. 19 and 21.

1010 ILC, Special Rapporteur Sreenivasa Rao, *Second report on international liability for injurious consequences arising out of acts not prohibited by international law (prevention of transboundary damage from hazardous activities)*, UN Doc. A/CN.4/501 (1999) 118, 119, para. 31.

1011 T. Dannenbaum, 'Dual Attribution in the Context of Military Operations', in A. S. Barros, C. Ryngaert and J. Wouters (eds.), op. cit. *supra* note 37, 127.

1012 See: 22 U.S. Code § 262m-7(a), which reads as follows: 'The Secretary of the Treasury shall instruct the United States Executive Director of each multilateral development bank not to vote in favor of any proposal ... which would result or be likely to result in significant impact on the environment.' A description of the first US abstention for environmental reasons can be found in: B. M. Rich, *supra* note 19, 734, 735.

1013 Restrictions can, for example, be politically charged, such as the requirement that US representatives oppose loans to Iran (recall the discussion in Section 1.1.1.2) and recently to Argentina in the IDB (Interview #XXXIII, 31 June 2015). For an overview of the types of legal restriction imposed upon US representatives, see: R. M. Nelson and M. A. Weiss, *supra* note 119, 8, 9.

1014 22 U.S. Code § 262d.

than four thousand families. The requesters claimed that Bank policies had been flagrantly disregarded, resulting in the forced eviction of more than twenty-two thousand people. Following the Inspection Panel's findings, which largely concurred with said claims,[1015] and the management's response thereof, acknowledging several failures on the Bank's side,[1016] the Bank sought for solutions with the Cambodian Government, without much success. In response to such stalemate, the Board set in place a lending freeze to the country in 2011.[1017] The decision was reversed in 2016, however, with the Board's approval of new loans to Cambodia, comprising a land allocation project. This happened while a public appeal had been issued that year, calling upon the Government to put an end to increasing human rights abuses, including with regard to land rights.[1018] Seen from a human rights due diligence lens, the role of Executive Directors in supporting the Inspection Panel's investigations and in subsequently responding to the action plans submitted to them by the Bank's management is of undeniable importance (see Section 3.4.2.2). Human rights due diligence calls for close oversight and the circumstances of the case could only lead to the Board's ultimate decision of halting new funds to the country. The problem lies in the approval of new loans whilst the Bank had not fully discharged its commitments (set out in the action plans) towards the victims impacted by the abovementioned project, and in the midst of significant controversy around Cambodia's human rights performance.[1019] All such elements provide enough material to discuss member State responsibility. It was, indeed, on the basis of human rights grounds that the US Executive Director abstained from voting the abovementioned new loans.[1020]

In sum, what member States' human rights due diligence obligations call for is that project- or programme-related documentation be examined through a human rights lens and that human rights in fact play a role in the Executive Director's final

1015 See, e.g.: Inspection Panel Investigation Report, *Cambodia: Land Management and Administration Project (Credit No. 3650 – KH)*, 23 November 2010, 59, where the Panel observed that the resettlement process 'in no way met the standards envisaged in the [Bank's Resettlement Policy Framework] or reflected in widely accepted international standards (such as enshrined in relevant human rights instruments). There was no consultative and participatory process, civil works commenced long before the resettlement process had been satisfactorily implemented, and project affected people were subjected to pressure to evacuate their houses without having had access to any grievance procedures.'

1016 Management Report and Recommendation in Response to the Inspection Panel Investigation Report – Cambodia: Land Management and Administration Project (IDA Credit No. 3605-KH), Doc. INSP/58016-KH, 21 January 2011.

1017 The Cambodia Daily news article, 'World Bank Will Resume Funding to Cambodia', 21 May 2016, available at: www.cambodiadaily.com/news/world-bank-will-resume-funding-to-cambodia-112866/, last consulted 15 October 2018.

1018 Ibid. See also: Maryknoll Office for Global Concerns, 'Cambodia: The World Bank and human rights' (2016), available at: http://maryknollogc.org/article/cambodia-world-bank-and-human-rights, last consulted 15 October 2018.

1019 Ibid.

1020 Ibid.

decision. In this vein, and following the findings of Section 3.4.1, it can generally be asserted that voting, or expressing consent, in favour of a loan where the member State has not taken any preventive measures to avoid possible harm, for example, by omitting any consideration of the human rights or environmental impacts of the project at hand, may give rise to State responsibility, for a violation of its positive obligation to exercise due diligence in protecting human rights extraterritorially. In the particular case at stake, a standard of care will have to be determined, by questioning whether the State either *knew* or *should have known* (on the basis of staff reports and bilateral meetings) that the adopted decision could result in harmful conduct, and whether it could have reasonably averted it.[1021] Importantly, such a standard of care is to be observed throughout the whole project cycle. As noted in Section 3.4.2.1, C, member States' 'authority management' role entails that they are required to duly account for the human-rights-related concerns that arise during project or programme implementation, as well as to ensure that the organisation mitigates any unintended or unanticipated adverse consequences stemming from its operations.

The contours of due diligence as a standard of care in institutional decision-making do not seem to go further than this. Day-to-day operational decisions, for example, may be taken by the international financial institution's staff outside the remit of member State decision-making power. With regard to these decisions, it does not seem possible to invoke member State responsibility for failure to exercise due diligence in preventing human rights harm. Rather, it is the international organisation that should be held responsible for its own wrongful conduct. This is not to say, however, that member State responsibility may not arise in relation to such types of issue: indeed, it might come into play where the creation of an entity with operational autonomy to take decisions along said lines is not followed by the setting up of dispute settlement mechanisms allowing victims to contest the organisation's conduct. Here, the member State could be held responsible not for a failure to protect the human rights that were particularly harmed by the staff's decision, but, rather, for a failure to protect the individual's right of access to justice as applied in an institutional setting. This point will be returned to in the following sections.

1021 In the *ITC* litigation before the then Court of Justice of the European Communities, referred *supra* note 343, one of the arguments raised by Maclaine Watson against ITC member States concerned their negligence in acting upon the knowledge they had about the precariousness of the buffer stock manager's operations. As was noted, more detailed knowledge could have been obtained had they supported the UK's initiatives in that respect: the UK had in fact alerted to the buffer stock manager's operations and attempted to obtain more detailed information to evaluate whether or not the buffer stock manager was acting outside his mandate but all such attempts were blocked by the member States (See: Opinion of Advocate General Darmon, 1 June 1989, points 35, 37). In this case, the UK can be said to have acted to the best of its ability and, thus, to have satisfied the reasonableness standard inherent in the duty of due diligence.

3.4.2.2 The Setting Up of the International Financial Institution's Operational and Institutional Framework

International human rights law conditions member States in terms that demand not only the representation of, but also responsiveness to, the interests of those impacted by institutional operations (recall Section 3.2). This brings to the fore the question of how to operationalise every individual's entitlement to have his or her rights determined before an 'independent and impartial tribunal' in the framework of the operations of international financial institutions.[1022]

As will be seen, various shortcomings exist in this respect, which can be traced back to the way in which member States set up, and make use of, the internal (and external) dispute settlement mechanisms of international financial institutions. It will be contended that the problem, in the main, pertains to what member States omit to do (or *decide* not to do) in said contexts. Notably, member States' failure to bring sufficient pressure to bear on international financial institutions to provide for adequate responses to human rights violations may engage their responsibility under international law.

A MEMBER STATES' 'NON-DECISIONS' AS A RESPONSIBILITY MATTER? A fundamental component of States' human rights obligations relates to the possession of a legal, judicial and administrative apparatus that is able to guarantee human rights protection.[1023] Once States create an international financial institution to perform public functions *on their behalf*, it is thus essential to unravel how such protection duties are to be transposed to institutional contexts, and, notably, how they affect the role of member States as creators of the organisation.

A big part of the response to ensuring responsiveness lies in the way in which member States set up the operational framework of the international financial institution, i.e., in the policies they approve, the feedback mechanisms they set in place, and the internal accountability mechanisms they establish. In this sphere, however, the shortcomings are numerous. Suffice it to note that by 2013 (almost seventy years following the creation of the Bretton Woods institutions), the CRC was still pleading for the setting up of procedures and mechanisms to identify, address and remedy violations of children's rights within international organisations such as the WB.[1024]

1022 See: Article 10 UDHR, *supra* note 816.
While the current section is centred on internal and external dispute settlement mechanisms of international financial institutions, Section 3.5.2.4 will briefly address the setting up of accountability mechanisms by member States relating to their own conduct, before which violations of human rights due diligence could be alleged.

1023 See: R. Pisillo-Mazzeschi, *supra* note 906, 25, 26, generally discussing the requirements of the duty to protect and how due diligence relates to it.

1024 General Comment No. 16, *supra* note 952, para. 48.

To understand how human rights may be better protected in institutional frameworks, it is prudent to grasp who sets the agenda and how this agenda sometimes omits certain options. This is mostly so because any Executive Director, at any moment, may propose that certain items be brought before the Board for consideration.[1025] Truth be told, with such power in hand, member States could have by now done much more to ensure responsiveness when it comes to the activities of international financial institutions. One could thus wonder, alongside Wilde, whether '[t]he relatively unaccountable nature of international organizations may be a key structural feature as far as their importance to states is concerned, not something that has come about by accident'.[1026] If reform of the governance of international financial institutions is required under international human rights law,[1027] the question is then how exactly the responsibility of member States may be engaged for failure to undertake it.

As has been explained with regard to the IMF, '[a]ny action or deliberate nonaction of the Executive Board is based on a "decision" in the broad sense. Not all of them are formalized and recorded as "Executive Board decisions" in the technical sense. Deliberate nonaction may be expressed by refraining from putting an item on the agenda of the Board, by informally requesting a member state to withdraw an application, or by adjourning discussion on the matter *sine die*.'[1028] In this vein, the non-inclusion of human rights considerations in the organisation's policy framework, or the non-creation of robust internal accountability mechanisms, could under certain circumstances be perceived as a *decision* not to pursue such concerns.[1029] It is true that (member) States omit many things all the time, and although some authors would emphasize that member States' 'non-decisions' pertain to the political realm of decision-making,[1030] it will be contended in the subsequent sections

1025 E. Hexner, *supra* note 587, 80; Interview #XIII, 5 June 2015; Interview #XVIII, 12 June 2015; Interview #XXIV, 19 June 2015; Interview #XXIX, 26 June 2015; Interview #XXX, 26 June 2015.

1026 R. Wilde, *supra* note 37, 411.

1027 See, generally: D. Bradlow, *supra* note 188; J. Stiglitz, *supra* note 16.

1028 E. Hexner, *supra* note 587, 87, 88.

1029 For example, throughout the WB's environmental and social safeguard review process (the ESF is referred *supra* note 187), which lasted for years, numerous CSOs approached the Bank, either through direct meetings or the submission of policy papers, to explain in detail the various shortcomings of its environmental and social policies in terms of human rights protection (an overview is available at: https://consultations.worldbank.org/consultation/review-and-update-world-bank-safeguard-policies, last consulted 15 October 2018). Importantly, summaries of the consultations were provided to the Executive Board.

Generally, CSOs hold bilateral (ad hoc) meetings with Executive Directors throughout the year, where human rights concerns are addressed. It is even not uncommon to hear senior management blaming the Board for its inaction over the human rights agenda. See: G. A. Sarfaty, *supra* note 206, 54, 55.

1030 See, inter alia: H. Schermers and N. Blokker, *supra* note 152, 501; S. Kadelbach, 'From Public International Law to International Public Law: A Comment on the "Public Authority" of International Institutions and the "Publicness" of Their Law', in A. Von Bogdandy, R. Wolfrum, J. V. Bernstorff, P. Dann and M. Goldmann (eds.), op. cit. *supra* note 50, 47, referring to the 'non-decision' of UN member States to set up an independent body to review the process of delisting of terrorism suspects as a political question.

that some of them do rise to the level of legal relevance.[1031] This is so where, in contravention of the right of access to justice, member States fail to ensure that the victims of institutional harm are able to pursue remedies against the wrongdoing international financial institution and/or the member States themselves for their own wrongful conduct.

While the following section will focus on the establishment of adequate internal mechanisms of enforcement, using the WB as a 'case-study', a preliminary note on member States' role in the design of its operational policies is in order. This is so, as human rights harm stemming from institutional operations may also find its source in loopholes contained in the policies approved by the Board.[1032] An example that can be provided in this respect concerns the new ESS2 on Labor and Working Conditions. The policy does not refer to ILO's core labour standards conventions and does not fully protect workers' freedom of association in Bank-funded projects, since it regards it as a domestic legal matter.[1033] It is therefore possible to finance projects in countries where the right to freedom of association is not recognised – while this labour standard is at the core of the ILO's values.[1034] Apart from possible questions of member State responsibility for the approval of a loan on such terms (as discussed above), other issues arise in this case. For instance, if the right to freedom of association were violated in the course of project implementation, the victim would not be able to make much use of the Inspection Panel, which is solely competent to judge the Bank's compliance with its own operational policies (see Section 3.4.2.2, B). This would result in a lack of protection afforded to the individual, which could be traced back to a failure of the member States to ensure that the institutional policies they approved were sufficiently protective of human rights. Hence, problems regarding the human rights compatibility of redress mechanisms may in reality more directly relate to the human rights incompatibility of the standards against which these mechanisms measure institutional performance.[1035]

1031 See further: M. Koskenniemi, *supra* note 94, 174–82, on the distinction between States' legal and purely political behaviour.

1032 Differently from multilateral development banks, where the Boards of Executive Directors are quite influential in both project and policy design, the role of the IMF Board is most evident in debating and amending changes in general policies (see: R. Stone, *supra* note 58, 77; Interview #XXVI, 22 June 2015). Responsibility for failure to exercise due diligence within the IMF can thus more often emerge in the latter contexts, as it is also then that more means are available to Executive Directors to effect change.

1033 Para. 16 of ESS2 on Labor and Working Conditions, *supra* note 187. Still, in order to afford some level of protection, the policy notes that project workers should not be hampered, by the borrower, from developing alternative mechanisms to protect their rights. The WB's Guidance Notes for Borrowers (2018) 11, 12, fill this gap only partially (the document is available at: https://bankinformationcenter.org/en-us/update/house-financial-services-committee-passes-world-bank/).

1034 See, inter alia, Principle I of the Declaration Concerning the Aims and Purposes of the International Labour Organization, annexed to the ILO's Constitution, 15 UNTS 40, adopted 1 April 1919.

1035 See: 'Glass Half Full Report', *supra* note 24, 63.

B THE INADEQUACY OF THE WORLD BANK'S INTERNAL DISPUTE SETTLEMENT MECHANISMS. The claim that 'power breeds responsibility' entails that victims of harm should have access to a remedy against whoever exercised power in a given circumstance. Besides the international organisation's power as perpetrator, it is important to recall that the power withheld by member States as creators remains a legally relevant factor to consider when evaluating the organisation's capacity to respond to the harm it caused. After all, here, as elsewhere, the organisation's performance most often emerges as the result of decisions (or 'non-decisions') taken by the member States.[1036] As will be contended, the responsibility of member States may notably be engaged by failing to bring sufficient pressure to bear on international organisations to provide for adequate (i.e., human-rights-consistent) dispute settlement mechanisms.[1037]

It should be noted that by 2010, all multilateral development banks had established one dispute settlement mechanism, with the mandate to investigate claims from victims of project-related harm (or risk thereof), owed to a failure of the organisation to comply with its operational policies and procedures.[1038] These initiatives are commendable, but are not necessarily indicative of effective human rights protection, as the WB example will demonstrate. The IMF constitutes the only international financial institution without any sort of accountability mechanism, inasmuch as, so the argument goes, the nature of its operations differs from that of the other organisations.[1039] One fails to see, however, how the absence of an accountability mechanism with competence to evaluate IMF performance, the quality of its advice and the accuracy of its assessments regarding the human rights impacts of its programmes[1040] has not yet come across in judicial fora as a violation, by member States, of their human rights protection duties. All the more so considering that the Executive Board is free to introduce such a mechanism on its own authority, without the need for a decision by the Board of Governors or an amendment to the IMF's Articles of Agreement.[1041]

In what concerns the WB, various mechanisms have been set in place to evaluate its performance, which are of relevance to the current discussion. To start with, failures of the Bank to comply with its operational policies may be signalled through regular reviews undertaken by the Independent Evaluation Group (IEG). On the basis of its assessment of the organisation's development performance, it can put forward recommendations for the Executive Board to consider, including policy revision or remedial action.[1042] The IEG plays a non-negligible role as reviewer of the overall operations of the Bank, but not of particular individual complaints.

1036 K. Wellens, *Remedies against International Organisations* (2002) 44.
1037 C. Ryngaert and H. Buchanan, *supra* note 37, 146.
1038 D. Bradlow, *supra* note 188, 56.
1039 Interview #XXXII, 30 June 2015.
1040 See, generally: J. Stiglitz, *supra* note 16, 119, 133.
1041 D. Bradlow, *supra* note 188, 57.
1042 See the IEG website, available at: http://ieg.worldbankgroup.org/about-us, last consulted 15 October 2018.

To a certain extent, such tasks were taken up by the Inspection Panel.[1043] This internal accountability mechanism constitutes an important avenue for aggrieved individuals to contest actions or omissions in the framework of Bank-financed projects. The Panel, however, only has recommendatory powers; and in examining the Bank's compliance with its operational policies, it neither applies human rights law nor is competent to establish human rights violations; it is therefore unable to offer reparation to victims.[1044] While project-related grievances may be addressed through project-level grievance mechanisms and the Grievance Redress Service,[1045] these mechanisms, too, fall short in applying human rights prescriptions.[1046] Similar considerations apply to the Compliance Advisor and Ombudsman (CAO), established by the IFC and the MIGA. It constitutes an independent recourse mechanism for projects supported by these institutions, and addresses the concerns of individuals and communities affected by the environmental or social impacts of those projects. The CAO may support the stakeholders involved in resolving the issues complained about and may also undertake compliance auditing of IFC/MIGA operations.[1047] The problem-solving competences of the CAO, however, do not extend to the provision of indemnity or compensation for any material harm.[1048]

Despite the significance of the above mechanisms, self-adjudication can lead to arbitrariness, and, thus, 'there is no guarantee of the sustainability of internal accountability mechanisms, however well intentioned, and no guarantee that where policies exist, they are necessarily enforced by the institutional enforcement mechanisms'.[1049] In fact, in a 2016 report authored by eleven CSOs on the practice of several internal accountability mechanisms,[1050] it is noted that 'more than half of complaints do not proceed past the registration or eligibility phase, and a significant number of those found eligible never proceed to a substantive phase of the pro-

1043 See: World Bank Executive Directors' Resolution No. IBRD 93-10 and Resolution No. IDA 93-6 'The World Bank Inspection Panel', adopted on 22 September 1993.

1044 Still, individual claims of human rights violations can be subjected to its appraisal. For instance, in the Chad-Cameroon pipeline investigation (from 2002), the Panel explicitly considered whether the human rights context in Chad would impede the implementation of the project in a manner consistent with Bank policies, particularly those regarding informed and open consultations. See: World Bank Inspection Panel, 'Accountability at the World Bank: The Inspection Panel at 15 Years', 2009, 50.

1045 See: www.worldbank.org/grs, last consulted 15 October 2018.

1046 It has moreover been noted that project-level grievance mechanisms, despite being useful, are not independent and they present as drawback the fact that 'project-affected people may not trust that a project-level mechanism would adequately address their issues because they are often designed and operated by the same actor that may have caused the harm'. See: 'Glass Half Full Report', *supra* note 24, 56, 57.

1047 See: IFC CAO Operational Guidelines 2013, available at www.cao-ombudsman.org/howwework/ombudsman/documents/EnglishCAOGuidelines06.08.07Web.pdf, last consulted 15 October 2018.

1048 The same applies to the AsDB Accountability Mechanism and the EBRD Project Complaint Mechanism.

1049 C. Tan, *supra* note 264, 23, 24.

1050 'Glass Half Full Report', *supra* note 24.

cess'.[1051] A comparison of concluded cases in the Inspection Panel and the CAO shows that the former found 63.5 per cent of concluded cases eligible and that 33 per cent of them reached a substantive phase and achieved results, whereas the CAO found 55 per cent of concluded cases eligible, with 30 per cent of them reaching a substantive phase and only 20 per cent achieving results.[1052] Next to this, the report points to the frequent failure of multilateral development banks to adequately respond to findings of non-compliance by their internal accountability mechanisms. As seen above, the findings of the Inspection Panel, for example, translate into recommendations,[1053] and, thus, part of the solution lies in the Board's willingness to take them on board. The end result is that '[c]omplainants must accept a decision handed down by the same body – namely, the board of directors – that approved the project at issue'.[1054]

From the above, it follows that there are clear limitations in holding the WB answerable for human rights violations. In commenting on the ECtHR's *Bosphorus* decision, and its application of the 'equivalent protection' criterion to the EU (recall the discussion in Section 3.3.1.1), De Schutter observed that so much reliance on the internal accountability mechanism (in this case the ECJ) of an international organisation that had not acceded to the ECHR was not merited, inasmuch as, even if remedies were available, full human rights protection could not be guaranteed.[1055] Next to this, the author asserted that a finding of 'equivalent protection' could not obliterate 'the added value that a form of judicial control *external* to the legal order concerned might represent'.[1056] De Schutter's observations with regard to the EU can be said to generally apply to international financial institutions – and even more so, considering that their accountability mechanisms are empowered neither to settle human rights disputes nor to provide judicial-type remedies, such as damages for non-compliance with institutional policies.[1057] Within the WB, 'equivalent protection' might thus be difficult to obtain. This is owed not only to the inexistence of an independent and impartial dispute settlement system within the Bank that is able to effectively protect human rights, as seen

1051 Ibid., 52, 53.
1052 Ibid., 46, 47.
1053 To be more precise, once the technical eligibility of a request for inspection is confirmed by the Panel, the latter submits a report recommending an investigation to the Board. If, in its discretion, the Board approves the report, the Inspection Panel undertakes the proposed investigation and prepares a concluding Investigation Report, once again for Board consideration. The latter report does not contain any recommendations as to which remedial action should be taken, since the Inspection Panel solely passes judgment upon the WB's non-compliance with its policies. This task is rather taken up by management, through the preparation of a separate report. Both reports are evaluated by the Board, and it is up to the Executive Directors to approve the plans of action that management may have included in its report. See: 'The Inspection Panel at the World Bank: Operating Procedures', April 2014, paras. 41–50 and 66–71 (Inspection Panel Operating Procedures).
1054 'Glass Half Full Report', *supra* note 24, 60.
1055 O. De Schutter, *supra* note 391, 83.
1056 Ibid. (emphasis in original).
1057 E. Suzuki and S. Nanwani, 'Responsibility of International Organizations: The Accountability Mechanisms of Multilateral Development Banks', 27 Mich J Int'l L (2005) 206.

above, but also to the absence of external mechanisms satisfying similar requirements, as will be briefly discussed in the following section.

C SUBJECTING THE WORLD BANK TO EXTERNAL DISPUTE SETTLEMENT MECHANISMS. When it comes to subjecting international organisations to the jurisdiction of domestic courts, it is well known that they usually enjoy 'full' functional immunity or other extended grants of immunity. International development banks constitute, however, an exception to this: in particular, the amenability of the WB to suit in national courts is envisaged in its Articles of Agreement.[1058] In practice, the scope of immunity depends on how functional immunity is interpreted in national courts – and these, as noted by Reinisch and Wurm, tend to interpret broadly the 'remaining' immunity in order to abstain from adjudicating a certain dispute.[1059]

Such a state of affairs may be in conflict with individuals' right of access to justice,[1060] which has been defined as the 'right to obtain the protection of the law and the availability of legal remedies before a court or other equivalent mechanism of judicial or quasi-judicial protection'.[1061] Although this right might be subject to limitations, *in casu*, for the legitimate purpose of protecting the independent functioning of international organisations, said limitations should 'not restrict or reduce the access left to the individual in such a way or to such an extent that the very essence of the right is impaired'.[1062]

The particular question of how the right of access to justice is juxtaposed with member State obligations was addressed by the ECtHR in the *Waite and Kennedy* case.[1063] There, the Court examined an employment-related claim regarding the

1058 See: Article VII, Section 3 of the IBRD Articles of Agreement, *supra* note 4; Article VI, Section 3 of the Articles of Agreement of the International Finance Corporation, 25 May 1955; and Article 44 of the Convention Establishing the Multilateral Investment Guarantee Agency, 24 ILM 1605, 11 October 1985.

1059 A. Reinisch and J. Wurm, 'International Financial Institutions before National Courts', in D. Bradlow and D. Hunter (eds.), op. cit. *supra* note 1, 103–35. With regard to international organisations in general, see: C. Ryngaert, 'The Immunity of International Organizations before Domestic Courts: Recent Trends', 7 IOLR (2010) 121. Recently, however, the US Supreme Court showed some signs of reversal of the above-mentioned tendency as it considered the IFC not to be absolutely immune from suit. See: *Budha Ismail Jam, et al, Petitioners v. International Finance Corporation*, 27 February 2019, 586 U.S. — (2019), a case involving a community of Indian fisherfolk, which sued the IFC for harm caused by a $450 million IFC-financed Tata Mundra coal-fired power plant in Gujarat, India.

1060 While prioritising the right of access to justice over institutional immunity is mainly a European approach, it has also been expressed by other international courts and tribunals, as well as administrative tribunals of international organisations, as noted by A. Reinisch, 'Immunity of Property, Funds, and Assets (Article II Section 2 General Convention)', in A. Reinisch and P. Bachmayer (eds.), *The Conventions on the Privileges and Immunities of the United Nations and Its Specialized Agencies: A Commentary* (2016) 72–9.

1061 F. Francioni, 'Access to Justice, Denial of Justice and International Investment Law', 20(3) EJIL (2009) 729, 729.

1062 ECtHR *Waite and Kennedy* case, *supra* note 842, para. 59, repeatedly highlighted by the court in subsequent case-law, such as, for example, the *Al-Dulimi* case, mentioned *supra* note 430, para. 129.

1063 Ibid.

European Space Agency and the question of whether the right of access to justice had been unduly impaired by Germany, for having granted immunity to the organisation. It then famously held that

> where States establish international organisations in order to pursue or strengthen their cooperation in certain fields of activities, and *where they attribute to these organisations certain competences and accord them immunities, there may be implications as to the protection of fundamental rights*. It would be incompatible with the purpose and object of the Convention, however, if the Contracting States were thereby absolved from their responsibility under the Convention in relation to the field of activity covered by such attribution. It should be recalled that the Convention is intended to guarantee not theoretical or illusory rights, but rights that are practical and effective. This is particularly true for the right of access to the courts in view of the prominent place held in a democratic society by the right to a fair trial.[1064]

For WB member States, what are, then, the human rights implications of granting the institution with immunity? It could be asserted that Executive Directors are required to undertake measures towards the waiver of the immunity of the WB, or one of its officials, when the latter's responsibility for human rights violations is invoked before a court.[1065] While the authority to decide upon waivers of immunity normally rests on the executive head of the organisation,[1066] it is clear that Executive Directors have enough leeway to steer institutional behaviour in this respect (recall Section 2.2). Importantly, the right to provide authoritative interpretation of the provisions contained in the constitutions of international financial institutions, including with regard to privileges and immunities,[1067] is normally granted to the Executive Board.[1068] Next to this, it could be argued that an individual's right of access to justice directs the requirement of rejection of immunity to national courts.[1069]

Still, member States' duty to safeguard the right of access to justice can be fulfilled through other means. Even if immunity from national jurisdiction is maintained, it

1064 Ibid., para. 67 (emphasis added).

1065 In the Convention on the Privileges and Immunities of the Specialized Agencies, *supra* note 210, the waiver of the organisation's immunity is foreseen in Article III, Section 4, and the waiver of the official's immunity in Article VI, Section 22. In the latter case, it is specified that such a waiver is required where 'maintaining the official's immunity would impede the course of justice' and provided that 'waiving his or her immunity would not jeopardize the interests of the institution'.

1066 See, inter alia: A. S. Barros and C. Ryngaert, 'Officials (Article VI Sections 18–23 Specialized Agencies Convention)', in A. Reinisch and P. Bachmayer (eds.), op. cit. *supra* note 210, 430–3.

1067 See, e.g.: Article VII of the IBRD Articles of Agreement, *supra* note 4, and Articles 50–9 of the Agreement Establishing the AfDB, *supra* note 567.

1068 See, e.g.: Article IX(a) of the IBRD Articles of Agreement, ibid. and Article 61(2) of the Agreement Establishing the AfDB, ibid.

1069 Given the principle of the unity of the State, domestic courts are to be considered organs of States whose conduct is attributable to the latter for the purposes of international responsibility. See: para. 5 of the commentaries to Article 4 ASR. See also: J. Crawford, *The International Law Commission's Article on State Responsibility: Introduction, Text and Commentaries* (2005) 91–3.

is surely not tantamount to immunity from the substance of the claim.[1070] What matters is that said means constitute a 'reasonable alternative' to protect human rights effectively, as also emphasized by the ECtHR in *Waite and Kennedy*,[1071] and subsequently tested in various cases, including the recent *Klausecker* v. *Germany*.[1072] Interestingly, the 'reasonable alternative' test has been applied as well by European courts in several disputes of an employment nature, and has a few times led to the prioritisation of the right of the claimant over the functional needs of the organisation, and, thus, to the rejection of the latter's immunity.[1073]

It is true that the 'question of immunity from legal process is distinct from the issue of compensation for any damages incurred', as asserted by the ICJ with respect to UN operations.[1074] And, in fact, the UN and NATO have already endorsed this understanding, by accepting responsibility for harm caused to individuals in the context of military interventions.[1075] With regard to international financial institutions, the assumption of responsibility – which is a decision that can certainly be triggered by the member States – would be helpful. From the perspective of the right of access to justice, however, it would not suffice. Indeed, what this right calls for is the provision, to individuals, of effective, alternative, procedural means to implement responsibility. The importance of setting up appropriate modes of dispute settlement as a counterpart to institutional immunity underlies Article IX Section 31

1070 A. Miller, 'The Privileges and Immunities of the United Nations', 6 IOLR (2009) 169, 98.

1071 *Waite and Kennedy*, *supra* note 842, para. 68.

1072 *Klausecker* v. *Germany*, App. No. 415/07, 6 January 2015, paras. 62–77 (where the court considered that the claimant's participation in an arbitral procedure constituted a reasonable alternative means to protect his rights under the ECHR).

1073 See, inter alia: *African Development Bank* v. *Haas*, French Court of Cassation (soc.), 25 January 2005, (2005) Journal des Tribunaux 454; *Western European Union* v. *Siedler*, Appeal Judgment, Cass No. S 04 0129 F, ILDC 1625 (BE 2009). In the context of peace and security operations, however, the *Wait and Kennedy* doctrine was for example rejected by the Dutch Supreme Court in *Mothers of Srebrenica et al.* v. *State of the Netherlands and the UN*, 13 April 2012, LJN: BW 1999; ILDC 1760 (NL 2012), a decision that was followed by the ECtHR in *Stiching Mothers of Srebrenica* v. *The Netherlands*, App. No. 65542/12, 11 June 2013.

When it comes to US case-law, institutional immunity tends to be upheld under a functional necessity rationale, as showed by the recent case *Amaratunga* v. *Northwest Atlantic Fisheries Organization*, 29 November 2013, 2013 SCC 66. In what particularly regards employment-related disputes against international financial institutions, the approach followed by US courts has been significantly influenced by the DC Court of Appeals' decision in *Mendaro* v. *World Bank*, 717 F.2d 610 (D.C.Cir. 1983). Here, based on policy reasons concerning the functional needs of the Bank, the court found the latter's amenability to suit in domestic jurisdictions to only apply in cases involving the external affairs of the institution with debtors, creditors or bondholders, and not in employment-related ones (see 615). For subsequent cases following such an approach, see: A. Reinisch and J. Wurm, *supra* note 1059, 130–6.

1074 ICJ *Cumuraswamy* opinion, *supra* note 171, para. 66.

1075 The UN has for example accepted legal liability for its activities in the Congo, as mentioned in the commentary to Article 36 ARIO. See also: C. F. Amerasinghe, *Principles of Institutional Law of International Organisations* (2004) 399–402. With regard to NATO, in 2000 it paid compensation to a Bulgarian family for damage to their property by a deflected missile during its military operations against Yugolsavia (see: H. Schermers and N. Blokker, *supra* note 152, 1013).

of the Convention on the Privileges and Immunities of the Specialized Agencies,[1076] which applies to, inter alia, disputes of a private law character, including tortious claims. Yet, there is no further specification of which means are to be resorted to.

As a reasonable alternative to domestic court litigation, a default mechanism for dispute settlement against international financial institutions should be provided for. According to Martha, arbitration could suitably serve such purpose.[1077] Suzuki moreover refers to the possibility, lying in the hands of Executive Directors, of creating an accountability mechanism in the form of a special tribunal capable of making binding decisions upon the international financial institution.[1078] Finally, a combination of settlement by negotiations, where required under a formalised conciliation process, could also be considered.[1079]

As put by a senior legal advisor of the WB,[1080] the provision of access to justice to individuals is not necessarily an immunity question, but, rather, one that calls for a decision by the Board to engage in responsibility matters, by ensuring that the organisation provides individuals with the necessary procedural means of redress.

D CONCLUDING REMARKS: ENGAGING MEMBER STATE RESPONSIBILITY FOR OMISSION OF THE REQUIRED CONDUCT. Sections 3.4.2.2, A–C show that it is pertinent to discuss the responsibility of member States for their 'non-decisions'[1081] implicit in the setting up of an international organisation that is not sufficiently able to respond to its wrongs, and that is moreover granted with immunity, by judging them against individuals' right of access to justice. As already noted in Section 3.3.1.1, the ECtHR's *Gasparini* case importantly contributed to the notion that structural lacunas in human rights protection within an international organisation may indeed invoke State responsibility for the terms in which powers were transferred to the organisation in the first place.

In answering the question of how to specifically argue for the establishment of member State responsibility, it should be noted that due diligence, as an element of member States' duty to protect, does not play a role when it comes to the institutionalisation, as such, of accountability mechanisms. With regard to the latter, the – right of access to justice – protection duties of member States thereby come forth as

1076 *Supra* note 210.

1077 R. Martha, 'International Financial Institutions and Claims of Private Parties: Immunity Obliges', in *The World Bank Legal Review: International Financial Institutions and Global Legal Governance* (2012) 124–6.

1078 E. Suzuki, 'Responsibility of International Financial Institutions under International Law', in D. Bradlow and D. Hunter (eds.), op. cit. *supra* note 1, 86.

1079 K. Schmalenbach, 'Dispute Settlement (Article IX Sections 31–32 Specialized Agencies Convention)', in A. Reinisch and P. Bachmayer (eds.), op. cit. *supra* note 210, 590.

1080 Communication on file with the author.

1081 As explained by S. Lukes, *supra* note 86, 77, 'whether we count an absence of action as an action depends on a judgement as to whether such action has significant causal consequences and on whether we are disposed to regard the actor who fails to act as responsible'.

obligations of result.[1082] In this vein, the responsibility of member States could be invoked where an individual, with prima facie grounds to claim a human rights violation against the WB, is unable to resort to any dispute settlement mechanism of the types referred to above, or is otherwise provided with an insufficient response thereof, which cannot be said to afford an equivalent human rights protection. Here, the responsibility of the member State would arise for omission, i.e., for creating and allowing these obstacles and barriers in institutional design to remain,[1083] and, thereby, for failure to ensure that victims of institutional harm would be able to pursue remedies against the offender (i.e., the international organisation).

A different – even if closely related – question pertains to how member States make *use* of the existing legal and administrative apparatus. It is here where due diligence comes in as an objective standard to evaluate member State behaviour against human rights prescriptions.[1084] To judge member State conduct along these terms is to evaluate, for example: the extent to which they effectively followed up project implementation (recall Section 3.4.2.1); the contours of their measures once informed about the findings and recommendations of the organisation's accountability mechanism;[1085] the terms in which they used their power internally to ignite institutional action when confronted with external (e.g., media) outcry concerning human rights matters[1086] – also considering that, in the WB at least, any Executive Director may submit a Request to the Inspection Panel 'in special cases of serious alleged violations of the Bank's policies and procedures';[1087] or the terms in which their representatives and national courts dealt with questions of immunity and the existence of alternative dispute settlement mechanisms.[1088]

Inherent in all these examples is an inquiry into the extent to which the member State undertook actions to 'investigate events' and to 'pursue those responsible'.[1089] Here, as before, its responsibility could arise for an omission, notably, for having failed to protect the individual's right of access to justice throughout the operations of the international financial institution.

1082 ILA Due Diligence Report, *supra* note 56, 16.

1083 See, UN Human Rights Council, Report of the Special Rapporteur on the right to food, *supra* note 23, para. 46, drawing on the (similar) human rights protection duties of States with regard to private conduct.

1084 R. Pisillo-Mazzeschi, *supra* note 906, 26–30.

1085 Recall *supra* note 1053, where, using the WB as example, an explanation is provided of the various instances where the Executive Board is involved in the Inspection Panel's assessment of complaints.

1086 As noted in *William E. Chapman (U.S.A.)* v. *United Mexican States*, 24 October 1930, UNRIAA IV, 636, 'the matter of warning obviously is important in connection with the question of responsibility'.

1087 Inspection Panel Operating Procedures, *supra* note 1053, para. 10(d).

1088 It is important to note that procedural duties of human rights protection do not rest solely upon the Executive Director, but rather weigh on the member State as a whole, as can be derived from the ECtHR's decision in *Mehida Mustafić-Mujić and Others* v. *The Netherlands*, App. No. 49037/15, 30 August 2016, para. 102.

1089 R. Pisillo-Mazzeschi, *supra* note 906, 29.

3.5 THE ESTABLISHMENT OF MEMBER STATE RESPONSIBILITY FOR FAILURE TO PROTECT HUMAN RIGHTS

Section 3.4 showed that a failure by member States to protect human rights as creators and participants in international organisations, and, notably, to observe due diligence prescriptions while performing such roles, engages their responsibility under international law. As repeatedly noted, the harmful activity of the international organisation is not per se attributable to the member State; it solely represents the external fact 'catalysing' a different wrongful act, i.e., the member State's failure to prevent or provide redress with regard to the organisation's acts.[1090] Two (wrongful) acts may thus be at stake: that of the international organisation, as perpetrator, and that of the member State, as careless 'authority manager'. Importantly, these spheres of responsibility are not substitutes to one another, as they both clearly respond to different things.

The current section will concentrate on the determination of wrongful member State behaviour (i.e., the breach of a due diligence duty by the member State) and its attendant legal consequences (i.e., the remedial forms that are available to those impacted by institutional operations). It will do so by discussing the various elements that determine the existence of a breach of the duty of due diligence, and, if harm is produced, the emergence of a subsequent duty to repair. Notably, proof must be made of member State's constructive knowledge and capacity to act, of what conduct is abstractly required of the State, and of the causality link between member State action and damage. As the latter will normally be indivisible, the allocation of responsibility among the various member States seems to remain outside the spectrum of the victim's burden of proof: he or she is required to demonstrate that the State *contributed* to the proscribed outcome, without, however, having to specify what the concrete contribution was. All these notions will be briefly discussed in Sections 3.5.1 and 3.5.2, which thereby provide a background for, and an overview of, the sort of technical arguments that could be raised when litigating member State responsibility. Questions of standing of course emerge, and, thus, some attention will likewise be devoted to identifying who, after, all, can be considered a 'victim' of institutional and member State behaviour.

[1090] Ibid., 26; and also: S. Heathcote, 'State Omissions and Due Diligence: Aspects of Fault, Damage, and Contribution to Injury in the Law of State Responsibility', in K. Bannelier, T. Christakis and S. Heathcote (eds.), *The ICJ and the Evolution of International Law: The Enduring Impact of the Corfu Channel Case* (2012) 301.

3.5.1 *Proof of Wrongfulness*

3.5.1.1 An Inquiry into Member States' Constructive Knowledge and Capacity to Act

As clarified in Section 3.4.1, in order to invoke member State responsibility for a breach of the duty due diligence, it is necessary to prove that the State either knew or should have known about the presence of risks in institutional operations, and that it had the capacity to influence the action of the international organisation with a view to preventing or redressing harm (or the threat thereof). This section discusses the concepts of knowledge and capacity as applied in international financial institutions only in generic terms, for due diligence is hardly an 'automatic standard for deciding, regardless of the circumstances, whether a State was "diligent" in discharging its duty of vigilance and protection'.[1091] Proof of a failure to exercise due diligence must thus always be made *in concreto*.[1092]

So as to understand the interaction between the principles of proof and responsibility in this sort of scenario, it is instructive to recall the ICJ's pronouncements in the *Corfu Channel* case.[1093] When inquiring into evidence of knowledge on the part of Albania, the Court held that 'it cannot be concluded from the mere fact of the control exercised by a State over its territory and waters that that State necessarily knew, or ought to have known, of any unlawful act perpetrated therein'.[1094] Along these lines, it could be claimed that the mere fact that member States remain powerful actors in international financial institutions does not necessarily entail (constructive) knowledge of the unlawfulness of institutional operations. Yet, the ICJ also asserted that the fact of control 'has a bearing upon the methods of proof available to establish the knowledge of that State as to such events. By reason of this exclusive control, the other State, the victim of a breach of international law, is often unable to furnish direct proof of facts giving rise to responsibility. Such a State should be allowed a more liberal recourse to *inferences of fact and circumstantial evidence*.'[1095] Following the ICJ's approach, this section will look into possible elements of fact characterising the relationship between international financial institutions and their members that allow for inferences to be made as to existence of the latter's knowledge.

Firstly, it is clear that Executive Directors are (or can be) generally well informed about the operations of international financial institutions throughout the whole project/programme cycle. In fact, in the phase of project appraisal and negotiation, interaction with management through bilateral meetings or informally is possible at

1091 ILC, Special Rapporteur García-Amador, *Second Report on State Responsibility*, *supra* note 409, 122, para. 7.
1092 *Genocide* case, *supra* note 779, para. 430.
1093 *Supra* note 912.
1094 Ibid., 18.
1095 Ibid. (emphasis added).

any time, allowing Executive Directors to raise varied questions and concerns – including in the IMF, where negotiations on the design of conditionality in individual programmes are normally held secretly.[1096] It is, thus not surprising to hear member State representatives admitting that the sense and outcome of Board meetings are often predictable, also for the staff. Notably, the latter is alive to the positions of Executive Directors regarding a given project or programme and will only submit it for Board approval once it becomes likely that the proposal will be accepted.[1097] Finally, when it comes to project implementation, the Board may likewise ask for updates at any moment[1098] – the phase prior to the approval of a loan's second tranche being particularly apposite for such purposes.[1099]

Knowledge about a given project or programme does not stop at the Executive Directors' offices. Rather, it is shared on a permanent basis with their capitals. Indeed, in several interviews conducted for this research it was corroborated that Executive Directors normally send information to the pertinent ministry(ies) when it comes to operational policies and politically sensitive matters. It was moreover clarified that capitals have permanent access, also through online platforms, to all project- or programme-related documentation, such as the reports prepared by management, and the buffs, greys or statements exchanged by Executive Directors.[1100]

It has been noted that the staff has some discretion in what it conveys to the Board through its reports: it may for instance downplay the severity of the risks entailed in a given project,[1101] and it may not even take into account certain factors, such as human rights risks, if the institution's operational policies do not require it to do so.[1102] Again, this points to the limits of what Executive Directors, and their national authorities, can *control* in institutional contexts (recall Section 1.2.1). In any event, and as previously mentioned, apart from staff reporting, other assessments are available to Executive Directors through their own sources and directly from management[1103] – not to mention the widely disseminated reports prepared by CSOs operating globally, and the meetings they themselves organise directly with

1096 R. Stone, *supra* note 58, 60, 135, 155; Interview #XIV, 8 June 2015; Interview #XVII, 12 June 2015; Interview #XXV, 22 June 2015; Interview #XXVII, 25 June 2015; Interview #XXVIII, 25 June 2015; Interview #XXX, 26 June 2015.

1097 Interview #II, 3 October 2013; Interview #IV, 3 June 2014; Interview #XXV, 22 June 2015; Interview #XXVII, 25 June 2015; Interview #XXVIII, 25 June 2015; Interview #XXX, 26 June 2015.

1098 Interview #XIII, 5 June 2015; Interview #XV, 11 June 2015; Interview #XVII, 12 June 2015.

1099 Interview #III, 2 June 2014.

1100 Interview #III, 2 June 2014; Interview #VI, 23 March 2015; Interview #XV, 11 June 2015; Interview #XXI, 17 June 2015; Interview #XXIII, 19 June 2015; Interview #XXVII, 25 June 2015; Interview #XXIX, 26 June 2015; Interview #XXXI, 29 June 2015.

1101 R. Stone, *supra* note 58, 66, describing how, during the Mexican crisis, IMF staff filtered the information it passed on to the Executive Board, by censoring data out of concern that it would be leaked or downplaying the severity of exchange rate risks in its reports.

1102 HRW, 'Abuse Free Development', *supra* note 25, 5.

1103 R. Stone, *supra* note 58, 69. According to the author, again in the context of the Mexican crisis, the fact that the Executive Board had access to more candid assessments through other means led to the unlikelihood of a different decision being taken, had staff reporting been more accurate.

Executive Directors.[1104] It can thus be asserted that knowledge, even if constructive, will more often than not be possible to prove.

The communication channels that link Executive Directors to the organisation's management and staff bring to the fore another element that is crucial for proof of undue diligence: that of member States' capacity to steer institutional behaviour. As acknowledged in various interviews, the conditioning of institutional conduct can actually be exerted throughout the whole project cycle.[1105] For instance, if publicity of human rights problems is solely made at the stage of project implementation, Executive Directors have the necessary discretion to suspend the financing of the second tranche (if the latter is still to be approved).[1106] This was one of the arguments raised in the abovementioned *Chixoy Dam* case:[1107] according to the petitioners, the fact that the second instalment for the project had been released after the occurrence of the massacres in Guatemala revealed the reckless disregard of the WB's Executive Board for the human rights of the Chixoy Dam communities, thereby engaging their international responsibility.[1108]

It is true, as repeatedly stated above, that there are limits as to what member States can *do* prior to, during, and in the follow-up to decision-making processes. Schermers and Blokker, for instance, have noted that rules on decision-making impose constraints on the freedom of member States to control, or take initiatives for, decisions in the organisation.[1109] To that, one should add that general rules safeguarding the independence of the organisation's officials and its well functioning likewise impose similar constraints.[1110] All this should be taken into account, since, as noted by the ICJ in the *Genocide* case, '[t]he State's capacity to influence must also be assessed by legal criteria, since it is clear that every State may only act within the limits permitted by international law'.[1111] That being so, it is also true that there are perfectly acceptable ways to combine respect for institutional autonomy with the operationalisation of member States' duties under international law, judging from all the examples mentioned in Section 3.4.2 on what human rights due diligence requires of member States.[1112] After all, 'capacity to influence effectively the action'[1113] of the international financial institution – in a human-

1104 Interview #VI, 23 March 2015.

1105 Interview #III, 2 June 2014; Interview #XII, 5 June 2015; Interview #XVI, 11 June 2015; Interview #XVII, 12 June 2015; Interview #XXI, 17 June 2015; Interview #XXV, 22 June 2015; Interview #XXVII, 25 June 2015; Interview #XXVIII, 25 June 2015; Interview #XXX, 26 June 2015; Interview #XXXIII, 31 June 2015.

1106 Interview #III, 2 June 2014.

1107 Mentioned *supra* note 48.

1108 Ibid., 17.

1109 H. Schermers and N. Blokker, *supra* note 152, 606.

1110 Recall Chapter I.

1111 *Genocide* case, *supra* note 779, para. 430.

1112 As a matter of fact, sometimes the response simply lies in contacting the staff and asking for clarifications concerning human rights-related matters, and acting upon the information provided if need be. Interview #III, 2 June 2014.

1113 *Genocide* case, *supra* note 779, para. 430.

rights-consistent manner – is a logical corollary of the role of member States as 'authority managers' (recall Section 1.3).

Finally, when it comes to the policy framework of the international financial institution, and, notably, to drivers of change within the organisation, several member State representatives interviewed for this research acknowledged that the Board certainly has a significant role to play.[1114] Impetus for change may come from various places, within the institution (e.g., its head) as well the outside world (e.g., national authorities, CSOs or the private sector), and the Board comes forth as the apposite instrument to materialise it.[1115] As seen in Section 3.4.2.2, the capacity to transform 'non-decisions' regarding the policy framework of international financial institutions in human-rights-consistent decisions lies in the hands of member States and, as admitted by one representative, 'the board can be powerful if it wants to'.[1116]

3.5.1.2 The (Ir)relevance of Subjective-Psychological Elements

To answer the question of whether subjective-psychological elements have a role to play in the establishment of a failure to exercise due diligence, it is instructive to briefly look into the regime of international responsibility devised by the ILC. At first glance, the ASR seem to have left out fault as an element required for the establishment of responsibility. Following what Anzilotti had proclaimed earlier, the issue is one that is left to the interpretation of primary norms.[1117] The question of whether subjective-psychological elements were entirely discarded in secondary rules of international law does not, however, have a clear-cut answer. As observed by D'Aspremont, all the hypotheses of attribution of responsibility to the State envisaged in the ASR and the ARIO (such as aid or assistance, direction and control or coercion) require *knowledge* of the circumstances of the wrongful act,[1118] which constitutes a subjective element.[1119] To complicate things further, in its commentaries to both the ASR and the ARIO regarding the establishment of complicity (i.e., aid or assistance), the ILC included a reference to the requirement of *intent*, meaning that the State's derived responsibility will only arise

1114 Interview #VI, 23 March 2015; Interview #XIII, 5 June 2015; Interview #XV, 11 June 2015; Interview #XVIII, 12 June 2015; Interview #XXIV, 19 June 2015; Interview #XXVI, 22 June 2015; Interview #XXX, 26 June 2015.

1115 Interview #XV, 11 June 2015.

1116 Interview #XXX, 26 June 2015.

1117 D. Anzilotti, *Corso di diritto internazionale*, Vol. I, *Introduzione-Teorie generali* (1955) 406–12. See also: para. 3 of the commentary to Article 2 ASR.

1118 J. D'Aspremont, 'The Articles on the Responsibility of International Organizations: Magnifying the Fissures in the Law of International Responsibility', 9 IOLR (2012) 15, 18, 25.

1119 See para. 3 of the commentaries to Article 2 ASR. See also A. A. Cançado Trindade, 'Complementarity between State Responsibility and Individual Responsibility for Grave Violations of Human Rights: The Crime of State Revisited', in M. Ragazzi (ed.), op. cit. *supra* note 48, 258, according to whom responsibility based on fault is not entirely dismissed from secondary rules, inasmuch as the subjective element may lead to the aggravation of the State's responsibility.

where it 'intended, by the aid or assistance given, to facilitate the occurrence of the wrongful conduct'.[1120]

The ILC's views on complicity diverge, to some extent, from those espoused by the ICJ in the *Genocide* case.[1121] Here, the Court asserted that for complicity to be established it would have to be proved that the accomplice 'acted knowingly', i.e., 'was aware of the specific intent (*dolus specialis*) of the principal perpetrator', and gave 'support in perpetrating the [wrongful act] with full knowledge of the facts',[1122] without, however, requiring that the *intention* of the principal perpetrator was reciprocated by the accomplice.[1123]

Beyond the framework devised by the ILC, the question could as well be raised: what is the role played by *knowledge*, even if constructive, in the establishment of a failure to exercise due diligence? In the *Genocide* case, the ICJ determined that for a State to incur responsibility, it would have to be proved that it 'was aware, or should normally have been aware',[1124] of the serious danger inherent in the circumstances at hand. In this vein, is foreseeability of harm (in the form of injurious human rights or environmental impacts) by member States, or *unreasonableness* in not foreseeing it, a 'culpable' factor, determinant for the establishment of responsibility?

An appraisal of the various understandings developed over time regarding the nature of the criterion of due diligence[1125] shows that several authors initially approached it as being subjective in nature. Accordingly, for responsibility to be established, it would have to be proved that the actor either wilfully determined the effect produced by its conduct (*dolus*), or failed to take the necessary measures to avoid the injurious outcome (*culpa*).[1126] As a subsequent development in the theorisation of fault responsibility, the notion of psychological-normative fault was advanced, whereby fault was to be found in the actor's dismissive attitude towards a specified duty to act diligently (rather than towards the harmful event).[1127]

In contrast with fault responsibility, increasingly more authors have come to interpret due diligence as materialising in an objective standard of behaviour.[1128] Through this approach, fault is 'objectivised', and, thus, responsibility does not require looking into the particular subjective-psychological attitude of the actor,

1120 See para. 5 of the commentaries to Article 16 ASR, as well as both para. 1 of the commentaries to Article 58 and para. 4 of the commentaries to Article 14 ARIO, where reference is made to article 16 ASR.

1121 Mentioned *supra* note 779.

1122 Ibid., paras. 421 and 432, respectively.

1123 For this reason, Corten and Klein deem the requirement of intent as not being adequately reflective of the state of the law. See: O. Corten and P. Klein, 'The Limits of Complicity As a Ground for Responsibility: Lessons Learned from the *Corfu Channel* case', in K. Bannelier, T. Christakis and S. Heathcote (eds.), op. cit. *supra* note 1090, 329, 330.

1124 *Genocide* case, *supra* note 779, para. 432.

1125 For an extensive overview, see: R. P. Mazzeschi, *supra* 56, 1–116.

1126 R. Pisillo-Mazzeschi, *supra* note 906, 9.

1127 R. Pisillo-Mazzeschi, *supra* note 56, 72–9.

1128 Ibid., 94–100. See also: S. Heathcote, *supra* note 1090, 302–5.

but rather relates to the very content of the international obligation: it arises as the sole consequence of conduct that is contrary to such obligation.[1129] As will shortly be seen, this form of responsibility can now be said to have been endorsed in the decisions of international tribunals and in State practice.[1130]

In fact, in cases decided by the ICJ involving State failure to exercise due diligence, such as the *Corfu Channel* and the *Genocide* cases, the Court did not purport to determine the presence of subjective fault on the side of individuals acting as organs of the State[1131] (in the former, the Albanian coast guard and in the latter, the Yugoslav federal authorities). In both cases, diligence had to be measured objectively.[1132] These precedents go on to show that the responsibility of the State for failure to exercise due diligence is not based on its 'wilful disregard',[1133] but, rather, on the objective fact of not having undertaken the required conduct.

In this vein, although elements such as 'awareness' or (constructive) 'knowledge' of possible damage are required for the establishment of responsibility, they are not used for the purposes of ascertaining the psychological attitude of the State, and the reasons underlying its failure to exercise the required conduct, despite its knowledge of risk. Rather, said references to knowledge are used to determine the moment at which the obligation of due diligence becomes applicable.[1134] Ultimately, other than scrutinising the State's motivations, what must be proved is that the State omitted the required conduct on the basis of what the primary norm in question would abstractly require from it. Foreseeability (of harm) thus serves the sole, crucial function of triggering the duty of due diligence: as soon as there is a situation of risk the member State should be aware of, it is compelled to act diligently (if it has the capacity to do so) with a view to avoiding, or at least mitigating, such risk.[1135]

1129 R. Pisillo-Mazzeschi, *supra* note 906, 9.

1130 J. Crawford, *Brownlie's Principles of Public International Law* (2012) 556–8.

1131 Ibid., 558.

1132 See: R. Barnidge, *supra* note 924, 105, noting that the ICJ's inquiry into Albania's knowledge ignited quite some controversy among authors as to whether the Court's decision was rooted in fault responsibility or objective responsibility.

1133 The term was used by the UK in the *Osman* case (*supra* note 888), where it alleged that the obligation to take preventive action to protect the right to life could only be deemed violated if the State's failure to take such action would amount to 'gross dereliction or wilful disregard of their duty' (para. 107). The ECtHR found this standard too rigid and incompatible with the requirements of the Convention and, in particular, the obligations of the contracting parties to 'secure the practical and effective protection of the rights and freedoms laid down therein' (para. 116).

1134 S. Heathcote, *supra* note 1090, 300, 301.

1135 As asserted by the ICJ in para. 431 of the *Genocide* case, *supra* note 779, 'a State's obligation to prevent, and the corresponding duty to act, arise at the instant that the State learns of, or should normally have learned of, the existence of a serious risk that genocide will be committed'. Similarly, the notion that knowledge constitutes a prerequisite for the duty of due diligence to come into being underlies the regime devised by the ILC in the Articles on Prevention of Transboundary Harm, mentioned *supra* note 923. This can be immediately concluded when reading Article 3.

3.5.1.3 The Breach of the Duty of Due Diligence

From Section 3.5.1.2 it can be concluded that the duty of due diligence is to be characterised as one of conduct and not of result, as one requiring States to deploy their best efforts to achieve a desired result (prevention of damage), without, however, having to absolutely guarantee such result.[1136] Recalling the words of the ICJ in the *Genocide* case, due diligence requires States to 'employ all means reasonably available to them' so as to prevent, as far as possible, a certain violation.[1137] As applied to the context of State participation in international financial institutions, it does not seem *reasonable*, indeed, to require from member States more than to *do all they can* to prevent harm. Inasmuch as the emergence of damage is dependent upon the unfolding of institutional operations, there is certainly a non-negligible amount of factors conditioning the outcome that go beyond the State's 'guaranteeing capacity' and 'authority management' role.[1138]

It remains to be seen when exactly the breach of due diligence materialises and, thus, at which moment it is possible to invoke member State responsibility. More specifically, the inquiry draws on whether States, through their participation in institutional decision-making processes, should only be held responsible when harm actually arises out of the operations of the international organisation, or whether their responsibility can already be invoked for not having done 'all they could' to prevent potential harm – harm constituting but a teleological element guiding member State behaviour.

If one considers the regime devised in the ASR, it is clear that damage is not a constitutive element of international responsibility[1139] – the elements of breach and attribution sufficing to engage State responsibility.[1140] However, in the *Genocide* case – where the ICJ described the obligation to prevent genocide as one of conduct, informed by due diligence prescriptions[1141] – the Court asserted that 'a State can be held responsible for breaching the obligation to prevent genocide only if genocide was actually committed. It is at the time when commission of the prohibited act … begins

1136 ILC, Special Rapporteur Crawford, *Second Report on State Responsibility*, *supra* note 752, 21, para. 57, referring to the distinction between obligations of conduct and result in civil law systems.

1137 *Genocide* case, *supra* note 779, para. 430. As noted by the Court, in such an assessment it is irrelevant to the breach of the obligation of conduct 'whether the State whose responsibility is in issue claims, or even proves, that even if it had employed all means reasonably at its disposal, they would not have sufficed to prevent the commission of [the wrongful act] … the more so since the possibility remains that the combined efforts of several States, each complying with its obligation to prevent, might have achieved the result … which the efforts of only one State were insufficient to produce'.

1138 See: V. Tzevelekos, *supra* note 925, 198. See also: R. P. Mazzeschi, *supra* note 56, 395, according to whom the distinction between obligations of conduct and of result in international law is based on the degree of the State's capacity to prevent harm and, thus, the likelihood of achieving the result protected by the law.

1139 Although it does play a role with regard to the invocation of responsibility by the injured State (see: Article 42 ASR).

1140 See: para. 9 of the commentaries to Article 2 ASR, as well as para. 6 of the commentaries to Article 31.

1141 *Genocide* case, *supra* note 779, para. 430.

that the breach of an obligation of prevention occurs.'[1142] Hence, according to the ICJ, if the external event does not occur, 'a State that omitted to act when it could have done so cannot be held responsible *a posteriori*'.[1143]

Visibly, such type of understanding is unattractive, in that States should not be able to neglect their due diligence duties on the grounds that the external event has not yet taken place and may never do so.[1144] Otherwise, there would be space for objectionable situations to occur, such as the impossibility of establishing the responsibility of the member State where it was aware of possible injurious human rights or environmental impacts stemming from the execution of a project (which ultimately did not occur for external factors) and it did nothing to prevent or at least mitigate them.

Truth be told, in *Genocide*, the ICJ's position is owed to the fact that the court resorted to a general rule of the law of State responsibility, as codified in Article 14(3) ASR, whereby 'the breach of an international obligation requiring a State to prevent a given event occurs when the event occurs'. The ICJ thus saw in the obligation to prevent genocide an obligation of a dual nature, which arises once the State learns of, or should normally have learned of, a serious risk of genocide, but which is capable of being breached only when genocide is actually committed.[1145] Somewhat paradoxically, then, an obligation described as being one of conduct was considered, at the same time, as a sub-category of obligations of result.[1146]

1142 Ibid., para. 431.

1143 Ibid. Such line of thought is also reflected in the ICJ *Pulp Mills* case, *supra* note 709. There, the Court described the obligation to 'preserve the aquatic environment, and in particular to prevent pollution by prescribing appropriate rules and Measures' as an obligation to act with due diligence, thereby engaging State responsibility 'if it was shown that it had failed to act diligently and thus take all appropriate measures to enforce its relevant regulations' (para. 197). However, once again, the Court would only find a breach of the obligation where the interest protected by the law had actually been harmed. Accordingly, in order to determine whether there had been a violation by Uruguay of its obligation to preserve the aquatic environment, the Court went on to examine the impacts of the pulp mill's discharges on the quality of the waters of the river and whether they could be qualified as damaging (see para. 262).

1144 The observation was made by ILC Special Rapporteur Crawford with regard to States' duty under Article 22(2) of the Vienna Convention on Diplomatic Relations, providing that '[t]he receiving State is under a special duty to take all appropriate steps to protect the premises of the mission against any intrusion or damage and to prevent any disturbance of the peace of the mission or impairment of its dignity'. This provision had been previously interpreted by ILC Special Rapporteur Ago as entailing an obligation of prevention in the form of obligation of result. See: ILC, Special Rapporteur Crawford, *Second Report on State Responsibility*, *supra* note 409, 28, paras. 85 and 86. See also: M. Milanovic, 'State Responsibility for Genocide: A Follow-up', 18(4) EJIL (2007) 669, 687, noting that '[t]here is a slight, if unavoidable, contradiction in defining the scope of the duty to prevent genocide as arising whenever there is awareness of a serious risk of genocide, yet requiring that genocide actually be committed in order that state responsibility for a breach of the obligation to prevent should ensue'.

1145 M. Milanovic, ibid., 687.

1146 Such an interpretation of prevention obligations was inherited from the views advanced by ILC Special Rapporteur Ago during the codification of the ASR. See: P.-M. Dupuy, 'Reviewing the

The concept of obligation of conduct, as understood in this book, does not correspond to the general category of obligations of prevention envisaged in Article 14(3) of ASR. It rather appraises the State's actual behaviour as the decisive element, and not the result attained.[1147] This interpretation is in line with the ICJ's earlier assertions in the *Tehran Hostages* case, where it held that the '*inaction* of the Iranian Government [vis-à-vis the injurious conduct of militants at the US Embassy] *by itself* constituted clear and serious violation of Iran's obligations'.[1148] Furthermore, it also follows the ICJ's decision in the more recent *FYROM* case (discussed in Chapter II),[1149] which specifically involved the participation of a member State in an international organisation. Here, the issue was raised of whether Greece's obligation not to object to FYROM's candidacy for membership in NATO – which was characterised as an obligation of conduct – was only to be scrutinised in case the member State was actually able to condition, on its own accord, institutional conduct. As had been suggested by FYROM, the obligation 'not to object' also covered situations where the respondent's act 'would not have the effect of preventing membership (where unanimity is not required for membership decisions). In other words … it [was] the act of objection itself that [was] prohibited, irrespective of its consequences.'[1150] Along these lines, the ICJ concluded that the question put before it was not whether NATO's decision regarding FYROM's candidacy was 'due exclusively, principally, or marginally' to Greece's objection, but, rather, whether the latter, 'by its own conduct, did not comply with the obligation not to object'.[1151]

It is therefore argued that the duty of due diligence is breached and member State responsibility is triggered for the (mere) failure to undertake the required preventive action: the *maintenance* of a situation of risk of damage to human rights should thus suffice for the establishment of responsibility.[1152] This is so because the *object* of the obligation is the diligent conduct itself and not the result.[1153] Emphasis should therefore be placed on 'process over outcome, conduct over result'.[1154]

Difficulties of Codification: On Ago's Classification of Obligations of Means and Obligations of Result in Relation to State Responsibility', 10(2) EJIL (1999) 371, 378–80.

1147 P.-M. Dupuy, ibid., 382. See also: YILC, 1978, Vol. II, Part Two, 82.

1148 ICJ *Tehran Hostages* case, *supra* note 920, para. 67 (emphasis added).

1149 *FYROM* case, *supra* note 528.

1150 Ibid., Memorial, 81, 82.

1151 Ibid., Judgment, para. 70.

1152 According to Salomon, it is not necessary to determine the occurrence of harm in order to establish State responsibility for a failure to comply with an obligation to assist and cooperate internationally. See: M. Salomon, 'Deprivation, Causation and the Law of International Cooperation', in M. Langford, W. Vandenhole, M. Scheinin and W. V. Genugten (eds.), op. cit. *supra* note 53, 281.
It is of note that, in an earlier commentary of the *Trail Smelter* arbitration and the application of the 'no-harm' rule, the ILC asserted that '[e]ven in the specific case of an obligation to prevent an event, the presence of damage is not an additional condition for the existence of an internationally wrongful act'. See: YILC 1978, Vol. II, Part Two, 82.

1153 R. P. Mazzeschi, *supra* note 56, 406, 407.

1154 M. Salomon, *supra* note 681, 132.

3.5.2 *Member State Responsibility and Victim Access to a Remedy*

3.5.2.1 Identifying the Victim

A fundamental aspect in the present discussion relates to the identification of the individuals that are to be considered *affected* by institutional operations – and that are thereby entitled to claim remedial action from member States. Who, after all, is to be considered a victim? A vague definition would point to the various 'stakeholders' whose lives are shaped by the situation in question.[1155] Yet, the question arises of whether all such 'stakeholders' have standing before a dispute settlement mechanism, such as a judicial human rights body.[1156] For example, does an individual not *directly* affected by institutional operations have standing?

In what concerns judicial dispute settlement of human rights matters in international fora, the question of standing is answered differently across regions.[1157] In the European human rights regime, admissible applicants are defined in Article 34 ECHR[1158] as any person, NGO or group of individuals claiming to be a victim of a violation of ECHR rights. The claimant must therefore present him or herself as a direct victim (or an indirect or potential victim)[1159] and allege a concrete violation of the rights contained in the convention. Article 35(3)(b) prescribes an additional admissibility criterion, whereby the applicant is required to prove that he or she has suffered a 'significant disadvantage' from the alleged human rights violation.[1160] The ECtHR has adopted a somewhat stringent approach to the finding of a violation of ECHR rights, requiring proof that the alleged damage 'directly affected' the rights of the applicant.

The Court's stringency is notably visible in cases involving environmental degradation, which may very well emerge in the context of the operations of international financial institutions.[1161] Indeed, there is a persistent and prevailing individualistic perspective in which the environmental dimension of human rights is envisaged and

1155 See: J. A. Scholte, *supra* note 795, especially 309, 329, 336, 340.

1156 It is certain that persons impacted by institutional and member State action may only resort to international remedies after all domestic remedies have been exhausted. See, inter alia: Article 35(1) ECHR, *supra* note 125.

1157 For an extensive overview of individual and collective complaint procedures in international and regional human rights systems, see: A. Vandenbogaerde, *Towards Shared Accountability in International Human Rights Law* (2016).

1158 *Supra* note 125.

1159 The ECtHR has shown some flexibility in the application of the victim requirement, by allowing, for example, applications where the direct victim had died after the application was lodged, by granting victim status to close relatives and, exceptionally, by allowing applications from claimants acting on behalf of a victim without any valid form of authority. See: *Case of Centre for Legal Resources on Behalf of Valentin Câmpeanu* v. *Romania*, App. No. 47848/08, 17 July 2014, paras. 97–100 and 102–14.

1160 On the meaning and implications of the 'significant disadvantage' requirement, see: D. Shelton, 'Significantly Disadvantaged? Shrinking Access to the European Court of Human Rights', 16 Hum Rts L Rev (2016) 303.

1161 For example, in *Kyrtatos* v. *Greece, supra* note 971, paras. 52, 53, the ECtHR did not find an illegal drainage and subsequent destruction of wetland to constitute an infringement of Article 8 ECHR

adjudicated, barring any consideration of the diffused repercussions that environmental harm may have on the collective life of the people living in and around injured areas.[1162] Petitions *in abstracto* or *actio popularis* for the sake of environmental and (general) human rights protection are therefore not allowed under Article 34, meaning that 'applicants may not complain against a provision of domestic law, a domestic practice or public acts simply because they appear to contravene the Convention'.[1163]

The Inter-American human rights regime does not differ much from the European one. According to Article 44 ACHR,[1164] any person, group of persons or NGO may lodge a petition with the Commission, containing denunciations or complaints of a violation of the Convention. Although this provision omits explicit reference to the 'victim requirement', the Inter-American Commission has rejected collective complaints and the use of *actio popularis*, under the understanding that the claimant has to be a victim, or, at least, to identify specific victims, and indicate a clear violation of ACHR rights.[1165]

Clear endorsement of human rights as a collective entitlement can rather be found in the African human rights system. This is only natural, as the whole ideology underlying the Banjul Charter is informed by the collective-social dimension of human rights as peoples' rights.[1166] The admissibility criteria contained in Article 56 of the Banjul Charter[1167] certainly contribute to this, as they do not require complainants to be the victims of a specific human rights violation. The well-known *Ogoniland* case,[1168] for example, was filed by two NGOs on behalf of the people of Ogoniland, Nigeria.

Undoubtedly, throughout the whole programme or project cycle, the operations of international financial institutions and their member States may *affect* the human rights of individuals, without this impact necessarily constituting a *direct* harm thereof. Impacts may also be cumulative or indirect (such as downstream impacts, e.g., from deforestation and land use conversion), and, as has been noted, in some projects these can even be greater than direct ones.[1169] Next to this, institutional

(prescribing the right to respect for private and family life), as it did not 'directly affect' the claimants' rights.

1162 F. Francioni, 'Realism, Utopia and the Future of International Environmental Law', in *EUI Working Papers*, Law 2012/11, 13, 14.

1163 *Valentin Câmpeanu* case, *supra* note 1159, para. 101.

1164 *Supra* note 819.

1165 See, e.g.: *Felix Roman Esparragoza Gonzalez et al.* v. *Venezuela*, Admissibility Decision, Inter-American Commission on Human Rights, Petition 12.210, Report No. 48/04, 13 October 2004, para. 40.

1166 F. Francioni, 'International Human Rights in an Environmental Horizon', 21(1) EJIL (2010) 41, 51.

1167 Mentioned *supra* note 820.

1168 Mentioned *supra* note 963.

1169 Several CSOs alerted to this fact during the WB consultations undertaken for the purposes of review of its safeguard policies. See: Summary of Phase 3 Consultations and Bank Management Responses, 16, available at: http://consultations.worldbank.org/Data/hub/files/consultation-template/review-and-update-world-bank-safeguard-policies/en/materials/summary_of_phase_3_consultations_and_

operations may represent a risk of interference with the enjoyment of human rights, or, otherwise, an incursion into individuals' legitimate interests. That being so, it is not a given whether judicial human rights bodies would qualify as a 'victim' of a violation an individual who *solely* had his or her 'interests' affected, or who was *solely* subjected to the risk of harm. This holds particularly true with regard to the ECtHR, which has been systematically reluctant to find State responsibility in cases where the risk of harm was not immediately evident.[1170]

It is noteworthy that the abovementioned Aarhus Convention[1171] accounts for all such concerns, as it grants access to a review procedure not only to those maintaining the impairment of a right, but also to whoever has a 'sufficient interest' in challenging the legality of State conduct under the requirements of the right of participation in environmental decision-making. When it comes to the right of access to information, standing is prescribed in even broader terms, in that the complainant is not required to assert an interest.[1172]

Interestingly, the notions of risk and public interest participation have been endorsed by various international financial institutions in their operational policies. With regard to the WB Inspection Panel, the entitlement to submit a Request is granted to 'two or more people with common interests and concerns who claim that they have been or are likely to be adversely affected by a Bank-financed operation'.[1173] More broadly, access to the EIB Complaints Mechanism is granted not only to those who allege direct negative impacts stemming from EIB decisions, actions or omissions, but also to those who simply allege the Bank's wrongdoing.[1174] A similar trend can be traced in the EBRD Project Complaint Mechanism, which defines as complainants seeking a 'Problem-solving Initiative': '[o]ne or more individual(s) located in an Impacted Area, or who has or have an economic interest, including social and cultural interests, in an Impacted Area'.[1175]

To be sure, in compliance review mechanisms (such as the Inspection Panel of the WB, the CAO of the IFC and the MIGA or the Independent Review Mechanism of the AfDB), more than in problem-solving mechanisms, it even seems to be more

bank_management_reponses_final_for_public_disclosure_post_board_august_4.pdf, last consulted 15 October 2018.

1170 For an example of an earlier, emblematic case, see: *L.C.B.* v. *United Kingdom*, App. No. 14/1997/798/1001, 9 June 1998 (where the applicant, diagnosed with leukaemia, alleged a violation of Article 2 on the right to life, for the State's failure to both monitor the extent of her father's exposure to radiation during atmospheric nuclear testing and prevent the applicant's life from being avoidably put at risk). For a more recent example, see: *Hardy and Maile* v. *United Kingdom*, App. No. 31965/07, 09 July 2012 (involving the construction and operation of two liquefied natural gas terminals and the alleged violation of Article 8 on right to respect for private and family life for the State's failure to undertake an appropriate assessment of the risks posed to the marine environment in case of a major release of liquefied natural gas from a delivery ship).

1171 Mentioned *supra* note 774.

1172 Ibid., Article 9(1)(2).

1173 Inspection Panel Operating Procedures, *supra* note 1053, para. 10.

1174 EIB, The EIB Complaints Mechanism Operating Procedures, August 2013, 5, 6.

1175 EBRD, Project Complaint Mechanism (PCM) Rules of Procedure, 7 May 2014, para. 1.

fruitful to file grievances where the impacts are not *too* individualised, precisely because the former are oriented towards addressing systemic problems or patterns in the organisation's operations.[1176] For instance, in its compliance appraisal of a grievance regarding the operations of a gold mine in Peru, the CAO asserted the following: 'CAO acknowledges the seriousness of the issues raised by the complaint at an individual level. However, after careful consideration of the information at hand, it is not apparent that the labor issues raised … are indicative of substantial concerns regarding the environmental and social outcomes of the project or issues of systemic importance for IFC that would merit a compliance investigation'.[1177]

These considerations allow for important extrapolations to be made to the human rights regime, for the purposes of interpretation and adjudication. If, as once put by the ECtHR, human rights treaties – *in casu* the ECHR – are 'intended to guarantee rights that are not theoretical or illusory, but practical and effective',[1178] their application to the member States of international financial institutions cannot be dissociated from the dynamics within which these institutions operate. To be more concrete, apart from the crucial need of preventing and redressing harm, it is also fundamental to ensure that both the member States and the organisation perform their respective roles in conformity with legality and, in that way, serve better the development purposes of the project at hand. One fails to see why the ECHR or the ACHR would not allow individuals not directly affected by institutional operations to challenge member State compliance with the law, if other pertinent regimes such as the Aarhus Convention (which is also a human rights treaty) and the accountability mechanisms of international financial institutions already do so.

As noted by Chinkin, 'where a State has entered into a treaty on behalf of an individual, or a group of individuals, it is self-evident that those individuals have an interest in its performance or non-performance'.[1179] Along these lines, it should be noted that a human right is not just a right not to be harmed; it is also a right to be protected, which entails not putting such right at risk. After all, member State failure to observe the required standard of care constitutes, on its own, a violation of human rights prescriptions, without it being necessary to prove the occurrence of harm. In these cases, the individual's right (of not having his or her life, health, property, or the environment where he or she lives endangered) translates into an interest in the restoration of the legality of State conduct in international affairs,[1180] more precisely,

1176 'Glass Half Full Report', *supra* note 24, 74, 75.

1177 CAO, Compliance Appraisal: Summary of Results, Yanacocha (IFC Project #2983), Complaints 04–07, 29 May 2015, 2, available at: www.cao-ombudsman.org/cases/document-links/documents/CAOAppraisalofYanacocha_May292015_forweb_000.pdf, last consulted 15 October 2018.

1178 *Matthews* case, *supra* note 500, para. 34.

1179 C. Chinkin, *supra* note 176, 14.

1180 The idea that human rights seek to protect legitimate collective interests can also be derived from the existence of formal interstate mechanisms for complaints to human rights bodies. As has been noted by the Human Rights Committee, the reason underlying the creation of these mechanisms relates to the fact that every State Party, albeit not a rights holder, has a legal interest in the performance by

the legality of State participation in institutional decision-making processes that will have an impact in their lives. This is so justified in a spirit conducive to a 'rule-based society in which responsibility fulfils the essential function of ensuring a return to legality and ensuring that the actors that acted in breach of international law will comply with their obligations'.[1181]

3.5.2.2 The Provision of a Remedy by the Member States

When institutional operations result in the infliction of harm upon an individual, and a given member State has not undertaken the required due diligence measures to prevent or punish it,[1182] said individual is entitled to obtain reparation for the damage suffered from the wrongdoing member State. In order to substantiate the member State's duty to repair, a causal link must be established between its conduct, in the form of omission, and the alleged damage.

As explained in the ASR commentaries, the requirement of causality is not necessarily the same with regard to every breach of an international obligation.[1183] Certainly, in this book's type of scenarios, direct or natural causality cannot be determined, since the legally proscribed outcome will have been perpetrated by the international organisation and not the member State. The member State's conduct may, however, constitute an 'indirect cause of the event', and thereby attest to the necessary causal relationship.[1184] For instance, the State's approval, with disregard for certain human rights issues, of a project that proves to be injurious can be regarded as a necessary step in a series of stages that lead to the implementation of the project on the ground. Within this chain of causality, the international financial institution emerges as a vehicle to the materialisation of the State's approval of the project[1185] and the damage, while not 'caused by' the member State, can be found 'within the risk of' its conduct.[1186] Here, causality is 'normative' – the link being established 'by a rule of law',[1187] namely, by asking whether the member State's actual conduct conformed with what would be abstractly required from a diligent State, when confronted with foreseeable harm.[1188]

every other State Party of their human rights obligations, which are, indeed, *erga omnes* obligations. See: Human Rights Committee, General Comment No. 31: Nature of the General Legal Obligation Imposed on States Parties to the Covenant, UN Doc. CCPR/C/21/Rev.1/Add.13 (2004) para. 2. More generally, Article 48 ASR accentuates the role of individual States in enforcing the international legal order, by entitling States other than the injured one(s) to invoke responsibility where the obligation breached is owed to the international community as a whole.

1181 A. Nolkaemper and D. Jacobs, *supra* note 72, 389.

1182 The question of the plurality of responsible (member) States will be addressed below.

1183 Para. 10 of the commentaries to Article 31 ASR.

1184 ILC, Special Rapporteur Ago, *Second Report on State Responsibility*, UN Doc. A/CN.4/233 (1970) 194, para. 52.

1185 CIEL Legal Analysis on International Financial Institutions & Human Rights Law, *supra* note 681, 5.

1186 See: H. L. A. Hart and T. Honoré, *Causation in the Law* (2002) 64.

1187 ILC, Special Rapporteur Ago, *Second Report on State Responsibility*, *supra* note 1184.

1188 See: S. Heathcote, *supra* note 1090, 310 and also R. P. Mazzeschi, *supra* note 56, 409.

Indeed, while the criterion of 'directness' may not be used, 'foreseeability' comes forth as a more appropriate one. The inquiry turns into whether, for example, the member State could have predicted or foreseen that its vote, and the subsequent implementing acts of the organisation, would result in negative interference with the enjoyment of human rights in the borrower State.[1189]

Importantly, for causality to be asserted, harm must not be too speculative or remote,[1190] which calls for a judgement regarding the definition of the project's scope and how its impacts are to be understood. What kind of harm and for what type of activity are, thus, questions that must be answered in this examination. Notably, a decision must be made as to whether the notion of 'project' encompasses only those activities directly financed by the international financial institution or whether it extends to other activities not financed by the organisation but necessary to the viability of the project, or which would not occur but for the existence of the organisation-financed project.[1191]

The hurdle of causation being overcome, determination must be made of the content of international responsibility, notably, of the appropriate form and extent of reparation. As far as possible, it must 'wipe out all the consequences of the illegal act and reestablish the situation which would, in all probability, have existed if that act had not been committed'.[1192] To that end, reparation may take the form of restitution, compensation or satisfaction[1193] – restitution having primacy over the latter forms of reparation.[1194]

As clarified in the ASR commentaries, restitution is understood as a means to re-establish 'the *status quo ante*, i.e., the situation that existed prior to the occurrence of the wrongful act'.[1195] For example, *legal restitutio in integrum* may be provided by an order of a judicial tribunal declaring the unlawfulness of a decision adopted by the member State without due account of the human rights and environmental risks of a given project. If the injury relates to project implementation and involves, for example, environmental harm and resettlement, restitution may be obtained through the provision of relief and resettlement assistance, combined with comprehensive restoration of the environmentally impacted area.[1196] In seeking for the most

1189 See: C. Tan, *supra* note 264, 113.

1190 Para. 10 of the commentaries to Article 31 ASR. The ILC makes clear that causality is a necessary, albeit not sufficient, condition for reparation, as the injury may be too remote or consequential to be the subject of reparation.
For an appraisal of the sort of difficulties in terms of remoteness that can arise in cases where the applicant seeks compensation for environmental and ESC rights harm, see: D. Shelton, 'Remedies and Reparation', in M. Langford, W. Vandenhole, M. Scheinin and W. V. Genugten (eds.), op. cit. *supra* note 53, especially 386–90.

1191 See: 'Glass Half Full Report', *supra* note 24, 72, 73.

1192 *Case concerning the Factory at Chorzów, Claim for Indemnity (Germany* v. *Poland)*, Publ. PCIJ Series A, No. 17 (1928) 47.

1193 See: Articles 31, 34–37 ARIO.

1194 Paras. 1 and 3 of the commentaries to Article 35 ASR.

1195 Ibid., para. 2.

1196 See the remedies identified by the IACHR in the *Ogoniland* case, *supra* note 963, 15.

appropriate solution, it can, in any event, be noted that remedial orders for specific member State performance seem to constitute a more appropriate and comprehensive remedy than the provision of compensation *stricto sensu*.[1197]

Still, whenever restitution is not possible, compensation emerges as the standard consequence for damage.[1198] As determined in Article 36(2) ASR, compensation 'shall cover any financially assessable damage including loss of profits' and generally consists of monetary payment. In what concerns the types of damage that may be compensable, the ASR leave such determination to the particularities of the case at hand.[1199] It has, for example, been noted that in cases involving displacement owing to the construction of dams, the notion of 'financially assessable damage' should include downstream impacts such as the victims' reduced access to productive resources, in that such types of projects can have disastrous and impoverishing impacts on fishing and agricultural communities.[1200]

At this point it shall be recalled that reparation is not, in any case, the sole 'new legal relation' that arises from the 'fact of responsibility'[1201] with pertinence to the current discussion. While pecuniary claims will highly likely be the most common ones,[1202] claims for cessation of the wrongful conduct and the provision of appropriate assurances and guarantees of non-repetition, as provided for in Article 30 ASR, may likewise arise. As explained by the ILC, 'cessation is, as it were, the negative aspect of future performance, concerned with securing an end to continuing wrongful conduct, whereas assurances and guarantees serve a preventive function and may be described as a positive reinforcement of future performance'.[1203] Importantly, these measures do not depend on injury for their existence,[1204] and, thus, the member State's internationally wrongful act constitutes sufficient remedial ground.[1205] This is so given that said measures are not meant to correct the wrong

1197 ILA Report on Accountability of International Organisations, *supra* note 50, 43, 44.

1198 Para. 1 of the commentaries to Article 36 ASR.

1199 Ibid., para. 7 et seq. In the case of environmental harm, for example, the commentaries note in para. 15 that 'environmental damage will often extend beyond that which can be readily quantified in terms of clean-up costs or property devaluation. Damage to such environmental values … is, as a matter of principle, no less real and compensable than damage to property, though it may be difficult to quantify.'

1200 Oxfam Comments on the Second Draft of World Bank Environmental and Social Framework, March 2015, 6, available at: https://consultations.worldbank.org/Data/hub/files/oxfam_comments_on_second_draft_wb_environmental_and_social_framework.pdf, last consulted 15 October 2018.

1201 A. Pellet, 'The Definition of Responsibility in International Law', in J. Crawford, A. Pellet, S. Olleson and K. Parlett (eds.), op. cit. *supra* 389, 3, 9.

1202 Para. 2 of the commentaries to Article 36 ASR.

1203 Para. 1 of the commentaries to Article 30 ASR. In para. 2, it is clarified that cessation is also relevant to State omissions.

1204 A. Pellet, *supra* note 1201.

1205 Cf.: C. Ahlborn, 'Remedies against International Organizations – A Relational Account of International Responsibility', in D. Sarooshi (ed.), op. cit. *supra* note 601, 525–76, arguing that, in consideration of the relational definition of international responsibility, the ILC should acknowledge more explicitly that injury is a necessary ground for international responsibility.

inflicted upon the injured party, but rather serve the purpose of restoring the legal order as a whole.[1206]

The more rare claimant without a case of direct harm to make (recall Section 3.5.2.1) may therefore also seek remedies in cases of member State failure to act diligently. These remedies could consist in requiring specific performance of the various components of the duty of due diligence.[1207] For instance, the aim of the complainant could be to trigger a change in the terms in which member States participate in decision-making processes – a remedy that may more appropriately be achieved by resorting to assurances and guarantees of non-repetition. The latter could entail the setting up of specific procedures within the offices of Executive Directors and their national authorities that allow for a more effective screening of the human rights impacts of projects subject to their approval, for example. This sort of restorative result is most welcome, in that it invites international actors, such as member States, to act with diligence and care, and reminds, once again, that international responsibility is also a form of constraint to restore and protect legality.[1208]

3.5.2.3 Division of Reparation Duties among Multiple Member States

Claims for reparation against the member States of international financial institutions (and any international organisation for that matter) will, more often than not, involve harm that can hardly be allocated to a specific actor. Indeed, various relevant relationships come into play, notably, among the member States and the international financial institution; among the member States themselves; and, finally, within each multi-party constituency. There is, thus, a multiplicity of actors that contributes towards a single harmful outcome: member States will normally act simultaneously – each member State's vote constituting a contributing cause to the injury; and the international financial institution's conduct will be consecutive to that of the member States – its implementing acts constituting, as well, a contributing cause to the injury. The crux of the problem in these cases of shared responsibility,[1209] i.e., where several contributing causes may be identified, lies in the fact

1206 As noted in para. 6 of the commentaries to Article 31 ASR, while in some cases 'the gist of a wrong is the causing of actual harm', in other cases 'what matters is the failure to take necessary precautions to prevent harm even if in the event no harm occurs'.

1207 ILC, Special Rapporteur Sreenivasa Rao, *Second report on international liability for injurious consequences arising out of acts not prohibited by international law (prevention of transboundary damage from hazardous activities)*, *supra* note 1010, 119, para. 35.

1208 J. D'Aspremont, *supra* note 71, 385.

1209 The complicated question of shared responsibility has been extensively analysed in a series of publications in the past years, under the auspices of the SHARES research project of the Amsterdam Center for International Law, led by Professor André Nollkaemper. A list of all publications can be found here: www.sharesproject.nl/publication, last consulted 15 October 2018.
For reasons of economy, the debate will not be reproduced in this book, also because the sole aim at this stage is to note that each member State is individually responsible for its own wrongful conduct – the

that there is no ready-made solution, through the test of causation, for the determination of who exactly is responsible, and for what consequences.[1210]

The types of human right and environmental violation at stake may therefore not easily lend themselves to the apportionment of responsibility among member States, for if harm is indivisible, it can be quite strenuous to establish causal links between each member State's individual conduct and the alleged damage.[1211] Notwithstanding, as an *indirect* cause of the event, said conduct passes the test of causation, not through the application of the widely used but-for test, but, rather, the 'necessary element of a sufficient set' (or NESS) test.[1212] In light of the latter, the act performed by the member State emerges as a 'necessary element of a set of antecedent actual conditions that was sufficient for the occurrence of the result'.[1213] In other words, the causal link between the proscribed outcome and the member State's vote is established since, in the circumstances, the latter forms a necessary part of a complex of conditions sufficient for the outcome[1214] – this complex of conditions consisting of all the other approving votes, together with the organisation's acts of implementation of the project on the ground.

Crucially, the acknowledgement that each member State's contribution, in itself, might have been insufficient to *cause* the harm – a situation termed '*cumulative* shared responsibility'[1215] – does not serve as an impediment to trigger their responsibility in individualised terms. Articles 47 ASR and 48 ARIO so confirm.[1216] Although both provisions refer to situations of shared responsibility for the same *act*, the commentaries to Article 47 assert that

> situations can also arise where several States by separate internationally wrongful conduct have contributed to causing the same damage. For example … ICJ held that Albania was responsible to the United Kingdom for the same damage on the

question of the allocation of responsibility among the member States not being of concern to the complainant.

1210 A. Nollkaemper and D. Jacobs, *supra* note 455, 2, 3.

1211 For a discussion of causation in the context of indivisible socioeconomic extraterritorial harm, see: M. Salomon, *supra* note 1152, 277, 278.

1212 For a distinction between both causation tests, see: E. Plakokefalos, 'Causation in the Law of State Responsibility and the Problem of Overdetermination: In Search of Clarity', 26(2) EJIL (2015) 471, 476–8.

1213 R. Wright, 'Causation, Responsibility, Risk, Probability, Naked Statistics, and Proof: Pruning the Bramble Bush by Clarifying the Concepts', 73 Iowa L Rev (1987–1988) 1001, 1019. As further explained by the author, 'to avoid including causally irrelevant conditions in this sufficient set, the antecedent conditions must be restricted to those that are necessary for the sufficiency of the set'. In fact, the 'necessary causal condition' begins with member States' approving votes, which grant the required authority for the organisation to act.

1214 See: A. Honoré and J. Gardner, 'Causation in the Law', *The Stanford Encyclopedia of Philosophy*, E. N. Zalta (ed.) (2010).

1215 A. Nollkaemper, 'Introduction', in A. Nollkaemper and E. Plakokefalos (eds.), *Principles of Shared Responsibility in International Law: An Appraisal of the State of the Art* (2014) 10.

1216 Article 47(1) ASR determines: 'Where several States are responsible for the same internationally wrongful act, the responsibility of each State may be invoked in relation to that act.'

basis that it knew or should have known of the presence of the mines and of the attempt by the British ships to exercise their right of transit, but failed to warn the ships. Yet, it was not suggested that Albania's responsibility for failure to warn was reduced, let alone precluded, by reason of the concurrent responsibility of a third State. In such cases, the responsibility of each participating State is determined individually, on the basis of its own conduct and by reference to its own international obligations.[1217]

In casu, member States' human rights due diligence obligations.[1218]

Each member State may, thus, be held to account for the wrongful conduct as a whole.[1219] It may then have recourse to the other responsible member States to ensure equitable distribution of the burden of reparation.[1220] As already noted, just how to apportion the latter is no easy affair. It has been suggested that such allocation be made in accordance with the share of member States' participation in the expenses of the organisation.[1221] As this participation reflects, in a way, the voice held by member States in international financial institutions, it could indeed serve as a fair allocation formula. The proportionality criterion was likewise supported by several authors in the context of the IDI Questionnaire on member State responsibility.[1222] Some noted, however, that the matter was not one with which the victim should struggle (as such internal arrangements would not in any event be opposable to the third party) and, thereby, upheld the principle of joint and several responsibility.[1223]

It is contended here that joint and several responsibility constitutes, indeed, the most appropriate allocation principle in these cases. Inasmuch as it allows the

1217 Para. 8 of the commentaries to Article 47 ASR.

1218 The understanding that member States' failure to observe due diligence obligations may give rise to a situation of cumulative causation, whereby each member State will be held individually responsible for the whole damage, has been upheld by Klein. The author, however, applies this notion to the particular context of member States' supervisory obligations concerning the (wrongful) use of their territory by the organisation. When it comes to member State participation in decision-making processes, Klein rather considers member States' approving votes as a whole, which would constitute one cumulative cause, together with the injurious act of the organisation (the other cumulative cause). In this case, the duty to repair would rest either on the international organisation, or on the *totality* of the member States – and not on each State individually (as contended in this book), given the weakened causality links that tie the State to the harm inflicted by the organisation. See: P. Klein, *supra* note 350, 589–93.

1219 Para. 2 of the commentaries to Article 47 ASR, and paras. 12 and 13 of the commentaries to Article 31 ASR. For a discussion of how to apportion responsibility in cases of 'cumulative causes', see: P. D'Argent, 'Reparation, Cessation, Assurances and Guarantees of Non-Repetition', in A. Nollkaemper and E. Plakokefalos (eds.), op. cit. *supra* note 1215, 227–32.

1220 C. Dominicé, 'Attribution of Conduct to Multiple States and the Implication of a State in the Act of Another State' in J. Crawford, A. Pellet, S. Olleson and K. Parlett (eds.) op. cit. *supra* note 389, 284.

1221 I. Seidl-Hohenveldern, *supra* note 678, 418.

1222 See: IDI Questionnaire on member State responsibility, *supra* note 655, 294, 307 (response of D. Vignes); 328 (response of K. Zemanek); 334, 336 (response of J. Crawford); 368 (response of I. Seidl-Hohenveldern).

1223 Ibid., 294, 307, 334.
It is of note that the regime of joint and several responsibility is already embraced in other international legal fields, such as the UNCLOS (in Article 139(2)).

injured individual to bring a claim against any of the wrongdoer member States for the whole damage, it does justice to reasons of equality between the parties,[1224] and avoids the shifting of the responsibility buck to the detriment of the injured party.[1225] As rightly noted by Hirsch, the member State that provides a remedy to a third party to an extent exceeding its share is undoubtedly in a better position, in comparison with the third party, to demand and receive from the other members their share, as it can resort to the various mechanisms provided for in the organisation's constituent instrument, which are in fact not available to the third party.[1226]

3.5.2.4 Putting into Effect Member States' Duty to Provide a Remedy

Having clarified how member State reparation duties come about, the question arises as to *where* their responsibility may be invoked. Here, as in the case of international (financial) institutions, victims are faced with a few legal, conceptual and practical difficulties. This, in any event, does not call into question the availability of avenues of action,[1227] some of which will be briefly discussed in the current section. The focus will be placed on mechanisms that the allegedly wrongdoing member State may provide itself, as guarantor of human rights responsiveness.[1228]

Domestic judicatures of the member State constitute obvious forums to litigate member States' responsibility for failure to comply with their human rights due diligence obligations. The subject-matter of the (tort) claim would regard the vote or position adopted by the State's Executive Director in the Board of the institution, as well as the accompanying executive decisions (if identified) taken by the State entities responsible for directing their representative's vote.[1229] As already discussed in Section 1.1.1.2, these factors could be judged against, for example, the Human Rights Act in the UK, the Act on Development Cooperation in Belgium, or the International Financial Institutions Act in the US.

An obstacle that emerges in this context relates to the tendency of courts to show some deference towards their governments, particularly when it comes to

1224 See: ILA Report on Accountability of International Organisations, *supra* note 50, 42, arguing that the pre-existing inequality between the international organisation and the third party calls for flexibility with regard to the burden of proof.

1225 C. Ahlborn, 'To Share or Not to Share? The Allocation of Responsibility between International Organizations and Their Member States', 88(3–4) *Journal of International Peace and Organization* (2013) 45.

1226 M. Hirsch, *supra* note 76, 168.

1227 For an overview of the various avenues of action to litigate member State responsibility, and attendant obstacles, see: F. Messineo, 'The Invocation of Member State Responsibility before National and International Courts: Rekindling Old Utopias', in A. S. Barros, C. Ryngaert and J. Wouters (eds.), op. cit. *supra* note 37, 193.

1228 It is certainly possible to resort to regional human rights systems but this option will not be discussed at this stage.

1229 M. Salomon, *supra* note 681, 178.

action taken in the realm of international cooperation.[1230] To challenge votes and instructions is tantamount to exercising judicial review over the executive's activities pertaining to issues closely associated with foreign (development) policy.[1231] Deemed political by their nature, these matters could, thus, be found unsuited to adjudication. Yet, while such was the dominant approach for most of the twentieth century, the claim can now be made that foreign relations law is undergoing a process of 'normalisation'.[1232] And, as has been noted, constitutional presumptions of non-intrusion into matters of foreign affairs may be set aside when faced with an appeal to core values such as human rights.[1233] Openness towards the acceptance of member State responsibility is thus also a product of how domestic courts approach State participation in international organisations. It is argued that the filing of a lawsuit in the court of the member State itself, instead of being interpreted as a request to supplant a foreign policy decision, should, rather, be viewed as an appeal to enforce specific rights recognised in domestic and international legal instruments.

Apart from the judicial settlement of disputes, other solutions could be put forward. Arbitration has, for instance, been proposed by Amerasinghe in the framework of the IDI Questionnaire on member State responsibility.[1234] Another option, which would have to be carefully tailored, would be the setting up of problem-solving mechanisms within member States' (at least the most engaged ones) own development agencies. The concept has, at least, been applied in bilateral development cooperation: for instance, the Japan International Cooperation Agency (JICA) has set up an independent 'objection procedure' based on its Guidelines for Environmental and Social Considerations.[1235] The procedure is basically centred on encouraging dialogue between the parties concerned, and is aimed at providing support 'in the prompt resolution of disputes concerning specific environmental and/or social problems caused by projects for which JICA provides assistance, which have

1230 F. Messineo, *supra* note 1227, 197.

1231 E. De Wet, *supra* note 291, 878.

1232 See: G. Sitaraman and I. Wuerth, 'The Normalization of Foreign Relations Law', 128(7) Harv L Rev (2015) 1897, describing the evolution of US courts' approach to foreign relations law and the paradigm shift from exceptionalism (i.e., the belief that legal issues arising from foreign relations are functionally, doctrinally and also methodologically distinct from those arising in domestic policy), which prevailed in the twentieth century, to 'normalisation'.

1233 See: T. De La Mare, 'Foreign Affairs: Forbidden Territory for the Courts' (2013), paras. 18–24, referring to the case-law of UK courts with regard to questions of foreign affairs involving human rights matters.

1234 C. F. Amerasinghe, response to the IDI Questionnaire on Member State responsibility, *supra* note 655, 351, 352.

1235 Japan International Cooperation Agency, *Objection Procedures based on the Guidelines for Environmental and Social Considerations*, April 2010, available at: www.jica.go.jp/english/our_work/social_environmental/objection/c8hovm0000013011-att/objection.pdf, last consulted 15 October 2018.

arisen due to JICA's non-compliance with the Guidelines'.[1236] Such types of conciliatory mechanism, including mediation, are most welcome. They give substance to member States' role as responsible global development actors, while at the same time de-dramatising the question of member State responsibility.

3.6 CONCLUSION OF CHAPTER III

It was once noted that '[t]he liberal states that shape the existing world order and its defining institutions imprint that order on the identity and interests of existing international organizations"[1237] – and, one would add, on the terms in which the latter operate. This holds true for what works well and not so well within these organisations. Indeed, under the normative baseline provided by human rights due diligence, Chapter III showed that part of the problem regarding the lack of human rights protection in international financial institutions lies in what member States *do* and *fail to do* within such contexts. Their decisions and 'non-decisions' can thus bring about their responsibility under international law.

Member States' duty to protect human rights was seen to derive from the general premise that States do not leave their international obligations at home after adhering to international organisations (Section 3.1). As argued, said duty is further substantiated by the notion that the creation of, and participation in, international organisations entails duly accounting for the interests of the beneficiaries of multilateral cooperation. The constitutional values of representation and responsiveness were thus introduced with a view to exploring the terms in which they proactively and retrospectively frame and tame member State governance (Section 3.2). It was shown that these values translate into the setting up of procedural guarantees of protection in institutional settings – an understanding that has been particularly advanced in the human rights field (Section 3.3). Still, not every individual wherever in the world somehow affected by member States will automatically fall under their jurisdiction. In order to determine the extraterritorial scope of member States' human rights obligations, certain links must therefore be established: the member State, operating at the 'macro' level of political management, strategy formulation and oversight over policy implementation, must have had capacity to *affect* an outcome on his own and thereby *condition* the impact of the organisation's activity on the lives of individuals.

The due diligence standard emerged in this context as a pertinent benchmark by which to judge member State performance. Indeed, Section 3.4.1 showed that the preventive procedural implications it imposes can be transposed without

[1236] Ibid., Article 2(2). See also: A. Kämpf, *supra* note 1003, arguing that German development cooperation should establish a human rights complaints mechanism.

[1237] M. Barnett and R. Duvall, *supra* note 207, 51.

much difficulty to the conduct of member States within international financial institutions (Section 3.4.2). Under said framework, it was asserted that member State guaranteeing obligations come into being with the design of the international financial institution's operational framework and accountability mechanisms, and endure throughout States' participation in the endeavours of the organisation. In particular, as creators, States are required to set up an international financial institution that is able to respond to its wrongs in a human-rights-consistent manner, or, otherwise, to ensure that external mechanisms fulfil such a role (Section 3.4.2.2); and, as participants, they are required to act on a fully informed basis, by appropriately assessing the human rights and environmental risks at stake in the projects or programmes subject to their approval, as well as to guarantee that human rights are not disproportionally interfered with throughout the whole project cycle (Section 3.4.2.1). In cases where human rights are affected, if the member State did all it could to ensure their protection, then its responsibility will no longer be at issue.

Otherwise, failure to protect human rights along the lines mentioned above may give rise to the invocation of member State responsibility. As discussed in Section 3.5, due diligence is breached as soon as the member State has not undertaken the required conduct, without it being necessary to demonstrate the occurrence of an external event (Section 3.5.1.3). Proof of fault is likewise not necessary; *solely* that member States had knowledge, even if constructive, of the possibility of harm (Section 3.5.1.2). This knowledge, as was noted in Section 3.5.1.1, is easily obtainable by Executive Directors and their national authorities through staff reporting, informal and formal bilateral meetings with staff and management, as well as through outside sources. Importantly, the existing communication channels between Executive Directors and the staff provide the necessary leeway for member States to steer institutional behaviour.

Member State responsibility may be invoked – be it in domestic courts, regional human rights bodies or through conciliation (Section 3.5.2.4) – for various sorts of reason. In all likelihood, most cases would be brought by individuals directly affected by institutional operations with a view to obtaining reparation for the injury endured. In such instances, under the principle of joint and several responsibility, the claimant would be entitled to bring a claim against any of the wrongdoer member States for the whole damage and would be required to demonstrate that a (indirect) causal link existed between the conduct of the member State and the legally proscribed outcome (Section 3.5.2). Still, as discussed in Section 3.5.2.1, direct harm is not a necessary condition for victimhood in the context of human rights violations. Relatedly, reparation may not be the sole aim underlying the invocation of member State responsibility for failure to observe due diligence. Individuals whose rights were not directly affected but were nevertheless put at risk during the implementation of a given project, should also be provided with the means to challenge member State behaviour when it runs counter to human rights prescriptions. If the law of responsibility is to operate as a powerful element to defend the principle of legality,[1238] such an interpretation of the human rights regime is certainly called for.

1238 P. Klein, *supra* note 350, 4.

Conclusion

1 THE SUBJECTION OF MEMBER STATE GOVERNANCE TO INTERNATIONAL LAW AND ADJUDICATION

Despite the decades-long, ubiquitously raised concerns regarding the injurious human rights impacts of the operations of international financial institutions and their member States, still today countless voices (unsuccessfully) claim violations in these contexts. At times, individuals seem to be treated as if there is no history and past mistakes cannot be undone.[1239] While much could be changed if only there were political will to do so,[1240] the problem also lies in an insufficient investigation of what can be achieved through international law. The scope and extent of States' human rights obligations as participants in international (financial) institutions have remained uncertain, and so too the terms of application of secondary international legal rules to these actors. In the main, the topic is challenging as it calls for legal particularity in a governance context that is idiosyncratically complex. Indeed, responsibility may be dispersed among different actors, such as the borrowing State, the international financial institution and its member States, and it is far from clear-cut who exactly is to be held responsible, under which terms, and for what. At the end of the day, what remains elusive under international law, and stands out as the major quandary in this book, is how to effectively protect individuals impacted by the operations of international financial institutions and their member States. It has been rightly noted that a proper legal arrangement would presuppose an adequate regime of responsibility, applicable law and remedies against international organisations.[1241] As this

1239 M. Salomon, *supra* note 26, 543, 544, referring to the human costs of structural adjustment measures in Greece, which stand in contrast with half a century of standard-setting in the area of international human rights law.

1240 For example, the discussion of whether or not to endorse human rights language in the WB's recently revised ESF (*supra* note 187) held among the member States reveals that the objection of some was based on the fear that it would lead to more complaints being submitted, and, thus, undermine the effectiveness of the institution's operations. Field notes, 24 June 2015.

1241 R. Wilde, *supra* note 37, 408.

book has attempted to show, this holds equally true with regard to the member States.

From a broader perspective, to discuss member States' responsibility is to question their role in global governance and its legitimacy. Once States create international financial institutions, and participate in their activities, what protection is to be afforded to those whose interests such cooperative endeavours are meant to serve? Is it legitimate, and legally acceptable, that States participating in institutional undertakings do not engage with those affected when formulating their decisions, and that the latter are not provided with appropriate mechanisms to both question the impact of these decisions and hold their authors to account? As transpires from these questions, the matter at hand is thus also one of how to achieve good (global) governance.[1242] The book picked up on such legitimacy concerns and attempted to frame them in international law, in terms that would guarantee that power is responsive to the individuals it affects. With a focus on member States as global actors, the book thus inserts itself in the wider debate of how to find *order* in the international legal system.[1243] Notably, how to unveil, in the latter, a framework which – drawing inspiration from the domestic rule of law tradition – is able to constrain public power as it is exercised by governments participating in international organisations, and thereby ensure that when States adhere to the latter, they do not leave their international obligations behind.

In this book's ethos, governance, as referring to member States, is not just a catchword: it is also a legal concept, inasmuch as it is inextricably linked to the way in which sovereignty is exercised at the global level – and sovereignty, as astutely noted almost a century ago by Verdross, exists *within* public international law.[1244] The concept of (global) governance is admittedly a dynamic and interactive one,[1245] insofar as it stretches back and forth among the various actors that inform the complex governing networks of today. This raises difficulties when it comes to subsuming the concept under international law, for the latter's formal ways demand static conceptual tools to operate with.[1246] In any event, as argued in Chapter I, linking governance to member States' role as 'authority managers' locates their power in a sufficiently clear sphere of conduct to accommodate in international legal terms. This matter will be revisited below.

1242 The subject of member State responsibility could also be treated from the perspective of global democratic governance. On the concept, see: S. Marks, *The Riddle of All Constitutions: International Law, Democracy and the Critique of Ideology* (2000).

1243 What brings *order* into law has of course been perceived differently across time. See: R. Foqué, 'Global Governance and the Rule of Law: Human Rights and General Principles of Good Global Governance', in K. Wellens (ed.), *International Law: Theory and Practice* (1998) 25.

1244 A. Verdross, 'Le Fondement du Droit International', 16 RCADI 1927/1, 247.

1245 S. K. Sell, 'Who Governs the Globe?', in T. Weiss and R. Wilkinson (eds.), op. cit. *supra* note 207, 83.

1246 This much has been noted by J. D'Aspremont, *supra* note 199, 77, with regard to the concept of institutional autonomy.

The argumentation espoused throughout the book's chapters reveals that it is possible to conjecture the contours of a responsibility regime targeting the governance role of member States of international financial institutions. Not only do member States have human rights obligations when participating in said contexts, but also, secondary rules of international law offer criteria to establish their responsibility in cases of non-compliance. A caveat, however, lies in having to rely on member States' 'willingness to accept this greater policy scrutiny and its operation through [dispute settlement] mechanisms'.[1247] To say member States is of course to go beyond Executive Directors and national governmental authorities, so as to encompass domestic courts as well.

The problem with national litigation may be the courts' general reluctance to exercise judicial review over their executive's activities pertaining to matters closely linked to foreign (development) policy. In the present context, the court would be required to scrutinise the vote or position adopted by the State's Executive Director on the Board of the institution, as well as accompanying executive decisions (if identified) taken by the State entities responsible for directing their representative's vote – all of which could be deemed non-justiciable. Still, the appeal to core values such as human rights has the potential to trump concerns of non-intrusion into matters of foreign affairs, as was noted in Section 3.5.2.4. The question is not one of requesting the domestic court to supplant a foreign policy decision of the member State, but, rather, one of appealing to the enforcement of specific rights recognised in domestic and international legal instruments. The subsequent difficulty, then, relates to how courts would interpret the jurisdictional scope of human rights norms (recall Section 3.3).

Domestic judicatures certainly have an important role to play in sustaining more openness towards the acceptance of member State responsibility. Dutch courts, for instance, have proved their readiness to widen the debate in contexts of international organisation-led peacekeeping operations.[1248] In the field of development cooperation, however, scarcely any case has been decided. One court ruling known to the author is the UK High Court *Pergau Dam* case of 1995, where a British grant under bilateral development cooperation was linked to the arms trade, and thereby judged impermissible.[1249] It remains to be seen how State conduct performed in the framework of multilateral development cooperation would be adjudicated, but the potential is certainly there to make a case out of it where valid allegations of human rights violations are at stake.

1247 R. Wilde, *supra* note 37, 415.

1248 Recall Section 2.1.2.2, B, referring to the 2011 *Nuhanović* and *Mustafić* decisions of the Dutch Supreme Court and the 2014 District Court of The Hague's decision *Mothers of Srebrenica* v. *Netherlands*.

1249 *Regina* v. *Secretary of State for Foreign Affairs ex Parte the World Development Movement Ltd*, Queen's Bench Division, [1995] 1 WLR 386.

Courts are not, in any event, the only forum available to solve disputes between member States and third parties. Member States' subjection to greater scrutiny can also be translated into alternative solutions, such as arbitration.[1250] Another option, based on conciliatory grounds, is the setting up of problem-solving mechanisms within member States' (at least the most engaged ones) own development agencies. As has been noted, the concept is not alien to bilateral development cooperation, at least.[1251]

All this, of course, is not to say that widening access to dispute settlement against member States will in and of itself provide sufficient protection of the human rights of individuals impacted by the operations of international financial institutions. Again, it is of utmost importance to clarify the international human rights obligations of these organisations, the terms in which secondary rules of international law apply to them, and, at a practical level, to ensure that they are imbued with appropriate mechanisms to remedy their own wrongs.[1252] Both entities partake in the governance of global development, and, thus, litigation against member States is but a mechanism that must be embedded in a broader system of effective oversight and protection.[1253]

2 OVERVIEW OF THE DISCUSSION

The book's chapters assembled a series of insights which, taken together, allowed for a theory of member State responsibility to gain shape. Without the intent of repeating what was already stated, it can be useful to recall the main findings reached. In so doing, attention will be paid, here and there, to the concept of member State power and how it came across in the various issues addressed throughout the book.

One of the first questions that comes to mind when approaching the topic of member State responsibility concerns the delineation of the borderline between member States and international organisations as subjects of international law. This exercise is essential, for international legal rules will apply to member States only when they act as States, and not as integral components of the organisation. Chapter I addressed the matter by firstly inquiring into the legal implications of State adherence to international organisations. Looking underneath the institutional veil, particularly of international financial institutions, it showed that member States remain powerful actors in their own right when participating in said contexts. Such legal visibility was notably linked to the perceived need for States to uphold their domestic preferences when acting in an institutional setting. It was thus concluded that the transfer of the exercise of sovereign powers to international organisations can be seen to unfold in a 'continuum', i.e., as a dynamic process,

1250 Recall Section 3.5.2.4.
1251 Ibid.
1252 See, inter alia: N. Blokker, *supra* note 37, 43–6.
1253 E. De Wet, *supra* note 291, 881, 882.

wherein member States (through their executive and, to the extent possible, their legislative branches) remain systemically engaged.

This has obvious implications for the application of international responsibility rules, as it brings to view the inevitability of finding, in institutional frameworks, a margin for sovereign action, and thus, a potential 'new' locus of responsibility, which is parallel – and of a lesser scope – to that of the international organisation. As the chapter concluded, when it comes to member State participation in international financial institutions, such locus of responsibility is to be found at a 'macro level' wherein member States exercise their power as 'authority managers', i.e., at the level of the governance mechanisms and procedures they establish and conduct.

The question subsequently addressed in Chapter II was how to account for member States' governance role in the regime of international responsibility. The analysis undertaken in the first part of the chapter on the evolution of doctrinal and judicial approaches to member State responsibility shed light on the conceptual underpinnings of the current regime; on how approaches may shift depending on the policy considerations prioritised (either third party protection or the preservation of institutional autonomy); and why certain gaps endure in the field. Some of these last can be explained by the fact that, since their inception, debates praised the international legal personality of international organisations as the main vantage point from which responsibility issues in an institutional context were to be addressed. An overzealous attitude towards the organisation's legal personality and autonomy, even if comprehensible, meant that State responsibility was seen only as a secondary option. Moreover, it brought with it an insufficient exploration of the terms in which the responsibility of the State is to be established for its own conduct performed in institutional settings.

This legacy was brought to Part V ARIO. It led, first and foremost, to the – valid – determination that member States cannot be held responsible for institutional conduct on the sole basis of membership; and, secondly, to the delineation of what are in the end quite exceptional circumstances of derived member State responsibility (recall Article 58 on aid or assistance, Article 59 on direction and control and Article 61 on circumvention). These instances are important reminders that member States cannot support, push or force international organisations to commit an act that is internationally wrongful. However, they were seen to not respond to the question of how to establish member State responsibility for their participation in institutional decision-making. Ultimately, all this means that the regime of international responsibility, as devised in the ARIO, does not offer clear criteria to accommodate the governance functions of the member States of international (financial) institutions. Still, it was also noted that the ARIO left the door open to approaching the matter from the viewpoint of member States' responsibility for their *own* conduct performed in institutional settings, and, thus, under the ASR. To make use of such an important hint, the chapter's inquiry turned into the question of how to identify legally relevant State conduct in an institutional context, i.e., into a question of attribution.

Given that, with a few exceptions, not much has so far been said about the operation of attribution rules in the governance bodies of international organisations, attention was paid to the treatment of these rules in contexts where member States emerge as troop contributors and as implementers of institutional decisions. A few important benchmarks applicable in such instances were seen to apply similarly in contexts of institutional decision-making: essentially, in attributing conduct to member States, the focus is placed on the margin that is left for them to act with discretion, under the postulation that 'only the entity which is at the origin of the alleged infringement of an obligation ... would be held responsible and could defend the measure concerned'.[1254] When it comes to case-law, it is worth recalling the ICJ's *FYROM* case,[1255] which is possibly the main instance, in international adjudication, where the individual conduct of a State in the process of institutional decision-making was so assertively identified. As seen, the case shows that while it cannot be doubted that the final acts emerging from decision-making processes constitute institutional decisions per se (for which the organisation may be held responsible), the exercise of voting rights by member States qualifies as an act of the State (which in turn may lead to a finding of State responsibility).

Such important findings fed into the final part of Chapter II, which specifically examined the participation of member States in the decision-making processes of international financial institutions. Given the wide uncertainty around the international legal status of Executive Directors, a thorough evaluation was made of the plausibility of their qualification as State organs, as opposed to officials of the organisation (with regard to which it is in any event certain that they owe fiduciary duties). As clarified, the existence of clear reporting lines between Executive Directors and their national authorities allows the latter to regulate, or constrain, the conduct of the former, thereby underpinning their legal status as State representatives. To be sure, it is the member States that put them in office and it is the member States that have a final say in cases where they misbehave. The propriety of attributing their conduct to States is further corroborated by the formal (and informal) dynamics of decision-making in said contexts. Indeed, the final part of Chapter II showed that the votes or positions taken by Executive Directors either can be traced back to member State instructions, or are otherwise generally presumed to have been endorsed by the latter. This holds true for Executive Directors of both single-party and multi-party constituencies. The exercise of voting rights thus emerges as a corollary of Executive Directors' power of sovereign representation.

The final step was to explore how member State governance functions, as performed by Executive Directors, are framed and tamed by the international legal order. After delving into the general requirement of preservation of legality, Chapter III invoked constitutionalist approaches to international law, and insights

1254 G. Gaja, *supra* note 482.
1255 *Supra* note 528.

from human rights law, to undergird the understanding that the principles of representation and responsiveness must inform member State conduct as creators and participants in institutional undertakings. This entails constraining their acts both proactively and retrospectively in order to offer an adequate level of protection to the beneficiaries of multilateral development cooperation. In their pronouncements regarding the human rights obligations of member States, human rights bodies have not provided sufficient guidance as to how the latter materialise in practice. They have, however, firmly appealed to the need to protect human rights extraterritorially in institutional frameworks. As the examination of these bodies' interpretations revealed, member State power is seen to have a bearing on the determination of the scope of their human rights obligations. In particular, owing to the influence they exert over international organisations, member States are required to act with due diligence with a view to ensuring that human rights are effectively protected throughout institutional operations.

Against this backdrop, the chapter moved on to a discussion of the concrete obligations of member States as creators of, and participants in, international financial institutions, and their attendant implications for responsibility purposes. Beyond Part V ARIO, which was seen to concentrate on excesses of power that member States may exert over international organisations, the chapter explored how member States' power can also be found in their failure to perform. It did so through the prism of due diligence as a standard to evaluate member State behaviour. As was discussed, when linked to human rights law, this standard brings with it procedural requirements of conduct that allow for the operationalisation of the abovementioned values of representation and responsiveness. Firstly, it constrains member States' use of their voting power, as well as their behaviour prior to the adoption of a decision, in terms that demand the representation of the interests of those impacted by institutional operations. Essentially, it calls upon member States to appropriately ascertain the human rights risks of the projects subject to their approval, and to safeguard both meaningful consultations and timely dissemination of information throughout the operations of the organisation. As was seen, member States' obligations extend not only to those affected, but also to those likely to be affected, or having an interest in, said operations. Secondly, when particularly linked to the right of access to justice, due diligence conditions the terms in which member States make use of the institutional and policy apparatus they set up in international financial institutions. Noting that various shortcomings exist with regard to internal (and external) dispute settlement mechanisms within these organisations, it was concluded that member State failure to bring sufficient pressure upon international financial institutions to provide for adequate responses to human rights violations could engage their responsibility under international law.

The concrete terms in which member States' responsibility may be invoked for failure to observe due diligence requirements in the performance of their governance role were analysed in the final part of the chapter. Attention was paid along the way to the various elements that lead to the establishment of wrongfulness, as well as to those elements defining the legal consequences of the internationally wrongful act. As was seen, a breach of due diligence may be established as soon as the member State has not undertaken the required conduct, without an external event having to be proven. When it comes to the existence of subjective-psychological elements, such as fault, these are also left out of the complainant's burden of proof, except the need to prove that member States had knowledge, even if constructive, of the risk of harm. A look into the links between Executive Directors, their national authorities and the activity of the staff revealed that proof of (constructive) knowledge may not be as hard as it would seem.

In claims where damage is alleged, it is of course also necessary to establish a causality link between the damage and member State conduct – in these cases, under the criterion not of 'directness', but, rather, of 'foreseeability'. Although damage was seen to be normally indivisible, it was concluded that the specific allocation of responsibility among the various member States (and the international financial institution) is not something of concern to the claimant: under the principle of joint and several responsibility, his or her claim may be brought against any of the wrongdoer member States for the whole damage. What has to be proved is that the member State *contributed* to the proscribed outcome. Still, it was also noted that direct harm is not a necessary condition of victimhood in the context of human rights violations. Relatedly, reparation may not be the sole aim underlying the invocation of member State responsibility for failure to observe human rights due diligence. Although these cases will certainly be more rare, the claimant's purpose might otherwise be restorative, and the remedies sought could, for instance, consist in requiring specific performance of the various components of the duty of due diligence. Importantly, then, to seek for remedies in these contexts might also represent an attempt to restore the legality of State conduct in international affairs.

The foregoing wrapping up of the various chapters serves as a reminder of the appropriateness of assessing member State human rights protection duties through the prism of due diligence. An individual whose rights were injured, or put at risk, in the context of international financial institution operations thus has a few paths to resort to in terms of international responsibility. Depending on the concrete circumstances of the case, he or she may invoke: a) the responsibility of the international organisation for wrongful conduct attributable to it; b) the responsibility of the member State(s) for excesses of power exerted over said conduct; c) the responsibility of the member State(s) for its own wrongful omission to protect human rights diligently. Adding the third option to the classical responsibility equation contained in the ARIO is of utmost usefulness, as it brings to view the notion that member States have a fundamental governance role to play in institutional settings, which exists on its own, and runs in parallel with the operations of the international financial institution. Due diligence thus creates a boundary between the power of member States and that of the international financial institution, structures their relations, and brings forth a novel framework for the analysis of member State responsibility.

3 MEMBER STATES' HUMAN RIGHTS DUE DILIGENCE DUTIES AS PROMOTERS OF LEGALITY AND PREDICTABILITY

As discussed in Chapter III, due diligence operates as an important *ex ante* tool that sets clear guidance and standards against which member State performance can be judged. With its emphasis on conduct and process, it brings about an international legal order that is also proactive in securing the rights of individuals, and not one that only comes into being to react to situations where harm has already occurred. In retrieving the constitutional values of representativeness and responsiveness, as translated in international human rights provisions (recall Chapter III's discussion on public participation rights), due diligence allows for the operationalisation of this protective framework in the governance of international financial institutions by their member States. While promoting legality, due diligence creates an incentive structure for member States to act in conformity with international human rights law. Next to this, it renders global development governance, as steered by member States, more predictable.[1256]

Subjecting member State participation in the representative organs of international financial institutions to obligations of conduct provides a balanced lens through which to demarcate the role of the organisation from that of the participating State. It responds to Escarameia's concern, expressed during the ILC debates preceding the adoption of the ARIO, that 'it would be unfair for a member State that had done everything in its power to prevent the international organization from committing a wrongful act to risk incurring responsibility once such an act had been committed'.[1257] All in all, where the State does all that is required by primary obligations of conduct when it votes or adopts a position in institutional decision-making processes, or while it monitors project implementation, it may no longer be found responsible under the ASR, even where the conduct subsequently performed by the international organisation proves to be harmful. This, again, shows that this form of member State responsibility is independent from that of the international organisation.

The obligations of member States for their own conduct will therefore apply only to a certain degree: from a certain point on, the law of State responsibility (which operates, in this context, on the basis of a failure to exercise due diligence) no longer

1256 As was discussed, predictability is linked to the notion that the operations of both international financial institutions and their member States should be conducted in a sufficiently open and clear manner (by following certain procedures), so that their actions are understandable to all stakeholders. See also: D. Bradlow, *supra* note 188, 50.

1257 UN Doc. A/CN.4/2892, YILC, 2006, Vol. I, 155, para. 6.

holds, and, thus, it is solely the law of international organisation responsibility that is at stake. This brings to mind the assertion, made elsewhere in this book, that sovereignty, in the framework of the binary relationship member States–international organisation, manifests itself in a plurarchic form, meaning that it is dispersed between distinct levels of authority.[1258] Which sites of governance can properly be identified as the most suitable or effective is thus a fundamental inquiry to undertake, also for the purposes of international responsibility.

As was seen in Section 1.3, sovereignty, as exercised by member States, manifests itself at a 'macro' level of political management, strategy formulation and oversight over policy implementation, alongside the technical decisions of management and staff. With regard to harmful operational staff decisions that were too remote for member States to be able to *control*, or that generally lay outside the remit of member State decision-making power, it does not seem possible to invoke member State responsibility for failure to exercise due diligence in preventing human rights harm. In seeking responsibility in these contexts, the solution may rather be found in the law of international organisation responsibility. It must be recalled that the legal personality and autonomy of international organisations imply that the latter are to be held responsible for their own wrongful conduct.[1259] This is not to say, however, that member State responsibility may not subsequently arise in relation to such types of issue, under different grounds: indeed, it might come into play where the creation of an entity with operational autonomy along said lines is not followed by the setting up of dispute settlement mechanisms through which victims could contest the organisation's conduct. Here, the member State could be held responsible, not for a failure to protect the human rights that were particularly hurt by the staff's decision, but, rather, for a failure to protect the individual's right of access to justice as applied in an institutional setting (recall Section 3.4.2.2).

Importantly, then, there is never a legal vacuum in the assessment of both actors' spheres of responsibility: rather, just the need to clarify the boundaries between them. Doctrinal support for this type of responsibility arrangement has been termed – and understandably so – 'irenic', inasmuch as it creates the necessary conditions to avoid conflicts of obligations between both subjects of international law.[1260] This is of utmost importance in the present context, in that international financial institutions are certainly not bound by the same human rights obligations as States.

The ILA Study Group on Due Diligence in International Law raised the question, in its First Report, of whether 'the existence of due diligence as a standard of behaviour (and of responsibility) across a range of areas of international law say[s]

1258 Recall A. Kuper, *supra* note 283.

1259 With a few exceptions, as discussed in Section 2.1.2.1.

1260 E. Lagrange, *supra* note 93, 419. The author, however, does not agree with the possibility of establishing member State responsibility in such terms.

anything more fundamental about the role of the State in regulating private and corporate behaviour in contemporary international law'.[1261] The query could likewise regard the role of member States in regulating institutional behaviour – and there is indeed something more fundamental in subjecting such a role to the standard of due diligence: it situates member State power vis-à-vis the international financial institution, structures their relations and creates a novel framework for the analysis of member State responsibility. Seen from a wider perspective, the responsibility regime espoused in this book responds to the need for legal security and imbues global development governance, as driven by said actors, with a sense of consistency and predictability.

4 THE CONSTRUCTIVE DIMENSION OF MEMBER STATE RESPONSIBILITY

The claim for human rights protection has a bearing on how member State responsibility is to be perceived. As discussed in Chapter III, such a claim is not solely a demand not to be harmed, but is also about not having one's rights put at risk. This logic points to the importance of ensuring the legality (i.e., human rights conformity) of processes, apart from their outcomes – in this case, the process of member State participation in international financial institutions.

There is something constructive in litigating member States' responsibility for their governance role in these settings. If, from one perspective, responsibility stands out as a punitive mechanism, from another viewpoint it is also a means to improve member States' performance as global development actors. As nicely put by Koskenniemi, a claim is not only the formulation of a particular grievance that has happened to the individual; it is also a claim of anyone that would be in such position.[1262] In this way, the claim becomes constructed in social terms and the private grievance is lifted to the 'level of public law violation, of concern not only to the victim but to the community'.[1263] International law, in the end, is not only about governing things; it also expresses a universalist principle of inclusion at the outset, inasmuch as it provides protection to individuals and groups whose interests are not sufficiently represented in governance bodies.[1264] In this book's context, a claim that is legally sound serves as an appeal as to what went wrong in a particular development project. In that sense, it steers dialogue and may constructively lead to better development outcomes in the future – for example, through the improvement of the procedural safeguards that will be followed by member States in a future project.

[1261] ILA Due Diligence Report, *supra* note 56, 1.
[1262] M. Koskeniemmi, 'Global Governance and Public International Law', *Kritische Justiz* (2004) 241, 249, 250.
[1263] Ibid.
[1264] Ibid.

It is particularly instructive to quote an excerpt of the United Nations Development Strategy Beyond 2015, which reads: 'Policy failures in developing countries should not be used as evidence of incapacity but rather as a learning resource. Trial and error are part of the process of continuous evaluation of the experience of policymaking and policy implementation; given that the domestic environment is complex and the international environment fast-moving. International institutions and practices need to exhibit greater humility, less certainty of correctness, and greater respect for local knowledge.'[1265] Failure thus translates into a learning opportunity. Furthermore, the implementation of member State responsibility becomes a useful tool to compel member States to engage in new institutional arrangements, and to bring pressure to bear on international financial institutions to change their ways. Member State responsibility can thereby serve a remedial, preventive and reformist purpose.[1266]

That being said, it is also important to note that, apart from its litigation, the very existence of a solid member State responsibility framework has a constructive dimension. While the concern is normally raised that widening such a regime would result in unwarranted interference by the member States with institutional decision-making processes (recall Chapter II), the argument could be turned on its head, to make way for the claim that member States 'will simply set up appropriate built-in safeguards to prevent potential liability'.[1267] As opportunely noted by Spijkers, the fact that the Netherlands was condemned in the *Nuhanović* and *Mustafić* judgments[1268] did not steer the country towards the avoidance of future responsibility by prohibiting the Dutch authorities from ever getting involved in peacekeeping missions; rather, it created an incentive for the prevention of failure, as the Netherlands committed to monitoring more intensely the peacekeeping missions in which it participates.[1269] A similar point was also made by Belarus during the ILC debates preceding the adoption of the ARIO: 'Recognition of the responsibility of States for internationally wrongful actions or omissions of an international organization would force States to take a more considered approach to their membership of international organizations and, in general, would strengthen legality in the activities of all international organizations.'[1270]

Within international financial institutions, a more serious commitment, by the member States, through observance of their protection duties under international

1265 The United Nations Development Strategy Beyond 2015, Committee for Development Policy, Policy Note (2012) 44.

1266 See: A. F. Lang, *supra* note 938, 65.

1267 Waelbroeck response to IDI Questionnaire on member State responsibility, *supra* note 655, 322, 323.

1268 Mentioned *supra* notes 82 and 1275.

1269 O. Spijkers, '*Nuhanović* v. *Netherlands*, Judgment, BZ9225, and *Mustafić* v. *Netherlands*, Judgment, BZ9228, Supreme Court of the Netherlands, 6 September 2013', in C. Ryngaert, I. Dekker, R. Wessel and J. Wouters (eds.), op. cit. *supra* note 101, 350.

1270 Comments of Belarus, UNGA Sixth Committee, 60th Session, Summary Record of the 12th meeting, UN Doc. A/C.6/60/SR.12 (2005) para. 51.

human rights law, can only enhance the success of their global development endeavours, while at the same time preventing potential responsibility. The standard of care imposed by human rights due diligence prescriptions surely provides relevant guidance in this respect (recall Chapter III). A meaningful engagement with this framework can already start at the moment of selection of the ministry responsible for the State's participation in such organisations, and of the attendant representative: simply put, these entities should have adequate knowledge of international human rights law. As a matter of fact, it was on the basis of such types of consideration that a legislative proposal was recently put forward in Belgium to transfer the competence for the country's mandate in the WB from the Ministry of Finance to the Ministry of Development Cooperation.[1271]

This book calls for a conscious approach to member State responsibility under the framework imposed by human rights due diligence. Responsibility need not be 'feared', for if member States are able to demonstrate that they took all reasonable steps to avoid human rights violations by appropriately following human rights due diligence requirements, they certainly endure fewer risks of being blamed for human rights harm,[1272] and of possible legal claims being brought against them in the future.[1273] The pursuit of human rights protection duties brings about a more collaborative relationship between member States and the beneficiaries of a given project or programme, and thereby develops a more stable 'license to operate'.[1274] After all, this is what the principles of *good* governance are about, more particularly, good global development governance. As put elsewhere in this book, if member States create and participate in international financial institutions to further global development needs, they can be fully credible in what they do only if they are prepared to assume responsibility for it.

1271 Chambre des Représentants de Belgique, *Proposition de Résolution relative au rôle de la Belgique au sein de la Banque mondiale*, Doc. 54 1836/001, 17 Mai 2016, 11.

1272 For example, in their recent Legal Brief on the Case of Greece, *supra* note 28, De Schutter and Salomon are particularly vocal in affirming the human rights responsibility of Euro Area member States (apart from the EU and the IMF) for the human rights violations stemming from the fiscal consolidation measures adopted in Greece (see, especially: 5–8, 14, 15).

1273 See: *UN Guiding Principles on Business and Human Rights*, commentary to principle 17, *supra* note 6.

1274 HRW Abuse Free Development Report, *supra* note 25, 18.

Bibliography

1 LITERATURE

1.1 *Books*

Allan, T., *Constitutional Justice: A Liberal Theory of the Rule of Law*, Oxford University Press, 2001.

Amerasinghe, C. F., *Principles of Institutional Law of International Organisations*, Cambridge University Press, 2004.

Anzilotti, D., *Corso di diritto internazionale, Vol. I, Introduzione-Teorie generali*, 5th edn, Padova, 1955.

Bekker, P., *The Legal Position of Intergovernmental Organizations: A Functional Necessity Analysis of Their Legal Status and Immunities*, Martinus Nijhoff, 1994.

Bordin, F., *The Analogy between States and International Organizations: Legal Reasoning and the Development of the Law of International Organizations*, Doctoral Dissertation defended at the University of Cambridge, 2014.

Boughton, J. M., *Tearing Down Walls: The International Monetary Fund 1990–1999*, International Monetary Fund, 2012.

Brölmann, C., *The Institutional Veil in Public International Law: International Organisations and the Law of Treaties*, Hart Publishing, 2007.

Brownlie, I., *Principles of Public International Law*, Oxford University Press, 2008.

Chinkin, C., *Third Parties in International Law*, Oxford University Press, 1993.

Clapham, A., *Human Rights Obligations of Non-State Actors*, Oxford University Press, 2006.

Crawford, J., *State Responsibility: The General Part*, Cambridge University Press, 2013.

Brownlie's Principles of Public International Law, Oxford University Press, 2012.

The International Law Commission's Articles on State Responsibility: Introduction, Text and Commentaries, Cambridge University Press, 2005.

Darrow, M., *Between Light and Shadow: The World Bank, the International Monetary Fund and International Human Rights Law*, Hart Publishing, 2003.

David, E., *Droit des Organisations Internationales*, Bruylant, 2016.

Escarameia, P., *Reflexões sobre Temas de Direito Internacional: Timor, a ONU e o Tribunal Penal Internacional*, Instituto Superior de Ciências Sociais e Políticas, 2001.

Fellmeth, A. X. and Horwitx, M., *Guide to Latin in International Law*, Oxford University Press, 2009.

Van Genugten, W., *The World Bank Group, the IMF and Human Rights: A Contextualised Way Forward*, Intersentia, 2015.

Gold, J., *Voting and Decisions in the International Monetary Fund: An Essay on the Law and Practice of the Fund*, International Monetary Fund, 1972.
Gounelle, M., *La Motivation des Actes Juridiques en Droit International Public: Contribution à Une Théorie de L'acte Juridique en Droit International Public*, Pédone, 1979.
Harrod, F., *The Life of John Maynard Keynes*, Oxford University Press, 1951.
Hart, H. L. A. and Honoré, T., *Causation in the Law*, Oxford University Press, 2002.
Held, D. and Mcgrew, A., *Globalization/Anti-Globalization: Beyond the Great Divide*, Cambridge University Press, 2007.
Higgins, R., *Themes and Theories: Selected Essays, Speeches and Writings in International Law*, Oxford University Press, 2009.
Problems and Process: International Law and How We Use It, Oxford University Press, 1994.
The Development of International Law through the Political Organs of the United Nations, Oxford University Press, 1963.
Hirsch, M., *The Responsibility of International Organizations toward Third Parties: Some Basic Principles*, Martinus Nijhoff, 1995.
Hurrel, A., *On Global Order: Power, Values and the Constitution of International Society*, Oxford University Press, 2007.
Jenks, C. W., *The Proper Law of International Organisations*, Stevens & Sons Limited, 1962.
Klabbers, J., *An Introduction to International Institutional Law*, Cambridge University Press, 2009 and 2015.
Klein, P., *La Responsabilité des Organisations Internationales dans les Ordres Juridiques Internes et des Droit des Gens*, Bruylant, 1998.
Koskenniemi, M., *From Apology to Utopia: The Structure of International Legal Argument*, Cambridge University Press, 2005.
Kuper, A., *Democracy beyond Borders: Justice and Representation in Global Institutions*, Oxford University Press, 2004.
Lagrange, E., *La Représentation Institutionnelle dans l'ordre International: Une Contribution à La Théorie de la Personnalité Morale des Organisations Internationals*, Kluwer Law International, 2002.
Lawson, R. and Schermers, H., *Leading Cases of the European Court of Human Rights*, Ars Aequi Libri, 1999.
Von Lindeiner-Wildau, K., *La Supranationalité en tant que Principe de Droit*, Sijthoff, 1970.
Lukes, S., *Power: A Radical View*, Palgrave Macmillan, 2005.
Marks, S., *The Riddle of All Constitutions: International Law, Democracy and the Critique of Ideology*, Oxford University Press, 2000.
Martin Martinez, M., *National Sovereignty and International Organizations*, Kluwer Law International, 1996.
McCorquodale, R., *International Law beyond the State: Essays on Sovereignty, Non-State Actors and Human Rights*, CMP Publishing, 2011.
Mearsheimer, J., *The Tragedy of Great Power Politics*, W. W. Norton, 2001.
Michaels, D. B., *International Privileges and Immunities: A Case for a Universal Statute*, Martinus Nijhoff, 1971.
Mikesel, R., The Bretton Woods Debates: A Memoir, Essays in International Finance, No. 192, Princeton University, 1994.
Mistry, P., *Multilateral Development Banks: An Assessment of Their Financial Structures, Policies and Practices*, Fondad, 1995.

Pisillo-Mazzeschi, R., *'Due Diligence' e Responsabilità Internazionale Degli Stati*, Giuffrè, 1989.

Plantey, A., *International Negotiation in the Twenty-First Century* (translated by Frances Meadows), Routledge-Cavendish, 2007.

Portman, R., *Legal Personality in International Law*, Cambridge University Press, 2010.

Reynolds, F. M. B., *Bowstead & Reynolds on Agency*, Sweet & Maxwell, 2014.

Reuteur, P., *Institutions Internationales*, Presses Universitaires de France, 1969.

Salomon, M., *Global Responsibility for Human Rights: World Poverty and the Development of International Law*, Oxford University Press, 2007.

Sands, P. and Klein, P., *Bowett's Law of International Institutions*, Sweet & Maxwell, 2009.

Sarfaty, G. A., *Values in Translation: Human Rights and the Culture of the World Bank*, Stanford University Press, 2012.

Sarooshi, D., *International Organizations and Their Exercise of Sovereign Powers*, Oxford University Press, 2005.

Scelle, G., *Précis de Droit des Gens. Principes et Systématique*, Vol. I, 1932, and Vol. II, 1934.

Schermers, H., *International Institutional Law*, Kluwer Law International, 1980.

Schermers, H. and Blokker, N., *International Institutional Law: Unity within Diversity*, Martinus Nijhoff, 2011.

Seidl-Hohenveldern, I., *Corporations in and under International Law*, Cambridge University Press, 1987.

Skogly, S., *Beyond International Borders: States' Human Rights Obligations in International Cooperation*, Intersentia, 2006.

Stone, R., *Controlling Institutions: International Organizations and the Global Economy*, Cambridge University Press, 2011.

Tzanakopoulos, A., *Disobeying the Security Council: Countermeasures against Wrongful Sanctions*, Oxford University Press, 2011.

Vandenbogaerde, A., *Towards Shared Accountability in International Human Rights Law*, Intersentia, 2016.

Wellens, K., *Remedies against International Organisations*, Cambridge University Press, 2002.

White, N., *The Law of International Organisations*, Manchester University Press, 2005.

Williams, J. F., *Chapters on Current International Law and the Law of Nations*, London: Longmans, Green & Co., 1929.

1.2 *Chapters in Books*

Adam, H. T., 'Les Organismes Internationaux Spécialisés: Contribution a la Théorie Générale des Établissements Publics Internationaux', in LGDJ, 1965, p. 130.

Ahlborn, C., 'Remedies against International Organizations – A Relational Account of International Responsibility', in D. Sarooshi (ed.), *Remedies and Responsibility for the Actions of International Organizations/Mesures de Réparation et Responsabilité à Raison des Actes des Organisations Internationales*, Brill–Nijhoff, 2014, pp. 525–76.

Allott, P., 'Intergovernmental Societies and the Idea of Constitutionalism', in J. M. Coicaud and V. Heiskanen (eds.), *The Legitimacy of International Organisations*, United Nations University Press, 2001, pp. 69–103.

Alvarez, J. E., 'International Organizations As Law-Makers', in W. P. Heere (ed.), *From Government to Governance: The Growing Impact of Non-State Actors on the International and European Legal System*, Hague Joint Conference on Contemporary Issues of International Law, 2003, pp. 11–20.

'Constitutional Interpretation in International Organizations', in J. Coicaud and V. Heiskanen (eds.), *The Legitimacy of International Organizations*, United Nations University Press, 2001, pp. 104–54.

D'Argent, P., 'Reparation, Cessation, Assurances and Guarantees of Non-Repetition', in A. Nollkaemper and E. Plakokefalos (eds.), *Principles of Shared Responsibility in International Law: An Appraisal of the State of the Art*, Cambridge University Press, 2014, pp. 208–50.

D'Aspremont, J., 'The Multifaceted Concept of the Autonomy of International Organizations and International Legal Discourse', in R. Collins and N. White (eds.), *International Organizations and the Idea of Autonomy: Institutional Independence in the International Legal Order*, Routledge, 2011, pp. 63–86.

De Baere, G., 'European Integration and the Rule of Law in Foreign Policy', in J. Dickson and P. Eleftheriadis (eds.), *Philosophical Foundations of European Union Law*, Philosophical Foundations of Law book series, Oxford University Press, 2012, pp. 354–83.

Barnett, M. and Duvall, R., 'International Organizations and the Diffusion of Power', in T. Weiss and R. Wilkinson (eds.), *International Organization and Global Governance*, Routledge, 2014, pp. 48–59.

'Power in Global Governance', in M. Barnett and R. Duval (eds.), *Power in Global Governance*, Cambridge University Press, 2005, pp. 1–32.

Barros, A. S., 'Member States and the International Legal (Dis)order: Accounting for the Notion of Responsible Governance', in A. S. Barros, C. Ryngaert and J. Wouters (eds.), *International Organizations and Member State Responsibility: Critical Perspectives*, Brill–Nijhoff, 2016, pp. 48–71.

'Application of the Interim Accord of 13 September 1995 (The Former Yugoslav Republic of Macedonia v. Greece), Judgment, [2011], ICJ Reports 644', in C. Ryngaert, I. Dekker, R. Wessel and J. Wouters (eds.), *Judicial Decisions on the Law of International Organizations*, Oxford University Press, 2016, pp. 56–65.

'Matthews v. The United Kingdom', in C. Ryngaert, I. F. Dekker, R.A. Wessel and J. Wouters (eds.), *Judicial Decisions on the Law of International Organizations*, Oxford University Press, 2016, pp. 286–99.

Barros, A. S. and Ryngaert, C., 'Officials (Article VI Sections 18–23 Specialized Agencies Convention)', in A. Reinisch and P. Bachmayer (eds.), *The Conventions on the Privileges and Immunities of the United Nations and Its Specialized Agencies: A Commentary*, Oxford University Press, 2016, pp. 395–438.

Blokker, N., 'Member State Responsibility for Wrongdoings of International Organizations: Beacon of Hope or Delusion?', in A. S. Barros, C. Ryngaert and J. Wouters (eds.), *International Organizations and Member State Responsibility: Critical Perspectives*, Brill–Nijhoff, 2016, pp. 34–47.

Blomeyer-Bartenstein, M., 'Due Diligence', in R. Bernhardt (ed.), *Encyclopaedia of Public International Law*, North Holland Amsterdam, 1987, pp. 138–43.

Von Bogdandy, A., 'General Principles of International Public Authority: Sketching a Research Field', in A. Von Bogdandy, R. Wolfrum, J. V. Bernstorff, P. Dann and M. Goldmann (eds.), *The Exercise of Public Authority by International Institutions: Advancing International Institutional Law*, Springer, 2009, pp. 727–60.

Von Bogdandy, A., Dann, P. and Goldmann, M., 'Developing the Publicness of Public International Law: Towards a Legal Framework for Global Governance Activities', in A. Von Bogdandy, R. Wolfrum, J. V. Bernstorff, P. Dann and M. Goldmann (eds.), *The Exercise of Public Authority by International Institutions: Advancing International Institutional Law*, Springer, 2009, pp. 3–32.

Bradlow, D., 'International Law and the Operations of the International Financial Institutions', in D. Bradlow and D. Hunter (eds.), *International Financial Institutions and International Law*, Kluwer Law International, 2010, pp. 1–30.

Brölmann, C., 'Member States and International Legal Responsibility: Developments of the Institutional Veil', in A. S. Barros, C. Ryngaert and J. Wouters (eds.), *International Organizations and Member State Responsibility: Critical Perspectives*, Brill–Nijhoff, 2016, pp. 72–94.

Brownlie, I., 'The Responsibility of States for the Acts of International Organizations', in M. Ragazzi (ed.), *International Responsibility Today: Essays in Memory of Oscar Schachter*, Martinus Nijhoff, 2005, pp. 355–62.

'State Responsibility: The Problem of Delegation', in K. Ginther, G. Hafner, W. Lang, H. Neuhold and L. Sucharipa-Behrmann (eds.), *Völkerrecht zwischen normativem Anspruch und politischer Realität: Festschrift für Karl Zemanek zum 65. Geburtstag*, Duncker&Humblot, 1994, pp. 299–306.

Campbell, 'Managing Conflicts of Interest and Other Ethics Issues at the IMF', in R. Lamdany and L. Martinez-Diaz (eds.), *Studies of IMF Governance: A Compendium*, IMF Independent Evaluation Office, 2009, pp. 254–75.

Della Cananea, G., 'Procedural Due Process of Law beyond the State', in A. Von Bogdandy, R. Wolfrum, J. V. Bernstorff, P. Dann and M. Goldmann (eds.), *The Exercise of Public Authority by International Institutions: Advancing International Institutional Law*, Springer, 2009, pp. 965–99.

Cançado Trindade, A. A., 'Prologue: An Overview of the Contribution of International Tribunals to the Rule of Law', in G. De Baere and J. Wouters (eds.), *The Contribution of International and Supranational Courts to the Rule of Law*, Edward Elgar, 2015, pp. 3–18.

'Complementarity between State Responsibility and Individual Responsibility for Grave Violations of Human Rights: The Crime of State Revisited', in M. Ragazzi (ed.), *International Responsibility Today: Essays in Memory of Oscar Schachter*, Martinus Nijhoff, 2005, pp. 253–70.

Cassese, A., 'Modern Constitutions and International Law', in *Académie de Droit International de la Haye*,192, Recueil des Cours, 1985/III, pp. 341–476.

Chen, Y., 'Attribution, Causation and Responsibility of International Organizations', in D. Sarooshi (ed.), *Remedies and Responsibility for the Actions of International Organizations/Mesures de Réparation et Responsabilité à Raison des Actes des Organisations Internationales*, Brill–Nijhoff, 2014, pp. 33–111.

Clark, D., 'Understanding the World Bank Inspection Panel', in D. Clark, J. Fox and K. Treakle (eds.), *Demanding Accountability: Civil-Society Claims and the World Bank Inspection Panel*, Rowman & Littlefield Publishers, 2003, pp. 1–24.

Collins, R. and White, N., 'International Organizations and the Idea of Autonomy: Introduction and Overview', in R. Collins and N. White (eds.), *International Organizations and the Idea of Autonomy: Institutional Independence in the International Legal Order*, Routledge, 2011, pp. 1–20.

Corten, O. and Klein, P., 'The Limits of Complicity As a Ground for Responsibility: Lessons Learned from the *Corfu Channel* Case', in K. Bannelier, T. Christakis and S. Heathcote (eds.), *The ICJ and the Evolution of International Law: The Enduring Impact of the Corfu Channel Case*, Routledge, 2012, pp. 315–34.

Dannenbaum, T., 'Dual Attribution in the Context of Military Operations', in A. S. Barros, C. Ryngaert and J. Wouters (eds.), *International Organizations and Member State Responsibility: Critical Perspectives*, Brill–Nijhoff, 2016, pp. 114–38.

Dominicé, C., 'Attribution of Conduct to Multiple States and the Implication of a State in the Act of Another State', in J. Crawford, A. Pellet, S. Olleson and K. Parlett (eds.), *The Law of International Responsibility*, Oxford University Press, 2010, pp. 281–9.

Dugard, J. and Vermeer-Künzli, A., 'The Elusive Allocation of Responsibility to Informal Organizations: The Case of the Quartet of the Middle East', in M. Ragazzi (ed.), *Responsibility of International Organizations: Essays in Memory of Sir Ian Brownlie*, Martinus Nijhoff, 2013, pp. 261–73.

Eagleton, C., 'International Organization and the Law of Responsibility', in *Académie de Droit International de la Haye*, 76, Recueil des Cours, 1950/I, pp. 319–425.

Fassbender, B., 'Article 2(1)', in B. Simma, D.Khan, G. Nolte and A. Paulus (eds.), *The Charter of the United Nations: A Commentary*, Oxford University Press, 2012, pp. 133–65.

'We the Peoples of the United Nations' Constituent Power and Constitutional Form in International Law', in M. Loughlin and N. Walker (eds.), *The Paradox of Constitutionalism: Constituent Power and Constitutional Form*, Oxford University Press, 2008, pp. 269–91.

Fratianni, M., Savona, P. and Pattison, J., 'Governance and Conflicts of Interest in International Financial Institutions', in M. Fratianni, P. Savona and J. Kirton (eds.), *Corporate, Public and Global Governance: The G8 Contribution*, Ashgate, 2007, pp. 127–48.

Gaja, G., 'Accession to the ECHR', in A. Biondi, P. Eeckhout and S. Ripley (eds.), *EU Law after Lisbon*, Oxford University Press, 2012, pp. 180–94.

'The Role of the United Nations in Preventing and Suppressing Genocide', in *The UN Genocide Convention: A Commentary*, Oxford University Press, 2009, pp. 397–406.

Gazzini, T., 'The Relationship between International Legal Personality and the Autonomy of International Organisations', in R. Collins and N. White (eds.), *International Organizations and the Idea of Autonomy: Institutional Independence in the International Legal Order*, Routledge, 2011, pp. 196–212.

Gemkow, T. and Zürn, M., 'Constraining International Authority through the Rule of Law: Legitimatory Potential and Political Dynamics', in M. Zürn, A. Nollkaemper and R. Peerenboom (eds.), *Rule of Law Dynamics – In an Era of International and Transnational Governance*, Cambridge University Press, 2012, pp. 68–89.

Gready, P. and Vandenhole, W., 'What Are We Trying to Change? Theories of Change in Development and Human Rights', in P. Gready and W. Vandenhole (eds.), *Human Rights and Development in the New Millennium: Towards a Theory of Change*, Routledge, 2014, pp. 1–27.

Guy Peters, B., 'Governance as Political Theory', in D. Levi-Faur (ed.), *Oxford Handbook on Governance*, Oxford University Press, 2012, pp. 19–32.

Hawkins, D. G., Lake, D. A., Nielson, D. L. and Tierney, M. J., 'Delegation under Anarchy: States, International Organizations, and Principal-Agent Theory', in D. G. Hawkins, D. A. Lake, D. L. Nielson and M. J. Tierney (eds.), *Delegation and Agency in International Organizations*, Cambridge University Press, 2006, pp. 3–38.

Heathcote, S., 'State Omissions and Due Diligence: Aspects of Fault, Damage, and Contribution to Injury in the Law of State Responsibility', in K. Bannelier, T. Christakis and S. Heathcote (eds.), *The ICJ and the Evolution of International Law: The Enduring Impact of the Corfu Channel Case*, Routledge, 2012, pp. 295–314.

Heieck, J., 'The Responsibility Not to Veto Revisited: How the Duty to Prevent Genocide as a *Jus Cogens* Norm Imposes a Legal Duty Not to Veto on the Five Permanent Members of the Security Council', in R. Barnes and V. Tzevelekos (eds.), *Beyond Responsibility to Protect: Generating Change in International Law*, Intersentia, 2016, pp. 103–22.

Heijer, M. and Lawson, R., 'Extraterritorial Human Rights and the Concept of "Jurisdiction"', in M. Langford, W. Vandenhole, M. Scheinin and W. V. Genugten (eds.), *Global Justice, State Duties: The Extraterritorial Scope of Economic, Social, and Cultural Rights in International Law*, Cambridge University Press, 2013, pp. 153–91.

Held, D., 'The Diffusion of Authority', in T. Weiss and R. Wilkinson (eds.), *International Organization and Global Governance*, Routledge, 2014, pp. 60–72.

Hilpold, P., 'Solange I, BverfGE 37, 291, 29 May 1974; Solange II, BverfGE 73, 339, 22 October 1986; Solange III, BverfGE 89, 155, 12 October 1993; and Solange IV, BverfGE 102, 147, 7 June 2000', in C. Ryngaert, I. Dekker, R. Wessel, and J. Wouters (eds.), *Judicial Decisions on the Law of International Organizations*, Oxford University Press, 2016, pp. 170–82.

Kadelbach, S., 'From Public International Law to International Public Law: A Comment on the "Public Authority" of International Institutions and the "Publicness" of Their Law, in A. Von Bogdandy, R. Wolfrum, J. V. Bernstorff, P. Dann and M. Goldmann (eds.), *The Exercise of Public Authority by International Institutions: Advancing International Institutional Law*, Springer, 2009, pp. 33–49.

Keohane, R. and Nye, J., 'Introduction', in J. S. Nye and J. D. Donnahue (eds.), *Governance in a Globalizing World*, Brookings Institution Press, 2000, pp. 1–42.

Khalfan, A., 'Division of Responsibility amongst States', in M. Langford, W. Vandenhole, M. Scheinin and W. V. Genugten (eds.), *Global Justice, State Duties: The Extraterritorial Scope of Economic, Social, and Cultural Rights in International Law*, Cambridge University Press, 2013, pp. 299–331.

Khalfan, A. and Seiderman, I., 'Extraterritorial Human Rights Obligations: Wider Implications of the Maastricht Principles and the Continuing Accountability Challenge', in W. Vandenhole (ed.), *Challenging Territoriality in Human Rights Law: Building Blocks for a Plural and Diverse Duty-Bearer Regime*, Routledge, 2015, pp. 13–43.

Klabbers, J., 'Autonomy, Constitutionalism and Virtue in International Institutional Law', in R. Collins and N. White (eds.), *International Organizations and the Idea of Autonomy: Institutional Independence in the International Legal Order*, Routledge, 2011, pp. 120–40.

'The Concept of Legal Personality', in F. Johns (ed), *International Legal Personality*, Ashgate, 2010, pp. 3–34.

'Setting the Scene', in J. Klabbers, A. Peters and G. Ulfstein (eds.), *The Constitutionalization of International Law*, Oxford University Press, 2009, pp. 1–44.

'The Changing Image of International Organizations', in J. Coicaud and V. Heiskanen (eds.), *The Legitimacy of International Organizations*, United Nations University Press, 2001, pp. 221–55.

Klein, P., 'The Attribution of Acts to International Organizations', in J. Crawford, A. Pellet, S. Olleson and K. Parlett (eds.), *The Law of International Responsibility*, Oxford University Press, 2010, pp. 297–315.

Kolb, R., 'Article 2(2)',in B. Simma, D. Khan, G. Nolte and A. Paulus (eds.), *The Charter of the United Nations: A Commentary*, Oxford University Press, 2012, pp. 166–80.

Kornhauser, L. A., 'Incentives, Compensation and Irreparable Harm', in A. Nollkaemper and D. Jacobs (eds.), *Distribution of Responsibilities in International Law*, Cambridge University Press, 2015, pp. 120–52.

Kuijper, P. J. and Paasivirta, E., 'EU International Responsibility and Its Attribution: From the Inside Looking Out', in M. Evans and P. Koutrakos (eds.), *The International Responsibility of the European Union: European and International Perspectives*, Hart Publishing, 2013, pp. 35–71.

Lang, A. F., 'Shared Political Responsibility', in A. Nollkaemper and D. Jacobs (eds.), *Distribution of Responsibilities in International Law*, Cambridge University Press, 2015, pp. 62–86.

Langford, M., Coomans, F. and Gómez Isa, F., 'Extraterritorial Duties in International Law', in M. Langford, W. Vandenhole, M. Scheinin and W. V. Genugten (eds.), *Global Justice, State Duties: The Extraterritorial Scope of Economic, Social, and Cultural Rights in International Law*, Cambridge University Press, 2013, pp. 51–113.

Lauterpacht, 'The Development of the Law of International Organization by the Decisions of International Tribunals', in *Académie de Droit International de la Haye*, 152, Recueil des Cours, 1976/IV, pp. 377–478.

Levi-Faur, D., 'From "Big Government" to "Big Governance"', in D. Levi-Faur (ed.), *Oxford Handbook on Governance*, Oxford University Press, 2012, pp. 3–18.

Lindahl, H. 'Constituent Power and Reflexive Identity: Towards an Ontology of Collective Selfhood', in M. Loughlin and N. Walker (eds.), *The Paradox of Constitutionalism: Constituent Power and Constitutional Form*, Oxford University Press, 2008, pp. 9–24.

Lock, T., 'Gasparini v. Italy and Belgium', in C. Ryngaert, I. F. Dekker, R.A. Wessel and J. Wouters (eds.), *Judicial Decisions on the Law of International Organizations*, Oxford University Press, 2016, pp. 328–35.

Magliveras, K. D., 'Membership in International Organizations', in J. Klabbers and Å. Wallendahl (eds.), *Research Handbook on the Law of International Organizations*, Edward Elgar, 2011, pp. 84–107.

Martinez-Diaz, L., 'Executive Boards in International Organizations', in R. Lamdany and L. Martinez-Diaz (eds.), *Studies of IMF Governance: A Compendium*, IMF Independent Evaluation Office, 2009, pp. 82–126.

McInerney-Lankford, S., 'International Development Actors and Human Rights', in M. Langford, A. Sumner and A. E. Yamin (eds.), *The Millennium Development Goals and Human Rights: Past, Present and Future*, Cambridge University Press, 2013, pp. 160–206.

'International Financial Institutions and Human Rights: Select Perspectives on Legal Obligations', in D. Bradlow and D. Hunter (eds.), *International Financial Institutions and International Law*, Kluwer Law International, 2010, pp. 239–86.

Messineo, F., 'The Invocation of Member State Responsibility before National and International Courts: Rekindling Old Utopias', in A. S. Barros, C. Ryngaert and J. Wouters (eds.), *International Organizations and Member State Responsibility: Critical Perspectives*, Brill–Nijhoff, 2016, pp. 193–209.

Mountford, A., 'Governance of the International Monetary Fund', in R. Lamdany and L. Martinez-Diaz (eds.), *Studies of IMF Governance: A Compendium*, IMF Independent Evaluation Office, 2009, pp. 15–42.

Naert, F., 'Binding International Organisations to Member State Treaties or Responsibility of Member States for Their Own Actions in the Framework of International Organisations', in J. Wouters, E. Brems, S. Smis and P. Schmitt (eds.), *Accountability for Human Rights Violations by International Organisations*, Intersentia, 2010, pp. 129–68.

Narula, S., 'International Financial Institutions, Transnational Corporations and Duties of States', in M. Langford, W. Vandenhole, M. Scheinin and W. V. Genugten (eds.), *Global Justice, State Duties: The Extraterritorial Scope of Economic, Social, and Cultural Rights in International Law*, Cambridge University Press, 2013, pp. 114–49.

Nollkaemper, A., 'Power and Responsibility', in A. Di Stefano (ed.), *Un Diritto Senza Terra? Funzioni e limite del principio di territorialità nel diritto Internazionale e dell'Unione europea*, Giappichelli, 2015, pp. 19–44.

'Introduction', in A. Nollkaemper and E. Plakokefalos (eds.), *Principles of Shared Responsibility in International Law: An Appraisal of the State of the Art*, Cambridge University Press, 2014, pp. 1–24.

Nollkaemper, A. and Jacobs, D., 'Introduction: Mapping the Normative Framework for the Distribution of Shared Responsibility', in A. Nollkaemper and D. Jacobs (eds.), *Distribution of Responsibilities in International Law*, Cambridge University Press, 2015, pp. 1–35.

Palchetti, P., '*Maclaine Watson & Co. Ltd v. International Tin Council*, 26 October 1989', in C. Ryngaert, I. F. Dekker, R. A. Wessel and J. Wouters (eds.), *Judicial Decisions on the Law of International Organizations*, Oxford University Press, 2016, pp. 28–37.

'Litigating Member State Responsibility: The Monetary Gold Principle and the Protection of Absent Organizations', in A. S. Barros, C. Ryngaert and J. Wouters (eds.), *International Organizations and Member State Responsibility: Critical Perspectives*, Brill–Nijhoff, 2016, pp. 178–90.

'Exploring Alternative Routes: The Obligation of Members to Enable the Organization to Make Reparation', in M. Ragazzi (ed.), *The Responsibility of International Organizations: Essays in Memory of Sir Ian Brownlie*, Martinus Nijhoff, 2013, pp. 303–12.

Pellet, A., 'The Definition of Responsibility in International Law', in J. Crawford, A. Pellet, S. Olleson and K. Parlett (eds.), *The Law of International Responsibility*, Oxford University Press, 2010, pp. 3–16.

Pescatore, P., 'Les Relations Extérieures des Communautés Européennes', in *Académie de Droit International de la Haye*, 103 Recueil des Cours 1961/II, pp. 1–242.

Peters, A., 'Membership in the Global Constitutional Community', in J. Klabbers, A. Peters and G. Ulfstein (eds.), *The Constitutionalization of International Law*, Oxford University Press, 2009, pp. 153–262.

Pierik, R., 'Shared Responsibility in International Law: A Normative-Philosophical Analysis', in A. Nollkaemper and D. Jacobs (eds.), *Distribution of Responsibilities in International Law*, Cambridge University Press, 2015, pp. 36–61.

Queneudec, J., 'Préface', in E. Lagrange (ed.), *La Représentation Institutionnelle dans L'Ordre International: Une Contribution à la Théorie de la Personnalité Morale des Organisations Internationales*, Kluwer Law International, 2002, pp. I–VII.

Reinalda, B. and Verbeek, B., 'Policy Autonomy of Intergovernmental Organizations: A Challenge to International Relations Theory?', in R. Collins and N. White (eds.), *International Organizations and the Idea of Autonomy: Institutional Independence in the International Legal Order*, Routledge, 2011, pp. 87–103.

Reinisch, A., 'Immunity of Property, Funds, and Assets (Article II Section 2 General Convention)', in A. Reinisch and P. Bachmayer (eds.), *The Conventions on the Privileges and Immunities of the United Nations and Its Specialized Agencies: A Commentary*, Oxford University Press, 2016, pp. 63–98.

Reinisch, A. and Wurm, J., 'International Financial Institutions before National Courts', in D. Bradlow and D. Hunter (eds.), *International Financial Institutions and International Law*, Kluwer Law International, 2010, pp. 103–35.

Risse, T. 'Governance in Areas of Limited Statehood', in D. Levi-Faur (ed.), *Oxford Handbook on Governance*, Oxford University Press, 2012, pp. 699–715.

Ryngaert, C., 'State Responsibility and Non-State Actors', in M. Noortmann, A. Reinisch and C. Ryngaert (eds.), *Non-State Actors in International Law*, Hart Publishing, 2015, pp. 163–204.

'Jurisdiction: Towards a Reasonableness Test', in M. Langford, W. Vandenhole, M. Scheinin and W. V. Genugten (eds.), *Global Justice, State Duties: The Extraterritorial Scope of Economic, Social, and Cultural Rights in International Law*, Cambridge University Press, 2013, pp. 192–211.

Said, W., 'Foucault and the Imagination of Power', in D. C. Hoy (ed.), *Foucault: A Critical Reader*, Blackwell Publishers, 1986, pp. 149–56.

Salomon, M., 'Deprivation, Causation and the Law of International Cooperation', in M. Langford, W. Vandenhole, M. Scheinin and W. V. Genugten (eds.), *Global Justice, State Duties: The Extraterritorial Scope of Economic, Social, and Cultural Rights in International Law*, Cambridge University Press, 2013, pp. 259–95.

'International Economic Governance and Human Rights Accountability', in M. Salomon, A. Tostensen and W. Vandenhole (eds.), *Casting the Net Wider: Human Rights, Development and New Duty-Bearers*, Intersentia, 2007, pp. 153–83.

Sari, A., 'Autonomy, Attribution and Accountability', in R. Collins and N. White (eds.), *International Organizations and the Idea of Autonomy: Institutional Independence in the International Legal Order*, Routledge, 2011, pp. 257–77.

Sari, A. and Wessel, R., 'International Responsibility for EU Military Operations: Finding the EU's Place in the Global Accountability Regime', in B. Van Vooren, S. Blockmans and J. Wouters (eds.), *The EU's Role in Global Governance: The Legal Dimension*, Oxford University Press, 2013, pp. 126–41.

Sarooshi, D., 'International Organizations and State Responsibility', in M. Ragazzi (ed.), *The Responsibility of International Organizations: Essays in Memory of Sir Ian Brownlie*, Martinus Nijhoff, 2013, pp. 79–87.

Schmalenbach, K., 'Dispute Settlement (Article IX Sections 31–32 Specialized Agencies Convention)', in A. Reinisch and P. Bachmayer (eds.), *The Conventions on the Privileges and Immunities of the United Nations and Its Specialized Agencies: A Commentary*, Oxford University Press, 2016, pp. 589–605.

Scholte, J. A., 'Global Governance, Accountability and Civil Society', in J. A. Scholte (ed.), *Building Global Democracy? Civil Society and Accountable Global Governance*, Cambridge University Press, 2011, pp. 8–41.

De Schutter, O., 'Human Rights and the Rise of International Organisations: The Logic of Sliding Scales in the Law of International Responsibility', in J. Wouters, E. Brems, S. Smis and P. Schmitt (eds.), *Accountability for Human Rights Violations by International Organisations*, Intersentia, 2010, pp. 51–128.

Scovazzi, T., 'Banković and Others v. Belgium and 16 other Contracting States', in C. Ryngaert, I. F. Dekker, R.A. Wessel and J. Wouters (eds.), *Judicial Decisions on the Law of International Organizations*, Oxford University Press, 2016, pp. 300–8.

Seidl-Hohenveldern, I., 'Responsibility of Member States of an International Organization for Acts of That Organization', in P. Lamberti Zanardi et al. (eds.), *International Law at the Time of Its Codification: Essays in Honour of Roberto Ago*, Dott. A. Giuffrè Editore, 1987, pp. 415–28.

Shelton, D., 'Remedies and Reparation', in M. Langford, W. Vandenhole, M. Scheinin and W. V. Genugten (eds.), *Global Justice, State Duties: The Extraterritorial Scope of Economic, Social, and Cultural Rights in International Law*, Cambridge University Press, 2013, pp. 367–90.

Skogly, S., 'The Human Rights Obligations of the World Bank and the IMF', in W. V. Genugten, P. Hunt and S. Mathews (eds.), *World Bank, IMF and Human Rights*, Wolf Legal Publishers (WLP), 2003, pp. 45–78.

Sornarajah, M., 'Linking State Responsibility for Certain Harms Caused by Corporate Nationals Abroad to Civil Recourse in the Legal Systems of Home States', in C. Scott (ed.), *Torture As Tort: Comparative Perspectives on the Development of Transnational Human Rights Litigation*, Hart Publishing, 2001, pp. 491–512.

Stein, T., 'Kosovo and the International Community: The Attribution of Possible Internationally Wrongful Acts: Responsibility of NATO or of Its Member States', in C. Tomuschat (ed.), *Kosovo and the International Community: A Legal Assessment*, Kluwer Law International, 2002, pp. 181–92.

Strand, J., 'The Regional Development Banks and Global Governance', in T. Weiss and R. Wilkinson (eds.), *International Organization and Global Governance*, Routledge, 2014, pp. 593–604.

Suzuki, E., 'Responsibility of International Financial Institutions under International Law', in D. Bradlow and D. Hunter (eds.), *International Financial Institutions and International Law*, Kluwer Law International, 2010, pp. 63–101.

Talmon, S., 'Responsibility of International Organizations: Does the European Community Require Special Treatment?', in M. Ragazzi (ed.), *International Responsibility Today: Essays in Memory of Oscar Schachter*, Martinus Nijhoff, 2005, pp. 405–21.

Toufayan, M., 'Between Solipsism and Empire (through Law): International Organizations and the Politics of Formalized Mimetism', in *Responsibility of Individuals, States and Organizations*, Proceedings of the 35th Annual Conference of the Canadian Council on International Law, Kluwer, 2006, pp. 182–210.

Tsagourias, N., 'Conceptualizing the Autonomy of the European Union', in R. Collins and N. White (eds.), *International Organizations and the Idea of Autonomy: Institutional Independence in the International Legal Order*, Routledge, 2011, pp. 339–52.

'Introduction – Constitutionalism: A Theoretical Roadmap', in N. Tsagourias (ed.), *Transnational Constitutionalism: International and European Perspectives*, Cambridge University Press, 2010, pp. 1–14.

'The Constitutional Role of General Principles of Law in International and European Jurisprudence', in N. Tsagourias (ed.), *Transnational Constitutionalism: International and European Perspectives*, Cambridge University Press, 2010, pp. 71–106.

Tzanakopoulos, A., 'Sharing Responsibility for UN Targeted Sanctions', in A. S. Barros, C. Ryngaert and J. Wouters (eds.), *International Organizations and Member State Responsibility: Critical Perspectives*, Brill–Nijhoff, 2016, pp. 139–58.

Vandenhole, W. and Genugten, W. V., 'Introduction: An Emerging Multi-Duty-Bearer Human Rights Regime?', in W. Vandenhole (ed.), *Challenging Territoriality in Human Rights Law: Building Blocks for a Plural and Diverse Duty-Bearer Regime*, Routledge, 2015, pp. 1–11.

Virally, M., 'La Notion de Fonction dans la Théorie de l'Organisation Internationale', in *Mélanges Offerts à Charles Rousseau – La Communauté Internationale*, Pédone, 1974, pp. 277–300.

Walker, N., 'Post-Constituent Constitutionalism? The Case of the European Union', in M. Loughlin and N. Walker (eds.), *The Paradox of Constitutionalism: Constituent Power and Constitutional Form*, Oxford University Press, 2008, pp. 247–69.

Weiss, T. and Wilkinson, R., 'International Organization and Global Governance: What Matters and Why', in T. Weiss and R. Wilkinson (eds.), *International Organization and Global Governance*, Routledge, 2014, pp. 3–17.

Wessel, R., 'International Governmental Organizations As Non-StateActors', in M. Noortmann, A. Reinisch and C. Ryngaert (eds.), *Non-State Actors in International Law*, Hart Publishing, 2015, pp. 185–203.

'Dissolution and Succession: The Transmigration of the Soul of International Organizations', in J. Klabbers and Å. Wallendahl (eds.), *Research Handbook on the Law of International Organizations*, Edward Elgar, 2011, pp. 342–62.

De Wet, E., 'Holding International Institutions Accountable: The Complementary Role of Non-Judicial Oversight Mechanisms and Judicial Review', in A. Von Bogdandy, R. Wolfrum, J. V. Bernstorff, P. Dann and M. Goldmann (eds.), *The Exercise of Public Authority by International Institutions: Advancing International Institutional Law*, Springer, 2009, pp. 855–82.

White, N., 'Decision-Making', in J. Klabbers and Å. Wallendahl (eds.), *Research Handbook on the Law of International Organizations*, Edward Elgar, 2011, pp. 33–55.

'Discerning Separate Will', in W. P. Heere (ed.), *From Government to Governance: The Growing Impact of Non-State Actors on the International and European Legal System*, Proceedings of the 2003 Hague Joint Conference on Contemporary Issues of International Law, 2004, pp. 31–8.

Yee, S., '"Member Responsibility" and the ILC Articles on the Responsibility of International Organizations: Some Observations', in M. Ragazzi (ed.), *Responsibility of International Organizations: Essays in Memory of Sir Ian Brownlie*, Martinus Nijhoff, 2013, pp. 325–36.

'The Responsibility of States Members of an International Organization for Its Conduct As a Result of Membership or Their Normal Conduct Associated with Membership', in M. Ragazzi (ed.), *International Responsibility Today: Essays in Memory of Oscar Schachter*, Martinus Nijhoff, 2005, pp. 435–54.

Zimmermann, A., 'Article 27', in B. Simma, D. Khan, G. Nolte and A. Paulus (eds.), *The Charter of the United Nations: A Commentary*, Oxford University Press, 2012, pp. 885–8.

Zürn, M., 'Global Governance As Multi-Level Governance', in D. Levi-Faur (ed.), *Oxford Handbook on Governance*, Oxford University Press, 2012, pp. 730–44.

1.3 *Articles in Journals*

Abbott, K. and Snidal, D., 'Why States Act through Formal International Organizations', *Journal of Conflict Resolution*, 1998, Vol. 42(1), pp. 3–32.

Ahlborn, C., 'The Rules of International Organizations and the Law of International Responsibility', *International Organizations Law Review*, 2011, Vol. 8, pp. 397–482.

'To Share or Not to Share? The Allocation of Responsibility between International Organizations and Their Member States', *Die Friedens-Warte/Journal of International Peace and Organization*, 2013, Vol. 88 (3–4), pp. 45–75.

Alger, C. F. and Kille, K.J., 'How Are, and Should, Parliamentarians of States Be Involved in Global Governance?', *Journal of International Organizations Studies*, 2014, Vol. 5(2), pp. 71–84.

Alvarez, J. A., 'International Organizations: Then and Now', *American Journal of International Law*, 2006, Vol. 100, pp. 324–47.

Amerasinghe, C. F., 'Liability to Third Parties of Member States of International Organizations: Practice, Principle and Judicial Precedent', *American Journal of International Law*, 1991, Vol. 85, pp. 259–80.

D'Aspremont, J., 'International Responsibility and the Constitution of Power: International Organisations Bolstered', *International Organizations Law Review*, 2015, Vol. 12(2), pp. 382–400.

'The Articles on the Responsibility of International Organizations: Magnifying the Fissures in the Law of International Responsibility', *International Organizations Law Review*, 2012, Vol. 9, pp. 15–28.

Barnidge, R., 'The Due Diligence Principle under International Law', *International Community Law Review*, 2006, Vol. 8, pp. 81–121.

Barros, A. S. and Ryngaert, C., 'The Position of Member States in (Autonomous) Institutional Decision-Making: Implications for the Establishment of Responsibility', *International Organizations Law Review*, 2014, Vol. 11(1), pp. 53–82.

Barnett, M. and Finnemore, M., 'The Politics, Power, and Pathologies of International Organizations', *International Organization*, 1999, Vol. 53(4), pp. 699–732.

Bederman, D., 'The Souls of International Organizations: Legal Personality and the Lighthouse at Cape Spartel', *Virginia Journal of International Law*, 1996, Vol. 36, pp. 275–377.

Blokker, N., 'International Organizations and Their Members', *International Organizations Law Review*, 2004, Vol. 1, pp. 139–61.

Von Bogdandy, A. and Platise, M. S., 'ARIO and Human Rights Protection: Leaving the Individual in the Cold', *International Organizations Law Review*, 2012, Vol. 9, pp. 67–76.

Boon, K., 'Are Control Tests Fit for the Future? The Slippage Problem in Attribution Doctrines', *Melbourne Journal of International Law*, 2014, Vol. 15, pp. 330–77.

'Regime Conflicts and the U.N. Security Council: Applying the Law of Responsibility', *George Washington International Law Review*, 2010, Vol. 42, pp. 787–833.

Boyle, A., 'Human Rights and the Environment: Where Next?', *European Journal of International Law*, 2012, Vol. 23, pp. 613–42.

'Human Rights or Environmental Rights? A Reassessment', *Fordham Environmental Law Review*, 2007, Vol. 18, pp. 471–511.

Bradlow, D., 'The Reform of the Governance of the IFIs: A Critical Assessment', *World Bank Legal Review: International Financial Institutions and Global Legal Governance*, 2012, pp. 37–58.

'Developing Countries Debt Crises, International Financial Institutions, and International Law: Some Preliminary Thoughts', *German Yearbook of International Law*, 2008, Vol. 51, pp. 111–43.

Brechin, S. and Ness, G., 'Looking Back at the Gap: International Organizations as Organizations Twenty-Five Years Later', *Journal of International Organizations Studies*, Special Issue: Sociological Perspectives on IOs, 2013, Vol. 4(2), pp. 14–39.

Brölmann, C., 'Member States and International Legal Responsibility: Developments of the Institutional Veil', *International Organizations Law Review*, 2015, Vol. 12(2), pp. 358–81.

Bugalski, N., 'The Demise of Accountability at the World Bank?', *American University Law Review*, 2016, Vol. 31(1), pp. 1–56.

Cassese, A., 'Administrative Law without the State? The Challenge of Global Regulation', *Journal of International Law and Politics*, 2006, Vol. 37, pp. 663–94.

'Remarks on Scelle's Theory of "Role Splitting" (*dédoublement fonctionnel*) in International Law', *European Journal of International Law*, 1990, Vol. 210, pp. 210–31.

Chan, P., 'A Keen Observer of the International Rule of Law? International Law in China's Voting Behaviour and Argumentation in the United Nations Security Council', *Leiden Journal of International Law*, 2013, Vol. 26, pp. 875–907.

Chesterman, S., 'An International Rule of Law?', *American Journal of Comparative Law*, 2008, Vol. 56, pp. 331–61.

Ciampi, A., 'L'Union Européenne et le Respect des Droits de L'Homme Dans la Mise en Ouvre des Sanctions Devant la Cour Européenne des Droits de L'Homme', *Révue Générale de Droit Internationale Public*, 2006, pp. 85–116.

Cori, G. and Kauff-Gazin, F., 'L'arrêt Matthews: Une Protection Globale des Droits de L'Homme par une Vision Réductrice de L'Ordre Juridique Communautaire?', *Europe*, Janvier, 2000, Vol. 1, pp. 1–10.

Dannenbaum, T., 'Dual Attribution in the Context of Military Operations', *International Organizations Law Review*, 2015, Vol. 12(2), pp. 401–26.

'Translating the Standard of Effective Control into a System of Effective Accountability: How Liability Should Be Apportioned for Violations of Human Rights by Member State Troop Contingents Serving as United Nations Peacekeepers', *Harvard International Law Journal*, 2010, Vol. 51(1), pp. 113–92.

Dworkin, T., 'The Rule of Law', *Law of Ukraine Legal Journal*, 2013, Vol. 4, pp. 7–13.

Dupuy, P.-M., 'Reviewing the Difficulties of Codification: On Ago's Classification of Obligations of Means and Obligations of Result in Relation to State Responsibility', *European Journal of International Law*, 1999, Vol. 10(2), pp. 371–85.

Epstein, D. and O'Halloran, S., 'Sovereignty and Delegation in International Organizations', *Law and Contemporary Problems*, 2008, Vol. 71, pp. 77–92.

Fassbender, B., 'Targeted Sanctions Imposed by the UN Security Council and Due Process Rights: A Study Commissioned by the UN Office of Legal Affairs and Follow-Up Action by the United Nations', reprinted in *International Organizations Law Review*, 2006, Vol. 3, pp. 437–85.

Francioni, F., 'Realism, Utopia and the Future of International Environmental Law', *EUI Working Papers*, Law, 2012/11.

'International Human Rights in an Environmental Horizon', *European Journal of International Law*, 2010, Vol. 21(1), pp. 41–55.

'Access to Justice, Denial of Justice and International Investment Law', *European Journal of International Law*, 2009, Vol. 20(3), pp. 729–47.

François Gianviti, F., 'Decision-Making in the International Monetary Fund', *Current Developments in Monetary and Financial Law*, IMF, 1999, Vol. 1, pp. 31–67.

Gazzini, T., 'NATO Role in the Collective Security System', *Journal of Conflict and Security Law*, 2003, Vol. 8, pp. 231–63.

Guzman, A. T., 'International Organizations and the Frankenstein Problem', *European Journal of International Law*, 2013, Vol. 24(4), pp. 999–1025.

Guzman, A. T. and Landsidle, J., 'The Myth of International Delegation', *California Law Review*, 2008, Vol. 96(6), pp. 1693–723.

Hachez, N., 'What Elements of the Rule of Law Can Be Put to Use at International Level?', *Revue Belge de Droit International*, 2013, Vol. 2, pp. 307–24.

Haftel, Y. and Thompson, A., 'The Independence of International Organizations: Concept and Applications', *Journal of Conflict Resolution*, 2006, Vol. 50(2), pp. 253–75.

Hexner, E., 'The Executive Board of the International Monetary Fund: A Decision-Making Instrument', *International Organization*, 1964, Vol. 18(1), pp. 74–96.

Hoffmeister, F., 'Litigating Against the European Union and Its Member States – Who Responds under the ILC's Draft Articles on International Responsibility of International Organizations?', *European Journal of International Law*, 2010, Vol. 21(3), pp. 723–47.

Jenks, C. W., 'The Legal Personality of International Organizations', *British Yearbook of International Law*, 1945, Vol. 22, pp. 229–37.

'Some Constitutional Problems of International Organizations', *British Yearbook of International Law*, 1945, Vol. 22, pp. 11–72.

Keith, K., 'The International Rule of Law', *Leiden Journal of International Law*, 2015, Vol. 28, pp. 403–17.

Kehoane, R., Macedo S. and Moravcsik, A., 'Democracy-Enhancing Multilateralism', *International Organization*, 2009, Vol. 63, pp. 1–31.

Kennedy, D., 'The International Style in Postwar Law and Policy', *Utah Law Review*, 1994, Vol. 7, pp. 7–104.

Kingsbury, B. and Casini, L., 'Global Administrative Law Dimensions of International Organizations Law', *International Organizations Law Review*, 2009, Vol. 6, pp. 319–58.

Klabbers, J., 'The EJIL Foreword: The Transformation of International Organizations Law', *European Journal of International Law*, 2015, Vol. 26(1), pp. 9–82.

'The Life and Times of the Law of International Organizations', *Nordic Journal of International Law*, 2001, Vol. 70, pp. 287–317.

'Constitutionalism Lite', *International Organizations Law Review*, 2004, Vol. 1, pp. 31–59.

'Two Concepts of International Organization', *International Organizations Law Review*, 2005, Vol. 2, pp. 277–93.

Koskenniemi, M., 'Constitutionalism As Mindset: Reflections on Kantian Themes about International Law and Globalization', *Theoretical Inquiries in Law*, 2007, Vol. 8, pp. 9–36.

'Global Governance and Public International Law', *Kritische Justiz*, 2004, pp. 241–54.

Kuijper, P. J., 'Introduction to the Symposium on Responsibility of International Organizations and of (Member) States: Attributed or Direct Responsibility or Both?', *International Organizations Law Review*, 2010, Vol. 7(2), pp. 9–33.

Kunz, J. L., 'Privileges and Immunities of International Organizations', *American Journal of International Law*, 1947, Vol. 41, pp. 828–62.

Larsen, K. M., 'Attribution of Conduct in Peace Operations: The "Ultimate Control and Authority" Test', *European Journal of International Law*, 2008, Vol. 19(3), pp. 509–31.

Loughlin, M., 'The Rule of Law: A Theme in Five Variations', *Frontiers of Law in China*, 2015, Vol. 10, pp. 437–48.

Mann, F. A., 'International Corporations and National Law', *British Yearbook of International Law*, 1967, Vol. 42, pp. 145–74.

Marchegiano, G., 'The Juristic Character of the International Commission of Cape Spartel Lighthouse', *American Journal of International Law* 1931, Vol. 25, pp. 339–47.

Martha, R. 'International Financial Institutions and Claims of Private Parties: Immunity Obliges', *World Bank Legal Review: International Financial Institutions and Global Legal Governance*, 2012, pp. 92–131.

McNair, A., 'The Functions and Differing Legal Character of Treaties', *British Yearbook of International Law*, 1930, Vol. 11, pp. 100–18.

Milanovic, M., 'Norm Conflict in International Law: Whither Human Rights?', *Duke Journal of Comparative & International Law*, 2009, Vol. 20(1), pp. 69–131.

'State Responsibility for Genocide: A Follow-up', *European Journal of International Law*, 2007, Vol. 18(4), pp. 669–94.

Miller, A., 'The Privileges and Immunities of the United Nations', *International Organizations Law Review*, 2009, Vol. 6, pp. 169–257.

Murray, O., 'Piercing the Corporate Veil: The Responsibility of Member States of an International Organization', *International Organizations Law Review*, 2011, Vol. 8, pp. 291–357.

Nollkaemper, A., 'Dual Attribution: Liability of the Netherlands for Conduct of Dutchbat in Srebrenica', *Journal of International Criminal Justice*, 2011, Vol. 9, pp. 1143–57.

Nolkaemper, A. and Jacobs, D., 'Shared Responsibility in International Law: A Conceptual Framework', *Michigan Journal of International Law*, 2013, Vol. 34(2), pp. 359–438.

Paasivirta, E., 'Responsibility of a Member State of an International Organization: Where Will It End? Comments on Article 60 of the ILC Draft on the Responsibility of International Organizations', *International Organizations Law Review*, 2010, Vol. 7, pp. 49–61.

Palchetti, P., 'Sulla Responsabilità di uno Stato per il Voto Espresso in Seno ad Un'Organizzazione Internazionale', *Rivista di Diritto Internazionale*, 2012, Vol. XCV, pp. 352–73.

Panke, D., 'Getting Ready to Negotiate in International Organizations? On the Importance of the Domestic Construction of National Positions', *Journal of International Organizations Studies*, 2013, Vol. 4(2), pp. 25–38.

Pellet, A., '"Human Rightism" and International Law', *Italian Yearbook of International Law*, 2000, pp. 3–16.

Peters, A., 'The Security Council's Responsibility to Protect', *International Organizations Law Review*, 2011, Vol. 8, pp. 15–54.

'Humanity As the A and of Sovereignty', *European Journal of International Law*, 2009, Vol. 20(3), pp. 513–44.

Pettit, V., 'Responsibility Incorporated', *Ethics*, 2007, Vol. 117, pp. 171–201.

Pisillo-Mazzeschi, R., 'The Due Diligence Rule and the Nature of the International Responsibility of States', *German Yearbook of International Law*, 1992, Vol. 35, pp. 9–51.

Plakokefalos, E., 'Causation in the Law of State Responsibility and the Problem of Overdetermination: In Search of Clarity', *European Journal of International Law*, 2015, Vol. 26(2), pp. 471–92.

Reinisch, A., 'Aid or Assistance and Direction and Control between States and International Organizations in the Commission of Internationally Wrongful Acts', *International Organizations Law Review*, 2010, Vol. 7, pp. 63–77.

Rich, B. M., 'The Multilateral Development Banks, Environmental Policy, and the United States', *Ecology Law Quarterly*, 1984–1985, Vol. 12, pp. 681–745.

Ryngaert, C., 'Oscillating between Embracing and Avoiding Bosphorus: The European Court of Human Rights on Member State Responsibility for Acts of International Organisations and the Case of the EU', *European Law Review*, 2014, Vol. 39(2), pp. 176–92.

'Apportioning Responsibility between the UN and Member States in UN Peace-Support Operations: An Inquiry Into the Application of the "Effective Control" Standard after Behrami', *Israel Law Review*, 2012, Vol. 45(1), pp. 151–78.

'The European Court of Human Rights', *International & Comparative Law Quarterly*, 2011, Vol. 60(4), pp. 997–1016.

'The Immunity of International Organizations before Domestic Courts: Recent Trends', *International Organizations Law Review*, 2010, Vol. 7, pp. 121–48.

Ryngaert, C. and Buchanan, H., 'Member State Responsibility for the Acts of International Organizations', *Utrecht Law* Review, 2011, Vol. 7, pp. 131–46.

Sadurska, R. and Chinkin, C., 'The Collapse of the International Tin Council: A Case of State Responsibility?', *Virginia Journal of International Law*, 1989–1990, Vol. 30, pp. 845–90.

Salomon, M. 'Of Austerity, Human Rights and International Institutions', *European Law Journal*, 2015, Vol. 21(4), pp. 521–45.

Sarooshi, D., 'The Essentially Contested Nature of the Concept of Sovereignty: Implications for the Exercise by International Organizations of Delegated Powers of Government', *Michigan Journal of International Law*, 2004, Vol. 25, pp. 1107–39.

Scholte, J. A., 'Reconstructing Contemporary Democracy', *Indiana Journal of Global Legal Studies*, 2008, Vol. 15, pp. 305–50.

De Sena, P., 'International Monetary Fund, World Bank and Respect for Human Rights: A Critical Point of View', *Italian Yearbook of International Law*, 2010, Vol. 20(1), pp. 247–74.

De Sena, P. and Vitucci, M. C., 'The European Courts and the Security Council: Between *Dédoublement Fonctionnel* and Balancing of Values', *European Journal of International Law*, 2009, Vol. 20(1), pp. 193–228.

Seyersted, F., 'Objective International Personality of Intergovernmental Organizations: Do Their Capacities Really Depend upon the Conventions Establishing Them?', *Nordic Journal of International Law*, 1964, Vol. 37, pp. 3–112.

Shelton, D., 'Significantly Disadvantaged? Shrinking Access to the European Court of Human Rights', *Human Rights Law Review*, 2016, Vol. 16, pp. 303–22.

Shihata, I., 'Role of Law in Economic Development: The Legal Problems of International Public Ventures', *Revue Egyptienne de Droit International*, 1969, Vol. 25, pp. 119–28.

Sitaraman, G. and Wuerth, I., 'The Normalization of Foreign Relations Law', *Harvard Law Review*, 2015, Vol. 128(7), pp. 1897–979.

Stein, E., 'International Integration and Democracy: No Love at First Sight', *American Journal of International Law*, Vol. 95, 2001, pp. 489–534.

Stiglitz, J., 'Democratizing the International Monetary Fund and the World Bank: Governance and Accountability', *Columbia Academic Commons*, 2003, pp. 111–39.

Stumer, A., 'Liability of Member States for Acts of International Organizations: Reconsidering the Policy Objections', *Harvard International Law Journal*, 2007, Vol. 48(2), pp. 553–80.

Suzuki, E. and Nanwani, S:, 'Responsibility of International Organizations: The Accountability Mechanisms of Multilateral Development Banks', *Michigan Journal of International Law*, 2005, Vol. 27, pp. 177–225.

Tan, C., 'Mandating Rights and Limiting Mission Creep: Holding the World Bank and the International Monetary Fund Accountable for Human Rights Violations', *Human Rights and International Legal Discourse*, 2008, Vol. 2(2), pp. 79–116.

Tzanakopoulos, A., 'Sharing Responsibility for UN Targeted Sanctions', *International Organizations Law Review*, 2015, Vol. 12(2), pp. 427–47.

Tzevelekos, V., 'In Search of Alternative Solutions: Can the State of Origin Be Held Internationally Responsible for Investors' Human Rights Abuses That Are Not Attributable to It?', *Brooklyn Journal of International Law*, 2010, Vol. 35, pp. 155–231.

Vandenhole, W., 'Extraterritorial Human Rights Obligations: Taking Stock, Looking Forward', *European Journal of Human Rights*, 2013, Vol. 5, pp. 804–35.

Venzke, I., 'International Bureaucracies from a Political Science Perspective – Agency, Authority and International Institutional Law', *German Law Journal*, 2008, Vol. 09(11), pp. 1401–28.

Waldron, J., 'The Rule of International Law', *Harvard Journal of Law & Public Policy*, 2008, Vol. 30, pp. 15–30.

De Wet, E., 'The International Constitutional Order', *International and Comparative Law Quarterly*, 2006, Vol. 55, pp. 51–76.

Wessel, R., 'Revisiting the International Legal Status of the EU', *European Foreign Affairs Review*, 2000, Vol. 5, pp. 507–37.

White, N., 'Separate but Connected: Inter-Governmental Organizations and International Law', *International Organizations Law Review*, 2008, Vol. 5, pp. 175–95.

Wilde, R., 'Enhancing Accountability at the International Level: The Tension between International Organization and Member State Responsibility and the Underlying Issues at Stake', *ILSA Journal of International and Comparative Law*, 2006, Vol. 12, pp. 395–415.

Woods, N., 'Global Governance after the Financial Crisis: A New Multilateralism or the Last Gasp of the Great Powers?', *Global Policy*, 2010, Vol. 1(1), pp. 51–63.

'Making the IMF and the World Bank More Accountable', *International Affairs*, 2001, Vol. 77(1), pp. 83–100.

Wouters, J., De Meester, B. and Ryngaert, C., 'Democracy and International Law', *Netherlands Yearbook of International Law*, 2003, Vol. XXXIV, pp. 137–98.

Wright, R., 'Causation, Responsibility, Risk, Probability, Naked Statistics, and Proof: Pruning the Bramble Bush by Clarifying the Concepts', *Iowa Law Review*, 1987–1988, Vol. 73, pp. 1001–77.

1.4 *International Financial Institution Reports*

Independent Evaluation Office of the IMF, 'The IMF and Social Protection', Issues Paper for an Evaluation by the Independent Evaluation Office, 2016.

Independent Evaluation Office of the IMF, Report, 'The IMF and the Crises in Greece, Ireland, and Portugal', 2016.

Independent Evaluation Office of the IMF, Report, 'Governance of the IMF: An Evaluation', 2008.

International Monetary Fund, 'Greece: Ex Post Evaluation of Exceptional Access under the 2010 Stand-By Arrangement', IMF Country Report No. 13/156, June 2013.

Mountford, A., 'The Formal Governance Structure of the International Monetary Fund', IEO Background Paper, BP/08/01, March 2008.

World Bank, 'Review and Update of the World Bank's Safeguard Policies Environmental and Social Framework (Proposed Second Draft)', Consultation Paper, 1 July 2015.

World Bank, Nordic Trust Fund, 'Study on Human Rights Impact Assessments: A Review of the Literature, Differences with other Forms of Assessments and Relevance for Development', February 2013.

World Bank, 'The World Bank's Safeguard Policies: Proposed Review and Update', Approach Paper, 10 October 2012.

World Bank Group Annual Report, Department of Institutional Integrity on 'Investigations and Sanctions of Staff Misconduct and Fraud and Corruption in Bank-Financed Projects', February 2005.

1.5 *Other Articles and Studies*

Van Aken, W., 'Voting in the Council of the European Union: Contested Decision-Making in the EU Council of Ministers (1995–2010)', Report published by the Swedish Institute for European Policy Studies, 2012.

Barros, A. S., 'EBRD Statement on Operational Approach in Russia', in Oxford International Organizations Database, 2017.

Canotilho, C., Study for the European Parliament LIBE Committee, 'The Impact of the Crisis on Fundamental Rights across Member States of the EU: Country Report on Portugal', 2015.

Center for International Environmental Law, Legal Analysis on 'International Financial Institutions & Human Rights Law', Public Hearing of the Inter-American Commission of Human Rights on Human rights violations and responsibility of international financial institutions, 127th Regular Period of Sessions, 1 March 2007.

Daniel, C., Genovese, K., Van Huijstee, M. and Singh, S. (eds.), 'Glass Half Full? The State of Accountability in Development Finance', SOMO, January 2016.

De La Mare, T., 'Foreign Affairs: Forbidden Territory for the Courts', paper presented to the Administrative Law Bar Association, 27 July 2013.

Emerson, M., Balfour, R., Corthaut, T., Wouters, J., Kaczyński, P. M. and Renard, T., 'Upgrading the EU's Role as Global Actor: Institutions, Law and the Restructuring of European Diplomacy', Centre for European Policy Studies, 2011.

ETO Consortium, Handbook, 'For Human Rights Beyond Borders: How to Hold States Accountable for Extraterritorial Obligations', September 2017.

ETO Consortium, Maastricht Principles on Extraterritorial Obligations of States in the area of Economic, Social and Cultural Rights, 28 September 2011.

Faini, R. and Grilli, E., 'Who Runs the IFIs?', Centro Studi Luca D'agliano, Development Studies Working Papers, N. 191, 2004.

Honoré, A. and Gardner, J., 'Causation in the Law', in *The Stanford Encyclopedia of Philosophy* (Winter 2010 edition), E. N. Zalta (ed.): https://plato.stanford.edu/archives/win2010/entries/causation-law/.

House of Commons European Scrutiny Committee, 'The European Scrutiny System in the House of Commons', May 2015.

Human Rights Watch, 'Abuse-Free Development: How the World Bank Should Safeguard Against Human Rights Violations', July 2013.

Independent Commission for Aid Impact (ICAI), 'How DFID works with multilateral agencies to achieve impact', Report 44, June 2015.

Japan International Cooperation Agency, *Objection Procedures based on the Guidelines for Environmental and Social Considerations*, April 2010.

Kämpf, A., 'Human Rights Require Accountability: Why German Development Cooperation Needs a Human Rights Complaints Mechanism', German Institute for Human Rights Policy Paper, 2015.

Koivura, T., 'Due Diligence', in *Max Planck Encyclopedia of Public International Law*, last updated February 2010: http://opil.ouplaw.com/.

Lagarde, C., 'Promoting Responsible Energy Pricing', Center for Global Development, 31 July 2014.

House of Commons European Scrutiny Committee, 'The European Scrutiny System in the House of Commons', May 2015.

Nelson, R. M. and Weiss, M. A., 'Multilateral Development Banks: How the United States Makes and Implements Policy', Congressional Research Service Report, 29 April 2014.

Organisation for Economic Co-operation and Development, 'Towards more effective development co-operation: Overview of monitoring findings', in *Making Development Co-operation More Effective: 2014 Progress Report*, 2 April 2014.

Ragazzi, M., 'International Financial Institutions', in *Max Planck Encyclopedia of Public International Law*, last updated October 2017: http://opil.ouplaw.com/.

Regeringskansliet, Ministry for Foreign Affairs Sweden, *Swedish Assessment of Multilateral Organisations: The World Bank*, 2008.

Schlütter, B., *Parliamentary group of the Party of Democratic Socialism in the German Federal Parliament* v. *Federal Government, Constitutional dispute between federal organs* (Organstreitverfahren), BverfG, 2 BvE 6/99; ILDC 134 (DE 2001), 22 November 2001.

De Schutter, O. and Salomon, M., Legal Brief Prepared for the Special Committee of the Hellenic Parliament on the Audit of the Greek Debt (Debt Truth Committee), 'Economic Policy Conditionality: Socio-Economic Rights and International Legal Responsibility: The Case of Greece 2010–2015', 2015.

Stein, E., 'Democracy Beyond Nation-State: On World Trade Organization and European Union', in *The Dean Rusk Lectures*, Occasional Papers of the Dean Rusk Center, 2002.

Stratulat, C. and Emmanouilidis, J. A. (EPC), Fischer, T. and Piedrafita, S. (CEPS), Discussion Paper, 'Legitimising EU Policymaking: What Role for National Parliaments?', 2014.

Szyszczak, E. and Lydgate, E., UK Trade Policy Observatory, Briefing Paper 4, 'Triggering Article 50 TEU: A Legal Analysis', 10 October 2016.
Weiss, M. A. and Sanford, J. E., Congressional Research Service Report, 'The World Bank and Iran', 28 January 2008.

2 INTERNATIONAL DOCUMENTS

2.1 *Treaties*

African Charter on Human and Peoples' Rights, 1520 UNTS 217, 27 June 1981.
Agreement between the United Nations and the United States of America regarding the Headquarters of the United Nations, 11 UNTS 11, 1947.
Agreement between the United Nations and the International Monetary Fund, 16 UNTS 328, 15 April 1948.
Agreement between the United Nations and the International Bank for Reconstruction and Development, 16 UNTS 328, 15 April 1948.
Agreement Establishing the Black Sea Trade and Development Bank, 30 June 1994.
Agreement Establishing the Asian Development Bank, 123 UNTS 571, 22 August 1966.
Agreement Establishing the African Development Bank, 3 UNTS 510, 4 August 1963.
Agreement Establishing the European Bank for Reconstruction and Development, 1646 UNTS 97, 29 May 1990.
Agreement Establishing the Inter-American Development Bank, 69 UNTS 389, 30 December 1959.
Agreement Establishing the Nordic Investment Bank, 4 December 1975.
American Convention on Human Rights, 9 ILM 673, 22 November 1969.
American Declaration on the Rights and Duties of Man, adopted by the Ninth International Conference of American States, Colombia, 1948.
Arab Charter on Human Rights, 999 UNTS 171, 22 May 2004.
Articles of Agreement of the Asian Infrastructure Investment Bank, 25 December 2015.
Articles of Agreement of the International Finance Corporation, 264 UNTS 118, 25 May 1955.
Articles of Agreement of the International Monetary Fund, 39 UNTS 2, 27 December 1945.
Charter of the United Nations, 1 UNTS XVI, 24 October 1945.
Consolidated version of the Treaty on European Union, *OJ* C 83/13, 30 March 2010.
Consolidated version of the Treaty on the Functioning of the European Union, *OJ* C 326/47, 26 October 2012.
Convention on Access to Information, Public Participation in Decision-Making and Access to Justice in Environmental Matters, 2161 UNTS 450, 25 June 1998.
Convention Establishing the Multilateral Investment Guarantee Agency, 24 ILM 1605, 11 October 1985.
Convention on International Liability for Damages Caused by Space Objects, 961 UNTS 187, 1 September 1972.
Convention on International Civil Aviation, 15 UNTS 295, 7 December 1944.
Convention for the Protection of Human Rights and Fundamental Freedoms, 213 UNTS 222, 4 November 1950.
Convention on the Privileges and Immunities of the United Nations, 1 UNTS 15 and 90 UNTS 327 (corrigendum to Vol. 1), 13 February 1946.

Convention on the Privileges and Immunities of the Specialized Agencies, 33 UNTS 261, 21 November 1947.
Convention on the Prevention and Punishment of the Crime of Genocide, 78 UNTS 277, 9 December 1948.
Convention (I) for the Amelioration of the Condition of the Wounded and Sick in Armed Forces in the Field, 75 UNTS 31, 12 August 1949.
Convention on the Organisation for Economic Co-operation and Development, 888 UNTS 179, 14 December 1960.
Convention on the Rights of the Child, 1577 UNTS 3, 20 November 1989.
Convention on the Rights of Persons with Disabilities, 2515 UNTS 3, 3 May 2008.
Council Decision 76/787/ECSC, EEC, Euratom: Decision of the representatives of the Member States meeting in the council relating to the Act concerning the election of the representatives of the Assembly by direct universal suffrage, *OJ L* 278, 8 October 1976.
Declaration Concerning the Aims and Purposes of the International Labour Organization, annexed to the ILO's Constitution, 15 UNTS 40, adopted 1 April 1919.
EC Act Concerning the Election of the Representatives of the European Parliament by Direct Universal Suffrage of 1976, *OJ L* 278, 8 October 1976.
Headquarters Agreement between FAO and the Italian Government, 1409 UNTS 521, 31 October 1950.
International Bank for Reconstruction and Development Articles of Agreement, 2 UNTS 134, 27 December 1945.
International Covenant on Civil and Political Rights, 999 UNTS 171, 16 December 1966.
International Covenant on Economic, Social and Cultural Rights, 993 UNTS 3, 16 December 1966.
International Development Association Articles of Agreement, 249 UNTS 439, 24 September 1960.
Optional Protocol to the International Covenant on Economic, Social and Cultural Rights, UN General Assembly Resolution A/RES/63/117, adopted on 10 December 2008.
Treaty Establishing the European Stability Mechanism, 2 February 2012.
Treaty on the Non-Proliferation of Nuclear Weapons, 729 UNTS 161, 1 July 1986.
Vienna Convention on the Law of Treaties, 1155 UNTS 331, 1969.
Vienna Convention on the Law of Treaties between States and International Organizations or between International Organizations, 25 ILM 543, 1969.
United Nations Convention on the Law of the Sea, 10 December 1982, 1833 UNTS 397.

2.2 *UN Documents*

'Addis Ababa Action Agenda of the Third International Conference on Financing for Development', 13–16 July 2015, endorsed by UNGA 69/313 of 27 July 2015.
Committee on Economic, Social and Cultural Rights, 'Public debt, austerity measures and the International Covenant on Economic, Social and Cultural Rights', UN Doc. E/C.12/2016/1, 24 June 2016.
Committee on Economic, Social and Cultural Rights, Fifth periodic report submitted by States parties under articles 16 and 17 of the Covenant, UN Doc. E/C.12/DEU/5, 27 July 2010.
Committee on Economic, Social and Cultural Rights, Guidelines on Treaty-Specific Documents to be Submitted by States Parties under Articles 16 and 17 of the International Covenant on Economic, Social and Cultural Rights, UN Doc. E/C.12/2008/2, Annex, 24 March 2009.
Committee on Economic, Social and Cultural Rights, 'An Evaluation of the Obligation to Take Steps to the "Maximum of Available Resources" Under an Optional Protocol to the Covenant', UN Doc. E/C.12/2007/1, 21 September 2007.

Committee on Economic, Social and Cultural Rights, General Comment No. 19 on the Right to Social Security, UN Doc. E/C.12/GC/19, 2008.
Committee on Economic, Social and Cultural Rights, General Comment No. 18 on the Right to Work, UN Doc. E/C.12/GC/18, 2005.
Committee on Economic, Social and Cultural Rights, General Comment No. 15 on the Right to Water, UN Doc. E/C.12/2002/11, 2002.
Committee on Economic, Social and Cultural Rights, General Comment No. 14 on the Right to the Highest Attainable Standard of Health, UN Doc. E/C.12/2000/4, 2000.
Committee on Economic, Social and Cultural Rights, General Comment No. 8 on the Relationship between Economic Sanctions and Respect for Economic, Social and Cultural Rights, UN Doc. E/C.12/1997/8, 1997.
Committee on Economic, Social and Cultural Rights, General Comment No. 2 on International Technical Assistance Measures, UN Doc. E/1990/23, 1990.
Committee on the Elimination of Discrimination against Women, Concluding Observations on the seventh periodic report of Greece, UN Doc. CEDAW/C/GRC/CO/7, 1 March 2013.
Committee on the Rights of the Child, General Comment No. 16 on State obligations regarding the impact of the business sector on children's rights, UN Doc. CRC/C/GC/16, 2013.
Concluding observations of the Committee on Economic, Social, and Cultural Rights on the Fourth Report of the U.K., UN Doc. E/C.12/1/Add.79, 5 June 2002.
Concluding observations of the Committee on Economic, Social, and Cultural Rights on the Second Periodic Report of France, UN Doc. E/C.12/1/Add.72, 30 November 2001.
Concluding observations of the Committee on Economic, Social, and Cultural Rights on the Fourth Periodic Report of Germany, UN Doc. E/C.12/1/Add.68, 24 September 2001.
Concluding observations of the Committee on Economic, Social, and Cultural Rights on the Second Periodic Report of Japan, UN Doc. E/C.12/1/Add.67, 24 September 2001.
Declaration on Principles of International Law Concerning Friendly Relations and Co-Operation Among States in Accordance with the Charter of the United Nations (GAR 2625), adopted by the UNGA Resolution 2625 (XXV) of 24 October 1970.
Letter of 28 Special Rapporteurs sent to World Bank President Jim Yong Kim in the context of the process of review of the Bank's safeguard policies, 12 December 2014.
Report of the Second Meeting of the Parties to the Convention on Access to Information, Public Participation in Decision-making and Access to Justice in Environmental Matters, *Promoting the Application of the Principles of the Aarhus Convention in International Forums*, UN Doc ECE/MP.PP/2005/2/Add.5, 20 June 2005.
Rules of Procedure of the General Assembly, UN. Doc. A/520/Rev.17, September 2007.
'Transforming our World: the 2030 Agenda for Sustainable Development', endorsed by UNGA Resolution A/RES/70/1 of 25 September 2015.
Universal Declaration of Human Rights, UN Doc. A/810 at 71, 10 December 1948.
UN Declaration on the Rights of Indigenous Peoples, adopted by UNGA Resolution A/61/L.67 and Add.1, on 13 September 2007.
United Nations Development Strategy Beyond 2015, Committee for Development Policy, Policy Note, June 2012.
United Nations Economic Commission for Europe, *Almaty Guidelines on Promoting the Application of the Principles of the Aarhus Convention in International Forums*, December 2005.
UN General Assembly, *Declaration of the High-level Meeting of the General Assembly on the Rule of Law at the National and International Levels*, UNGA Resolution A/RES/67/1, 24 September 2012.

UN General Assembly Final Report of Subcommittee 1 of the Sixth Committee, *Co-Ordination of the Privileges and Immunities of the United Nations and of the Specialized Agencies*, UN Doc. A/C.6/191, 15 November 1947.

UN General Assembly, Follow-up to the outcome of the Millennium Summit, *Keeping the promise: united to achieve the Millennium Development Goals*, UN Doc. A/65/L.1, 17 September 2010.

UN General Assembly Sixth Committee, 61st Session, Summary Record of the 15th meeting, UN Doc. A/C.6/61/SR.15, 15 November 2006.

UN General Assembly Sixth Committee, 60th Session, Summary Record of the 11th meeting, UN Doc. A/C.6/60/SR.11, 24 October 2005.

UN General Assembly Sixth Committee, 59th Session, Summary Record of the 22nd meeting, A C.6/59/SR.22, 16 November 2004.

UN General Assembly, 'World Summit Outcome Document', adopted by UN General Assembly Resolution A/RES/60/1, 24 October 2005.

UN Human Rights Committee, General Comment 29, States of Emergency (article 4), UN Doc. CCPR/C/21/Rev.1/Add.11, 2001.

UN Human Rights Committee, General Comment No. 31: Nature of the General Legal Obligation Imposed on States Parties to the Covenant, UN Doc. CCPR/C/21/Rev.1/Add.13, 26 May 2004.

UN Human Rights Council, Report of the Independent Expert on the effects of foreign debt and other related international financial obligations of States on the full enjoyment of all human rights, particularly economic, social and cultural rights, Juan Pablo Bohoslavsky, UN Doc. A/HRC/34/57, 27 December 2016.

UN Human Rights Council, Report of the Independent Expert on the effects of foreign debt and other related international financial obligations of States on the full enjoyment of human rights, particularly economic, social and cultural rights, Juan Pablo Bohoslavsky, UN Doc. A/HRC/31/60, 12 January 2016.

UN Human Rights Council, Report of the Special Rapporteur on Extreme Poverty and Human Rights, Philip Alston, UN Doc. A/70/274, 4 August 2015.

UN Human Rights Council, Report of the Special Rapporteur on the right to food, Hilal Elver, *Access to Justice and the Right to Food: The Way Forward*, UN Doc. A/HRC/28/65, 12 January 2014.

UN Human Rights Council, Report of the Special Rapporteur on adequate housing as a component of the right to an adequate standard of living, and on the right to non-discrimination in this context, Mission to the World Bank, Raquel Rolnik, UN Doc. A/HRC/22/46/Add.3, 15 February 2013.

UN Human Rights Council, Report of the Independent Expert on the Issue of Human Rights Obligations Relating to the Enjoyment of a Safe, Clean, Healthy and Sustainable Environment, John H. Knox, UN Doc. A/HRC/25/53, 30 December 2013.

UN Human Rights Council, Report of the Special Rapporteur on Extreme Poverty and Human Rights, Magdalena Sepúlveda Carmona, *Mission to Timor-Leste*, UN Doc. A/HRC/20/25/Add.1, 24 May 2012.

UN Human Rights Council, Report of the Independent Expert on the effects of foreign debt and other related international financial obligations of States on the full enjoyment of all human rights, particularly economic, social and cultural rights, Cephas Lumina, *Guiding Principles on Foreign Debt and Human Rights*, UN Doc. A/HRC/20/23, 10 April 2011.

UN Human Rights Council, Report of the Special Representative of the Secretary-General on the Issue of Human Rights and Transnational Corporations and Other Business Enterprises, John Ruggie, *Guiding Principles on Business and Human Rights:*

Implementing the United Nations "Protect, Respect and Remedy" Framework, UN Doc. A/HRC/17/31, 21 March 2011.
United Nations Millennium Declaration, UNGA Resolution A/RES/55/2, UN Doc. A/55/L.2, 8 September 2000.
UN Office of the High Commissioner for Human Rights, *The Corporate Responsibility to Respect Human Rights: An Interpretive Guide*, 2012.
UN Office of the High Commissioner for Human Rights, *UN Guiding Principles on Business and Human Rights*, 2011.
UN Secretariat, 'The Practice of the United Nations, the Specialized Agencies and the International Atomic Energy Agency Concerning their Status, Privileges and Immunities', UN Doc. A/CN.4/L.118 and Add. l and 2, 8 March, 5 May and 23 May 1967.
UN Security Council Resolution 1874, North Korea, UN. Doc. S/RES/1874, 12 June 2009.
Vienna Convention on the Representation of States in their Relations with International Organizations of a Universal Character, UN Doc. A/CONF. 67/16, 14 March 1975.

2.3 *International Law Commission Documents*

Articles on Prevention of Transboundary Harm from Hazardous Activities, in Report of the International Law Commission, Fifty-Third session, Official Record of the General Assembly, Fifty-Sixth session, Supplement n. 10, UN Doc. A/56/10, 2001.
Articles on the Responsibility of International Organizations, with commentaries, in Report of the International Law Commission, Sixty-Third Session, April 26–June 3, July 4–August 12, UN Doc. A/66/10, 2011.
Articles on Responsibility of States for Internationally Wrongful Acts, with commentaries, Yearbook of the International Law Commission, Vol. II (Part Two), *Fifty-Third Session*, UN Doc. A/CN.4/SER.A/2001/Add.1, 2001.
'Identification of customary international law', Text of the draft conclusions as adopted by the Drafting Committee on second reading, UN Doc. A/CN.4/L.908, 17 May 2018.
Report of the ILC on the work of its Sixty-sixth Session, Official Records of the General Assembly, UN Doc. A/69/10, 5 May–6 June and 7 July–8 August 2014.
Report of the ILC on the work of its Sixty-first Session, Official Records of the General Assembly, 64th Session, Supp. 10, UN Doc. A/64/10, 2009.
'Responsibility of International Organizations', Addendum: Titles and texts of draft articles 25 to 30 adopted by the Drafting Committee on 19 July 2006', UN Doc. A/CN.4/L.687/Add.1, 31 May 2006.
'Responsibility of International Organizations', Comments and Observations Received from International Organizations, UN Doc. A/CN.4/637, 14 February 2011.
'Responsibility of International Organizations', Comments and Observations Received from International Organizations, UN Doc. A/CN.4/556, 12 May 2005.
'Responsibility of International Organisations', Comments and Observations Received from International Organisations, UN Doc. A/CN 4/545, 25 June 2004.
Special Rapporteur Ago, *Seventh Report on State Responsibility*, UN Doc. A/CN.4/307 and Add.1 and 2, 29 March, 17 April and 4 July 1978.
Special Rapporteur Ago, *Third Report on State Responsibility*, UN Doc. A/CN.4/246 and Add.1–3, 30 June 1972 and 9 April 1973.
Special Rapporteur Ago, *Second Report on State Responsibility*, UN Doc. A/CN.4/233, 20 April 1970.
Special Rapporteur Cedeño, *Fifth Report on Unilateral Acts of States*, UN Doc. A/CN.4/525 and.1 and 2, 4 and 17 April and 10 May 2002.

Special Rapporteur Cedeño, *Third Report on Unilateral Acts of States*, UN Doc. A/CN.4/505, 17 February 2000.
Special Rapporteur Cedeño, *Second Report on Unilateral Acts of States*, UN Doc. A/CN.4/500 and Add.1, 14 April and 10 May 1999.
Special Rapporteur Cedeño, *First Report on Unilateral Acts of States*, UN Doc. A/CN.4/486, 5 March 1998.
Special Rapporteur Crawford, *Second Report on State Responsibility*, UN Doc. A/CN.4/498 and Add.1–4, 17 March, 1 and 30 April, 19 July 1999.
Special Rapporteur El-Erian, *Sixth Report on Relations between States and International Organizations*, UN Doc. A/CN.4/241 and Add.1–6, 2 March, 29 March, 5 April, 9 April, 26 April, 12 May, 14 May 1971.
Special Rapporteur Gaja, *Eighth Report on Responsibility of International Organizations*, UN Doc. A/CN.4/640, 14 March 2011.
Special Rapporteur Gaja, *Seventh Report on Responsibility of International Organizations*, UN Doc. A/CN.4/610, 27 March 2009.
Special Rapporteur Gaja, *Fourth Report on Responsibility of International Organizations*, UN Doc. A/CN.4/564/Add.1–2, 12 and 20 April 2006.
Special Rapporteur Gaja, *Third Report on Responsibility of International Organizations*, UN Doc. A/CN.4/553, 13 May 2005.
Special Rapporteur García-Amador, *Second Report on State Responsibility*, UN. Doc. A/CN.4/106, 15 February 1957.
Special Rapporteur García-Amador, *State Responsibility*, UN Doc. A/CN.4/96, YILC, 1956, Vol. II.
Special Rapporteur Sreenivasa Rao, *Second report on international liability for injurious consequences arising out of acts not prohibited by international law (prevention of transboundary damage from hazardous activities)*, UN Doc. A/CN.4/501, 5 May 1999.
Special Rapporteur Wood, *Third Report on Identification of Customary International Law*, UN Doc. A/CN.4/682, 27 March 2015.
Summary record of the 2891st meeting, UN Doc. A/CN.4/2891, YILC, 2006, Vol. I.
Summary record of the 2892nd meeting, UN Doc. A/CN.4/2892, YILC, 2006, Vol. I.
Summary record of the 2902nd meeting, UN Doc. A/CN.4/2902, YILC, 2006, Vol. I.
Summary record of the 2933rd meeting, UN Doc. A/CN.4/2933, YILC, 2007, Vol. I.

2.4 *International Financial Institution Documents*

African Development Bank, Code of Conduct for Executive Directors, adopted as amended in September 2007.
African Development Bank, Africa Group I Constituency World Bank Group, Rules, Guidelines and Procedures, adopted in August 2010 and amended in October 2012.
African Development Bank, Handbook on Stakeholder Consultation and Participation in ADB Operations, 2001.
Asian Infrastructure Investment Bank, Environmental and Social Framework, February 2016.
Asian Development Bank, Code of Conduct for Directors, Alternates and the President, June 2011.
Asian Development Bank Safeguard Policy Statement, June 2009.
European Bank for Reconstruction and Development, Project Complaint Mechanism (PCM) Rules of Procedure, approved in 7 May 2014.

European Bank for Reconstruction and Development, Information Disclosure and Stakeholder Engagement, May 2014.
European Bank for Reconstruction and Development, Code of Conduct for Officials of the Board of Directors, revised in February 2012.
European Bank for Reconstruction and Development, By-laws, 15 April 1991.
European Investment Bank, The EIB Complaints Mechanism Operating Procedures, August 2013.
International Bank for Reconstruction and Development, By-laws, 26 September 1980.
International Finance Corporation, Compliance Advisor Ombudsman, Operational Guidelines 2013.
Inter-American Development Bank, Operational Policy on Gender Equality in Development, 3 November 2010.
Inter-American Development Bank, Operating Guidelines for the Conduct Committee of the Board of Executive Directors of the Inter-American Development Bank, the Inter-American Investment Corporation and the Donors Committee of the Multilateral Investment Fund, adopted on June 2004, amended on April 2009.
Inter-American Development Bank, Code of Ethics for the Boards of Executive Directors of the Inter-American Development Bank, the Inter-American Investment Corporation and the Donors Committee of the Multilateral Investment Fund, adopted on 2003, amended on 2009.
International Monetary Fund, By-Laws, Rules and Regulations, Sixty-Third Issue, April 2016.
International Monetary Fund, Revised Operational Guidance to IMF Staff on the 2002 Conditionality Guidelines, 23 July 2014.
International Monetary Fund, Code of Conduct for the Members of the Executive Board of the International Monetary Fund, adopted on 14 July 2000, revised on 12 December 2003 and 1 August 2012.
International Monetary Fund, Code of Conduct for Staff, adopted on 31 July 1998.
World Bank Guidance Note for Borrowers, Environment & Social Framework for IPF Operations, 'ESS2: Labor and Working Conditions', June 2018.
World Bank Environmental and Social Framework, August 2016.
World Bank Group Corporate Secretariat, Board Operations and Administration Manual, November 2014.
World Bank Operations Manual, August 2014.
World Bank Inspection Panel, 'Accountability at the World Bank: The Inspection Panel at 15 Years', 2009.
World Bank, Code of Conduct for Board Officials, 1 November 2007.
World Bank Resolution No. IBRD 93-10 and Resolution No. IDA 93-6, 'The World Bank Inspection Panel', 22 September 1993.

2.5 *International Law Association*

International Law Association Study Group on Due Diligence in International Law, First Report, Duncan French (Chair) and Tim Stephens (Rapporteur), 7 March 2014.
International Law Association, *Accountability of International Organisations Committee*, Final Report, Report of the Seventy-First Conference held in Berlin, 2004.

2.6 *Institut de Droit International*

'Draft Questionnaire', June 1989, and 'Questionnaire', September 1990, *Annuaire de l'Institut de Droit International*, Session de Lisbonne, Vol. 66-I, 1995, pp. 289–371.

Higgins, R. 'The Legal Consequences for Member States of the Non-Fulfilment by International Organizations of Their Obligations toward Third Parties – Preliminary Exposé and Draft Questionnaire', in *Annuaire de l'Institut de Droit International*, Session de Lisbonne, Vol. 66-I (1995) 288 (Preliminary Exposé).

Resolution on Member State Responsibility, *The Legal Consequences for Member States of the Non-fulfilment by International Organizations of their Obligations toward Third Parties, Annuaire de l'Institut de Droit International*, Session de Lisbonne, Vol. 66-I, 1995.

2.7 *Miscellaneous*

Council of Europe Final Report to the CDDH, Appendix 1 (2013), *Draft revised agreement on the accession of the European Union to the Convention for the Protection of Human Rights and Fundamental Freedoms*.

European Commission, 'Proposal for a Council Decision laying down measures in view of progressively establishing unified representation of the euro area in the International Monetary Fund', COM(2015) 603 final, 21 October 2015.

European Commission, 'Commission Staff Working Paper, Operational Guidance on taking account of Fundamental Rights in Commission Impact Assessments', SEC(2011)567 final, Brussels, 6 May 2011.

G20/OECD Principles of Corporate Governance, OECD Report to G20 Finance Ministers and Central Bank Governors, September 2015.

OECD, 'Busan Partnership for Effective Development Co-Operation, Fourth High Level Forum on Aid Effectiveness, Busan, Republic of Korea', 29 November–1 December 2011.

3 DOMESTIC LEGISLATION

3.1 *Belgium*

Loi Relative à la Coopération [belge] au Développement, 19 March 2013.

3.2 *Germany*

Act on Cooperation between the Federal Government and the German Bundestag in Matters concerning the European Union (EUZBBG), 4 July 2013.

3.3 *United Kingdom*

House of Commons Standing Order No. 143 on the European Scrutiny Committee, 27 October 2016.

Human Rights Act, 9 November 1998.

3.4 *United States*

Bretton Woods Agreements Act, as amended through P.L. 114-113, Enacted 18 December 2015. U.S. Code § 262.
Iran Counter Proliferation Act, 2007.
Iran Sanctions Act, 2008.

4 CASES

4.1 *International Courts, Tribunals and International Financial Institution Accountability Mechanisms*

4.1.1 International Court of Justice

Application of the Interim Accord of 13 September 1995 (The Former Yugoslav Republic of Macedonia v. *Greece)*, ICJ Reports 2011.
Barcelona Traction, Light and Power Company, Limited (Belgium v. *Spain)*, Judgment, ICJ Reports 3 (1970).
Case Concerning Application of the Convention on the Prevention and Punishment of the Crime of Genocide (Bosnia and Herzegovina v. *Serbia and Montenegro)*, Judgment, ICJ Reports 2007.
Case Concerning Certain Phosphate Lands in Nauru (Nauru v. *Australia)*, ICJ Reports 240 (1992).
Case Concerning Military and Paramilitary Activities in and against Nicaragua (Nicaragua v. *United States Of America)*, Merits, Judgment, ICJ Reports 1986.
Case Concerning Pulp Mills on the River Uruguay (Argentina v. *Uruguay)*, Judgment, ICJ Reports 2010.
Certain Expenses of the United Nations (Article 17, paragraph 2 of the Charter), Advisory Opinion, ICJ Reports 151 (1962).
Conditions of admission of a State to membership in the United Nations (Article 4 of Charter), Advisory Opinion, ICJ Reports 57 (1948).
Conditions of admission of a State to membership in the United Nations (Article 4 of Charter), Mémoires, Plaidoiries et Documents, Part II, Exposé de M. le Professeur Georges Scelle, 22 Avril 1948.
Corfu Channel Case (United Kingdom v. *Albania)*, Merits, ICJ Reports 4 (1949).
Difference Relating to Immunity from Legal Process of a Special Rapporteur of the Commission on Human Rights, Advisory Opinion, ICJ Reports 62 (1999).
Effects of Awards of Compensation made by the United Nations Administrative Tribunal, Advisory Opinion, ICJ Reports 47 (1954).
Interpretation of the Agreement of 25 March 1951 between the WHO and Egypt, Advisory Opinion, ICJ Reports 73 (1980).
Legality of the Use by a State of Nuclear Weapons in Armed Conflict, Advisory Opinion, ICJ Reports 66 (1996).
Reparation for Injuries Suffered in the Service of the United Nations, Advisory Opinion, ICJ Reports 174 (1949).
United States Diplomatic and Consular Staff in Tehran (United States of America v. *Iran)*, Judgment, ICJ Reports 1980.
Yugoslavia v. *Belgium et al*, Verbatim Record, CR/99/14, 10 May 1999.

4.1.2 Permanent Court of International Justice

Case concerning the Factory at Chorzów, Claim for Indemnity (Germany v. *Poland)*, Publ. PCIJ Series A, No. 17 (1928).
Case Relating to the Territorial Jurisdiction of the International Commission of the River Oder, Publ. PCIJ Series A, No.23, No. 16 (1929).
Case of the SS Lotus, Publ. PCIJ, Series A, No. 10 (1927).
Certain German Interests in Polish Upper Silesia (Germany v. *Poland)*, Publ. PCIJ Series A, No. 7 (1925).
Interpretation of Article 3 para 2 of the Treaty of Lausanne, Publ. PCIJ Series B, No. 12 (1925).
Interpretation of the Greco-Turkish Agreement of December 1st, 1926, Publ. PCIJ, Series B, No. 16 (1928).

4.1.3 International Criminal Tribunal for the former Yugoslavia

Prosecutor v. *Dusko Tadić*, IT-94-1-AR72, Appeals Chamber, 2 October 1995.

4.1.4 African Commission on Human & Peoples' Rights

Social and Economic Rights Action Center & the Center for Economic and Social Rights v. *Nigeria*, Communication No. 155/96, 27 May 2002.

4.1.5 European Court of Human Rights

Agim Behrami and Bekir Behrami v. *France*, App. No. 71412/01, 2 May 2007.
Al-Dulimi and Montana Management Inc v. *Switzerland*, App No 5809/08, 26 November 2013.
Al-Jedda v. *United Kingdom*, App.No. 27021/08, 7 July 2011.
Al-Skeini and others v. *United Kingdom*, App No. 55721/07, 7 July 2011.
Avotiņš v. *Latvia*, App. No. 17502/07, 23 May 2016.
Banković and Others v. *Belgium and 16 other Contracting States*, App. No. 52207/99, 12 December 2001.
Bosphorus Hava Yollari Turizm veTicaret Anonim Sirketi v. *Ireland*, App. No. 45036/98, 30 June 2005.
Case of Centre for Legal Resources on Behalf of Valentin Câmpeanu v. *Romania*, App. No. 47848/08, 17 July 2014.
Confedération Française Démocratique du Travail v. *The European Communities*, App. No. 8030/77, 10 July 1978.
Galić v. *the Netherlands*, App. No. 22617/07, 9 June 2009.
Gasparini v. *Italy and Belgium*, App. No. 10750/03, 12 May 2009.
Golder v. *The United Kingdom*, App. No. 4451/70, 21 February 1975.
Guerra and Others v. *Italy*, App. No. 116/1996/735/932, 19 February 1998.
Hassan v. *United Kingdom*, App. no. 29750/09, 16 September, 2014.
Hardy and Maile v. *United Kingdom*, App. No. 31965/07, 09 July 2012.
Hatton and others v. *United Kingdom*, App. No. 36022/97, 8 July 2003.
Ilascu and others v. *Moldova and Russia*, App. No. 48787/99, 8 July 2004.
Jaloud v. *Netherlands*, App. No. 47708/08, 20 November, 2014.

Klausecker v. *Germany*, App. No. 415/07, 6 January 2015.
Kyrtatos v. *Greece*, App. No. 41666/98, 22 May 2003.
L.C.B. v. *United Kingdom*, App. No. 14/1997/798/1001, 9 June 1998.
Lopez Ostra v. *Spain*, App. No. 16798/90, 9 December 1994.
Matthews v. *United Kingdom*, App. No. 24833/94, 18 February 1999.
Matthews v. *United Kingdom*, App. No. 24833/94, European Commission of Human Rights Report, 29 October 1997.
Mehida Mustafić-Mujić And Others v. *The Netherlands*, App. No. 49037/15, 30 August 2016.
Michaud v. *France*, App. No. 12323/11, 6 December 2012.
M. & Co. v. *Germany*, App. No. 13258/87, 9 February 1990.
Nada v. *Switzerland*, App. No. 10593/08, 12 September 2012.
Öneryildiz v. *Turkey*, App. No. 48939/99, 30 November 2004.
Osman v. *United Kingdom*, 87/1997/871/1083, Judgment, 28 October 1998, para. 116.
Rambus Inc. v. *Germany*, App. No. 40382/04, 16 June 2009.
Ruzhdi Saramati v. *France, Germany and Norway*, App. No. 78166/01, 2 May 2007.
Segi and others & Gestoras Pro-Amnistia and others v. *15 States Of The European Union*, App. No. 6422/02 and App. No. 9916/02, 23 May 2002.
Senator Lines v. *Austria, Belgium, Denmark, Finland, France, Germany, Greece, Ireland, Italy, Luxembourg, the Netherlands, Portugal, Spain, Sweden, and the United Kingdom*, App. No. 56672/00, 10 March 2004.
Stiching Mothers of Srebrenica v. *The Netherlands*, App. No. 65542/12, 11 June 2013.
Tatar v. *Romania*, App. No. 67021/01, 27 January 2009.
Taskin v. *Turkey*, App. No. 46117/99, 10 November 2004.
Waite and Kennedy v. *Germany*, App. No. 26083/94, 18 February 1999.
X v. *the FRG*, Decision of 10 June 1958, App. No. 235/56, Yearbook 2.

4.1.6 Inter-American Court of Human Rights

Kichwa Indigenous People of Sarayaku v. *Ecuador*, Judgment of 28 November 2007, Series C No. 245.
Velasquez Rodriguez, Preliminary Objections, Judgment of 26 June 1987, Series C No. 1.

4.1.7 Inter-American Commission on Human Rights

Appeal submitted by The Global Initiative for Economic, Social and Cultural Rights, Rights Action and the International Human Rights Clinic at Western New England University School of Law, on behalf of the Survivors of the Río Negro community and similar Chixoy Dam harmed communities in the Chixoy river basin, Guatemala (Petitioners), Case P-894-04, 7 December 2011.
Armando Alejandre Jr. et al v. *Cuba*, Case No. 11.589, 29 September 1999.
Coard et al v. *United States*, Case No. 10.951, 29 September 1999.
Felix Roman Esparragoza Gonzalez et al. v. *Venezuela*, Admissibility Decision, Petition 12.210, Report No. 48/04, 13 October 2004.
Maya Indigenous Communities of the Toledo District v. *Belize*, Case 12.053, Report N° 40/04, 12 October 2004.
Report No. 17/12, Petition P-900–08, Admissibility, Djamel Ameziane, United States, 20 March 2012.

4.1.8 European Court of Justice

Court of Justice (formerly European Court of Justice) and General Court (formerly Court of First Instance).
AMT (Tin Recoveries) v. *Council and Commission of the European Communities*, Case C-19/89, 32 O.J.E.C. (No. C 62) 7 (1989).
Commission and United Kingdom v. *Yassin Abdullah Kadi*, Joined Cases C-584/10 P, C-593/10 P and C-595/10 P, Judgment of the Court (Grand Chamber), 18 July 2013.
Flaminio Costa v. E.N.E.L., Case 6/64, 15 July 1964.
Ledra Advertising Ltd and Others v. *European Commission and European Central Bank*, Joined Cases C-8/15 P to C-10/15 P, 20 September 2016.
Maclaine Watson v. *Council and Commission of the European Communities*, Case C-241/87, 30 O.J.E.C. (No. C 262) 5 (1987).
Opinion 2/13, ECLI:EU:C:2014:2454, 18 December 2014.
Peter Gauweiler and Others v. *Deutscher Bundestag*, Case C-62/14, 2015.
Thomas Pringle v. *Ireland*, Case C-370/12, 27 November 2012.
Yassin Abdullah Kadi v. *European Commission*, Case T-85/09, [2010] ECR II-5177.
Yassin Abdullah Kadi and Al Barakaat International Foundation v. *Council of the European Union and the Commission of the European Communities*, Joined Cases C-402/05 P and C-415/05 P [2008] ECR I-6351.
Yassin Abdullah Kadi v. *Council of the European Union and Commission of the European Communities*, Case T-315/01 [2005] ECR II-3649.

4.1.9 European Committee of Social Rights

Federation of pensioners IKA-ETAM v. *Greece*, Decision on the Merits, Complaint No. 76/2012, 7 December 2012.

4.1.10 Arbitral Awards

Alabama Claims of the United States of America against Great Britain, 14 September 1872.
Trail Smelter Case (United States v. *Canada)*, Award, 1941, 3 U.N.R.I.A.A. 1905.
Westland Helicopters Ltd v. *Arab Organization for Industrialization, United Arab Emirates, Kingdom of Saudi Arabia, State of Qatar, Arab Republic of Egypt and Arab British Helicopter Company*, Arbitration, 5 March 1984, 23 ILM (1984) 1071.
William E. Chapman (U.S.A.) v. *United Mexican States*, 24 October 1930, UNRIAA IV.

4.1.11 International Finance Corporation Compliance Advisor Ombudsman

Compliance Advisor Ombudsman, Compliance Appraisal: Summary Of Results, Yanacocha (IFC Project #2983), Complaints 04–07, 29 May 2015.

4.1.12 World Trade Organization

Canada – Measures Affecting the Importation of Milk and the Exportation of Dairy Products, Appellate Body Report, WTO Doc. WT/DS103/AB/R, AB-1999–4, 13 October 1999.
European Communities and certain Member States: Measures Affecting Trade in Large Civil Aircraft, Report of the Panel, WT/DS316/R, 30 June 2010.

4.1.13 World Bank Administrative Tribunal

Aida Shekib, Decision No. 358 (2007).

4.1.14 World Bank Inspection Panel

Investigation Report, *Ethiopia: Promoting Basic Services Phase III Project (P128891)*, Report No. 91854-ET, 21 November 2014.

Investigation Report, *Cambodia: Land Management and Administration Project (Credit No. 3650 – KH)*, 23 November 2010.

Management Report and Recommendation in Response to the Inspection Panel Investigation Report – Cambodia: Land Management and Administration Project (IDA Credit No. 3605-KH), Doc. INSP/58016-KH, 21 January 2011.

4.2 *National Courts*

France

African Development Bank v. *Haas*, French Court of Cassation (soc.), 25 January 2005, (2005) Journal des Tribunaux 454.

Association Les Verts Parti Ecologiste, Conseil d'Etat, Case N° 54359 54360, CLI:FR: CEASS:1984:54359.19841123, 23 November 1984.

Western European Union v. *Siedler*, Appeal Judgment, Cass No. S 04 0129 F, ILDC 1625 (BE 2009).

Germany

BVerfG, 2 BvR 2728/13, 4 January 2014.

BVerfG, 2 BvR 2729/13, 2 BvR 2730/13, 2 BvR 2731/13, 2 BvE 13/13, 21 June 2016.

BVerfG, 2 BvE 2/07, 3 July 2007.

BVerfG, 2 BvE 6/99, 22 November 2001.

BVerfGE 37, 271, 2 BvL 52/71, 29 May 1974 (Solange I).

BVerfGE 73, 339, 2 BvR 197/83, 22 October 1986 (Solange II).

BVerfG 89, 155, 2 BvR 2134/92, 12 October 1993 (Solange III).

BVerfG 102, 147, 2 BvL 1/97, 7 June 2000 (Solange IV).

Netherlands

Mothers of Srebrenica v. *Netherlands*, Rechtbank's-Gravenhage, LJN: 8748/c/09/295247, 16 July 2014.

Mothers of Srebrenica et al v. *State of the Netherlands and the UN*, 13 April 2012, LJN: BW 1999; ILDC 1760 (NL 2012).

Mustafić v. *Netherlands*, Judgment, BZ9228, Supreme Court of the Netherlands, 6 September 2013.

Mustafić v. Netherlands, Gerechtshof's-Gravenhage, Appellate Judgment, LJN: BR5386, 5 July 2011.

Nuhanović v. *Netherlands*, Judgment, BZ9225, Supreme Court of the Netherlands, 6 September 2013.

Nuhanović v. Netherlands, Gerechtshof's-Gravenhage, Appellate Judgment, LJN: BR 5388, 5 July 2011.

Switzerland

Arab Organization for Industrialization and others v. *Westland Helicopters Ltd*, Swiss Federal Supreme Court (First Civil Court), 19 July 1988, 80 ILR 652.

Youssef Nada v. *State Secretariat for Economic Affairs and Federal Department of Economic Affairs*, Swiss Federal Tribunal, Administrative Appeal Judgment, Case No. 1A 45/2007, 14 November 2007.

United Kingdom

J H Rayner (Mincing Lane) Ltd v. *Department of Trade and Industry and Other* and Related Appeals *Maclaine Watson & Co Ltd* v. *Department of Trade and Industry* and *Maclaine Watson & Co Ltd* v. *International Tin Council*, United Kingdom House of Lords, 26 October 1989, 81 ILR 670.

Maclaine Watson & Co Ltd v. *Department of Trade & Industry*, [1988] 80 ILR 47.

Regina v. *Secretary of State for Foreign Affairs ex Parte the World Development Movement Ltd*, Queen's Bench Division, [1995] 1 WLR 386.

United States

Amaratunga v. *Northwest Atlantic Fisheries Organization*, 29 November 2013, 2013 SCC 66.

Budha Ismail Jam, et al, Petitioners v. International Finance Corporation, 27 February 2019, 586 U.S._(2019).

Mendaro v. *World Bank*, 717 F.2d 610 (D.C.Cir. 1983).

Prewitt Enterprises Inc and ors v. *Organization of Petroleum Exporting Countries*, Appeal judgment, 353 F3d 916 (11th Cir 2003).

5 ONLINE SOURCES

5.1 *International Financial Institutions*

Asian Infrastructure Investment Bank:

—www.aiib.org/en/about-aiib/governance/members-of-bank/index.html.

International Monetary Fund:

—https://www.imf.org/en/About/Factsheets/A-Guide-to-Committees-Groups-and-Clubs#IC.

—https://www.imf.org/external/about/govstruct.htm.

—Factsheet, 'IMF Support for Low-Income Countries', 8 March 2018: www.imf.org/en/About/Factsheets/IMF-Support-for-Low-Income-Countries.

—www.imf.org/external/np/exr/facts/govern.htm.

—www.imf.org/external/np/fad/environ/.

—www.imf.org/external/np/sec/memdir/eds.aspx#2.

World Bank:

—https://consultations.worldbank.org/consultation/review-and-update-world-bank-safeguard-policies.

—http://ieg.worldbankgroup.org/about-us.
—www.worldbank.org/en/about/leadership/directors.
—www.worldbank.org/en/about/leadership/members.
—www.worldbank.org/en/about/what-we-do.
—http://www.devcommittee.org/.

5.2 *News Articles*

Brettonwoods Project, 'Korean Workers Lawsuit against IMF Thrown Out', 15 April 2000, available at: www.brettonwoodsproject.org/2000/04/art-15638/, last consulted 15 October 2018.

Devex, 'No Easy Path for the World Bank's Safeguards', 9 December 2014: www.devex.com/news/no-easy-path-for-the-world-bank-s-safeguards-84887.

European Union Newsroom, 'EU Sanctions against Russia over Ukraine Crisis': http://europa.eu/newsroom/highlights/special-coverage/eu_sanctions/index_en.htm.

Financial Times, 'Brazil Calls for IMF Eurozone Rrescue Programmes Revision', 8 August 2013: https://next.ft.com/content/8fb83f5 c-004b-11e3-9c40-00144feab7de.

NATO Press Release, 'Bucharest Summit Declaration Issued by the Heads of State and Government Participating in the Meeting of the North Atlantic Council in Bucharest on 3 April 2008': www.nato.int/cps/en/natolive/official_texts_8443.htm.

Reuters, 'Ugandan Parliament Set to Re-introduce Anti-Gay Law', 6 August 2014: www.reuters.com/article/us-uganda-gay-idUSKBN0G60ZX20140806.

The Cambodia Daily, 'World Bank Will Resume Funding to Cambodia', 21 May 2016: www.cambodiadaily.com/news/world-bank-will-resume-funding-to-cambodia-112866/.

The Moscow Times, 'G7 Leaders Agree to Prolong Anti-Russian Sanctions', 27 May 2016: www.themoscowtimes.com/news/article/g7-leaders-agree-to-prolong-anti-russian-sanctions/570670.html.

5.3 *Others*

Belgium Parliament, De Kamer/La Chambre, Commissie Voor de Buitenlandse Betrekkingen van Dinsdag 7 Juni 2016/Commission des Relations Extérieures du Mardi 7 Juin 2016: www.dekamer.be/doc/CCRI/html/54/ic437x.html.

Bretton Woods Project, 'The UK's role in the World Bank and IMF Department for International Development and HM Treasury', 13 March 2013: www.brettonwoodsproject.org/2013/03/ukinbwi/.

Council of Europe: www.coe.int/en/web/conventions/full-list/-/conventions/treaty/005/signatures.

Danish Parliament Foreign Affairs Committee: www.thedanishparliament.dk/en/committees/committees/uru.

German Institute for Human Rights:

—'Submission for the Review of the World Bank's Environmental and Social Framework (ESF): Comments on the Draft Environmental and Social Framework as published in July 2014', 27 February 2015, https://consultations.worldbank.org/Data/hub/files/20150227_gihr_wb_sg_submission_esp_-_ess_1–2–7–10_commentary_-_gesamt.pdf.

—'Consultation on AIIB Environmental and Social Framework (ESF): Comments on the AIIB's Draft Environmental and Social Framework dated 3rd August 2015': www.institut-fuer-menschenrechte.de/fileadmin/user_upload/Publikationen/Stellungnahmen/Comments_on_the_AIIBs_Draft_Environmental_and_Social_Framework_23_October_2015.pdf.

EU, COSAC: www.cosac.eu/national-parliament-european-c/.
ILC, Analytical Guide to the Work of the International Law Commission on State Responsibility: http://legal.un.org/ilc/guide/9_6.shtml.
Jiechi, Y., 'Implementing the Chinese Dream', in *The National Interest*, 10 September 2013: http://nationalinterest.org/commentary/implementing-the-chinese-dream-9026.
Maryknoll Office for Global Concerns, 'Cambodia: The World Bank and human rights', September-October 2016: http://maryknollogc.org/article/cambodia-world-bank-and-human-rights.
Oxfam Comments on the Second Draft of World Bank Environmental and Social Framework, March 2015: https://consultations.worldbank.org/Data/hub/files/oxfam_comments_on_second_draft_wb_environmental_and_social_framework.pdf.
Parliamentary Network on the World Bank & the International Monetary Fund: www.parlnet.org/.
Social Justice Connection: https://sjc-cjs.org/wp-content/uploads/2015/11/ED-statement-on-safeguards-draft.pdf.
SHARES project: www.sharesproject.nl/publication.
The Global Initiative for Economic, Social and Cultural Rights, 'Guatemala: Holding the World Bank Accountable for Human Rights Violations': http://globalinitiative-escr.org/advocacy/guatemala-holding-the-world-bank-accountable-for-human-rights-violations/.
US Treasury:
—https://home.treasury.gov/policy-issues/international/multilateral-development-banks.

Index